CORNISH STUDIES

Second Series

TEN

INSTITUTE OF CORNISH STUDIES

Sardinia Pilchardus
(The Pilchard)

EDITOR'S NOTE

Cornish Studies (second series) exists to reflect current research conducted internationally in the inter-disciplinary field of Cornish Studies. It is edited by Professor Philip Payton, Director of the Institute of Cornish Studies at the University of Exeter, and is published by the University of Exeter Press. The opinions expressed in *Cornish Studies* are those of individual authors and are not necessarily those of the editor or publisher. The support of Cornwall County Council is gratefully acknowledged.

Cover illustration: Architect's impression of the roofscape of the proposed new Combined Universities in Cornwall building at the hub campus, Tremough, near Penryn, which from 2004 will accommodate the University of Exeter in Cornwall—including the Institute of Cornish Studies—and elements of the Falmouth College of Arts. (This image kindly provided by the architects for the project, Percy Thomas Architects.)

CORNISH STUDIES

Second Series

TEN

Edited by

Philip Payton

UNIVERSITY
of
EXETER
PRESS

First published in 2002 by
University of Exeter Press
Reed Hall, Streatham Drive
Exeter, Devon EX4 4QR
UK
www.ex.ac.uk/uep/

© Philip Payton 2002

British Library Cataloguing in Publication Data
A catalogue record for this book is
available from the British Library

ISBN 0 85989 733 8
ISSN 1352-271X

Typeset in 10/12pt Times by Kestrel Data, Exeter

Printed and bound in Great Britain by
Short Run Press Ltd, Exeter

Contents

INTRODUCTION

It seems hardly any time at all since the first volume of *Cornish Studies* (Second Series) appeared from University of Exeter Press in December 1993, just in time to find its way into bookshops before Christmas of that year. Something of a gamble for both the Institute of Cornish Studies and the Press, *Cornish Studies* set itself an ambitious agenda, its Editor's Note in *Cornish Studies: One* explaining that the series 'exists to reflect current research conducted internationally in the interdisciplinary field of Cornish Studies'. Thereafter, the declared intention to publish *Cornish Studies* as an annual paperback volume was achieved, while the 'international' and 'interdisciplinary' aims were pursued with some determination.

Before long, *Cornish Studies* was consisting routinely of a dozen or more major articles in each volume (with a tendency to grow fatter with the passage of the years), with contributions from individuals in institutions across the United Kingdom and in Ireland, Continental Europe, North America, and Australia. Subjects varied from Margaret James-Korany's ' "Blue Books" as Sources for Cornish Emigration History' in *Cornish Studies: One* to David Crowther and Chris Carter's 'Community Identity and Cyberspace: A Study of the Cornish Community' in *Cornish Studies: Nine* in 2001. Many of these contributions were consciously interdisciplinary in tone or approach, attempting to match in practice the rhetoric of what was known increasingly as 'New Cornish Studies', together with that of its twin offspring the 'new Cornish historiography' and the 'new Cornish social science'. As well as ushering in a growing focus on the modern and the contemporary, this 'newness' in *Cornish Studies* (Second Series) reflected a wider ambition within the discipline of Cornish Studies to learn from and contribute to important current academic debates in the humanities and social sciences, such as those surrounding 'Britishness' and the territorial identities and politics of modern Western European states. Implicit (and sometimes explicit) within this was not only an assumption that Cornwall and the Cornish were intrinsically worthy of study in their own right, but also a conviction that such study was of comparative value in studying other territories and peoples.

But although 'new' in these several senses of the word, *Cornish Studies* (Second Series)—like Cornish Studies itself—owed much to what had gone before. Following the foundation in January 1971 of the Institute of Cornish Studies, a collaborative venture by the University of Exeter and Cornwall County Council, Charles Thomas, the Institute's first Director, in 1973 launched what was to be the first series of *Cornish Studies*. This was conceived initially as an in-house journal for the Institute's staff, Honorary Research Fellows and Associates, a means of publishing material that might not sit happily in existing scholarly journals such as *Cornish Archaeology* (also founded by Professor Thomas) and the *Journal of the Royal Institution of Cornwall.* '[P]icking rather at random', as Thomas put it in his editorial note in *Cornish Studies* 1 (1973), 'the philology of the Cornish language, dialect studies, geography, and bibliography' were all subject areas rarely represented in Cornish journals, while others such as social and military history hardly ever appeared 'save in small doses and in competition with many other topics'. Within its sixty-four pages, *Cornish Studies* 1 (1973) included seven relatively short articles, ranging from Frank Turk's 'Distribution Patterns of the Mammalian Fauna of Cornwall' to Charles Thomas's own 'An Officer's Napoleonic Shoulder-belt Plate of the Cornish Yeomanry'. In the same edition, there appeared Oliver J. Padel's article 'Cornish Language Notes: 1, The Assibilation of Final Dental Stops. 2, RD 1232, Old Cornish *odencolc*, "lime kiln" ', heralding Padel's sustained contribution to Cornish language and associated place-name and medieval studies over three decades—both within and beyond the Institute of Cornish Studies.

Following this important but relatively modest start, under Charles Thomas's guidance *Cornish Studies* continued to broaden its scope, venturing into the areas that he had identified in 1973 but also developing as a forum where new work across the discipline, irrespective of subject matter, might receive an airing. This increasingly important role culminated in *Cornish Studies* 16 (1988), the last in the series, a 'Special Edition' of 'Tintagel Papers' which drew together new thinking on Tintagel and the results of recent excavations which, as Professor Malcolm Todd (then Chairman of the Institute's Board of Cornish Studies) explained in his Foreword, 'clear the ground for further work, which is to include renewed archaeological examination. Our understanding of the premier monument of medieval Cornwall is about to enter a new and fascinating phase.' Indeed it was, with the fruitful partnership of the Institute and the Cornwall Archaeological Unit resulting in 1990–1 in excavations in Tintagel churchyard, with later work in the mid-1990s reverting to the Island, and leading in turn to Charles Thomas's book *Tintagel: Arthur and Archaeology* (1993).

However, even as this work was reaching its climax, important changes within the Institute of Cornish Studies were happening, notably the retirement of Charles Thomas and his replacement as Director by the present author. The important advances of recent years were carried forward by the Cornwall Archaeological Unit, with its own impressive programme of publications, but at the Institute itself a thorough-going reassessment of its role led, amongst other things, to the new focus noted above. The first fruit of this new focus, the edited volume *Cornwall Since the War: The Contemporary History of a European Region*, published jointly by the Institute and Dyllansow Truran, brought together a team of scholars inside and outside Cornwall to look at issues from housing and the family to language revival and voting behaviour. But there was also the decision to re-launch *Cornish Studies*, this time under the aegis of University of Exeter Press as an annual paperback series, available at a reduced rate to Associates as part of their subscription but also marketed aggressively at home and overseas, so much so that one was as likely to find copies in Barnes & Noble in Walnut City, California, as in Truro's bookshops! Academic reviews were favourable, as were sales, setting *Cornish Studies* (Second Series) firmly in the right direction.

As intended, *Cornish Studies* (Second Series) proved an important vehicle for the 'New Cornish Studies' that had emerged, and with the publication of this present volume, *Cornish Studies: Ten*, there is now the opportunity to look back upon a decade's activity. This, in essence, is the collective purpose of *Cornish Studies: Ten*. But two important points need to be made. First of all, in reviewing ten year's work in Cornish Studies, it is important to recognize that much work in the field has appeared elsewhere, in the lists of local publishers here in Cornwall but also in scholarly journals as far away as Australia. Secondly, in reviewing this activity, it is necessary to resist the temptation to indulge in uncritical self-congratulation. For while the appearance of *Cornish Studies: Ten* is something of a publishing milestone and tribute to a decade's toil, it is plain that much has been left undone, whilst that which has been done should not escape the critical and, if necessary, sceptical eyes of both internal and external observers. This volume, then, aims to achieve just such a critical appraisal, to review the activities of the last ten years (including that which has appeared beyond the pages of *Cornish Studies*), pointing to significant advances in the field but highlighting shortcomings or failings and sketching an agenda for the future. The collection begins, fittingly, with an overview by Bernard Deacon, himself one of the leading architects of Cornish Studies as currently practised. Taking to task the concept of New Cornish Studies and 'the twin descriptors', as he calls them, of 'the new Cornish social science' and 'the new Cornish historiography', he suggests that together they constitute a 'rhetorically defined space' rather than a genuinely 'new' methodological approach, so that far from there being a disjunction between the 'old' Cornish Studies of the pre-1990s and the more recent 'new', there is actually a continuity between the two. But in offering this observation he hastens to add that 'the rhetoric of the New Cornish Studies also reflects and clarifies real shifts in the context of Cornish Studies over the past decade'. Interdisciplinarity, comparison and context are three key elements in New Cornish Studies, argues Deacon, while there is also a greater readiness to embrace social theory, bringing Cornish Studies as practised by many today closer to the social sciences.

In pursuing his analysis, Deacon concentrates on 'the new Cornish historiography', leaving 'the new Cornish social science' safely in the hands of Michael Williams, whose article follows on from Deacon's in this collection. Deacon objects that 'the new Cornish historiography' may have been insufficiently critical of the 'new' British history (of which it is ostensibly a part) given that, with the important exception of Mark Stoyle's work, it has not allowed Cornwall any more space than did earlier, Anglocentric views of British history. Moreover, he suggests that it has by and large ducked the postmodernist critiques of 'objectivist' history, avoiding the deconstructionist interrogation of both the past and the historians who seek to recreate it. Instead, he insists, the real 'newness' of 'the new Cornish historiography' lies not in any methodological innovation but rather in its normative assumptions. Here the project is to rehabilitate 'the Cornish' and 'Cornishness' in the writing of Cornish history, an admission which is, he says, an open and candid honesty which stands in marked contrast to a conservative, uncritical local history which, 'while clinging to a naïve empiricism, is strangely coy about its own assumptions'. Thus 'the new Cornish historiography', and the New Cornish Studies of which it is a part, is as much an ontological as an epistemological project, 'as much concerned with values and visions as with novel methodological approaches'.

This accepted, Deacon goes on to suggest a Cornish Studies agenda for the future, one which promotes the worth of 'micro-history', encourages a shift from 'Celtic' to 'cultural' studies, attempts to break out of ghettoes of its own making into the 'mainstream', and is pre-pared to 'embrace the more fragmentary, fluid and heterogeneous accounts of society that have become fashionable in many academic circles'. Here, 'those working within the New Cornish Studies field see that, by setting out to deconstruct certain powerful paradigms of Cornwall, they will also open up new possibilities for local actors'. As Deacon concludes:

> In short, the New Cornish Studies accepts that Cornish Studies is, inevitably, part of a struggle for place, part of an ongoing re-creation and conservation of that place we call Cornwall. It recognizes that Cornwall is neither essential nor unchanging but it also sets out to assert the right of the Cornish themselves to be involved in that process of change. It is part of a discourse that states that the Cornish no longer wish to be marginalized, casually misrepresented or appropriated for other agenda. They are not just passive constructions of outside discourses. They are agents who have made . . . their own history. The task of the New Cornish Studies is to recover the sense of agency, put it in a comparative context, open up our knowledge of the past and, ultimately, to empower people in Cornwall so that they are in a better position to make choices about their own future.

Malcolm Williams embraces a number of these themes in his treatment of the 'new Cornish social science', echoing the belief of Charles Thomas, Ronald Perry and others that part of the role of social science analysis in Cornwall is to furnish critiques of those policies and forces that are moulding the deleterious socio-economic conditions of contemporary Cornwall and to offer alternative agendas. But as Williams also explains, the emergence of the visibility and confidence of this 'new Cornish social science' has occurred alongside significant change within Cornwall itself, from the trauma represented by the final closure of South Crofty (Cornwall's last tin mine) to the passion generated by the Cornwall rugby football team's success in reaching the 'county finals' at Twickenham on several occasions in the late 1980s and 1990s. In other words, from Williams's perspective, the conditions necessary for a Cornish social science to be successfully established were created in the 1980s and 1990s, while the increasing preparedness of universities and local authorities to welcome (or at least tolerate) Cornish social science researchers has added to the climate of acceptance and relevance. A key part in this, Williams explains, was Judy Payne's 1995 study *Interpreting the Index of Local Conditions in Devon and Cornwall*, something of a 'Trojan horse' which was funded by the Westcountry Development Corporation and was intended to demonstrate poverty in both Devon and Cornwall but ended up by proving that Cornwall was very much poorer than Devon.

Again echoing Deacon's analysis, Williams notes the paradox of 'objectivity' and 'commitment' in Cornish social science research, observing that in this respect Cornish Studies is like Women's Studies, Irish Studies or Indian Studies, with their ideological assumptions based on 'foundation myths' designed to influence the policy process. Although Deacon is sceptical of the ability of Cornish Studies to influence planners and policy-makers, except at the most arcane level, Williams is more optimistic, noting (for example) the penetration of local housing authority agendas by Cornish analysts who were able to point unequivocally to serious and complex Cornish housing need. More generally, Williams notes the existence of an 'oppositional Cornish economics', designed to convince planners and politicians that a new model of economic planning is needed for the future, while he also observes that recent studies of in-migration and out-migration indicate an important shift in the aspirations of the indigenous Cornish, especially amongst the young who no longer aspire to emigration as a means of advancement. Despite the paucity of empirical research, Williams suggests that recent work on identity has also served to advance the understanding of 'Cornishness' and to influence policy, with Cornwall County Council on a number of occasions in the 1990s publishing major documents which articulated Cornish identity as a significant factor in influencing its discussions and recommendations.

Additionally, Malcolm Williams notes that '[t]he historic and contemporary political arrangements of Cornwall provide some of the best evidence of Cornish distinctiveness', pointing to recent work on Cornish nationalism, anti-metropolitanism and voting behaviour but also expressing disappointment that, despite the generally good coverage up until the early 1990s, the sea change in Cornish politics at and after the 1997 General Election has largely gone unremarked. Tourism, too, has not attracted the attention that one might have expected, though Williams detects a link between tourism and in-migration and draws attention to both Paul Thornton's and Ron Elzey's work in this field, the former on the 'tourist gaze' that potentially subverts that which it comes to see, the latter teasing out the (probably atypical) relationship between migration, tourism and seasonal employment in one major Cornish town—Newquay. For the future, Williams argues that 'new Cornish social science' should continue to engage with current Cornish issues, further establishing its relevance and credibility and continuing to insist upon its contextual significance in the socio-economic and political climate of contemporary Cornwall, especially in 'regeneration' issues such as

Objective 1, the Combined Universities in Cornwall, and the projected Cornish Assembly.

Deacon and Williams represent uncompromisingly 'insider' views of Cornish Studies. For a sympathetic 'outsider's' view, we turn to Colin H. Williams's article 'On Ideology, Identity and Integrity', a supportive yet critical assessment of Cornish Studies over the last decade or so. Williams considers that '[t]he growth of "New Cornish Studies" within the current generation is a remarkable achievement'. Perceptively, he recognizes that '[t]his academic project has been an attempt to re-define both the content and the relevance of Cornish Studies in the wake of social and political changes in the late twentieth century', but he also argues that 'ultimately it has been also, and continues to be, an ideological project searching for group recognition and collective self-realization'. He notes too the movement of Cornish Studies to the interface between the humanities and the social sciences, and argues that the big challenge for the future for Cornish Studies is the contemplation of the relationship between Cornwall and the rest of the United Kingdom—the relationship between Cornwall and the other Celtic nations but also the relationship between Cornwall and England. Here the 'Celticity' of the Cornish is, perhaps, a key consideration, although constructions of Celticity are themselves fraught with contradictions and difficulty, so that imaginings of the 'Cornish Celt' are often hazy. Moreover, the engagement of Cornish Studies with Celtic Studies was in the past, in Williams's estimation, often unimaginative and uninspiring. Thus '[c]onventionally preoccupied with questions of language, archaeology and local history, Cornish Studies followed the canons of Celtic Studies scholarship but looked tired and flat by comparison with the more dynamic Irish and Welsh efforts'. New Cornish Studies by contrast, however, 'has been characterized by a quantum leap in both ambition and fulfilment', although there is yet much to achieve before aspiring to the achievements of Welsh or Irish Studies let alone the dizzy heights of Quebec or Catalonia.

More generally, Colin H. Williams warns of the danger of becoming 'semi-detached' from the public that Cornish Studies purports to serve, in its isolation failing to inform the 'civil society' it hopes to shape, in its aspiring to 'golden age' perfection unable to influence those planners and policy-makers charged with the pragmatic and compromise-driven business of managing Cornwall's future. He notes too the institutional poverty of Cornwall, the lack of Cornish institutions around which cultural and socio-economic regeneration might occur, forcing Cornish Studies all too often back upon the constituencies of the disaffected and the disempowered. And then there is the 'dissonance created by the ambition of having a unified ideology coupled with internal contradictions'. Although '[w]hat drives Cornish Studies forward is an ideological commitment to honour Cornwall's place in the history of these isles and to serve its citizens today', there is in the tension between the pursuit of ideological unity and the reality of internal contradictions an implicit danger of intellectual coercion, an oppressive form of 'positive' liberty. Nonetheless, Cornish Studies practitioners should do more 'to deepen their association with civil society and government in the coming decade' because 'the general need to continue the argument, to engage, to be active and committed, to cajole and convince, is one we all share as involved citizens. It is part of the refashioning of plural Britain, and for that reason I wish Cornish Studies well in the next and successive decades.'

From the meld of 'insider' and 'outsider' perceptions of the current state of Cornish Studies, we turn to the discipline in detail, commencing in chronological fashion with Charles Thomas's discussion of 'Cornish Archaeology at the Millennium'. Here Thomas chooses to emphasize continuity above change in Cornwall, to paint a picture of burgeoning archaeological activity and the role of the Cornwall Archaeological Unit (now subsumed in the Historic Environment Unit) in managing it, though stressing that at the UK national level much has altered in the way archaeology is conducted. Paradoxically, television 'digs' have popularized archaeology while the reality is that amateur enthusiasts have been frozen out of the excavation process, no longer able to work alongside the 'experts' as they might have done in the 1970s. In Cornwall, however, the Cornwall Archaeological Society has been able to continue its programme of outings and lectures, including its Young Archaeologist activities, and its journal *Cornish Archaeology* continues to publish long technical reports of recent work. Industrial archaeology, too, has enjoyed considerable attention in Cornwall during the last decade, evidenced in the activities of both the Trevithick Society and the Trevithick Trust and in the attention now of the Cornwall Archaeological Unit as it constructs (with the aid of partners throughout Cornwall, including the Institute of Cornish Studies) a bid to UNESCO for World Heritage Site status for the Cornish mining landscape.

But despite this activity, Thomas is concerned about the continuing difficulty of disseminating accurate material to the general reading public without the fear of 'dumbing down', and he is also uncomfortable with the way in which 'archaeological evidence' has been inappropriately co-opted in the tiresomely frequent local press contests between the pro-Cornish and the anti-Cornish, the former attempting to locate contemporary Cornishness in some essentialist Iron Age Celticity, the latter unable to grasp the basic tenets of Cornish 'difference'. In amongst this popular blur there is Tintagel, on the one hand implicated in a vast array of imaginings of the 'Arthurian' and the 'Celtic' but on the other central to much of what has made Cornish archaeology in the last decade or so. As Thomas rightly observes, Tintagel is Cornwall's Tower of London or Stonehenge. But beyond this are intriguing questions about Tintagel's purpose, about the agenda that was behind this strategically useless but symbolically powerful edifice which hints, perhaps, at the accommodation of the Cornish in the Anglo-Norman compact of medieval England. Before this:

> It is at least possible that pre-Geoffrey [of Monmouth], before the 1120s, the relevant legends here were of King Mark, Tristan and Iseult; that the post-Roman occupants were the regional kings of *Dumnonia*, a region that by the 700s included and distinguished *Cornubia*, Cornwall; and that in these and other respects Tintagel is a primary emotional focus of what became medieval Cornwall.

Against this background, Professor Thomas shares the sensitivities of many others in Cornwall: 'The rash of unsightly notices and signs with "English Heritage" causes genuine offence and distress and the recent expunging of the first word probably aroused more applaud than condemnation'. And yet, the examination of medieval 'identities' (whatever that might mean in that period) has not influenced Cornish Studies to any great degree, the pioneering work elsewhere of R.R. Davies (for example) failing to impact thus far on consideration of Cornish 'difference' or particularism in the medieval period. The only sustained exception is the work of David Harvey, with its focus on issues of authority and territorialization in West Cornwall. But that is not to suggest that Cornish medieval studies are in any way moribund; far from it. As Allen Buckley illustrates in this volume, medieval Cornwall retains its attractions for many researchers, its very remoteness and impenetrability deterring the faint-hearted but encouraging the determined and the intrigued. Amongst the latter are scholars such as Nicholas Orme, Joanna Mattingly, James Whetter and Oliver Padel, who together have contributed much over the last decade or so to the reconstruction of medieval Cornwall. Nicholas Orme's illumination of the medieval church and Cornish saints, for example, has been complemented by Joanna Mattingly's painstaking work on medieval gilds and, especially, the remarkable stained glass windows of St Neot, her researches telling us much about the social and economic as well as religious life of Cornwall in that period.

Buckley singles out for particular comment the work of Oliver Padel and Harold Fox on *The Cornish Lands of the Arundells of Lanherne, Fourteenth to Sixteenth Centuries*, based on the remarkable Arundell Collection of manorial records acquired by the Cornwall Record Office a little over a decade ago. Here, according to Buckley, Padel and Fox have 'opened up a hitherto barely touched aspect of Cornish history . . . Probably not since the time of Charles Henderson has such a monumental task been undertaken in the study of medieval Cornwall.' And as Buckley adds, one of the particular benefits of the Padel and Fox study is the insight it provides into how the manorial system developed long after the medieval period, with echoes of the landlord–tenant relationship remaining down to our own time. He also emphasizes the importance of the *Arundell* work for our understanding of surname formation. There are occupational names in the Cornish language, such as Trehar (tailor) and Angove (Smith), nicknames such as Pengwyn (whitehead) and Vyan (small), and aliases such as 'Richard Kearne alias Tresillian', together with 'three part' patronymic (familial) or toponymic (place-name) surnames like 'John Thomme Harry' and 'John Petit Predannek'. For the future, Buckley looks to the recently formed medieval seminar group, set up under the aegis of the Institute of Cornish Studies, and notes that the *Victoria County History* project (again with the assistance of the Institute) will be a major opportunity to investigate aspects of Cornwall's medieval past. He also acknowledges the need for new work to set Cornwall in its comparative 'European, Celtic and Anglo-Cornish context', in particular the place of Bretons in medieval Cornish society, and argues that more should be done to engage the wider public in the pursuit of Cornish medieval history.

If the Cornish public as a whole has been hesitant in approaching the rarefied world of medieval studies, it has had no such inhibitions in contributing to the vigorous debate surrounding the early modern period, the local press periodically carrying heated correspondence about (for example) what did or did not happen in the Cornish rebellion of 1549, and several amateur publications making exaggerated claims of one sort or another about that and other events. The latter, with their overt political agenda, have alarmed Oliver Padel, who has complained (in the *Newsletter of the Cornish History Network*, 13, March 2002) of the 'manipulation of history for political or other ends . . . I regret that, from what I have seen of it, some of what has been dubbed "the new Cornish historiography" appears to be rather prone to this weakness.' Of course, all history is in some sense 'political', and even those who deny or conceal their normative assumptions are routinely selective in their use of 'facts' as well as being unhesitant in their choice of contexts and interpretations and their use of their own historical imaginations. Even the most bland and uncritical local history, apparently innocent and apolitical, will—in its emphasis on continuity rather than change and with its focus on 'manor' and 'church' and 'gentry'—consciously or unconsciously perpetuate a deferential, partial view of the socio-economic, cultural and political past. But there is a distinction between 'good' and 'bad' history, and if Oliver Padel is concerned about the excesses of some contributions to the debate surrounding the early modern period, then he need look no further than the outstanding scholarly contributions of Mark Stoyle for reassurance.

Nobody has made a greater contribution to the 'new Cornish historiography' than Mark Stoyle, who during the last decade has produced a string of important articles on Cornwall in the early modern period, culminating in the appearance in 2002 of his masterly book *West Britons: Cornish Identities and the Modern British State.* Welcomed by Ronald Hutton, doyen of Civil War studies, as '[a] significant and original contribution to British history', the book (as its dustcover notes attest) has also caught the attention of John Morrill, an architect of the 'new British historiography', who recognizes in Stoyle 'a distinguished historian of Cornwall and a scholar who can relate the history of Cornwall to the history of Britain'. In this present collection, Mark Stoyle offers an overview of the recent historiography of early modern Cornwall, arguing that the felicitous coincidence of the recent upsurge of Cornish historical writing and the growing influence nationally and internationally of the 'new British historiography' has created exactly the right conditions in which scholars might be encouraged to return to the period dominated for so long by A.L. Rowse's *Tudor Cornwall* and Mary Coate's *Cornwall in the Great Civil War and Interregnum.*

Although Stoyle notes the influence of a variety of perspectives in this new focus on early modern Cornwall, he stresses the importance of those accounts that emphasize Cornish 'difference', especially those that concentrate on the Tudor rebellions of 1497 and 1549 and the Civil War of 1642–6. But he also acknowledges the importance of the cultural studies that form much of the background to this period, singling out for particular praise the work of Matthew Spriggs on the Reverend Joseph Sherwood of St Erth, a contribution which indicates that much still remains to be discovered about the Cornish language in its 'Late' or 'Modern' phase and is 'one of the shrewdest and most enjoyable pieces to have been published on early modern Cornwall in recent years'. Stoyle is also full of admiration for the work of Paul Cockerham on Cornish funerary memorials in the early modern period, Cockerham's painstaking researches having demonstrated that the 'passion for memorialization' so evident in Cornwall was highly un-usual, if not unique, in Tudor and Stuart Britain, and the memorials themselves (as Stoyle puts it) important 'signifiers of Cornish cultural difference'. As Stoyle concludes, 'Cockerham's pioneering research has underlined the valuable contribution which these not-so-mute stones can make to the study of Cornwall's early modern past'.

But it is rebellion and Civil War that commands Stoyle's greatest interest and attention, and it is here that the major contributions to our understanding of Cornwall's place in the wider upheavals in the making-of-Britain can be detected. Stoyle acknowledges the work of Ian Arthurson, who has suggested that Yorkist sympathies amongst the local gentry may have precipitated the uprisings of 1497, but he finds more persuasive the 'very different thesis' that the two rebellions of that year were 'fuelled by Cornish resistance to the intruding power of the English state'. Similarly, in the often heated debate that surrounds the Prayer Book rebellion of 1548–9, Stoyle is convinced by those arguments that suggest that Cornish resistance to English intrusion and 'cultural aggression' motivated many in Cornwall at that time. He refutes Whiting's claim that 'the Prayer Book rebels did not represent majority opinion in Cornwall', dismissing it as 'clearly implausible'. In the same way, Stoyle in his treatment of the Civil War, while noting the religious and political plurality stressed by Anne Duffin, also identifies a majority opinion in Cornwall during the conflict in support of the Royalist cause. Here Cornish particularism is once again a significant factor, with the Parliamentarian cause seen in Cornwall (as in Wales) as associated with 'a narrowly English interest' while 'Charles I was seen as the King of Great Britain, the defender of the rights and privileges of all his subject peoples'.

Mark Stoyle concludes with a warning that although accounts which emphazise Cornish 'difference' in the early modern period have become increasingly fashionable, '[t]he Kernowsceptic backlash may be just around the corner', a backlash whose primary objectives would be 'to thrust the historiography of early modern Cornwall back into the box labelled "English local history", and to nail down the lid'. Stoyle considers that such an effort would be doomed to failure, for 'this particular genie is now out of the bottle for good', but he welcomes the opportunity for debate that such a reaction would provide as Cornish scholarship moves on to address new issues in this period. Stoyle stresses the urgent need for a reassessment of the Church in Cornwall between the Reformation and the Civil War, but one might add that the transition from 'early modern' to 'modern' also requires attention, those years between the release of Bishop Trelawny from the Tower and the coming of the Wesleys, the movement from the world Stoyle has described to the English-speaking, Methodist industrial Cornwall whose reformulated identity has captured the attention of Bernard Deacon and others.

Cornish identity in the age of technological prowess is the subject of my own contribution in this collection, where I review much of the work that has been accomplished in the last decade or so in the study of industrial Cornwall but where I concentrate specifically on the relationship between industrialization and identity reformulation. Drawing upon my earlier *The Making of Modern Cornwall* (1992) and Bernard Deacon's more recent work, the article argues that Cornwall's experience was in some respects akin to that of other British industrial regions as the industrial process redefined and perpetuated regional differentiation and distinctiveness, but that 'Cornishness' had also a strong 'ethnic' element in its identity. This was an ethnicity inherited from earlier times but it was also one made explicit in this period by commentators such as Samuel Drew and Fortescue Hitchins who constructed an 'ethnic history' around the 'subjugation of the Cornish by the English'. Pride in Cornish industrial prowess fuelled this ethnicity but, paradoxically, it also became entwined in the dominant imperial discourses (sometimes competing, sometimes complementary) of 'Englishness' and 'Britishness', producing within Cornwall a hybrid and complex identity which could be both 'English' and 'non-English' as well as 'British' and 'Cornish'.

To this complexity was added the emerging discourse of 'Celticity', one which impacted upon Cornwall in its industrial period but which became dominant in the post-industrial era, the anti-industrial, 'rural idyll' ideology of this new Celticism filling the space left by the decline of mining. As I argue, the Cornish experience is in some respects an exemplar of the wider Celtic experience, not least in dealing with the contradictory image of the 'industrial Celt', and is of value in considering the histories (and contemporary identities) of Ireland, Scotland and Wales where the industrial/Celtic contradictions have been of profound importance to both nation-building ideologies and national historiographies. However, with one or two notable exceptions, recent examinations of the Cornish experience have failed thus far to penetrate broader debates, a failing most apparent in Christopher Harvie's intriguing paper, delivered in 2000, on 'Larry Doyle and Captain MacWhirr: The Engineer and the Celtic Fringe', which, while examining many of the themes central to any discussion of Celtic identity and industrialization in Cornwall, devoted but three words to Cornwall. It has been left to Amy Hale to offer a more explicit analysis of the Cornish case and, as I note, in her contribution to David Harvey *et al.*'s 2002 book *Celtic Geographies*, she illustrates how in recent decades industrial symbols important to contemporary Cornish identity, such as ruined engine houses and china clay dumps, have been reinterpreted popularly as 'Celtic icon's, the 'industrial Celt' paradox by now having come full circle.

Central to the industrial identity of nineteenth-century Cornwall was the 'myth of Cousin Jack', an assertion born of technological prowess and deployed the world over to secure employment in the face of ethnic competition which insisted that the Cornish were innately qualified above all others as hard-rock miners. This, in turn, was central to Cornwall's 'Great Emigration', the extraordinary mass movement over a century and more of men and women from Cornwall to almost all corners of the globe as well as to other parts of these islands, much of it (but by no means all) associated with the establishment and growth of an international mining economy. Long established as an important element of Cornish historical study, examination of the Great Emigration has quickened during the last decade, with the publication here in Cornwall of volumes such as *The Cornish Overseas* (1999) mirrored in the appearance amongst the international Cornish-Australian and Cornish-American communities of titles such as Patricia Lay's *One and All: The Cornish in New South Wales* (1998) and Gage McKinney's *When Miners Sang: The Grass Valley Carol Choir* (2001). Much of this new work has been to 'fill in the gaps' in the narrative of Cornwall's emigration but there has also been an increasing emphasis on synthesis and explanation, as well as a tentative search for theoretical and comparative frameworks in which to place and better understand the Cornish experience. In this way, as Sharron Schwartz notes in her article in this collection, '[m]igration has . . . become a central plank in the platform upon which "the new Cornish historiography" has been constructed'.

Indeed, Sharron Schwartz has herself been pivotal in all this, her several articles and her doctoral thesis on the Cornish in Latin America illuminating a hitherto distinctly under-researched area of the Great Emigration and her insistence upon the importance and positive impact of both return migration and 'remittances' (monies sent home from abroad) challenging and altering conventional wisdoms. As if to under-line the process, even as she criticized those 'researchers [who] either ignored or downplayed the role of remittances', empirical evidence was emerging to support her view. For example, Larry Cenotto and Robert Richards have described the recent discovery in the old Post Office at Sutter Creek, in the heart of California's 'Motherlode' gold mining country, of details of 'foreign money orders', including lists of Cornish people who sent money home to Cornwall in the years 1898 to 1907. Now safely in the Amador County Archives, these lists indicate the activities of individuals such as M. Venning, who channelled part of his earnings back to one 'Mary Jane' of Torpoint, or Lewis Kempthorne who remitted funds to 'Martha' at St Agnes, or James Berryman who sent money to 'Beatrice' at Ponsanooth.

However, the critique that Schwartz presents in this volume is not limited to these concerns but expresses her wider disquiet that Cornish emigration studies, while increasingly prepared to consider comparative perspectives, have failed to respond sufficiently to the interdisciplinary spirit of New Cornish Studies by looking across the boundaries of the several disciplines with an interest in migration. In reviewing the progress of Cornish emigration studies over the last ten years, she notes the absence of many theoretical insights offered elsewhere in the academy and alights upon the work of scholars such as Oded Stark who in their 'new economics of labour migration' emphasize, as Schwartz explains, 'that out-migration, onward migration and return migration may be interlinked, part of a conscious strategy of risk diversification and capital accumulation by households and communities'. Here 'transnational collectivities' become important, as do the return migration and remittances noted above, affording new ways of looking at the Cornish experience and of understanding 'the continuing ramifications of the "Great Migration" on the modern Cornish, *both* at home and overseas'. As she concludes, '[a] corpus of excellent work has been built around the immigrant Cornish experience, but it is now time to adopt a fresh epistemological approach'.

As Schwartz freely acknowledges, she has been influenced strongly in her research and in her thinking by Ronald Perry, and working together Schwartz and Perry have made a significant contribution to Cornish Studies in recent years. Over a longer period, Ronald Perry has established a fine reputation as a Cornish economist, pioneering the study of many of the areas that have come to define the 'new Cornish social science', notably 'counter-urbanization' and 'opposition economics', but he has also ventured successfully into the realms of economic history, offering amongst other things a more nuanced understanding of late Victorian and Edwardian Cornwall. In his article in this volume, Perry brings together these several specialisms to provide what he calls a 'geo-economic perspective' of the making of modern Cornwall in the period 1800–2000. Noting the social, cultural and political as well as economic generalizations of the period offered by Bernard Deacon and myself, he argues for the particular relevance of an economic perspective. As he explains:

The far-reaching and imaginative interpretations of Payton and Deacon encompass a whole range of political, cultural and social, as well as spatial and economic issues, stretching back in time to medieval Cornwall. This article, however, focuses upon geo-economic aspects and covers the period from the late eighteenth century to the present day, offering a different perspective, through the use of a path-dependent model in which economic options in one period result from events and decisions in previous periods.

In so doing, Perry examines, for example, the centre–periphery model as an aid in understanding Cornwall's recent economic history, cautiously accepting its validity for certain periods but rejecting it for others. In contrast, he sets out to emphazise the important role of Cornwall in the early nineteenth century in the transfer of capital, technology and skilled labour to Latin America (mining) and South Wales (smelting), together with the key mid-century strategy to construct a direct rail link from Falmouth to Exeter—a means of maintaining Falmouth's pre-eminent maritime trading position in south-west Britain. But the latter scheme failed, the 'direct' route when it came being built via Plymouth (Falmouth's competitor) and furnishing merely a branch line from Truro to Falmouth. The Cornish port was thus eclipsed, combining with the decline of mining after the crash of copper to restrict Cornwall's opportunities for diversification. Paradoxically, 'it was the very responsiveness of earlier entrepreneurial actions—export of up-stream technology to the New World, transfer of down-stream technology to South Wales—combined with the failure to avoid a rail route that reinforced Plymouth as a regional Naval base and industrial port' that had prevented such diversification.

However, in contradistinction to other writers, Perry does identify sustained and often successful (at least in the short term) efforts (including those by return migrants) to achieve diversity in the Cornish economy, arguing that it was only later in the twentieth century that Cornwall became fully immersed in what he calls the 'institutionalization of core–periphery dependency'. The regional development policies of the 1960s were the first tangible institutions of dependency, followed by the 'counter-urbanization' and 'branch-factory' economy which led in turn to the early twenty-first-century marginalization recognizable today. He notes that there are now moves afoot to combat this dependency and marginalization, not least (in his estimation) the demands for a Cornish Assembly. But he also calls for an end to the imbalance in the economic study of Cornwall which has been unduly mining-centric, neglectful of intra-Cornwall differences and comparisons, and unaware of the significance of Plymouth as a barrier to Cornish economic development.

Ronald Perry's work on the economic history of modern Cornwall has been complemented by Garry Tregidga's on the political, and in this volume Tregidga offers a concise overview of 'personality, party and place' in Cornwall's often distinctive political experience. He contends that '[o]ne of the central features of Cornish Studies over the past ten years has been a growing interest in political issues', pointing to 'anti-metropolitanism' as both the focus of this interest and as a defining feature of what we may call 'Cornish political culture'. Synthesizing the ostensibly different approaches of political historians and political scientists from Edwin Jaggard to Adrian Lee, Tregidga detects aspects of coherence and unity in their work, with their emphases on 'difference' and on the emergence, sustenance and then survival of 'the Cornish radical tradition' over two centuries and its 'export' to other areas of the world, notably South Australia. Much of this work has focused on the fortunes (or otherwise) of the Liberal Party in Cornwall, including its complex relationship with the politics of anti-metropolitanism (and the nationalist party, Mebyon Kernow), but Tregidga argues that it is now time to turn to the other parties active in Cornwall which have been rather neglected—perhaps because they have seemed somehow 'less Cornish' than the Liberals and therefore less attractive as subjects for research for those with an interest in 'difference' and 'identity'.

Be that as it may, despite this call for a more catholic approach to the study of Cornish politics (including too the now obligatory call for recognition of intra-Cornwall distinctions), Tregidga considers that it is the ethno-regionalist imperative that is likely to continue to attract the attention of researchers over the years ahead 'as Cornwall attempts to meet the challenge of the new constitutional reorganization that is currently developing throughout the United Kingdom'. Here, he argues, there is evidence in Cornish Studies of a 'renewed interest in contemporary politics [which] comes at a critical time in the constitutional development of the United Kingdom', a time when the Combined Universities in Cornwall project has heralded institutional renewal in Cornwall and when there are major tensions between the Cornish Constitutional Convention's vision of a Cornish Assembly and the Labour government's plans to include Cornwall as an integral part of a seven-county regional structure.

But as well as emphasizing the importance of contemporary work, Garry Tregidga calls for more biographical studies of key figures in Cornish political history, arguing that such work can shed important light on political events, attitudes and trends. Here he has in mind historical figures such as Isaac Foot and perhaps A.L. Rowse, but 'political biography' of a different sort is exhibited in Edwin Jaggard's short 'biographical' article marking the important contribution to Cornish political studies of the late Brian Elvins, who died in 2001. As both Tregidga and Jaggard note, Elvins's contribution was of long standing, his early work providing much of the inspiration for Jaggard's own efforts, but it was only with the launch of *Cornish Studies* (Second Series) as a scholarly and accessible forum that he returned to writing and research in earnest. Working hard to adapt his work to new thinking and the latest research findings, Brian Elvins made an important but sadly eleventh-hour contribution to the flowering of activity described by Tregidga, shedding important new light on the history of the Liberals and on Cornish political culture in general.

It is but a short step from political culture to other cultural forms, and Alan M. Kent in his article takes us comprehensively into the realms of Cornish literature and literary studies, reviewing the development of both over the last ten years. Wide-ranging as well as exhaustive, Kent uses as his route map his excellent book *The Literature of Cornwall: Continuity, Identity, Difference 1000–2000* (2000), based in turn on his University of Exeter Ph.D. thesis, where he argues that 'in order for the literary imagining of Cornwall to be revitalized, writers must end the lament for what is lost and seek new ways of "de-Revivalizing" the literature'. He also sees the development of both Cornish literature and Cornish literary studies as necessarily mirroring that of Cornish history and other areas of Cornish Studies, where new 'Archipelagic' perspectives and contemporary political and economic change are creating new agendas and interests. Similarly, he notes the engagement of Cornish literature and literary studies with those elsewhere in the 'newly configured Britain' which are also responding to the new discourses of the 'Anglo-Celtic archipelago'. But he notes too that in Cornwall's 'unresolved duality of place' in the United Kingdom, something still undergoing constant negotiation at several levels and in various spheres (literary, historical, political, constitutional, and so on), there is a particular Cornish 'uniqueness' which makes the study of Cornwall so fascinating.

As a result of this 'unresolved duality of place', Cornish literature and literary studies are 'in some state', sometimes 'confused and sometimes unfocused, but also vibrant, contemporary and dynamic'. In this condition, argues Kent, it is crucial for Cornish literature to try to break out of its self-imposed straitjackets (many of them 'Revivalist' in nature) with the aim of truly transcending the Tamar, in effect making the 'local' into the 'international' and affirming the global worth and relevance of Cornish identity rather than compromising it. Meanwhile, the task of Cornish literary studies remains formidable. Like many others, Kent regrets the lack of a reliable, comprehensive, scholarly and annotated edition of the texts of the corpus of Cornish-language literature, with good English translations, and he is keen to see studies of the literature on and by the Cornish overseas. Echoing Tregidga's call for political biographies, Kent argues that many of Cornwall's literary figures remain shadowy and in need of biographical treatment. And, like Tregidga, Perry and others elsewhere in this volume, Alan M. Kent sees this particular moment in Cornwall's history as being of crucial significance, in this case for the future of Cornish literature in which a resolution of Cornwall's duality, or at least its more balanced expression, may alter Cornish writing 'irrevocably'.

In surveying the wider world of Cornish cultural studies, Amy Hale acknowledges that 'Cornish Studies, like most "area studies", are based on the central premise of cultural differentiation', and she admits too that it is 'engaged in a normative project to locate a distinctively Cornish identity'. However, she also contends that the approach of Cornish Studies (as expressed institutionally in the Institute of Cornish Studies) to cultural differentiation has changed over the years, focused initially on material culture and linguistics, moving by the 1990s to theoretically led historical inquiry to explain the persistence of Cornish identity over time, and then attempting a more uncertain engagement with cultural studies and anthropology. But much of this recent engagement has involved historical and documentary or secondary source material, with the possibilities for ethnographic field-based research largely unrecognized or unaddressed, the only major exceptions being the work of Mary McArthur, Caroline Vink and Amy Hale herself.

Hale recognizes that there are a number of reasons for this state of affairs, some internal and some external, and some to do with the current nature of anthropology, the trend within the discipline to focus its activities beyond Western Europe rendering the Cornish invisible to its scholarship, a position reinforced by the reluctance of ill-informed grant-awarding bodies to allocate resources to the study of those perceived to be 'white people in England'. Yet, in terms of folklore studies, Cornwall has always occupied a particular niche, in its early days little more than antiquarianism but more recently exhibiting a certain sophistication which, in identifying and asserting Cornish folkloric 'difference', may also act as the confidence-building legitimation that anthropology needs to be persuaded of to allow a more sustained engagement with Cornish Studies. Here, Hale insists, ethnographic research in Cornwall should move away 'from an examination of the phenomenon of Cornish identity as based in lived experience to exploring the sometimes competing identities constructed within a wider discourse of identity'. She also identifies room in Cornwall for 'cultural studies' itself, calling for a greater engagement with the sub-discipline and recognizing the need to build upon Ella Westland's ground-breaking collection *Cornwall: The Cultural Construction of Place* (1997). In mapping the way forward she calls for greater accep-tance of the fact that 'Cornwall does not contain a homogeneous mass of people. It never has and there are a number of hybrid Cornish identities which could profitably be researched.' Moreover, she adds, '[t]he Cornish are themselves not one single, easy-to-define population . . . Aside from the various ethnicities residing in the peninsula, there are gender groupings, class groupings, religious groups, industry-based groupings and sexual identities all of which overlap and combine'.

In several important respects the problems raised by Amy Hale and her challenges for the future are being met, albeit from a radically different perspective, by the work of the Cornish Audio Visual Archive (CAVA) project, a 'movement' (as Treve Crago describes it in his article) based in the Institute of Cornish Studies but drawing its strength from a major Cornwall-wide partnership and now the recipient of a very substantial grant from the Heritage Lottery Fund. Here, as Crago explains, the research method is indeed field work but the academic context is oral history. Rather like folklore, oral history has always enjoyed a niche in Cornish Studies, the desire to record the memories of 'old folk' before they pass on complemented by specific research aims such as dialect surveys or documenting agricultural practices. Indeed, as Crago also explains, there is in this an important continuity in the activities of the Institute in both its pre-1991 and later guises, the oral history recordings conducted under Charles Thomas's direction now forming a valuable part of the CAVA collection.

However, there are some important differences between the 'old' and the 'new', not least in CAVA's explicit engagement in current debates about the nature and purpose of oral history. Here 'oral history' is not merely the collecting of 'reminiscences' for particular research aims ('dialect' or 'agricultural practices'), nor even an activity designed to add to and diversify the repertoire of primary research material available to the historian, but is a *genre* in its own right. Echoing the work of Alessandro Portelli, Crago argues that the 'distortions' of history thrown up sometimes by memories 'failing' or 'altering' with the years (a phenomenon that has made many con-servative historians suspicious of oral history) is, far from being problematic, an valuable insight into eyewitness accounts that are neither 'true' nor 'false' but reveal an individual's 'composure'. This 'composure' is the way in which an individual strives to place himself or herself successfully within a story, creating (in Penny Summerhill's words) 'a coherent narrative and version of oneself which can be lived within relative psychic comfort'.

If the work of Treve Crago seems innovative, not to say radical, then there is some reassurance that some things in Cornish cultural studies do not change, not least the continuing preoccupation with the Cornish language and its Revival. The late 1980s and the 1990s were dominated by the 'language debate' about the relative merits of the three principal forms of Revived Cornish ('Unified', 'Kemmyn' and 'Modern') and, by extension, about the relative academic worth of the work of their principal advocates (Nicholas Williams, Ken George and Richard Gendall). However, although that debate shows no signs of abating, there are important indications that new agendas and new possibilities are emerging. First of all, there was in 2002 the exciting discovery of a hitherto unnoticed, apparently sixteenth-century Cornish-language document, a *Life of St Kea (Beunans Ke)*, which turned up in the personal papers of the late Professor J.E. Caerwyn Williams when donated to the National Library of Wales in Aberystwyth. Thought at first to be two separate plays, the document is now recognized as one (incomplete) play, the first part detailing the life of St Kea, a Celtic saint venerated in both Cornwall and Brittany, the second based on Geoffrey of Monmouth's tale of King Arthur's quarrel with the Roman emperor Lucius Hiberius, a tale which culminates in Arthur's triumph and the emperor's death in battle, together with the clandestine affair between Arthur's nephew Modred and Queen Guenevere. As well as expanding the corpus of Middle Cornish literature by some 20 per cent, the play sheds new light on the cult of St Kea in Cornwall and (echoing Charles Thomas's estimation of the emotional importance of Tintagel to the medieval Cornish) provides impressive new evidence of the strength of Cornish interest in the Arthurian tradition.

In its way equally important was the successful completion in 2002 of Jon Mills's doctoral thesis at the University of Exeter on the 'Computer-Assisted Lemmatisation of a Cornish Text Corpus for Lexicographical Purposes'. At a time when much of contemporary Revived Cornish is lexicographically problematic, to say the least, Mills's rigorous intervention in Cornish language studies promises a surer footing for the future. As well as facilitating a more objective assessment of Revived Cornish usages, Mills's work paves the way at last for a full Cornish dictionary and for scholarly editions of the corpus of Cornish in its original spelling and with good English translations.

Hot on the heels of *Beunans Ke* and the Mills thesis came the intimation in July 2002 that the British government had, after lengthy consideration, decided that it would shortly add Cornish to the list of indigenous 'minority' languages in the United Kingdom recognized within the context of the European Charter of Minority or Regional Languages of which the UK is already a signatory. This too opens up a range of new possibilities for both the study of historical Cornish and the development of the Revived language, and is directly attributable to the intervention in the debate about the status of Cornish by Professor Kenneth MacKinnon. Already known for his important work on Scots Gaelic and on language-planning advice for the Scottish Executive, MacKinnon was commissioned by the Government Office of the South-West to undertake an independent academic study of Cornish. In his article in this collection, he explains this process, offering a summary of the report he went on to produce and also (unlike the original report) offering recommendations and thoughts for the future.

Significantly, a number of Kenneth MacKinnon's recommendations is echoed in Neil Kennedy's article 'Fatel Era Ny a Kee?' (How are we doing?), where Kennedy attempts to 'reflect on the contemporary needs of the revival as a whole rather than getting bogged down in factional interests or the historical focus of most Celticists'. Here his concern is that 'a small set of preoccupations and distractions is diverting the energies of revivalists from the task of constructing a social context for Cornish'. Accepting both the plurality of the Cornish language situation and the surprising degree of convergence between the researches of Williams, George and Gendall, he concludes that it may be possible for many in the language movement to accept now that no-one can impose an absolute standard. He echoes Ray Chubb's belief that personal freedom is preferable to coercion, and believes that in such a climate of tolerance and acceptance language practitioners will not only be able to work together in a way that has not been possible in the recent past but will be able to supplement historical research with newly developed studies of learning and teaching: 'Above all, we need to create an atmosphere of reflective, practice-based research amongst teachers and encourage the ongoing, critical examination of resources and methods. This needs to recognize that many, if not most, of the answers lie outside the classroom and may be addressed by revivalists themselves.'

Intimations of governmental recognition of the 'official' status of the Cornish language were a considerable boost for the language-planning aspirations of Neil Kennedy and others, and reinforced the perception—expressed by many in this volume—that there is something especially significant in the present moment. The creation of the Combined Universities of Cornwall project, with the movement in 2004 of the Institute of Cornish Studies to the new campus at Tremough, is tangible evidence of institutional renewal, a significant reversal of the post-war trend in Cornwall of institutional deconstruction and decay. At the same time there is a strong Cornish contribution, exemplified in the activities of the Cornish Constitutional Convention with its demand for a Cornish Assembly, to the debate about the future of regionalization and devolution in the UK, especially with regard to the possibility of asymmetrical solutions (such as those applied in Spain) rather than the imposition of templates based on the 'standard' planning regions. Colin H. Williams has stressed the importance for the future relevance of Cornish Studies that it should engage in debate about the 'civil' future of Cornwall and its external relationships, a view echoed throughout this volume by scholars who see in Cornwall's place in the re-defining United Kingdom unparalleled opportunities for the future. The last decade's work has seen much activity, excitement and achievement but all this may pale into insignificance as we contemplate what lies ahead.

Philip Payton,
Professor of Cornish Studies and
Director, Institute of Cornish Studies,
University of Exeter.

THE NEW CORNISH STUDIES: NEW DISCIPLINE OR RHETORICALLY DEFINED SPACE?

Bernard Deacon

INTRODUCTION

The decades around the turns of centuries (even more so in the case of millennia) are perfect breeding grounds for the cult of the 'new'. In the 1900s New Liberalism emerged, to be succeeded in the 1990s by its distantly related offspring 'New Labour'. Meanwhile, 'new turns' and 'new directions' proliferate in academic disciplines.[1] Amongst these progeny of *fin-de-siècle* anxieties and *début-de-siècle* clean-slate enthusiasms, the last ten years have seen the emergence of the New Cornish Studies, together with its sub-genres of the 'new Cornish social science' and the 'new Cornish historiography'. These explicit labels made their simultaneous appearance in 1995,[2] although they had been prefigured as early as 1993 when it was claimed that Charles Thomas, the first Professor of Cornish Studies, had effectively been 'arguing for the development of a critical Cornish social science' back in 1972.[3] Since 1995 the twin descriptors of 'new Cornish social science' and 'new Cornish historiography' have been regularly invoked. It is, therefore, high time these concepts were subjected to some interrogation.

In relation to New Labour, Steven Lukes has proposed that the 'third way' is neither a concept nor an ideology; instead it is better viewed as a 'rhetorically defined space'.[4] This is a space that bounds a number of different, even contradictory concepts and has expansive and shifting boundaries defined in terms of a set of broad values rather than rigid ideological traditions. The New Cornish Studies may not, as we shall see, share the ambiguity produced by the capacious 'rhetorical space' of New Labour. Nevertheless, it retains a certain elusiveness and the analogy suggests one apposite line of criticism. This might revolve around perceived gaps between the rhetoric of claims and the substance of achievements. In this review I shall present an 'insider', yet nonetheless critical, reflection on the New Cornish Studies. I shall indeed argue that the New Cornish Studies does, in many respects, fit the description of a 'rhetorically defined space'. Moreover, I shall also suggest that surveying the actual corpus of work produced within Cornish Studies in the past decade leads us to the conclusion that, rather than a sharp discontinuity between 'old' and 'new' Cornish Studies, we might detect a continuum between them. The New Cornish Studies builds on, re-emphasizes and develops some of the concerns of the 'old' Cornish Studies. However, the rhetoric of the New Cornish Studies also reflects and clarifies real shifts in the context of Cornish Studies over the past decade. In doing so it presents opportunities for a research agenda that, although currently only in the process of fulfilment, offers exciting pointers for the next decade of work in Cornish Studies.

In Lukes's formulation, boundary formation is crucial to all kinds of rhetorically defined spaces, whether political projects or academic disciplines. Just as New Labour might be viewed as having porous and flexible boundaries, so the boundaries around Cornish Studies have not remained static. In this article I begin by defining some possible boundaries, briefly tracing the etymology of the New Cornish Studies and contrasting it with 'old Cornish Studies'. In the process I identify some reasons why Cornish Studies adopted certain new directions after the 1980s. I then move on to identify some tensions within the New Cornish Studies project before focusing more specifically on the 'new Cornish historiography'. This course is adopted not because the 'new Cornish historiography' is more important than the 'new Cornish social science', but rather because Malcolm Williams elsewhere in his volume reviews the 'new Cornish social science' and offers his own view of its 'foundational myths'. The article concludes by pulling together some possible pointers for the future direction of Cornish Studies. These are necessarily speculative and should be approached as preliminary observations on the present and future state of Cornish Studies, in the hope of stimulating and energizing further debate about its direction.

THE ROOTS OF CORNISH STUDIES

In their volume *New Directions in Celtic Studies*, Amy Hale and Philip Payton ask the question 'what is Celtic Studies'? We also need to turn this question back onto Cornish Studies itself. In asking what it is, we have first to establish what it was and what else it might have been.

Those involved in academic Cornish Studies based in and around the Institute of Cornish Studies, part of the University of Exeter but situated in Cornwall and part-funded by Cornwall County Council, represent Cornish Studies in its institutionalized variant. But institutionalized Cornish Studies, although inevitably the focus of this review, has a relatively short history and, furthermore, only represents one possible strand among several. We might, for example, identify at least three models of Cornish Studies that are available to us: Cornish Studies as local studies, Cornish Studies as national(ist) studies, and Cornish Studies as Celtic Studies. These variants provide possible boundaries for its rhetorically defined space.

Cornish Studies as local studies originated in the antiquarian moment of the eighteenth and nineteenth centuries, when gentlemanly amateurs began painstakingly to reconstruct the historical traces of their parishes. This gradually evolved into the local history groups of the late twentieth and early twenty-first centuries. In contemporary Cornwall the model is perhaps most clearly seen in the Cornwall Association of Local Historians. But it has also informed the explicitly more 'Cornish' activities of the Old Cornwall societies. While local historians valorize the 'local', other academic disciplines employ the local within a spatial hierarchy which treats it as a quarry for the wider academic community, providing the empirical data that informs wider perspectives and contexts and tests generalizations, models and theories. The application of this model to Cornish Studies has had two implications. First, it tends to lead to an emphasis upon the single place, parish or community. In this way it bears out John Marshall's observation that places are often 'examined without a visible territorial framework'.[5] Moreover, places can sometimes be studied with no discernable comparative context whatsoever. Second, it tends to put Cornish Studies into a box labelled 'local' while the really important academic work goes on elsewhere. This attitude was implied by the remark of a former Principal of Cornwall College in 1990: 'we use Cornwall and its environment as a resource but we are also aware of wider concerns'.[6] Past or present Cornwall, from this perspective, only provides a series of case studies that might illuminate broader academic generalizations.[7] Seeing Cornish Studies in this way strips away its 'Cornish' aspect and renders it as mere local studies, with a resultant lowly positioning within the academic hierarchy.

The second possible approach is that of Cornish Studies as national(ist) studies. At the time of the formation of the Institute of Cornish Studies in 1971, Charles Thomas's own connections with the Cornish Revival and the support of the revivalist movement in the Institute's establishment guaranteed that issues dear to the Revival's heart, most obviously the Cornish language, played a considerable part in the content of academic Cornish Studies.[8] During the 1990s a less culturally confined and more politically focused strand of Cornish Studies as nationalist studies began to emerge. This adopted a colonial framework for viewing Cornwall's history and for explaining the waning of the Cornish language.[9] But, while vigorously articulated, the polemical tone of this writing and its cavalier treatment of historical evidence put it outside the mainstream of academic Cornish Studies, although many of its concerns and some of its assumptions are, as we shall see later, shared by that Cornish Studies community.

Finally, there is Cornish Studies as Celtic Studies. This clearly overlapped in the 1970s with Cornish Studies as national studies, both having a common interest in the Cornish language and dialect. It also provided the early Institute with a ready-made academic legitimacy. However, Celtic Studies has its own disciplinary centre, one that revolves around linguistics and medieval literature. Those Celtic languages that have a rich set of resources for study, like Irish and Welsh, lie at the core of the discipline. Languages such as Cornish, with a smaller literature and a much smaller medieval language community, are of more marginal interest. In addition, the role of Revived Cornish was looked at by Celtic scholars with great suspicion and even hostility.[10]

Because of these problems, academic Cornish Studies was never situated in its entirety within the Celtic Studies canon of 'Celtic' linguistics and medieval literature. While two of its first three staff did work in those fields, the definition of Cornish Studies adopted by Charles Thomas was always much broader: 'the study of all aspects of man and his handiwork in the regional setting (Cornwall and Scilly), past, present and future. The development of society, industry and the landscape in our fast-changing world is as much of concern . . . as the history of those vast topics in the recent and remote past.'[11] In theory this meant that Cornish Studies could encompass a huge range of disciplinary concerns across the humanities and social sciences. In practice Cornish Studies was a pragmatic amalgam of traditional Celtic Studies, plus Charles Thomas's own specialism, archaeology, and, drawing from the Cornish Studies as local studies paradigm, local history.

THE NEW CORNISH STUDIES AND ITS CONTEXT

But what is the New Cornish Studies and how does it differ from the old? While, as we have seen, the descriptors 'new Cornish social science' and 'new Cornish historiography' were regularly applied by Philip Payton to Cornish Studies from 1995 onwards, there is no key text that sets out the basis of the New Cornish Studies. Nevertheless, its main elements can be identified from Philip Payton's writings. While his evolving stance on New Cornish Studies can be gleaned most easily from the Introductions to the series *Cornish Studies* from 1996 onwards,[12] one of the most succinct statements appeared in a less accessible source, the Australian journal *Locality,* in 2000. Here, focusing on the 'new Cornish historiography', Payton claims that it leaves behind the 'stifling bonds of antiquarianism' and turns from that 'inward looking and uncritical chronicling of events west of the River Tamar' to a more interdisciplinary and more contextual approach, giving a sense of both people and place and setting these firmly into their comparative background.[13]

Interdisciplinarity, comparison and context are the three central concepts of the New Cornish Studies. Indeed, we can incorporate these aspects into an ideal model of the contrast between 'new' and 'old' Cornish Studies, at least as articulated in the writings of Philip Payton (see Table 1). Perhaps the starkest contrast is in the attitude to social

	Old Cornish Studies	New Cornish Studies
theory	empiricist	informed by social theory
content	the past	the contemporary
	Cornish particularities	Cornish difference and identity
methods	insights of specialist disciplines	multidisciplinary and interdisciplinary
	pure	applied/policy engagement

theory. The plea for a direct engagement with social theory indicates a vision of Cornish Studies as closer to the social sciences than to the humanities. In his own major synthesis of Cornwall's past, *TheMaking of Modern Cornwall,* published in 1992, Payton adopts an explicit centre–periphery model.[14] More recently, the preferred model has become that of the 'new British history', suggesting that academic frameworks can be adopted from history and the humanities as well as the more theory-orientated social sciences.[15]

On taking over as Director of the Institute of Cornish Studies in October 1991, Philip Payton alerted its Associates to his desire to move the focus of activity of Cornish Studies 'towards contemporary Cornwall', towards its socio-economic condition, issues of governance and politics, and the cultural state of its communities.[16] In history, similarly, there was a shift from the concern with the very distant past, as expressed in archaeological studies, to that of the modern period.[17] Two issues have been prominent in the preferred content of the New Cornish Studies. At first the issue was 'difference': 'when all is said and done it is this Cornish "difference" that is at root the *raison d'être* of Cornish Studies as an area of academic inquiry'.[18] Because sensitivity to 'difference' raises the question of 'identity', a second strand to the content of New Cornish Studies increasingly apparent from 1997 was that of 'identity formation'. By 1998 it was being asserted that 'elucidation and analysis of [the Cornish identity] is perhaps the prime task of Cornish Studies as an academic discipline'.[19] Methodologically, the call was for interdisciplinarity and the 'genuine cross-disciplinary transfer' of methods.[20] The aim was to move beyond multidisciplinary studies to a more deliberately integrative approach to understanding Cornwall. The purpose of this quest for integrated knowledge was 'to marshal, synthesize and explain hitherto disparate knowledge'. Together with its interdisciplinary emphasis, the 'new Cornish social science' was claimed to be both empirical and applied.[21]

Superficially, as the references so far indicate, the New Cornish Studies seems heavily dependent on one person. Academic Cornish Studies has always been a small field in terms of personnel. This means that, to explain its development, we have to give an important place to individuals. And none more so than the Directors of the Institute of Cornish Studies. As editors of *Cornish Studies* (in both its [first series] guise as an in-house journal and in its current [second series] existence as annual volumes), and as spokespersons for the Institute, they have occupied a strategic role in interpreting and advancing the form that Cornish Studies takes. But, inevitably, the limited resources of the Institute and the marginal place of Cornish Studies within the academy also require Directors of the Institute to adopt a rhetorical stance on the field, attempting to steer its potential future as well as articulate its achievements in the present.[22] This both reminds us of, and partly explains, the rhetorical aspect of the New Cornish Studies, as a statement of a desired epistemological position rather than as a necessarily accurate description of current practice.

However, the rhetorical nature of the New Cornish Studies project should not prevent us, on the other hand, from recognizing that a real shift in the focus of Cornish Studies has occurred over the past decade.

This shift has been accomplished by a group of scholars working in a loose network, if not exactly bonded by the close contact and shared aims sometimes imagined or projected. The other contributions to this volume go a long way to record the breadth of coverage and the number of people who have, directly or tangentially, worked in and around the field of Cornish Studies over the past decade. Moreover, there are good, contextual reasons why we should expect Cornish Studies to have changed direction since the 1980s, reasons that exist over and above changes in personnel at the Institute of Cornish Studies. These intellectual and social shifts have altered the terrain within which Cornish Studies has to survive.

The first of these has been provoked by growing academic debates in the humanities and social sciences around the notion of post-modernism. Postmodernist theorists have made explicit a scepticism about those 'grand narratives', such as liberalism or Marxism, that formerly held sway within the social sciences and which attempted to construct over-arching theories of society. Instead of the generalizing thrust of 'grand narratives', it is argued that scholars should return to a concern with the unexpected and the contingent, the heterogeneous rather than the homogenous. This shift has had a profound effect and one that goes far beyond the often inaccessible work that passes itself off as 'postmodernist'. In general terms it has helped to produce an uncertainty about the former taken-for-granted canons and procedures of various academic disciplines. More specifically, it opens up a space for studying areas formerly viewed as marginal or liminal.[23] In this respect, as a result of a changing intellectual climate, the highly specialized and rigidly compartmentalized disciplines of social science and historical studies are under pressure. Some observers see this change as leading to a growth of interest in 'regional and local approaches'.[24] The broad turn to the regional and local makes it easier for Cornish Studies to claim credibility and establish its legitimacy within an academic community that has sometimes tended to approach Cornwall and Cornish Studies with a certain amount of wariness.

Furthermore, the turn to the local and the regional is often accompanied by the adoption of concepts of fluidity and hybridity. It is this that has multiplied uncertainties about formerly cherished assumptions. Celtic Studies is a disciplinary field that has, arguably, been more affected by growing uncertainty than many others. The work of Malcolm Chapman and Simon James has, from their vantage points of anthropology and archaeology, raised fundamental objections about the category 'Celtic' as a historical reality in the early medieval and preceding periods.[25] Their critique rests on the claim that those groups we now define as 'Celtic' did not use the word 'Celtic' to describe themselves. Instead, they propose that the Celts are a modern 'invented tradition' rather than the past reality they are uncritically taken to be. Such questioning of the core definitions of the discipline has opened up room for alternative definitions and approaches. This is perhaps best illustrated by the recent volume of essays edited by David Harvey *et al.* as *Celtic Geographies*.[26] Here hybridity and contestation are the name of the game as former certainties about what and who are 'Celtic' are displaced by more fluid notions of 'Celticity'. Moreover, Cornish Studies played its full part in this shift towards 'ambiguity and complexity' in Celtic Studies, hosting two conferences on the 'New Celtic Studies' and publishing a volume of the same name.[27] In addition, the 'Cornish' chapters by Amy Hale and Alan M. Kent in *Celtic Geographies* succeed in establishing a more hybrid recognition of 'the Celt' and by implication 'the Cornish', helping readers to resist the temptation to resort to simplistic and essentialist concepts of the 'Cornish Celt' and alerting them to other perspectives.[28]

Perhaps because of the marginal position of Cornish Studies within traditional Celtic Studies, the New Cornish Studies was hitched to the movement of Irish Studies (from 1985) and Welsh Studies away from an exclusive concern with language and literature and towards history, sociology, anthropology and geography.[29] This movement reflects New Cornish Studies' concern with the contemporary, but also recognizes a second major contextual shift—that of society more generally. In conditions of 'postmodernity' or 'late modernity', it has been suggested that issues of identity politics and identity formation become more central, as 'social identities, geographical locations, and national allegiances all tend to be out of sync, at least more so now than in the recent past'.[30] This has certainly been the case in the Celtic territories of Western Europe. The establishment of devolved assemblies in Scotland and Wales and the formation of the British-Irish Council of the Isles were belated responses by an over-centralized British state to the re-assertion of identity in Scotland, Wales and Northern Ireland that gathered pace after the 1960s. This background 'lent an urgency and relevance to the discipline [of Celtic Studies]'.[31] In a similar way, a growing confidence in Cornishness during the 1980s and 1990s underpinned the challenges to the status quo and conventional wisdom that ultimately resulted in the granting of Objective 1 European funding and the impressive declaration of support for the idea of a devolved Cornish Assembly tapped by the Cornish Constitutional Convention's campaign in 2000/01. In these circumstances, the contemporary concerns of Cornish Studies become a matter of urgent relevance.

THE NEW CORNISH STUDIES: SOME PROBLEMS
A changing context produced the circumstances in which Cornish
Studies launched itself in new directions. The resultant New Cornish
Studies has sought to channel this movement into a particular path.
However, there exist some rarely discussed tensions around this
project. This section will briefly review a few such issues before moving
on to look in a little more depth at the case study of the 'new Cornish
historiography'. First, we ought to note the practical questions that face
the New Cornish Studies project. Who do we write for? The popular
view of Cornish Studies is still one dominated by language and history,
looking to the past and sharing some ground with notions of 'heritage'.
Is Cornish Studies, in moving towards a more theoretically engaged
and contemporary stance, in danger of losing this non-specialist
audience? And who exactly owns it? Is it the property of the Institute
of Cornish Studies or is it something broader? If it is something
broader, then what are the processes and the arenas whereby the field
is developed further and its direction shaped? As noted above, the
relative lack of Cornish Studies personnel has always meant that its
output turns out to be narrower than its declared aims. Thus, despite
Charles Thomas's wide definition of Cornish Studies in 1972, the actual
academic work of the Institute was much more narrowly centred on
archaeology and place-name research in the 1970s and 1980s, with
other projects dependent on the vagaries of short-term grant funding.
Similarly, the current output of the Institute appears more focused
on historical studies than the broader social sciences favoured by the
New Cornish Studies. Is this a problem? And if it is, what do we do
about it?

I do not intend to attempt to answer these questions here. But it is
worth noting that it is not only lack of resources that has set up
tensions between the rhetoric of the New Cornish Studies project and
its fulfilment. By way of illustration, we might here identify two contradictions that cohere around the New Cornish Studies. As we have seen
above, Philip Payton claims an applied aspect for the 'new Cornish
social science'; for 'such a process cannot fail to inform, influence and
guide planners and policy makers at every level, should they care to
listen'.[32] But do they? The vision of an applied Cornish Studies that
informs policy-makers in Cornwall and elsewhere may conflict with the
preferred content of the New Cornish Studies and its links to social
theory. Some of the latter will no doubt be critical of the assumptions
that lie behind policy-making in local government, or critical of the
centralized framework within which this occurs. In many respects an
open coalescence between policy actors in Cornwall and work inspired
by critical social theory is an unlikely scenario. This is particularly so

when we consider the context of Cornish policy-making over the past half-century. Cornwall has lacked that critical civil society within which transparent debate over policy can routinely take place. The absence of a genuinely investigative media, the missing university, the more general institutional vacuum, and the want of public space within which strategic debate can take place have combined to stifle real discussion about policy. In such a context 'applied Cornish Studies' can easily be reduced to the production of empirical data to reinforce and legitimate policy decisions rather than the insertion of academically grounded policy options that might inform the local process of governance and challenge the taken-for-granted assumptions of policy actors. On a broader, more philosophical note we might also identify a con-tradiction between renewed intellectual uncertainties and the reasser-tion of identity politics that provides the context for possible political change in Cornwall and in other 'Celtic' peripheries. In challenging popular narratives of Cornishness and Celticity, academics tread a perilous tightrope between being alert to heterogeneity and decon-structing claims that may underlie the struggles of disempowered and voiceless groups. Bridging this potential gap will be a delicate task for the New Cornish Studies over the coming decades.

Luke Gibbons has written that 'a culture has not found its own voice until it has expressed itself in a body of critical as well as creative work'.[33] In cognate fashion, it can be suggested that an academic discipline has not come of age until it contains a critical edge, both about its own 'foundational myths'[34] and about the concepts and theories it utilizes. In relation to this latter, the New Cornish Studies has been insufficiently critical hitherto of the various frameworks it employs. For example, the idea of centre and periphery might not allow for the situation where there is more than one centre or core, as was arguably the case in eighteenth-century industrializing Britain.[35] Similarly, the 'new Cornish historiography' might be insufficiently critical of the 'new' British history. This latter perspective, despite its apparent openness to diversity, often gives Cornwall little more space than did 'old' English histories.[36] More fundamentally, Pittock has pointed out how 'four nations' new British history is unconsciously subject to the status quo, for example overplaying Ireland's colonial past at the same time as it downplays that of Scotland and Wales. For Pittock, the 'new' British history is 'camouflaged anglocentrism', a point echoed by Nicholas Canny, who adds a methodological dimension to his critique of the new British history, which he sees as widening the gulf between political and social/economic history and emphasizing similarity at the expense of difference.[37] The 'new Cornish historiography' could engage with these criticisms, lending its voice to support or to qualify them. Even the turn to identity may be problematic. For example, Richard Handler has suggested that identity is a 'reified concept' that is imposed on past places and times even though it is actually 'peculiar to the modern western world'.[38] Handler's suspicion of identity echoes Colin Kidd's doubt about ethnic identities in the pre-modern British Isles. He proposes instead that ethnic identity was of 'second order' importance while the 'very notion of "identity" . . . might itself be anachronistic' when applied to the period before 1700.[39] The rhetorical aspect of the New Cornish Studies should not mean that the project cannot assimilate such criticisms of the concepts and models that it employs.

Furthermore, the rhetorical space of New Cornish Studies contains an inbuilt tendency to draw clear contrasts between the 'old' and the 'new'. While a necessary rhetorical device, this results in practice in overdrawing distinctions and erasing continuities. We can pursue this aspect more easily in relation to the specific case of the 'new Cornish historiography'. This will also allow us to investigate that possible gap between the rhetoric of the 'new Cornish historiography' and its substance. But, more important, it also reveals an important but often understated basis of the New Cornish Studies.

THE NEW CORNISH HISTORIOGRAPHY

The description 'new Cornish historiography' begs a number of questions: namely, in what way is it 'new', how is it 'Cornish', and why 'historiography'? This section deals with these three questions, although not quite in this same order.

In what ways is the 'new Cornish historiography' new? Colin H. Williams has pointed out in relation to Celtic Studies that 'new approaches' do not always deliver what they claim.[40] The claims for the 'new Cornish historiography' are similar to those for the generic New Cornish Studies—it has to engage with and contribute to 'new discourses . . . such engagement should be our over-arching research strategy for the future'. And it should set developments in Cornwall 'firmly in a comparative context'.[41] Perhaps the most successful example of this is Mark Stoyle's recent volume *West Britons*.[42] But is the broad historical work that appears in *Cornish Studies* so clearly 'new'? Does it contrast markedly and unambiguously with the published work in, say, the *Journal of the Royal Institution of Cornwall (JRIC)*, with its roots in antiquarianism and local studies? For example Volume 3 of New Series II of the *JRIC* contained several articles with a historical theme.[43] These allow it to draw a picture of the 'old' Cornish history. The articles are based for the most part on a detailed close reading of primary sources, tend towards the descriptive, are heavily empirical and focus on the agency of individuals rather than structural processes. In adopting this approach, they reproduce 'evocative tableaux rather than explanatory accounts of historical processes and structures'.[44] But many of the articles in *Cornish Studies*, while more likely to contain comparative academic and spatial references, are not that different in style. As has been noted of Celtic Studies in general, they give us detailed case studies rather than engage in theory construction.[45] Occasionally, indeed, the same authors publish in both places, the *JRIC* and *Cornish Studies*.[46] Consequently, on this evidence the boundary between the 'new Cornish historiography' as represented by *Cornish Studies* and the 'old' Cornish history of the *JRIC* is often more difficult to discern in practice than in theory.

As the claim to 'newness' rests on methodology, this aspect overlaps considerably with that of 'historiography'. The choice of this word suggests methodological novelty, with its implicit contrast between the new methodologically alert 'historiography' and the old unreflective 'history'. But historical writing in both *Cornish Studies* and the *JRIC* adopts recognizably 'historical' methods of source-critical interpretation and reconstruction through inferential or deductive reasoning within a narrative account.[47] Of course, it is possible to detect some differences. Contributions to *Cornish Studies* may be more marked by interpretation (by narrational emplotment) than reportage (by the what, where, when or who disclosed by the evidence). Articles in *Cornish Studies* are also more likely to adopt an explicit academic framework, grounding themselves in a wider academic literature, although this is not exactly absent from many contributions to the *JRIC*. In any case, this is more academic 'good practice' than methodological innovation, a marginal stylistic as opposed to a major methodological contrast. Thus it would appear that there remains considerable overlap between the 'old' and the 'new'.

Furthermore, if the old is 'old' in that it is untouched by some of the debates rippling through the academy, so the new appears not so 'new', or only episodically new, in its engagement with these debates. Nowhere is this more striking than in the way both 'old Cornish history' and 'new Cornish historiography' appear to avoid the historiographical debates triggered off by postmodernist critiques of 'objectivist' history as merely a fabricatory product of the present.[48] Even the local historians have tinkered, albeit rather gingerly, with this debate.[49] By way of concluding this comparison, and adopting Munslow's classification of historical perspectives, both 'old Cornish history' and 'new Cornish historiography' would appear to be broadly 'reconstructionist' in tenor ('seeking the most probably truthful . . . interpretation inherent in the documents of the past') as opposed to 'deconstructionist' (interrogating discourses both of the past and of historians).[50]

If the epistemological radicalism of the 'new Cornish historiography' is more subtle than the rhetorical definition may lead us to expect, we find a greater distance between it and older variants in its ontological stance, in its underlying assumptions. Indeed, it is when seeking to establish how the 'new Cornish historiography' is precisely 'Cornish' that I contend that we meet the real 'newness' of the project. This lies not in its methodology but in its explicit normative assumptions. Philip Payton, in the Introduction to *Cornwall*, sums this up directly: 'until recently, *our* history has been so often the history of Cornwall without the Cornish people, and it is high time that we offered a corrective'.[51] There are echoes here of the work of the late Gwyn Alf Williams in Wales or the feminist position that asserts 'the right to name ourselves, to act as subjects rather than objects of history'.[52] Just as some feminists would argue that women have a 'privileged knowledge' that enables them to write about women's history with an insight unavailable to men, however sympathetic, there is more than a hint here that the 'new Cornish historiography' offers a privileged, though nonetheless rigorous, vantage point on the Cornish past.

In claiming this, the 'new Cornish historiography' clearly parts company with 'old Cornish history', which is heavily influenced by local history. The latter, while clinging to a naïve empiricism, is strangely coy about its own assumptions. Lacking critical reflection on these, it ends up taking a conservative and/or romantic definition of Cornwall and its territoriality for granted, rarely admitting its origins in a deferential English local historical tradition that stresses order, stability and rurality. By way of contrast, the 'new Cornish historiography', looking as much perhaps for inspiration to the emigrant communities and the more open societies of the Cornish diaspora as to the class-bound hierarchies of rural nineteenth-century Britain, is less deferential and more critical.

THE FUTURE OF CORNISH STUDIES

My argument, therefore, is that the New Cornish Studies is as much an ontological as an epistemological project, as much concerned with values and visions as with novel methodological approaches. In view of this, how might the field develop over the next decade? Here I will briefly sketch out four potential shifts for the New Cornish Studies. These are, first, from British history to micro-history; second, from Celtic Studies to cultural studies; third, from comparative work to extraversion; and fourth, from Cornwall to Cornwalls.

While the new British history has provided a springboard for some of the most exciting work of the 'new Cornish historiography' during the 1990s and early 2000s, we need to build on this and engage with other frameworks in order to develop our understanding of historical periods and themes beyond the early modern period. One such approach is that of micro-history. Micro-history is a new, more analytical, more theory-sensitive type of historical study, one that proposes 'to say a great deal about the wider world but from a less abstract perspective rooted in vernacular expression and experience'.[53] Micro-history recognizes that 'big problems exist in small spaces' and aims to unite the general social processes and the local uniqueness that arise from them.[54] It studies the totality of people's lives, rather than privileging either the public sphere over the private or the economic over the cultural or vice versa. Done well, as in the work of Barry Reay,[55] micro-history achieves precisely what the 'new Cornish historiography' sets out to do—influence wider generalizations and theories about the social world. There is a clear overlap here with anthropology and with the work currently growing up around the Cornish Audio Visual Archive project, with its emphasis on oral history and the vernacular.[56] But micro-history is not confined to the twentieth century; it can be applied to any period.[57]

My second shift is from Celtic Studies to cultural studies. However, to advocate this is not to propose the wholesale jettisoning of the 'Celtic'. It is merely to admit that the New Cornish Studies has already broken the always tenuous link between Cornish Studies and the 'canon' of Celtic Studies. But the 'Celtic' remains one strand in Cornwall and in Cornish life. What the New Cornish Studies might fruitfully do now is explicitly to engage with aspects of cultural studies. The concern of the latter with the diversity of cultures within the British Isles and with the limitations of the concept 'British' provides obvious points of connection.[58] In many ways the 'new Celtic Studies' is a bridge between Cornish Studies and cultural studies. The three issues that Harvey *et al.* claim that a concern with 'Celticity' can illuminate —the politics and economics of exclusion and division, the promotion of 'difference' in political, cultural and economic terms, and the search for identity in a consumerist society—are broad cultural issues and ones that are equally important in studies of contemporary Cornwall. For example, the commodification of Cornishness is an area that desperately requires more interdisciplinary attention.

Third, Cornish Studies must progress beyond being comparative to being actively outward-looking. To engage fully with new discourses means breaking out of self-imposed ghettos, publishing in wider arenas and reaching larger audiences. One possible development would be to begin to apply Cornish Studies perspectives to 'mainstream' aspects, to deconstruct the assumptions and discourses of majority claims and imaginations.[59]

Finally, the New Cornish Studies will have to embrace the more fragmentary, fluid and heterogeneous accounts of society that have become fashionable in many academic circles. These offer the opportunity to re-think the very ways we imagine Cornwall and, by implication, ourselves.[60] As the practitioners of Cornish Studies, through helping to construct differences and identities, we are inevitably 'forced to confront the construction of ourselves'.[61] To adopt this more reflective approach is to accept that the New Cornish Studies may be place-based, but it is not place-bounded. Like newer, broader definitions of Celticity, studies of Cornwall and Cornishness can also 'provide an opportunity through which more inclusive, multifacted, multi-ethnic, non-territorially bounded expressions of social cohesion can operate'.[62] I have argued in an earlier contribution to *Cornish Studies* that in the next phase of Cornish Studies we might move from the spatial scale of Cornwall to both spatial and cultural 'Cornwalls', becoming increasingly alert to the multiple representations of Cornwall that exist both now and in the past.[63] For instance, while Harvey *et al.* identify two spatial realms of Celticity, we might claim three spatial realms of Cornishness. There is the roots and tradition-seeking Cornishness of the diaspora, the romantic and wistful Cornishness of metropolitan England, and the Cornishness of Cornwall. And while the last of these includes the familiar, nostalgic view of Cornwall and its heritage that tends to be moulded by a sense of loss and 'hireth', there is another under-theorized aspect of the Cornishness of Cornwall. This is a more civic, open and inclusive Cornishness, one that looks to democratic institutions and to aspects of the European project for a re-forged and progressive sense of regional identity. All these Cornwalls are potential points of analysis for the New Cornish Studies.[64]

CONCLUSION

I have pointed to some potential directions the New Cornish Studies might take. In this way, this review article is ultimately located squarely within the New Cornish Studies approach. For, in foregrounding the potential of Cornish Studies, based on its underlying values, which stress that Cornwall, its communities, its past and its present are suitable subjects to study, we return to the heart of the Cornish Studies project. I have suggested in this article that New Cornish Studies is, indeed, as much a rhetorically defined space as a set of discrete methodologically novel academic productions. Nevertheless, its rhetorical character should not disguise the fact that it both informs and reflects real shifts in the field of Cornish Studies since the 1980s. Some of those shifts, which to an extent mirror wider intellectual and social change, may have occurred independently, without the rhetorical space of the New Cornish Studies. But the importance of the latter is that it has imposed some overall sense of direction and purpose upon them and provided an aspiration or vision for Cornish Studies practitioners to aim at.

Moreover, those working within the New Cornish Studies field see that, by setting out to deconstruct certain powerful paradigms of Cornwall, they will also open up new possibilities for local actors. In short, the New Cornish Studies accepts that Cornish Studies is, inevitably, part of a struggle for place, part of an ongoing re-creation and conservation of that place we call Cornwall.[65] It recognizes that Cornwall is neither essential nor unchanging but it also sets out to assert the right of the Cornish themselves to be involved in that process of change. It is a part of a discourse that states that the Cornish no longer wish to be marginalized, casually misrepresented or appropriated for other agenda. They are not just passive constructions of outside discourses. They are agents who have made, within obvious constraints, their own history. The task of the New Cornish Studies is to recover that sense of agency, put it into a comparative context, open up our knowledge of the past and, ultimately, to empower people in Cornwall so that they are in a better position to make choices about their own future. The contrast with the 'old Cornish history' should be apparent. But 'old Cornish history' is not the same as 'old' Cornish Studies. Old Cornish Studies shared the same ontological assumptions about Cornwall as does the New, viewing it as a fit object of study in its own right. What New Cornish Studies does is to make this more explicit.

NOTES AND REFERENCES

1. For example John Brannigan, *New Historicism and Cultural Materialism*, Basingstoke, 1998; Roger Backhouse (ed.), *New Directions in Economic Methodology*, London, 1994; Amitai Etzioni (ed.), *New Communitarian Thinking: Persons, Virtues, Institutions and Communities*, Charlottesville, VA, 1995.
2. Philip Payton, *ICS Associates Newsletter* 4, May 1995, p. 5; Philip Payton, 'Introduction', in Philip Payton (ed.), *Cornish Studies: Four*, Exeter, 1996a, p. 1.
3. Philip Payton, 'Introduction', in Philip Payton (ed.), *Cornish Studies: One*, Exeter, 1993, p. 1.
4. Steven Lukes, 'The Last Word on the Third Way', *The Review*, March 1999, pp. 3–4.
5. J.D. Marshall, *The Tyranny of the Discrete*, Aldershot, 1997, p. 3.
6. Communication reported at Perranporth Conference, 1990.

7. For some examples see James Vernon, 'Border Crossings: Cornwall and the English (Imagi)nation', in Geoffrey Cubitt (ed.), *Imagining Nations*, Manchester 1998, pp. 153–72; James Potter, 'External Manufacturing Investment in a Peripheral Rural Region: The Case of Devon and Cornwall', *Regional Studies* 27.3, 1993, pp. 193–206.

8. For Charles Thomas's links with the Revival see his 'An Dasserghyans Kerenwek', *Old Cornwall* 6.5, 1963, pp. 196–205.

9. John Angarrack, *Breaking the Chains: Propaganda, Censorship, Deception and the Manipulation of Public Opinion in Cornwall*, Camborne, 1999: Pol Hodge, *Cornwall's Secret War: The True Story of the Prayer Book Rebellion*, Truro, n.d. pp. 14–15.

10. See Glanville Price, *The Languages of Britain*, London, 1984, pp. 134–145.

11. Charles Thomas, *Bulletin of the ICS 1* June 1972.

12. And see Philip Payton, 'Cornwall in Context: The New Cornish Historiography', in Philip Payton (ed.), *Cornish Studies: Five*, Exeter, 1997, pp. 9–20.

13. Philip Payton, 'Local and Regional History: The View from Cornwall', *Locality* 11.3, 2000, pp. 18–22.

14. Philip Payton, *The Making of Modern Cornwall: Historical Experience and the Persistence of 'Difference'*, Redruth, 1992.

15. For work using the 'new British history' as a framework see Mark Stoyle, *West Britons: Cornish Identities and the Early Modern British State*, Exeter, 2002. For other examples of the use of theories and frameworks in Cornish Studies see Bernard Deacon, 'The Reformation of Territorial Identity: Cornwall in the Late Eighteenth and Nineteenth Centuries', unpublished Ph.D. thesis, Open University, 2001, and Alan M. Kent, *The Literature of Cornwall: Continuity, Identity, Difference 1000–2000*, Bristol, 2000.

16. Philip Payton, Letter to Associates of ICS, 6 January 1992. This trend can be seen in Amy Hale and Philip Payton (eds), *New Directions in Celtic Studies*, Exeter, 2000. But it is best illustrated in the contributions to David C. Harvey, Rhys Jones, Neil McInroy and Christine Milligan (eds), *Celtic Geographies: Old Culture, New Times*, London, 2002.

17. See Garry Tregidga, *The Liberal Party in South-West Britain Since 1918*, Exeter, 2000.

18. Payton, 1993, pp. 2–3.

19. Philip Payton, 'Introduction', in Philip Payton (ed.), *Cornish Studies: Six*, Exeter, 1998, p. 1. Despite these calls to study identity formation, Cornish Studies has yet to produce anything resembling Le Coadic's interdisciplinary study of the contemporary Breton identity (Ronan Le Coadic, *L'Identité Bretonne*, Rennes, 1998).

20. Payton, 1993, p. 1.

21. Payton, 1996a, p. 1.

22. Resource factors can also constrain the desired outcomes. For instance, the series *Cornish Studies*, given the small size of the disciplinary field, is forced into an eclecticism, both in terms of subject and of contributors, which to some extent blurs the vision of the ideal rhetorically defined space of the New Cornish Studies.

23. Academic journals are now noticeably more willing to accept Cornish Studies related submissions. For example, see Philip Payton, 'Cousin Jacks and Ancient Britons: Cornish Immigrants and Ethnic Identity', *Journal of Australian Studies* 68, 2001, pp. 54–64; Bernard Deacon, 'Imagining the Fishing: Artists and Fishermen in Late Nineteenth-Century Cornwall' *Rural History* 12.2, 2001, pp. 159–78; Ella Westland, 'D.H. Lawrence's Cornwall: Dwelling in a Precarious Age', *Cultural Geographies* 9, 2002, pp. 266–85.

24. Pat Hudson, 'Regional and Local History: Globalisation, Postmodernism and the Future', *Journal of Regional and Local Studies* 20, 1999, pp. 5–24.

25. Malcolm Chapman, *The Celts: The Construction of a Myth*, London, 1992; Simon James, *The Atlantic Celts: Ancient People or Modern Invention?*, London, 1999. See Patrick Sims-Williams, 'Celtomania or Celto-scepticism', Cambrian Medieval Celtic Studies, 36, 1998, pp. 1–35 for a response from within the field.

26. Harvey *et al.* (eds), 2002.

27. Hale and Payton (eds), 2000.

28. Amy Hale, 'Whose Celtic Cornwall? The Ethnic Cornish meet Cornish Spirituality', and Alan M. Kent, 'Celtic Nirvanas: Construction of Celtic in Contemporary British Youth Culture', in Harvey *et al.* (eds), 2002, pp. 157–70 and 208–26.

29. *The Times Higher Education Supplement*, 1 February 2002, p. 18.

30. Vicente L. Rafael, 'Regionalism, Area Studies and the Accidents of Agency', *American Historical Review* 104, 1999, pp. 1208–220.

31. Hale and Payton (eds), 2000, p. 4.

32. Payton, 1996a, p. 1.

33. Luke Gibbons, *Transformations in Irish Culture*, Cork, 1996, p. xi.

34. See Malcolm Williams in this volume.

35. See Bernard Deacon, 'Proto-regionalisation: The Case of Cornwall, *Journal of Regional and Local Studies* 18, 1998, pp. 27–41.

36. John Morrill, 'The British Problem, c1534–1707', in Brendan Bradshaw and John Morrill (eds), *The British Problem, c1534–1707: State Formation in the British Archipelago*, London, 1996. See pp. 1 and 6. Cornwall also gets little mention in Glenn Burgess (ed.), *The New British History: Founding a Modern State*, London, 1999.

37. Murray Pittock, *Celtic Identity and the British Image*, Manchester, 1999, pp. 98–100; Nicholas Canny, 'Irish, Scottish and Welsh Responses to Centralisation, c.1530–c.1640: A Comparative Perspective', in Alexander Grant and Keith Stringer (eds), *Uniting the Kingdom? The Making of British History*, London, 1995, pp. 147–8.

38. Nicholas Handler, 'Is "Identity" a Useful Cross-Cultural Concept?', in John R. Gillis (ed.), *Commemorations: The Politics of National Identity*, Princeton, 1994, pp. 27–40.

39. Colin Kidd, *British Identities before Nationalism: Ethnicity and Nationhood in the Atlantic World, 1600–1880*, Cambridge, 1999, p. 291.

40. Colin H. Williams, 'New Directions in Celtic Studies: An Essay in Social Criticism', in Hale and Payton (eds), 2000, p. 202.

41. Payton, 1997, p. 12.
42. Stoyle, 2002. See also Philip Payton, *Cornwall*, Fowey, 1996b.
43. *Journal of the Royal Institution of Cornwall*, 3.3–4, 2000. These ranged from studies of the medieval period to nineteenth-century political history.
44. Joseph M. Bryant, 'On Sources and Narratives in Historical Social Science: A Realist Critique of Positivist and Postmodernist Epistemologies', *British Journal of Sociology*, 51.3, 2000, p. 511.
45. Williams, 2000, p. 205.
46. For example, see Joanna Mattingly, 'The Helston Shoemakers' Gild and a Possible Connection with the 1549 Rebellion', in Payton (ed.), 1998, pp. 23–45, and Joanna Mattingly, 'Stories in the Glass—Reconstructing the St Neot Pre-Reformation Glazing Scheme', *Journal of the Royal Institution of Cornwall* 3.3–4, 2000, pp. 9–55, or Ronald Perry, 'The Changing Face of Celtic Tourism in Cornwall, 1875–1975', in Philip Payton (ed.), *Cornish Studies: Seven*, Exeter, 1999, pp. 94–106, and Ronald Perry, 'Silvanus Trevail and the Development of Modern Tourism in Cornwall', *Journal of the Royal Institution of Cornwall* 3.2, 1999, pp. 33–43.
47. Cf. Bryant, 2000.
48. For an introduction to this debate see Keith Jenkins (ed.), *The Postmodern History Reader*, London, 1997; Richard Evans, *In Defence of History*, London, 1997; Arthur Marwick, *The New Nature of History: Knowledge, Evidence, Language*, Basingstoke, 2001.
49. See George Sheeran and Yanina Sheeran, 'Reconstructing Local History', *The Local Historian* 29.4, 1999, pp. 256–62 and the responses in *The Local Historian* 31.1, 2001, pp. 47–50.
50. Alan Munslow, *The Routledge Companion to Historical Studies*, London, 2000.
51. Payton, 1996b, p. vi.
52. Geraint H. Jenkins, *The People's Historian: Professor Gwyn A. Williams (1925–1995)*, Aberystwyth, 1996, p. 7; Nancy Hartstock, 'Rethinking Modernism: Minority vs Majority Theories', *Cultural Critique* 7, 1987, pp. 187–206.
53. Hudson, 1999, p. 15.
54. Neil Evans, 'Writing the Social History of Modern Wales: Approaches, Achievements and Problems', *Social History* 17.3, 1992, p. 492; Day and Murdoch, 1993, p. 82.
55. Barry Reay, *Micro-Histories: Demography, Society and Culture in Rural England 1800–1930*, Cambridge, 1996.
56. The academic outcomes of the CAVA project are still unclear. But it promises to be a major potential growth area of Cornish Studies over the next decade, not least because of its success in attracting Heritage Lottery Fund support.
57. See Keith Wrightson and David Levine, *Poverty and Piety in an English Village*, Oxford, 1979.
58. Susan Basnett (ed.), *Studying British Cultures: An Introduction*, London, 1997.

59. For an example see Bernard Deacon, *Building the Region: Culture and Territory in the South West of England*, Milton Keynes, 2002.
60. See Kent, 2002.
61. Peter Jackson and Jan Penrose (eds), *Constructions of Race, Place and Nation*, London 1993, p. 209.
62. Harvey *et al.* (eds), 2002, p. 12.
63. Barnard Deacon, 'In Search of the Missing "Turn": The Spatial Dimension and Cornish Studies', in Philip Payton (ed.), *Cornish Studies: Eight*, Exeter, 2000, pp. 213–30.
64. See, for example, chapter 8 in Philip Payton, *A Vision of Cornwall*, Fowey, 2002.
65. Cf. Michael Keith and Steve Pile (eds), *Place and the Politics of Identity*, London, 1993, p. 6.

THE NEW CORNISH SOCIAL SCIENCE

Malcolm Williams

INTRODUCTION

Since the first volume of the new series of *Cornish Studies* ten years ago much has happened culturally and politically in Cornwall, and much of what has happened has attracted the interest of social scientists and subsequently been presented and discussed in *Cornish Studies*. Moreover, there is evidence to suggest that the emergence of what has been termed 'the new Cornish social science' has had wider implications in Cornish society. This article is, therefore, a review of the emergence and the output in the last ten years of the 'new Cornish social science'.

As a social scientist who, sometimes uncomfortably, straddles policy research, social statistics and sociology, I am aware that disciplinary boundaries are often fluid and ill-defined, but also that what keeps us in our jobs is the relevance of what we do. In the first case, this means any review of the last ten years, for this writer, will be from a interdisciplinary perspective which will inevitably lead to selectivity of topic over academic obeisance. In the second case, relevance is a subjective construct, which may be contested by different stakeholders, but the bottom line is that if Cornish social science matters only to its practitioners and not a wider society then it is irrelevant and likely doomed. My review of the last ten years begins from these premises.

The term 'new Cornish social science' was coined originally by Philip Payton[1] and has since come to be used to describe an inter-disciplinary approach to the study of a range of subjects, from manifestations of poverty in Cornwall to the nature of contemporary Cornish culture. Its remit of both subject and method is wide and perhaps, therefore, it is not unreasonable to ask wherein lies any theoretical or even taxonomic coherence? Thus in the first section of the article I will ask the question of what can we mean by 'new Cornish social science' (henceforth NCSS), not the least in relation to a putative older version.

In the second and greater part of the article I will review some of the themes and specific writings in NCSS, in terms of both their relevance to a better understanding of Cornwall and the Cornish, and their relationship to the context in which they arose. In other words, what is the relationship of NCSS to (most importantly) Cornish society and also to the wider academic and policy community? The latter is important, because by no means all social science conducted in Cornwall is reported in the pages of *Cornish Studies*. A great deal of it is bread and butter research, often seen as too humble to be thought of as social science at all—even by those who do it—but nevertheless a crucial source of data.[2]

Lastly, I will take a brief critical look at where we are, where we might go in the next ten years, and what might be the difficulties in that journey.

WHAT IS NEW CORNISH SOCIAL SCIENCE? ORIGINS AND LEGITIMATION

What might be broadly termed 'social studies of Cornwall' have been around a long while, though for the most part these were studies of social and economic history. One might cite, for example, the work of A.L. Rowse, John Rowe and A.K. Hamilton Jenkin,[3] but although influential in a foundational sense in establishing Cornish particularity this work never really gave rise to a contemporary social science. Through the 1970s and 1980s there was a handful of sociological and economic studies—for example Herman Giligan's community study of Padstow and McNabb *et al.*'s work on unemployment in West Cornwall.[4] In none of the cases were the studies self-consciously Cornish social science, but rather they were social science that happened to be done in Cornwall, or about Cornwall. Cornish particularism often emerged from the findings but for the most part the subject matter was an exemplar for a wider manifestation of the phenomena investigated. It was not that there was an absence of a desire to do Cornish social science; indeed the past Director of the Institute of Cornish Studies, Charles Thomas, maintained that one role for the discipline was to furnish a critique of those policies and forces that were moulding the socio-economic characteristics of contemporary Cornwall.[5] Ironically, however, the work that came closest to this ideal during Thomas's directorship was that of Ronald Perry and his associates on 'counter-urbanization' migration,[6] and that of the Cornish Social and Economic

Research Group (CoSERG) on various aspects of policy and identity.[7] At the time the latter work was seen as politicized and found no ready acceptance in mainstream Cornish Studies, though in all fairness CoSERG probably had little interest in such acceptance.

Yet if we want to find a beginning of a NCSS it is within this work, which takes as a starting point the 'fact' of Cornwall's existence as a distinct ethnic community. This assumption and its acceptance was an important step in the establishment of Cornish social science as a serious academic and policy discipline. Prior to this, contemporary social critique of policy and even research that began from this starting point was seen as politicized and parochial[8]—certainly its political and policy influence was limited. Conversely, and despite Thomas's desire for relevance, Cornish Studies remained a historical and in many respects conservative discipline. As Payton put it, Cornish Studies as practised for much of the twentieth century was 'concerned principally with the mechanisms of language "Revival" and, like the Old Cornwall movement, busied itself in an antiquarian quest to gather all the fragments of identity before they were lost in the rush to post-industrial modernity',[9] a position which, though entirely respectable within academic Celtic Studies, was not at the cutting edge of the contemporary social analysis of Cornwall.

Making a bridge between contemporary research and analysis, seen as politicized, and a respectable but conservative antiquarian discipline, required a particular historic moment upon which the present writer can only speculate, but which others may see as a suitable object for future research. Thus what follows is more by way of a historical hypothesis connecting events than a description of a causal process.

Between the publication of CoSERG's *Cornwall at the Crossroads* in 1988 and Payton's edited volume *Cornwall Since the War* in 1993, Cornwall experienced the trauma of the collapse of mining and a great deal of the industry associated with it, but also the affirming solidarity of victory for the Cornish rugby team at Twickenham in 1991. The two events were perhaps not unconnected. The closure of Geevor and Wheal Jane and the contraction of South Crofty were more important psychologically than they were economically (though, of course, one should not belittle the enormous local economic impact of closures), for even in the early 1980s extractive industries accounted for less than 10 per cent of the Cornish economy and this included china clay. The collapse of mining put an important and (at that time) mostly unexamined aspect of Cornish identity into the past tense.[10] Yet even as this was happening there was evidence of a new sense of solidarity evolving that drew eclectically on the symbols of an industrial past, those of the Celtic revival and contemporary aspects of popular culture, and fused these into new complex forms of Cornish identity.[11] The collapse of mining may well have produced a rallying point for the Cornish community, but what is a little more certain is that a new, more confident form of identity was in evidence at Twickenham in 1991. Identity was also becoming respectable on the policy agenda. Bernard Deacon, in *Cornish Studies: One*, noted a change in attitude towards identity by Cornwall County Council. In a 1992 strategy document, for example, the County Council spoke of the many who 'still see Cornwall as having a distinct "national" identity', and a year later, sensitive to criticisms that territory, ethnicity and cultural identity had not been given sufficient weight in the past, the Council entitled its Structure Plan consultative document *Cornwall: A Land Apart.*[12]

The crisis in mining was, of course, just one manifestation of economic failure in Cornwall and the beginning of a realization amongst some politicians and local government officers that things were not working out. Although some planners could speak of Cornwall's success in creating new jobs, these seemed to have little impact on long-term unemployment trends, whilst GDP and household income were stagnant or actually falling.[13] The extent of the housing crisis was made plain in Andrew George's *Homes for Locals in Cornwall*,[14] and in the Parish Housing Surveys of the Cornwall Rural Community Council. The analytic starting point for this work was largely that of CoSERG but the audience was a policy and political one far wider than that of CoSERG.[15] Even if the critique of mainstream economic and social policy was not embraced by those in power, there was a growing legitimacy in oppositional arguments. Perhaps an indication of the emerging respectability of what might be termed the 'Cornish case' was that the Liberal Democrats chose George, a founder member of CoSERG and joint author of *Cornwall at the Crossroads,* as their parliamentary candidate for St Ives in 1992 (he was subsequently elected in 1997).[16]

My claim, then, is that in this period the social conditions necessary for a Cornish social science to be established were fulfilled. In a more concrete sense, this probably took the form of a preparedness of universities and local authorities to encourage or at least tolerate researchers undertaking Cornish social science, and a willingness of the media to report what they had to say. These changed attitudes were perhaps the best evidence of legitimation.[17]

Moreover, the social acceptance of the 'Cornish case' has increased considerably since the first volume of *Cornish Studies*. For example, the Campaign for Cornwall in 1994,[18] the 1997 An Gof commemoration, the 1997–9 campaign for Objective 1 status, and the

ongoing campaign for a Cornish Assembly received significant establishment and media support, which in turn has made them and the
societal trends they represent suitable and respectable objects of study.
Perhaps more concretely, there has been an increasing symbiosis and
cross-over between academics working overtly in aspects of NCSS and
policy researchers in the public sector. This has included not just data
exchange as a basis for further research by each, but also cross-sector
funding and dissemination. Perhaps the best example of this was Judy
Payne's 1995 *Interpreting the Index of Local Conditions in Devon and
Cornwall*.[19] This was something of a Trojan horse, for although funded
by the Westcountry Development Corporation and intended to be a
statistical basis for the claim of poverty in both Devon and Cornwall, it
actually and conclusively showed Cornwall to be very much poorer
than Devon. As such, it played a key role in the argument for a
statistical disagregation between Cornwall and Devon and subsequently the ability to provide a statistical argument for Objective 1
status.[20]

The NCSS has been theoretically and methodologically eclectic.
The more theoretical work has been informed by a range of positions,
from Foucauldian-inspired post-structuralism and Gramscian Marxism
to neo-classical economic views of migration, approaches which in
other areas of social science would have been seen as contradictory
yet in NCSS seem to co-exist peacefully. Likewise, methods have
embraced statistical modelling of large and complex data sets,
ethnographic interviewing and historical genealogy. Such theoretical
and methodological heterogeneity of NCSS raises the question of what
makes it distinctive?

The straightforward answer to this is that there is something
distinctive about Cornwall and Cornishness that marks them out as a
special object of study, as a key variable, in much the same way as
feminists have taken the distinctive experience of women as a justification for a separate discipline of Women's Studies. Moreover, the
assertion of the legitimacy of a discipline claiming such ontological
distinction must, as I have argued, be grounded in its acceptance in
significant sectors of society, but also it cannot help but underwrite
political claims in that society made as a result of such distinctiveness.
Thus as feminism is a politicized discipline that opposes androcentricity
and favours empowerment for women, so a Cornish social science will
inevitably, in at least a generalized way, endorse political claims to
ethnic recognition and arrangements which favour the empowerment
of the Cornish. NCSS in particular, and Cornish Studies in general, are
in that sense politicized disciplines which depend for their legitimacy
upon the social acceptance of certain founding principles. It is these

which mark out NCSS from the earlier and above-mentioned social studies of Cornwall.

The disciplinary foundation in turn leads to a potential paradox of objectivity and commitment that is present throughout social science, but is particularly conspicuous in those disciplines which embrace specific ideological assumptions (e.g. Women's Studies, Irish Studies, Indian Studies). These are based upon a value system that requires the continued commitment of its adherents, yet as such is the antithesis of investigative disciplines which stress the centrality of a search for truth. For example, claims of ethnicity or nationhood will have foundational myths, or at least folk beliefs, that underwrite popular expressions of culture. In the case of Cornwall we might cite the various claims of historical nationhood, or claims to a distinct ethnic identity. In disciplines that begin from ideological assumptions there is a contradiction between adherence to these assumptions as a disciplinary foundation and their appropriateness as objects of study by the discipline. This becomes much more than a philosophical issue when what is at stake is the wish and intention of the discipline to influence policy processes. Despite the exhortations of Thomas to the contrary, the old Cornish Studies lacked such commitment, but NCSS is made relevant by it.

Many writers believe that one should try to accommodate such a paradox by philosophical sleights of hand that justify ideological positions as being themselves 'more objective'.[21] But as Ismay Barwell has remarked in respect of feminism, commitment is better served by objectivity[22] in the end, and indeed it is the mark of a mature discipline that it can afford such objectivity. In this respect, whilst NCSS is theoretically and methodologically eclectic, it has managed to do quite well as a critical discipline. There are instances where contemporary or historical research has challenged even the hard core of disciplinary assumptions. Two examples serve to illustrate this. The first concerns what might be the termed the 'Celtic tension' in Cornish Studies generally. The traditional and still partially prevailing view that Cornish Studies is a 'Celtic discipline' has been undermined to a great extent by new work in Cornish historiography which lays at least as much emphasis on the contemporary cultural shaping of Cornwall by a nineteenth-century neo-industrial society that eschewed or neglected the Celtic heritage.[23] To a great extent, yet nevertheless important from the perspective of social solidarity, the Celtic aspect of contemporary identity is largely (though not completely) synthetic in the sense that much of it revolves around recently 'invented' traditions, from the Gorseth to the Cornish tartan. One could mount a reasonable argument to suggest that although this has been known since the 1970s, what is different now and perhaps marks both disciplinary and social maturity is that such 'invented tradition' can be confronted without any particular identity damage to the discipline.

The second example is more squarely in the policy arena of housing. Prior to the mid-1990s, it was widely assumed that a dichotomy of housing opportunity existed between the Cornish and in-migrants. This was emphasized by CoSERG publications and, perhaps surprisingly, internalized by many housing workers. Research from the mid-1990s onwards painted a much more complex picture. On one hand, many in-migrants did enjoy housing advantage by selling in a dearer market and buying in a cheaper one, and likewise most people who had lived all their lives in Cornwall did not. However, housing need survey work indicated that the former group (though substantial) were mostly in-migrants from the South-East, and other groups of migrants from (say) the North did not always enjoy such advantage. Furthermore, the people in greatest housing need included not just those who had lived in Cornwall for a long time, but also new arrivals.[24]

To sum up so far: 'new' Cornish social science is distinct from social science in Cornwall prior to the 1990s. The latter was either social science that was done in Cornwall, though not from a Cornish perspective, and socio-economic history that was respectable but of limited contemporary relevance, or it was politicized investigation that had its origins in nationalism, anti-metropolitanism and oppositional economics. NCSS has fused elements of all three, gaining legitimacy from changes in Cornish society in the late 1980s which had created a new space for contemporary social science. At the same time, however, NCSS was also a successor to a longer-established historical tradition in Cornish Studies. Finally, there is evidence in the output from NCSS that it is becoming a self-critical discipline, willing and able to challenge its own foundational assumptions.

In the next section I will critically review some of the output of NCSS since 1993.

NEW CORNISH SOCIAL SCIENCE: THE FIRST TEN YEARS
In a single article one could not hope to review in any depth the prolific output of NCSS in the past ten years, so using my two starting points —interdisciplinarity and contemporary relevance—I will briefly discuss some key developments in six areas.

Cornish Economics
Cornish economics is perhaps misnamed, for it is really an extension of economic planning and is not yet a particularly sophisticated discipline—but then it does not need to be. In terms of its contribution

to shaping Cornwall's future, it has yet fully to transcend the first stage of convincing planners and politicians that a new economic model is needed. There has been some success and the pursuit and eventual acquisition of Objective 1 status can certainly be partially attributed to a sustained economic critique of the status quo.

Ronald Perry's 1993 chapter 'Economic Change and "Opposition Policies" ' in *Cornwall Since the War* was an elegant summary, backed up with numeric data that traced the doomed Keynesian project of 'population led growth' from its inception to the present. Although a similar argument had been made five years before in *Cornwall at the Crossroads*, here Perry enjoyed the legitimacy of what came to be considered a seminal collection in NCSS. As it stood, the first part of Perry's argument was pretty well unanswerable (and indeed was not answered): that the economic policies pursued by planners in Cornwall and those foisted upon Cornwall from Bristol and elsewhere had manifestly not worked.[25] The second part of his chapter was a plea for an alternative approach based upon population growth management and the exploitation of Cornwall's geographical advantages. Nevertheless, in order to move from critique to influence, Cornish economics required even more evidence of economic failure. Much of this was hard to obtain for two reasons: firstly, that on many measures Cornwall and Devon data were aggregated,[26] and secondly, that ward-based measures of deprivation favoured urban settlement patterns not found in Cornwall. For example, the ACORN classification of residential neighbourhoods has 37 categories and two-thirds of Cornwall was 'described' by just two of them![27] Similarly 'car ownership', a standard indicator of poverty, showed Cornwall to be doing very well. The aforementioned research by Payne successfully exploited the newly published Department of Environment Index of Local Conditions to produce a range of proxies and indices that better measured the widespread low-level deprivation experienced by Cornwall,[28] and differentiated this from the more concentrated local urban poverty experienced in parts of Plymouth.

Since this time, the statistical disaggregation of Cornwall and Devon and a greater sophistication in the use of proxies has permitted a far better statistical description of the Cornish economy and society. This has been enormously important in attracting a range of regeneration funding for initiatives including the Health Action Zone, the Education Action Zone, Sure Start and of course Objective 1.

Whilst the last decade has seen a great deal of descriptive research on the Cornish economy, there has been hardly any new academic work. An important exception to this was Peter Wills's 1998 article on economic development in a European context. Here Wills brought up to date the picture painted by Perry five years previously but took the more speculative part of Perry's work on alternatives further by considering various models of economic development pursued elsewhere in Europe. His conclusion was that whatever models are adopted, those regions that do best in economic development 'also have autonomy and flexibility that allow them to devise their own solutions'.[29]

Migration Studies
Though academic output in the economic field has been sparse, it has nevertheless had an important influence on studies of migration. One possible reason for the paucity of the former is that to understand what went wrong economically since the 1960s it is necessary to understand the nature of in- and out-migration, for arguably population change has been a crucial economic determinant. Unsurprisingly, then, studies of migration and economy intersect, as do studies of migration and housing.

Whilst much of the core research in NCSS has been based at the Institute of Cornish Studies, work in the latter two areas has been centred on the Cornwall Planning Department at Cornwall County Council (specifically research undertaken by Peter Mitchell[30]) and the Department of Sociology at the University of Plymouth. The migration studies referred to above have mostly used longitudinally linked individual level census data to track the movement and economic performance of in- and out-migrants compared with each other and with non-migrants.[31] This work and that of Perry and associates in the 1980s[32] has shown Cornwall to be a very unusual case, whereby large-scale in- and out-migration (with zero natural growth) has accompanied economic decline. More recently, a further twist in the counter-urbanization story in Cornwall was uncovered by Philipa Aldous in her longitudinal study of migration intentions amongst year 9 and year 11 school children.[33] A hypothesis that the 'migration' culture that had existed for over 100 years would still be extant was falsified by the finding that Cornish children were much less likely to wish to migrate than the sons and daughters of in-migrants. That in-migrant parents were much more likely to belong to non-manual classes and be university-educated than the Cornish parents, confirms the classical migratory elite hypothesis,[34] Aldous claimed. This holds that those who migrate in Western societies are those with the cultural and/or economic resources to do so. During the 'Great Emigration' of the nineteenth century, the migratory elite consisted of those Cornish people who had skills in demand elsewhere and had the cultural and economic means to migrate to those places. The finding that young Cornish people no longer aspire to migrate thus serves as a coda to the extensive work on historical migration. The latter work has featured prominently in *Cornish Studies* since the first volume and forms an important basis for the understanding of the contemporary Cornish economy and identity. Space does not permit a discussion of this work here, for strictly speaking it shades into the sister branch of Cornish Studies sometimes termed the 'new Cornish historiography'.[35]

Housing Studies

A persistent and serious side-effect of population-led growth has been that of housing need. Two studies conducted by Plymouth-based researchers, those of Mary Buck and associates and Carol Williams,[36] sought to establish both the roots of the housing crisis and the identity of the groups who succeeded or failed in the housing market. This led to and influenced other local housing need studies funded by the public and voluntary sector[37] and might be cited as examples of how an acceptance of Cornish socio-economic particularism has entered the mainstream. The 1990s also saw district housing need studies conducted in Kerrier, Carrick, Restormel and Penwith. The latter was one of the largest District housing studies in Britain and provided important confirmatory data on the successful and unsuccessful competitors in the housing market. District housing studies are notoriously parochial, but greater understanding of the wider Cornish context of need and its origins in population-led growth have to one extent or another informed district policies, though like so much social policy it is hard to identify the exact processes in which research—especially academic research—has had influence. It is nevertheless the case that housing has been an important research interface between NCSS in the academy and in the public sector.

One area in which one would have expected a great deal of work to have been done is that around the extent and problem of second homes. Surprisingly, only one article has appeared addressing this topic, from Paul Thornton in 1996.[38] As he rightly notes, this is a difficult area to research, with the only recent data for all of Cornwall imputable from the 1991 Census. Nevertheless, Thornton reports on a micro-study of Port Isaac, which (unsurprisingly) found that only 46 per cent of the lower village was permanently occupied and that whilst permanent residents mainly worked in manual occupations or were unemployed, second home owners worked in non-manual occupations and none was unemployed.

Identity

The area in which there has been the most progress, both in terms of the advancement of the understanding of 'Cornishness' and the ability of research to influence policy, has been that of identity. Of course, one could hold that in a discipline such as NCSS identity is both an input and an output in every research project or writing, so here I will confine myself to discussing some of the work that has overtly addressed identity issues. For the most part, there has been less discussion about whether the Cornish are a distinctive ethnic group, than about what is the nature of that distinctiveness. One exception to this rule was Ivey and Payton's 1994 paper which tackled the kind of view commonplace some years ago—that there was no such thing as a Cornish ethnic identity.[39] Such a view, it was argued, resulted from ethnicity and identity being viewed through the lenses of a British or Anglocentric perspective. Ivey and Payton's alternative builds on previous work by Cross, Ivey and more recently Caroline Vink,[40] to advocate an identity theory that has the aim of 'the generation of a positive sense of self and a positive sense of Cornwall's cultural history'.[41] The move here is precisely from description to advocacy, but one that begins from a premise often ignored or denied by writers in the British or Anglocentric tradition that Cornish people *feel* themselves to be different.

Yet despite the wealth of writing about the particularity of Cornish identity and culture in the past decade, empirical research has been scarce. For sure there has been an enormous wealth of historical data on Cornish diasporas and migration,[42] on the nature of difference in Cornish politics (e.g. the work of Elvins, Jaggard and Tregidga), on historical divisions of labour, on the particularity of the family and gender, and on Celticity and the Cornish revival (such as that by Hale). The aforementioned studies by Buck *et al.* and Carol Williams provided numeric data and ethnographic evidence on the distinctiveness of household arrangements and in-migration, and Philipa Aldous's work on youth and out-migration provided useful data on ethnic identity. But this is the extent of empirical work on identity and in each of these cases this was a by product of other work (on housing and migration). Nevertheless, Aldous's study,[43] though not the first survey to use an ethnic identifier, was the first to do so in a study across each Cornish district. The self-identification of young people as either Cornish or members of another ethnic group provided solid evidence for the existence of a distinct identity and furthermore seemed to confirm a long-held hypothesis that there was a West–East distance decay in 'Cornishness' (at least as measured here). The ways in which the sense of difference is manifested in individuals remains under-researched.

Nevertheless, despite the paucity of empirical work, there have been some important achievements in theorizing the changing nature of identity and these are potentially a basis from which testable hypotheses may be derived. In this respect the theoretical work of Bernard Deacon has been important. His 1993 article (with Payton) 'Re-Inventing Cornwall' describes the development of popular culture in Cornwall from the nineteenth century 'industrial' culture to the postmodern culture of (in his words) 'Majorette Troupes and the Mexican Wave', these latter referring to the hybrid forms popular culture now takes. Here Deacon is confronting the above-mentioned foundational myths of the revival, but whilst these might indeed be myths, they are crucially important to contemporary identity. It matters not at all that the Gorseth and the tartan were invented, or that the language and the music have been revived, but rather the way in which people in Cornwall use these symbols of identity. Deacon's later work has taken up the issue of space and place in Cornish culture; specifically he examines hypotheses of cultural difference and similarity in East and West Cornwall.[44] Though this work is firmly grounded in a historical context, it does provide an interesting marker for just those differences found in Aldous's contemporary work.

Just how far has the work on identity influenced policy? The historical researcher will be faced in this respect with a 'black box'. On one hand, as I have suggested, the writing on identity in the last ten years has been prolific, and on the other hand there are numerous examples of identity being seen as an important variable in policy-making. Cornwall County Council has long used the rhetoric of 'difference' both in documents for internal Cornish consumption and in documents intended for external consumption, most notably the submission to the Local Government Commission in 1994.[45] Cultural aims grounded in Cornish distinctiveness are built into Objective 1 documentation, and the preparedness of the County Council to back the bid for the separate coding of 'Cornish' as an ethnic category in the 2001 Census emphasizes the internalization, or at least acceptance, of distinctiveness by public bodies. How much this has been a direct result of NCSS and how much a manifestation of Cornish popularism, we just do not know. It is possible to cite two 'cross-over' documents, however: the first was the 1994 Campaign for Cornwall submission to the Local Government Commission and the second was the 1999 report to the Council of Europe Framework Convention for the Protection of National Minorities.[46] Both firmly took identity difference as a starting point for their argument and each in their different ways represented a legitimation of that difference. The first brought together (physically in County Hall most of the time) policy-makers, politicians, representatives of major businesses and academics in NCSS. The second, again widely supported by such groups, was part funded by the Joseph Rowntree Foundation.

Politics
The historic and contemporary political arrangements of Cornwall provide some of the best evidence for Cornish distinctiveness. Indeed, this has been a topic that has interested political scientists for some while, though curiously it has not been a major preoccupation in the last ten years. One searches in vain for any academic analysis of the historic 1997 election, or recent writings on the contemporary national-ist-autonomist movement. Whilst there has been little new work, both Philip Payton[47] and Adrian Lee[48] tell the story of political distinctive-ness well up until the early 1990s. Three things in particular stand out from Payton's and Lee's analyses that mark out Cornish politics as atypical: the very different party alignment present in Cornwall through the twentieth century; the strength of anti-metropolitan feeling in Cornwall; and the presence of a nationalist movement.

Party alignment: General election results between 1945 and 1992, as Lee notes, do not look so very different to those of many English counties. Since that time Conservatives have held four out of five constituencies on seven occasions and on the other seven occasions (until 1992) they have held three seats. Labour held one seat until 1970 (and regained that seat in 1997). Up until 1997 the Liberals (and later Liberal Democrats) managed to only hold one or two seats. However Lee's analysis is 'bottom up', rather than one that sees parties from a centralist national perspective. As Lee notes, one of most striking differences historically is the failure of the Labour Party to make significant inroads during the period of the 'great realignment' when they replaced the Liberals through much of England and South Wales. Indeed, the alignment in Cornwall was rather different, with Conservatives, rather than Labour, replacing Liberals during the 1930s. Between 1885 and 1910 the Conservatives had few victories, but by the 1950s Cornwall consistently returned four Conservatives and one Labour member.

The politics of the early decades of the twentieth century are complex and, as Garry Tregidga has shown, were influenced strongly by Cornish Methodism. Ironically, whilst its manifestation in Cornwall was seen by commentators as a very 'Celtic' phenomenon, its adherents identified more closely with Northern Irish Protestantism during the Home Rule campaign than they did with the southern Catholics. Consequently, the Cornish electorate shifted much of its allegiance to anti-Home Rule Liberal Unionists. Labour intervention in Cornwall was not significant until after 1945 and then it is notable that they were successful only in the Falmouth–Camborne constituency, where (unlike the rest of Cornwall) there was a relatively strong trades union movement. Yet despite the post-war success of the Conservative Party (though sailing under the National Liberal flag of convenience in St Ives constituency), the Liberal vote held up much better in Cornwall than nationally.

Anti-metropolitanism: Why did the Liberal vote hold up? The most obvious reason is, of course, the absence of Labour as a credible opposition through much of the period, but Payton emphasizes the Liberals' success in assuming the mantle of Cornish anti-metropolitanism and (citing Deacon) their ability to mobilize local patriotism in Cornwall. Labour, on the other hand, was seen as centralist and un-Cornish. The strength of this anti-metropolitanism is demonstrated in the data Payton cites from the 1970 British Election Survey. This showed nearly twice the level of agreement to the statement 'Government is too centralised in London' in Cornwall compared to the South-West (which itself differed from the rest of the country by only two percentage points in favour of the statement). But of course none of this so far adds up to more than local difference and an accentuated version of anti-metropolitanism found in parts of England. The key difference is that in Cornwall anti-metropolitanism is underwritten by a sense of identity difference that has given rise to a vigorous regionalist or nationalist movement.

The nationalist movement: Compared to the other Celtic countries, nationalism came late to Cornwall. Garry Tregidga's work has been an important milestone in helping us to understand why, and by extension why nationalist candidates do less well in the present day than they do in Wales or Scotland. Whilst, as he shows, nationalist sentiment was not altogether absent during the Celtic Revival, a combination of opposition to this by leading cultural figures such as Jenner, the (above-mentioned) rejection of 'Home Rule' politics in Cornwall on religious grounds, and the failure of the Celtic Revival to capture the imagination of what continued to be a nineteenth-century industrial culture meant that its impact was limited. This is not to suggest that Cornish 'patriotism' did not exist in that culture, but perhaps like that of the South Wales valleys it was a local patriotism that did not have 'national' aspirations. Nationalism had to wait until the 1950s for the revival to produce a political cadre, and at least until the 1980s for there to be fusion of revival and industrial cultures sufficient to produce a significant number of people in favour of regional devolution.

Nationalism has largely been the ghost in the machine of Cornish politics. With a few local government election exceptions, it has never been an electorally important force, though its influence on Cornish politics has been far in excess of that achieved directly through the ballot box. The most successful party, Mebyon Kernow, began life as a pressure group in the 1950s and during the 1960s could boast Liberal MPs Peter Bessell and John Pardoe as members and even the (somewhat maverick) Conservative David Mudd. Payton provides a number of examples of how, through the intervening period, the Liberals (mostly) but also the Labour and Conservative parties have sought to play the Cornish card, and indeed where Conservative and Labour candidates who have been perceived to be anti-Cornish (or even not Cornish enough) have lost their seats or failed to be elected. There is an argument to be made, and it is at least implicit in Payton's writing, that Cornwall's most successful 'nationalist' party has been the Liberals. Since the 1960s its MPs and most (though not all) of its councillors have supported 'Cornish' causes such as a university for Cornwall, opposition to Plymouth expansion into south-east Cornwall, a Cornwall-only European constituency and, in more recent times, a Cornish Development Agency and the most treasured nationalist prize —a Cornish Assembly. Embracing this agenda has not been just about electoral tactics, to neutralize Mebyon Kernow electoral interventions, because in many cases Liberal candidates were electorally unassailable and, in the case of the late David Penhaligon, revered by nationalists. This is perhaps now more than ever the case since the election of Andrew George as a Liberal Democrat MP in 1997.

The relationship between overt nationalist politics and the Liberal Party is underdescribed and undertheorized, as is the role of Mebyon Kernow in the various campaigns (and others) mentioned above. What in particular has kept nationalism such an active (and influential) force in Cornish politics for so long? Whilst one can explain the motivation towards the possibility of a political career in the UK parties, no such rewards beckon in joining Mebyon Kernow and the very best an activist can hope for is election to a local council. Yet since the 1950s with varying success the latter party has retained a visible presence in Cornish politics. The enduring nature of nationalism in Cornwall and its explicit and implicit effects on Cornish politics are surely a manifestation of a distinct sense of identity. Nevertheless, in the absence of empirical evidence we can only speculate on the processes which connect identity with politics in the Cornish case—though of course there are plenty of models elsewhere that may provide us with hypotheses.[49]

Tourism

The service sector in Cornwall accounts for over 30 per cent of employment,[50] much of which is in the tourist industry, yet its growth since the 1960s has by no means been regarded as an economic or cultural blessing in Cornwall. Indeed there is fairly conclusive evidence that it has been the most important motor of in-migration, the latter increasingly seen as economically deleterious. Nevertheless, as a major economic actor tourism is important to Cornish social science, both in its negative and positive economic contributions and in its direct and indirect influence on contemporary culture.

Though tourism has not been a prominent feature of NCSS since 1993, there have been a few important contributions. As Paul Thornton shows in a survey of recent research,[51] we actually know quite a lot about tourism in Cornwall and quite a lot of what we know comes from the Cornwall Tourist Visitor Surveys, latterly the Cornwall Holiday Survey. Between 1987 and 1993 data on 37,868 cases was collected. From this research we learn that (for example) in 1993 visitors to Cornwall spent an average of £193 per day and that 34 per cent of visitors make return visits the next year. Unsurprisingly, there has been a consistent trend away from serviced accommodation toward self-catering and there is some evidence of a shift away from beach holidays toward activities and sight-seeing. Despite the economic importance of the tourist industry, Thornton alights on some key questions that need to be addressed. Should the industry go for a hard driving campaign to maximize profitability and reach new markets? Should Cornwall generally ask what it wants from tourism? As he notes, if the aim is a more general prosperity and a reduction in unemployment, how can this be squared with the clear evidence that tourism has the effect of making Cornwall a desirable place to live, with the consequence that the industry is owned and operated largely by in-migrants?

The relationship between in-migration and tourism in one town —Newquay—was explored by Ron Elzey in a study in the mid-1990s. His focus was on seasonal workers who moved (mainly from the North of England) in the spring and for the most part returned in the autumn. Elzey found that whilst many did return, a growing number did not and 'signed on' in Newquay during the winter months. Elzey's in-migrants were untypical of those to Cornwall generally, though perhaps indicative of a new migrant stream attracted by tourism. Mostly they were under 30 and from working-class backgrounds, though like their older, wealthier counterparts from the South-East, lifestyle attractions inspired by earlier holidays were important motivations to migrate.

Tourism is potentially one of the most divisive issues Cornwall will face in the next quarter-century. The 'tourist gaze' potentially subverts that which it comes to see and the stereotyped images are fed back to and absorbed by the locals, though we do not really know how or to what extent this happens in Cornwall. More measurable are environmental consequences of tourism. Tourism needs better communications, which means more roads, and more roads bring more people, both of which lead to further environmental stress. Finally, tourism has done nothing to increase Cornwall's prosperity, or even maintain the economic level prior to the 'great in-migration'. Economically, one could argue it has been a spectacular failure, yet as Shaw and Williams conclude in their *Cornwall Since the War* chapter, 'blaming the tourist for all of the ills, or a blanket constraint on new tourism developments',[52] will solve nothing. Instead, they advocate the development of an effective strategy for tourism that is sensitive to both the needs of an existing industry and the Cornish community.

In this section I have tried to give a sense of the kind of work that has been done in NCSS in the past ten years or so. In the areas that I have discussed I have not always mentioned all of the work that has been done (this was particularly the case in respect of identity) and, moreover, there are a several areas I have not discussed at all. Gender and division of labour and gender and identity are emerging themes, whilst at various times during the decade the issue of regions and regionalism has produced some important work. Of course, the most obvious omission has been that of language and its relationship to culture, for despite the vigorous language debate in the pages of *Cornish Studies*, no author has discussed the role of the Cornish language revival in contemporary identity formation.

NCSS TEN YEARS ON AND THE NEXT TEN YEARS
In reading the previous section it will have become clear that whilst a great deal has been done in NCSS, there is much to do. Before considering the latter, let us review some of the positive achievements:

- NCSS has become established as a discipline legitimated both by the academic community and by wider Cornish society. It is embedded in Cornish society, strongly influenced in its research and analysis by contemporary events and able to have some societal influence.
- It has been successful in attracting academics from a number of other disciplines to carry out research and contribute papers.
- It is a critical discipline prepared to examine core assumptions about its subject matter.
- It is a methodologically eclectic discipline with the potential for fruitful research collaborations.

There are some areas in which less progress has been made:

- Whilst it is possible to identify NCSS as a discipline, defined by a commitment to social science investigations of Cornwall, this subject matter is too broad to provide methodological or theoretical coherence. In practical terms, this makes the production of research programmes difficult and less attractive to external funders.
- Subject matter clearly reflects practitioners' interests, but in *Cornish Studies* itself there has been an over-representation of 'historical' material. Of course, this shades into historiography and not strictly NCSS at all, but if we allow that all of the historically focused papers should be located within historiographical traditions rather than seen as social science, then NCSS becomes a relatively minor part of *Cornish Studies*.
- Allied to this is the paucity of empirical work, an issue I have touched upon several times in the previous section. The empirical research that has been done has mostly been in the areas of tourism, migration and housing. Despite its enormous importance little has been done on identity and although research was done at the beginning of the period in politics, nothing has been done in the much more interesting second half of the decade.

What Is To Be Done?
There is not space, nor would it be appropriate for me to set out prescriptions for research priorities, though my own views on these are perhaps implicit in the foregoing. Rather, I want to end this article with some brief thoughts on the context of research in the NCSS.

Social scientists are constantly goaded by government to make their research relevant and from my remarks above it might be thought I had joined this same chorus. However, relevance in the sense I intend is not adherence to a narrow economic project of wealth creation, but relevance in a broader sense to the issues that matter to the Cornish community. Now this of course assumes that we know what matters in Cornwall. In my review I have indicated some key areas where we cannot make such assumptions. Thus an important part of a relevant Cornish social science is to be able to describe what contemporary Cornwall is like and to understand what people in Cornwall think. This is a reasonable goal for any discipline that is centred upon a distinctive community.

Much of this kind of work will inevitably be about Cornwall as a whole, because the claim is that there is something distinctive about the social-spatial community that is Cornwall. A greater part of the work I have described above would fit this description. This might be seen as a first level of analysis in Cornish social science and perhaps by extension in the historical arena, Cornish Studies more generally.

A second level of research and analysis must be comparative work within Cornwall. Although people live within a larger Cornish community, their interface with economy and culture is at a more local level. Some of this work, such as that of Deacon (above) on the spatial dimension of Cornish culture, will inform the first level by demonstrating the heterogeneity of Cornish culture and economy, whilst other work will be about issues unique or specific to one locality. This may be work on regeneration strategies, housing policy, issues related to tourism or environmental questions. NCSS can bring to these localized studies a deeper theoretical understanding of how they relate to wider issues of economy or how conditions compare with elsewhere in Cornwall. Although less represented in the pages of *Cornish Studies* (what might be termed) local policy studies actually account for a considerable amount of research undertaken in Cornwall, though the extent to which these are explicitly informed by a *Cornish* social science approach varies considerably.

Finally, comparative studies of Cornish society with other societies helps us to understand differences and similarities. This kind of work is the least well developed, but an area that holds great potential for a theoretical understanding of Cornish issues and provides external credibility for Cornish social science.

Yet there are challenges for any research programme or programmes and at the risk of ending on a note of pessimism I will mention the ones I see as most important.

Credibility: NCSS is not yet home and dry as an established discipline or sub-discipline. It has to remain and become more credible to a number of constituencies: to policy-makers and politicians inside and outside of Cornwall and to academia. The latter is important both in respect of appointments and funding, but also in respect of individual careers. Publications on Cornish subjects or Cornish publications unfortunately do not yet carry as much academic weight as in other areas. Consequently, most people currently doing work in NCSS are 'part-timers' in this area. Finally, the work that is done must have public credibility and trust. In this regard the Institute of Cornish Studies has been very successful in reaching out to the public with educational programmes and events, but there is still important work to be done in the public understanding of Cornish social science.

Funding: Research programmes require funding and to obtain funding they must demonstrate credibility, but to do this there must be a body of research that has been funded. This may sound like Catch 22, but it is not quite that bad. Research *does* get funded. But the principal reason there is a deficit of empirical work in NCSS is a lack of substantial research grants. If the discipline is to grow and work successfully at the three levels I have suggested, then such substantial funding grants will be needed.

Context: In the first part of this article I argued that the emergence of NCSS has been at least partially a reflection of changes in Cornish society; in other words it does not exist in a political or socio-economic vacuum. Cornwall is undergoing greater changes now than we have seen in a generation: these include the unification and expansion of higher education facilities in Cornwall, and various regeneration projects—particularly Objective 1 and likely changes in the political settlement for Cornwall that will see it either with its own assembly or its governance merged into a seven-county assembly. These together will form the context of the next ten years for social science in Cornwall, but perhaps just as importantly the challenge for NCSS is to be a key actor in these changes.

NOTES AND REFERENCES

1. P. Payton, 'Introduction', in Philip Payton (ed.), *Cornish Studies: Six*, Exeter, 1998, p. 1.
2. For example, the Research and Information Unit in Cornwall County Council's Planning Department has been an important source of descriptive data. See http://www.cornwall.gov.uk/facts/socio-ec/ SE008.htm.
3. A.L. Rowse, *A Cornish Childhood*, London, 1975; J. Rowe, *Cornwall in the Age of the Industrial Revolution*, St Austell, 1993; A.K. Hamilton Jenkins, *The Cornish Miner*, 3rd edn, Newton Abbot 1972.
4. H. Gilligan, 'The Rural Labour Process: A Case Study of a Cornish Town', in Tony Bradley and Philip Lowe (eds), *Locality and Rurality: Economy and Society in Rural Regions*, Norwich, 1984; R. McNabb, J. Barry and N. Woodward, *Unemployment in West Cornwall*, London, Department of Employment, 1978.
5. P. Payton 'Post-War Cornwall: A Suitable Case for Treatment?' in Philip Payton (ed.), *Cornwall Since the War*, Redruth, 1993a, p. 7.
6. R. Perry, K. Dean and B. Brown, *Counterurbanisation*, Norwich, 1986. Though this work was foundational to later studies of migration into Cornwall, it is also considered a key contribution to the literature on counter-urbanization.
7. CoSERG published a number of working papers on various aspects of the Cornish economy and society in the 1980s. Much of its argument was summarized in B. Deacon, A. George and R. Perry, *Cornwall at the Crossroads*, Redruth, 1988.
8. The attitude of the Cornish political establishment towards social research and critique at this time mirrored the Thatcherite view of social science simply as an apologia for socialism—though in this case CoSERG was

seen to be making the nationalist case, as in its discussion paper *The Cornish Community: Reclaiming our Destiny*, Redruth, 1987.

9. Payton, 1993a, p. 7.
10. The social history of mining, as I indicated above, has been an important strand in Cornish Studies since the early twentieth century, yet until very recently there has been hardly any analysis of the relationship of this history to contemporary identity.
11. See B. Deacon and P. Payton, 'Re-inventing Cornwall: Cultural Change of the European Periphery', in Philip Payton (ed.), *Cornish Studies: One*, Exeter, 1993b, pp. 62–79.
12. Deacon and Payton, 1993, p. 75.
13. M. Williams, 'The Invisible People', *Radical Statistics* 52, 1992, pp. 21–8.
14. A. George, *Homes for Locals in Cornwall: Chyow rag Genesygyon yn Kernow*, Truro, 1987.
15. Parish housing surveys are joint ventures between the Cornwall Rural Community Council and civil parish councils in Cornwall. See A. George, *Review of the Current Situation in Cornwall and the Isles of Scilly*, Report to the 'Meeting House Need Conference', 1990.
16. George was the most overt in his promotion of 'Cornish issues', but Caroline Vink points out that in the 1992 election of 'each of the candidates in Cornish constituencies had Cornish issues on top of their agendas': C. Vink, '"Be Forever Cornish!" Some observations on the Ethnoregional Movement in Contemporary Cornwall', in Payton (ed.), 1993b, p. 116.
17. Media endorsement of the 'Cornish case' has been complex and contradictory. Analysis of newspaper coverage of Cornish affairs in the mid-1990s, in the Department of Sociology at Plymouth University, indicated a Janus-like endorsement of both 'Westcountry' and Cornish institutions and identity. Only relatively recently have Cornish newspapers, of the Harmsworth Press (publishers of the *Western Morning News*), endorsed campaigns such as that for the establishment of a Cornish Assembly.
18. Campaign for Cornwall, *A Sense of Difference—A Submission to the Local Government Commission for England*, Truro, 1994.
19. J. Payne, *Interpreting the Index of Local Conditions: Relative Deprivation in Devon and Cornwall*, Plymouth, 1995.
20. Cornwall County Council, *Objective One for Cornwall & Scilly: Key Statistics Report*, Truro, 1998.
21. See for example S. Harding, 'Rethinking Standpoint Epistemology: What is "Strong Objectivity"?', in E. Fox Keller and H. Longino (eds), *Feminism and Science*, Oxford, 1996.
22. I. Barwell, 'Toward a Defence of Objectivity', in K. Lennon and M. Whitford (eds), *Knowing the Difference: Feminist Perspectives in Epistemology*, London, 1994.
23. See for example P. Payton, *The Making of Modern Cornwall: Historical Experience and the Persistence of 'Difference'*, Redruth, 1992, chapter 4; S. Schwartz, 'In Defence of Customary Rights: Labouring Women's

Experience of Industrialization in Cornwall c1750–1870', in Philip Payton (ed.), *Cornish Studies: Seven*, Exeter, 1999, pp. 8–31; P. Payton, ' "Vote Labor and Rid South Australia of a Danger to the Purity of Our Race": The Cornish Radical Tradition in South Australia, 1900–1939', in Philip Payton (ed.), *Cornish Studies: Nine*, Exeter, 2001 pp. 173–203.

24. From a housing point of view this was worse news, because demand for affordable housing was not just internal as was previously believed.
25. R. Perry, 'Economic Change and "Opposition" Economics', in Payton (ed.), 1993a.
26. Williams, 1992, p. 22.
27. Williams, 1992, p. 25.
28. Payne, 1995, p. 9.
29. P. Wills, 'Cornish Regional Development: Evaluation, Europe and Evolution', in Payton (ed.), 1998, p. 159.
30. See P. Mitchell 'The Demographic Revolution', in Payton (ed.), 1993a; M. Williams, B. Cheal, P. Mitchell and L. Bryant, *Movers and Stayers: Migration and Social Change in Cornwall 1971–1991*, Plymouth, 1995.
31. See for example M. Williams and P. Champion, 'Cornwall, Poverty and In-Migration', in Payton (ed.), 1998, pp. 118–26.
32. Perry, 1993; Perry, Dean and Brown, 1986.
33. P. Aldous, 'Young People and Migration Choices in Cornwall', unpublished Ph.D. thesis, University of Plymouth, 2001.
34. F. Mugrove, *The Migratory Elite*, London, 1963.
35. See Bernard Deacon's article in this volume.
36. M. Buck, L. Bryant and M. Williams, *Housing and Households in Cornwall*, Plymouth, 1993; C. Williams, 'Housing in Cornwall: A Two Tier System', in Philip Payton (ed.), *Cornish Studies: Three*, Exeter, 1995, pp. 194–206.
37. See for example Penwith District Council, *Penwith Housing Needs Survey*, Penzance, 1997.
38. P. Thornton, 'Second Homes in Cornwall', in Philip Payton (ed.), *Cornish Studies: Four*, Exeter, 1996, pp. 147–51.
39. A. Ivey and P. Payton, 'Towards a Cornish Identity Theory', in Philip Payton (ed.), *Cornish Studies: Two*, Exeter, 1994.
40. Vink, 1993.
41. Ivey and Payton, 1994.
42. See for example R. James, 'Defining the Group: Nineteenth-Century Cornish on the North American Mining Frontier', in Payton (ed.), 1994, pp. 32–47; P. Payton, ' "Reforming Thirties" and "Hungry Forties": The Genesis of Cornwall's Emigration Trade', in Payton (ed.), 1996, pp. 107–27; S. Schwartz, 'The Making of a Myth: Cornish Miners in the New World in the Early Nineteenth Century', in Payton (ed.), 2001, pp. 105–26.
43. P. Aldous and M. Williams, 'A Question of Ethnic Identity', in Payton (ed.), 2001, pp. 213–26.
44. B. Deacon, 'In Search of the Missing Turn: The Spatial Dimension and Cornish Studies', in Philip Payton (ed.), *Cornish Studies: Eight*, Exeter, 2000, pp. 213–30.

45. Cornwall County Council, *Submission to the Local Government Commission (2 Parts)*, Truro, 1994.
46. B. Deacon (ed.), *The Cornish and the Council of Europe Framework Convention for the Protection of National Minorities*, Redruth, 1999.
47. Payton, 1992.
48. A. Lee, 'Political Parties and Elections', in P. Payton (ed.), 1993a.
49. See for example M. Guibernau, *Nationalisms: The Nation State and Nationalism in the 20th Century*, Cambridge, 1996.
50. *Cambridge Econometrics*, 1999, cited in Cornwall County Council, *Socio Economic Profile*, Truro, 2002, http://www.cornwall.gov.uk/facts/socio-ec/SE008.htm.
51. P. Thornton, 'Tourism in Cornwall: Recent Research and Current Trends', in Payton (ed.), 1994, pp. 108–27. See also P. Thornton, 'Cornwall and Changes in the Tourist Gaze', in Payton (ed.), 1993b, pp. 80–96.
52. A. Williams and G. Shaw, 'The Age of Mass Tourism', in Payton (ed.), 1993a, p. 97.

ON IDEOLOGY, IDENTITY AND INTEGRITY

Colin H. Williams

INTRODUCTION

The growth of 'New Cornish Studies' within the current generation is a remarkable achievement. This academic project has been an attempt to re-define both the content and the relevance of Cornish Studies in the wake of social and political changes in the late twentieth century. Yet in this article I argue that ultimately it has been also, and continues to be, an ideological project searching for group recognition and collective self-realization. Consequently it is hard, if not impossible, to review the field in any objective manner, for that would be a perversion of reason. It would force the material products of the sub-discipline into logical categories that serve more mature disciplines such as history, geography and biological science. Of course, at one level one can readily point to distinct and distinguished contributions within the fields of, for example, historical geography, tourism studies, Celtic linguistics and literature and folklore.[1] Such contributions can be judged on their own merit as contributing both to our collective knowledge of the place, Cornwall, and to the respective discipline, whether literature, history or linguistics. But over and above such individual contributions there is the larger question of what is Cornish Studies seeking to achieve? How tightly focused is it? How original is it in its genesis, methodology and application?

The roots of New Cornish Studies are discussed from an insider's perspective by Bernard Deacon[2] and have been elaborated upon in successive editorial Introductions to the flagship series *Cornish Studies* by its innovative and dynamic editor, Philip Payton.[3] Both Payton and Deacon have raised the possibility of alternative trajectories for the development of Cornish Studies from those three which have emerged in the modern period. In this current volume yet further twists and avenues have been suggested which may yet prove fruitful in engaging Cornish Studies scholars with postmodernist uncertainties and socio-economic realities.

We have seen that Cornish Studies may be treated as local studies, as national(ist) studies, and as an element within Celtic Studies. For understandable reasons connected with scale, key personalities, institutional resources and academic networks, the New Cornish Studies that emerged in the last quarter of the twentieth century was an idiosyncratic admixture of interests straining to deal with fundamental issues of authenticity, legitimacy, relevance and purchase. Having failed to address such issues within its conventional guise, a 'New' version of the sub-discipline was gradually constructed from the early 1990s onwards. This version, as Deacon makes clear, was a conscious attempt to re-locate Cornish Studies at the interface between the humanities and the social sciences.[4] The physical sciences, marine biology and environmental problems which characterized much work on Cornwall in the early post-war period, and certainly attracted a significant amount of attention in the first phase of the establishment of the Institute of Cornish Studies, have slipped from the pages of *Cornish Studies* in recent issues. This is a function, no doubt, of the disengagement of the Cornwall Biological Records Unit from the University of Exeter and its reinvestment within the Cornwall Wildlife Trust, but it may also reflect the inability or unwillingness of environmental researchers to engage fully with the re-location described by Deacon. Despite this, of course, scientific research continues apace and will continue to inform the context of Cornish Studies even if the synergy between physical and human sciences so characteristic of the late 1960s and early 1970s is no longer dominant within the Cornish academic network.

Having moved Cornish Studies to the interface between the humanities and the social sciences, the big issue it must face is the relationship between Cornwall and the rest of the United Kingdom. And in their related ways this means both England and the Celtic nations in tandem. This is the crux of the claim to an independent Cornish Studies existence, that we are dealing with a place which has a unique location and relationship within these isles.

In recent times the formation of the United Kingdom as a constitutional monarchy and as an identity-ascribing polity has been subject to intense debate. Not surprisingly, Cornish Studies scholars have sought to tease out Cornwall's role within this evolving matrix. Employing the core values of territory, identity and political consciousness, Deacon and Payton have offered persuasive accounts of

Cornwall's attempts to navigate into the mainstream of constitutional reform without losing its distinct 'sense of difference.'[5] Building on the more recent devolutionary pressures within the UK will be a major challenge to academics and policy-makers within Cornwall. Currently, most British schemes for regional reform within England base their regional delimitations on an admixture of functional economic regions and a sense of identity. Conventionally, Cornwall would thus comprise a sub-region of the South-West with its capital in Bristol. And yet of all the 'English' regions/counties, Cornwall has arguably the greatest sense of distinctiveness, the greatest articulation of a separate sense of place. The stumbling block, of course, from a centralist perspective is the relative weakness of its demographic and economic base to sustain a political settlement coterminous with its socio-cultural boundaries. No wonder then that the social and political theories championed by scholars of regionalism and nationalism have found a ready audience west of the Tamar. The challenge facing Cornish Studies scholars is first to integrate their version of national historiography within the broader sweep of British history and then to achieve the same goal with respect to Western European history and geography[6] and contemporary European Union policies, a process that Payton has begun in his recent *A Vision of Cornwall.*[7] Westminster and Brussels, then, are key to the determination of Cornwall's future and Cornish Studies would do well to invest much time and intelligence into articulating the contours and implications of these evolving relationships. But what of the conventional concern with the Celts, the 'significant others' which have figured so large in the Whig-imperialist vision of Britain?

'THE STRAIGHTENING OF BENT BACKS'

How Celtic are the Cornish? This is a pivotal question for it presupposes that one can legitimately still talk of national and ethnic divisions within the south-west peninsula. Over the years Cornwall has asserted and has been accepted as one of the constituent six Celtic nations of these isles. It is, after all, the basis for much of Cornwall's claim to being distinct, unique and authentic within the plural identities of this realm. In modern times, however, the various components of this Celtic identity have atrophied (as they have, to be fair, in most so-called Celtic contexts). Let us go back to basics, to DNA, blood types and the phenotypic features so beloved of Victorian anthropologists, ethnologists and geographers. Recent concerns with the origin and longevity of the constituent peoples of these isles, especially the Danes and the Vikings, have been expressed in very good television documentaries based on scholarly research monographs. What of the Celtic Cornish? Do they retain their distinctive characteristics?

Cole has argued that modern research in genetics, specifically the work of Harvey *et al.*,[8] which discussed the thesis that the Cornish were a distinctive genetic group, needs to be handled with great care.[9] For example, research evidence, based upon a sample of 250 Cornish people surveyed in May 1984 to investigate their physical and genetic attributes, concluded that:

> such characteristics as general body size, head size, hair and eye colour point to greater affinities with the Celtic-language speaking peoples of Wales, Ireland and Scotland than with neighbours of the Cornish to the east. On the other hand, the blood group evidence shows that the Cornish sample occupies a somewhat intermediate position between 'Celtic' and 'Anglo-Saxon' populations, but with a definite tendency to be aligned with the latter.[10]

This is, perhaps, a fitting postmodernist conclusion, full of ambiguity and nuanced interpretation that allows one to emphasize those features which suit the general argument proposed.

The oppositional elements of 'Cornish' and 'Anglo-Saxon' are also woven into the metanarrative formed from myths of ethnic descent. This is crucial for the legitimization of the New Cornish Studies project as both a contribution to, and in turn deriving from, the underlying Celticity of the population. In common with other regions of Europe the structure and content of these foundational, if mythical, ideas constitute the material evidence for the development of social movements. For Cornish Studies to be more than an exercise in local or county history, the prior legitimacy of the Cornish nation has to be established. Earlier attempts at proto-nation-building, including a defence of the Cornish language and its variant, revivalist character, or institution building, as with the Institute of Cornish Studies itself, are noted elsewhere in this volume. Yet more contemporary theorizing based on core–periphery differentials, internal–colonial theory and ethnic-regionalism, whilst rich in interpretative analysis, has been criticized as tending toward the polemical and is consequently perhaps less academically sound than might otherwise have been the case.[11] But this is often the fate of writings on nationalism and regionalism, for the discourse itself is by definition counter-hegemonic and counter-state, therefore oppositional, radical and disturbing.

In a characteristically rich treatment of myths of ethnic descent, Anthony Smith has distinguished between myths that cite genealogical ancestry and those which identify a more ideological descent, a distinction between 'biological' and 'cultural-ideological' myths.[12] He identifies six components of ethnic myths as follows: (1) a myth of temporal origins, or when we were begotten; (2) a myth of location and migration, or where we came from and how we got here; (3) a myth of ancestry, or who begot us and how we developed; (4) a myth of the heroic age, or how we freed ourselves and became glorious; (5) a myth of decline, or how we fell into a state of decay; (6) a myth of regeneration, or how to restore the golden age and renew our community as in 'the days of old'. In their various ways, earlier Cornish Studies scholars have tackled each of these elements and offered a plethora of answers.

The basic components of nationalism's belief system revolve around issues of identity, dignity, territory and autonomy. That is, it seeks to explain and interpret a question that has exercised many of the contributors to the New Cornish Studies. To what extent is the rhetorical nature of Cornish Studies a reflection of the limited number of personnel involved, as Deacon claims, above, and/or to what extent is it a reflection of the intellectual immaturity of the field? Hectoring and exaggerating for effect are a common tendency in order to quicken the location of one's subject matter toward the centre of the universe of interest. If the ultimate aim is also to straighten bent backs so as to walk tall in the company of both friends and strangers, then it is all the more imperative that the speed of rehabilitation be helped along by whatever means possible. And here we have a logical dilemma. By coupling New Cornish Studies to the revival of Celtic Studies writ large, practitioners have 'prized the Shadows of the Many over the Darkness of the One'.[13] Yet such a rhetorical device has also exposed the limited basis of previous scholarship on Cornwall, both from within and without. Conventionally preoccupied with questions of language, archaeology and local history, Cornish Studies followed the canons of Celtic Studies scholarship but looked tired and flat by comparison with the more dynamic Irish and Welsh efforts. This was not surprising, given both the original materials to hand and the very limited number of professional scholars in the field.[14]

In contrast, New Cornish Studies has been characterized by a quantum leap in both ambition and fulfilment. Yet in order to emerge from the 'Shadows of the Many' it has cast its fresh light on a whole range of topics and issues that until relatively recently lay outwith 'legitimate' Celtic Studies, whatever that may mean. Having recently written on this search for legitimacy through novelty, I will not repeat my observations here.[15] Rather, I will defer to Bernard Deacon's more generous treatment when he characterizes the hybrid nature of these newer contributions as being reflective of the postmodernist turn. With an emphasis on fluidity, ambiguity and complexity, volumes such as

Hale and Payton's *New Directions in Celtic Studies* (2000) certainly offer a breath of fresh air and take the Celtic/Cornish connection much further. But inherent in the linking of Cornish Studies to the latest thinking on critical theory, new Celtic spirituality, ethnomusicology and the like is the danger that a necessary meso step in the construction of the new sub-discipline is being neglected. I refer to evidence-based scholarship that is vital if such efforts are to be sustained over the long term. Contestation of older certainties are to be welcomed as an essential element of academic progress, but such contestations have to be built on more than rhetorical and polemical claims. If not, the search for a straight back will collapse into a genetic osteoporosis for the want of a balanced diet now as the sub-discipline is in a critical growth stage. I am conscious that writing this from my current bastion in Oxford/Cardiff might seem to be unforgivingly patronising for insiders. But in our own turn we in Wales look to the next higher order example in the spatial hierarchy of self-confident identities, and the heights of Quebec or Catalonia, far from appearing too daunting, are a welcome challenge to which we also aspire through imitation and struggle. Thus an essential element of the Cornish Studies agenda today would seem to be to further prioritize what the contours of the collective project should be, and then to seek the necessary resources and data to achieve this ambition.

A strong framework for future work has already been sketched out by Hale, Payton and Deacon among others, and is refined further in this present volume. However, we still need the quiet, persistent, polite critic to ask periodically, 'But to what does it all add up?', not so that we can wash our hands and rend our clothes, but rather so that at least once every decade or so, as now, we can measure how far we have come and, more significantly, anticipate how far we have yet to travel if the journey be worthwhile.

'STRANGERS TO OURSELVES'

'We are strangers to ourselves because we have no clear idea of the real, the historic, self, the collective identity formed many generations back, from which each and every individual identity takes its life and meaning. Hence self-exile and communal aimlessness.'[16] It may be objected that Cornish Studies has neither really fulfilled its ambition nor communicated its concerns to the general public in whose name it is seeking to regenerate a 'lost past'. That is, it is in danger of being semi-detached from the involved public and consequently not so potent a force as it might be in shaping civil society. In such circumstances, it is argued that it becomes the special responsibility of the enlightened ethnic intelligentsia to recover a lost past, to metamorphize a decayed present into a future 'golden age'. Such prescriptive ideologies are the *sine qua non* of ethnic regionalist and nationalist movements. Smith has pointed to a basic flaw in the rational of collective mobilization, namely:

> these notions can only represent ideal states, unattainable in an imperfect world; given the nature of social and geopolitical relations, they must always remain unfulfilled. Psychologically compelling if logically incoherent they present the 'drama' of nationalism and its quasi-messianic promises alongside other quite realistic and concrete goals, such as attaining independence, creating the conditions for self-sustaining growth, building up national institutions, demarcating the 'homeland', and creating a world of cultural diversity and pluralism.[17]

We can read into the motivation for pursuing Cornish Studies a desire to redress past injustices, to expose historical discrimination, the slighted 'national' character of the Cornish and the unfulfilled potential of a co-equal Celtic nation. The wounds of past oppression or even benign neglect need to be identified and picked over before being healed so that the extent of the pain and the hurt is delimited. But if remedial action is one of the dominant motivations, how is this translated into action, into policy, into progress so that we no longer inhabit a community of strangers?

The applied policy claims of the New Cornish Studies are a legitimate object of critical analysis. Deacon, Payton, Williams and others have queried to what extent such claims have been realized as fact. Deacon has pointed to the limited impact imposed by both the lack of personnel available and the lack of obvious infra-structural support and civil-society opportunities to engage with real decision-makers. Understandably, this is a very difficult and contentious issue for there are very few self-consciously Cornish social networks that are pressing for more reform of (for example) the education system or demanding language lessons in Cornish. The language issues have occupied much print space within Cornish Studies. Over and above the purely linguistic contributions, the Cornish language debate has resonance for wider issues to do with interpretations of being Cornish. As noted by N. Ford, common threads include the counterpoint of reality and imagination, and authenticizing and mythologizing.[18] Nowhere is the latter more pertinent than in the internal divisions that surround the language debate. Deacon has provided an insight into this through a discussion of the arguments presented by Tim Saunders.[19]

Saunders has rightly condemned this wholesale use of
'authenticity', along with notions of 'purity'. These, he argues,
'are categories from the realm of ethics and aesthetics, and to
import them into a scientific discourse is to impose value-
judgements where dispassionate and cool analysis are
essential'. However, while Saunders, writing from within a
scientific and modernist discourse, is correct in pointing to the
logical contradictions of combining authenticity and science,
he nevertheless misses a broader point here. Authenticity, like
science, is a product of modernity. And the problem of
modernity is a peculiarly modern problem.[20]

The other problem with modernity for contemporary Cornish is
that many of the essential building blocks necessary for language
reproduction and cultural enrichment are simply absent, both as
a resource and as a dynamic element in civil society. Thus, unlike
Ireland, Wales and to a lesser extent Scotland, Cornwall does not
possess a Celtic language-medium teaching profession at both primary
and secondary level; neither does it have a Celtic language-medium
religious/denominational network, public administration or media
industry. The lack of such institutional and professional support bases
severely limits the conditions of possibility for the actual revival of
Cornish and its ultimate use as a medium of social communication
in everyday life. It goes without saying that this also hampers the
development of linguistics and its various branches, notably socio-
linguistics and comparative linguistics. Without such constituents as
students within state schooling, bilingual employees or media
personnel, the special target audience of Cornish language studies is
perforce reliant on the marginal and the disaffected, as indeed is much
else that comprises the wider canon of Cornish Studies. It is to these
that activists claim the applied nature of their policy is aimed.
    But who exactly are the disempowered and voiceless groups which
practitioners of Cornish Studies scholarship are meant to serve? One
can accept the broad answer offered by this current volume in terms of
the new Cornish historiography's task to 'recover that sense of agency,
put it into comparative context, open up our knowledge of the past
and, ultimately, to empower people in Cornwall so that they are in a
better position to make choices about their own future' (p. 39). But the
argument that New Cornish Studies must be a valid contribution to
scholarship because it aims to empower the disenfranchised, is much
weaker than it seems. Over and above ostensibly liberal aims, what
specifically can/will Cornish Studies seek to do to change the direction
of society? More prosaically, having identified a number of key themes

and issues, what mechanisms are available to translate such aims into practical policy and/or a motor for action?

In similar vein, the overcoming of the limitations of seeing Cornish Studies as a sub-set of Celtic Studies rather than also being a form of cultural studies and applied social science is to be welcomed. But yet again to offer a prescriptive agenda which emphasizes 'the politics and economics of exclusion and division, the promotion of 'difference' in political, cultural and economic terms and the search for identity in a consumerist society' could be construed as being over-ambitious and certainly well beyond the capacity of Cornish Studies as presently constituted. Deacon would object and argue that such reasoning is to misrepresent the project. He has a point, which is well made in the following quotation:

> Those critics who might note a gap between the rhetorically defined space of New Cornish Studies and the actual work of Cornish Studies and then proceed to condemn the former as some form of chimera are, therefore, fundamentally mistaken. New Cornish Studies should be judged not in terms of its achievements so far but in terms of its aspiration or vision for Cornish Studies to aim at. On the grounds of coherence and relevance the New Cornish Studies provides that vision. Its first decade has set down some foundations. It is now up to Cornish Studies scholars in the next decade to complete these foundations and go on to construct the building.[21]

This plea for patience and tolerance is understandable and reminiscent of many projects in the early phase of maturation, whether we are discussing the initial post-independence phase of African nations in the 1970s or the development of former polytechnics as new universities. But it can also be disingenuous if such arguments have the effect of deflecting critical attention away from the details of what needs to be done both in terms of general trajectory and specific prioritizing within the subject.

Another troubling issue is the extent to which Cornish Studies is a self-consciously unified and unifying sub-discipline. A field of study which can range as far and wide as Hyatt's contribution on 'The Acarine Fauna of the Isles of Scilly,' in the first edition of *Cornish Studies*[22] through to Hayden's article on 'Cornwall: A Very Difficult Woman?' in *Cornish Studies: Nine* tends to attract generalists rather than specialists.[23] Or maybe it attracts specialists with a catholic taste for the intriguing and the erudite? I do not have problems with this eclectic range, for surely this is the stock in trade of so many other area-based series and journals, such as the *British Journal of Canadian Studies*.

Pluralism, properly conceived, should encourage an openness and a wonderment so that cultures are not shut up within themselves and afraid of reaching out to embrace the significant other. At present, because of its fragile nature, Cornish Studies is avowedly self-conscious; at times it is culpable of eking out the most tenuous connections with the 'larger world', itself a pejorative phrase which puts Cornwall in a subservient, dependency relationship with other places. It has not always been so, for in the nineteenth century nothing could be further from the truth, as studies on emigration and overseas trade and settlement by Payton[24] and others make abundantly clear. And it need not be so in the future if many of the ambitious plans for the sub-discipline come to fruition.[25]

What drives Cornish Studies forward is an ideological commitment to honour Cornwall's place in the history of these isles and to serve its citizens today. At root this is an issue of integrity for the lead scholars involved who have chosen to develop the field in a systematic manner. Therefore, it is not in the least surprising that the range of interests and topics encompassed within the sub-discipline should be as varied as any other place-centred endeavour. That the ideological commitment is neither sufficiently defined nor mature does not invalidate its role as a motor for action. But we should not be surprised at the dissonance created by the ambition of having a unified ideology coupled with internal contradictions. Writing in a quite different context but with the same force attached, Isaiah Berlin argued that any unified ideology that promises to reconcile all contradictions ends up imposing that vision on its citizens as an oppressive form of what he called 'positive' liberty. Governments should recognize that all values conflict, and all conflicts require negotiation. The best hope is that there might be liberty without undue imposition, a form of 'negative' liberty. Berlin's operative maxim was taken from Immanuel Kant: 'Out of timber so crooked as that from which man is made, nothing entirely straight can be built.'[26]

CONCLUSION

I anticipate a philosophical objection to these conclusions, concerned as they are with rather abstract notions of nation and identity rather than evidence-based public policy. It is now commonplace to hear Cornish Studies specialists arguing, as Ella Westland does, that '[r]epresentations of Cornwall, in the end, often tell us more about the needs of the nation than about the people living west of the Tamar'.[27] How could it not be otherwise? Place-centred disciplines in the early stages of maturation are by definition about boundary-formation and boundary-maintenance. They struggle with comparative analyses and universal notions for at root they must deal with inclusion and exclusion, at both a human and a philosophical level: i.e. what counts as Cornish is the acid test of the relevance of the issue for this field of study, at least for the present. There may seem to be a paradox in these comments, for I have simultaneously argued that we need both a more persuasive justification for the existence of Cornish Studies and far more data and evidence on contemporary Cornish social and economic patterns so as to relate the concerns of scholarship to public policy, economic development, regional planning and the like. We must consider, therefore, what Cornish Studies scholars can and should now do to deepen their association with civil society and government in the coming decade. The details, of course, I leave to the eminent scholars working within and around Cornwall, but the general need to continue the argument, to engage, to be active and committed, to cajole and convince, is one which we all share as involved citizens. It is part of the refashioning of a plural Britain, and for that reason I wish Cornish Studies well in the next and successive decades.

ACKNOWLEDGEMENT

This essay was written while I was a Visiting Fellow at Jesus College and Mansfield College, Oxford University, 2002.

NOTES AND REFERENCES

1. For representative examples of each of these see W.A. Morris, 'An Investigation into Migration Patterns for the Parish of Zennor in Cornwall During the Second Half of the Nineteenth Century', in Philip Payton (ed.), *Cornish Studies: Seven*, Exeter, 1999, pp. 32–48; P. Thornton, 'Cornwall and Changes in the Tourist Gaze', in Philip Payton (ed.), *Cornish Studies: One*, Exeter, 1993a, pp. 80–96; J. Mills, 'Reconstructive Phonology and Contrastive Lexicology: Problems with the *Gerlyver Kernewek Kemmyn*' in Payton (ed.), 1999, pp. 193–218; G. Price, 'Negative Particles in Cornish', in Philip Payton (ed.), *Cornish Studies: Four*, Exeter, 1996, pp. 147–51; J. Hurst, 'Literature in Cornwall', in P. Payton (ed.), *Cornwall Since the War*, Redruth, 1993b, pp. 291–308. For one volume which surveys many of these themes see E. Westland (ed.), *Cornwall: The Cultural Construction of Place*, Penzance, 1997.
2. See B. Deacon, 'The New Cornish Studies: New Discipline or Rhetorically Defined Space?' in this volume.
3. See for example his elaboration of the postmodernist turn in Cornish Studies in his editorial Introduction to Payton (ed.), 1996, pp. 1–5.
4. Introduction, Payton (ed.), 1996, p. 5 and B. Deacon, 'The Reformation of

Territorial Identity: Cornwall in the Late Eighteenth and Nineteenth Centuries', unpublished Ph.D. thesis, Open University, 2001.

5. See the excellent accounts by B. Deacon, 'And Shall Trelawny Die? The Cornish Identity', in Payton (ed.), 1993b, pp. 200–23; and P. Payton, 'Territory and Identity', in Payton (ed.), 1993b, pp. 223–52.

6. Representative literature would be J. Lawrence, 'The Politics of Place and the Politics of Nation', *Twentieth Century British History* 11.1, 2000, pp. 83–94; and K. Robbins, 'Britain and Europe: Devolution and Foreign Policy', *International Affairs* 74.1, 1998, pp. 105–18.

7. See Andrés Rodriguez-Pose, *The EU: Economy, Society and Polity*, Oxford, 2002; and P. Payton, *A Vision of Cornwall*, Fowey, 2002.

8. R.G. Harvey, M.T. Smith, S. Sherren, L. Bailey and S.J. Hyndman, 'How Celtic are the Cornish? A Study of Biological Affinities', *Journal of the Anthropological Institute* 21.2, June 1986, pp. 178–99.

9. R. Cole, 'The Cornish Identity and Genetics—An Alternative View', in Philip Payton (ed.), *Cornish Studies: Five*, Exeter, 1997, pp. 21–9.

10. Harvey *et al.*, 1986, p. 10.

11. See Deacon in this volume.

12. See A.D. Smith, 'National Identity and Myths of Ethnic Descent', chapter 2 of his *Myths and Memories of the Nation*, Oxford, 1999, pp. 56–95.

13. This phrase is discussed in relation to the ideas of I. Berlin as described by E. Rothstein, 'Fresh Debates on the Legacy of Isaiah Berlin', *New York Times*, 14 November, 1998, p. 2.

14. Despite the politically correct tendencies of ethnic/national assertion, is it really fair to compare and contrast Cornish Studies with Irish Studies or Breton Studies as opposed to 'Pembrokeshire Studies' or 'Leinster Studies'?

15. See C.H. Williams, 'Conclusion: New Directions in Celtic Studies: An Essay in Social Criticism', in A. Hale and P. Payton (eds), *New Directions in Celtic Studies*, Exeter, 2000, pp. 197–229.

16. Smith, 1999, p. 67.

17. Smith, 1999, p. 67–8.

18. N.J. Ford, 'Celticism, Identity and Imagination', *Ecumene* 6.4, 1999, pp. 471–3.

19. T. Saunders, 'Authenticity, Purity and Ideology', *Kernow* 30, 1995.

20. B. Deacon, 'Language Revival and Language Debate: Modernity and Postmodernity', in Payton (ed.), 1996, pp. 88–106.

21. Deacon in this volume.

22. K.H. Hyatt, 'The Acarine Fauna of the Isles of Scilly', in Payton (ed.), 1993a, pp. 120–61.

23. C. Hayden, 'Cornwall: A Very Difficult Woman? A Feminist Approach to Issues aof Cornish Identity', in Philip Payton (ed.), *Cornish Studies: Nine*, Exeter, 2001, pp. 204–12.

24. P. Payton, ' "Reforming Thirties" and "Hungry Forties": The Genesis of Cornwall's Emigration Trade', in Payton (ed.), 1996, pp. 107–27; see also P. Payton, 'Cornish Emigration in Response to Changes in the International Copper Market in the 1860s', in Philip Payton (ed.), *Cornish*

Studies: Three, Exeter, 1995, pp. 60–82; and P. Payton, *The Cornish Overseas*, Fowey, 1999.

25. For a personal contribution to this debate see my agenda for future comparative work in C.H. Williams in Hale and Payton (eds), 2000, pp. 197–229.
26. This is taken from Rothstein, 1998, p. 2.
27. Westland (ed.), 1997, p. 4.

CORNISH ARCHAEOLOGY AT THE MILLENNIUM

Charles Thomas

INTRODUCTION

At this start of our third millennium, Christian era, archaeology whether practised in Cornwall or anywhere else comprises two things. The first is the invention, the mastery and the exercise of a wide range of *techniques* designed to recover information about the otherwise unrecorded past—from Victorian times right back to the emergence of the first hominids. The second is the composition of *narratives* short and long, in print or other media (and to some extent museum displays), that present the results of all those techniques—ideally doing so dispassionately and in a form that ordinary people can understand.

In its first respect archaeology overlaps with the physical and natural sciences, and this is why, except perhaps from field-surveys, it increasingly excludes the amateur enthusiast whose role now tends to be confined to the bucket-and-shovel aspect. In its second aspect, once beyond a preliminary stage of purely factual reports, archaeology overlaps with intensive historical research, comparative linguistics and other specialized fields. It becomes difficult and time-consuming to undertake, which is why 'synthetic' writings, books with titles like *The Earliest Wheeled Transport* and *Christianity in Roman Britain to AD 500*, can seldom be produced by busy professionals at the work-face. These definitions—entirely relevant to archaeology in Cornwall—are not often voiced. Today they are complicated by further factors, one being that 'the past', the supposed reality of a local or national past, has very properly become public property. One cannot lightly destroy our ancient monuments, demolish historic structures and cut swathes through virgin landscapes (if we still have any). We expect, and we get, huge attendances at exhibitions featuring Ancient Egypt (or dinosaurs, which belong to palaeontology, another discipline altogether). There is a price to pay for this added publicity, welcome as it has been because a growth in public interest can produce more public funding. For millions of us, 'archaeology' means what happens in a *Time Team* television programme. It is almost impossible to point out that a *Time Team* foray is an artificially compressed sample investigation with associated surveys, that the real work involves months of processing the finds and results as a part of the untelevised clear-up, and that to assume any programme is truly representative is like picturing all medical science as a series of hasty appendectomies. Other complications are the rise of theoretical archaeology, borrowing from philosophy and the social sciences, which can deny the existence of any truly objective account of the past because it will be distorted by the author's own ineradicable prejudices; and indeed what can be called the political misuse of archaeological findings, real or imagined.

A DECADE OF CORNISH ARCHAEOLOGY

Given this plonking, but necessary, preamble, what can be said about archaeology in Cornwall during the last decade? The short answer is: quite a lot. But it has to be appreciated in something more like the last half-century, or the span since the successive foundations of the Cornwall Archaeological Society and its annual journal *Cornish Archaeology* (1962); the Institute of Cornish Studies and the first series, 1 to 16, of its annual volume *Cornish Studies* (1971/72); the Cornwall Committee for Rescue Archaeology (1975), later subsumed into the County Council as Cornwall Archaeological Unit (CAU), most recently the Historic Environment Unit (HEU); and from the late 1970s the expansion and general re-alignment of the Royal Institution of Cornwall, matrix of the Royal Cornwall Museum and the Courtney Library.

On paper, Cornwall is well provided for archaeologically, and one can add historically by counting in the splendid Cornwall Record Office. All these organizations were centred, or have become centred, in one place—Truro, as the city and administrative centre. Over many years a discreet, subdued, but unbending policy exercised by those in command has meant that the fragmentation once bedevilling larger counties like Somerset has been avoided. Cornwall does not have a rash of small, very localized, archaeological 'field clubs' beavering away in happy isolation. It does not have its enormous stock of archaeological matériel—records as well as physical finds—dispersed among dozens of usually vulnerable, often privately-run, town or village museums. The Royal Cornwall Museum at Truro,

Penlee House at Penzance and necessarily the Isles of Scilly Museum on St Mary's are the safe recognized repositories. From 1971, if not from 1962 when editing *Cornish Archaeology*, my overt archaeological aim in directing both the Institute of Cornish Studies and the Cornwall Committee for Rescue Archaeology was to bring Cornish (and Scillonian) archaeology into the broader professional world of the late twentieth century. Relinquishing, I hope for ever, a muddle of Phoenicians, sun-worship, druids, ley-lines, 'King Arthur' and the rest of the picturesque legacy, I and others set out to obtain central or external funding on a large scale; to train suitable graduates as professional archaeologists (most of them are now senior staff with CAU/HEU); to create Sites and Monuments Records for both Cornwall and Scilly; to indicate by example new standards of published results and at the same time to introduce new levels for ancillary features like place-name recording and linguistic (dialect) investigations. As a distinctive territory, a peninsula some 80 miles long with an appended archipelago, a region exceptionally rich in remains of its past, a population nearing the half-million mark, and not much money, Cornwall should be—again, on paper—very well off, archaeologically speaking.

In this year of AD 2002, is everything in the garden rosy? It should be. Nationally, from about the 1950s, with the inevitable rise of specialization many interests that used to be subsumed in the remit of, say, the Council for British Archaeology broke away, and were encouraged to break away, forming their own national bodies with journals and conferences. I forget the actual order of happenings but these included medieval and post-medieval archaeology, nautical archaeology, industrial archaeology, landscape studies and church archaeology, with some further minor movements like Roman pottery studies. In Cornwall the prime need was of course attention to the industrial legacy: mostly metalliferous mining with its associated machinery and constructions, but also quarrying, tin-streaming and the china clay industry. Its needs were met by the formation of the Trevithick Society, and later the Trevithick Trust, and the Wheal Martyn Museum. (Note that, alarmingly, we still lack specific museums of fisheries, quarrying, mining as a historically developed industry, and—if this is possible—agriculture). On the conventional front, the CAU or HEU, if now perforce more of an archaeological management unit, has not only survived the demise of many comparable, 1970s-originating units elsewhere in Britain, but is today among the largest operators, with its own impressive range of publications.

What has taken place, certainly since 1992 and in fact since more like 1972, is a complete national change in the way that archaeology is conducted. True, at least a dozen old universities and some of the new ones offer degrees in variegated archaeology, though perhaps without stressing that full-time careers in archaeology are now hard to find. These courses, along with increasing popular interest generated by television—and vast sales of books on pseudo-archaeology, seem to fill a gap left by the sad and steady demise of archaeological courses in adult education in much of Britain, at one time very much the brand leaders in that field. But amateur (i.e. unpaid, non-professional, not necessarily unqualified) participation in British archaeology has been steadily frozen out. Up to the 1970s the main focus of hundreds of archaeological societies, winter lectures apart, was some form of annual excavation. Opportunities to get out and dig, often alongside 'real' archaeologists, teemed for a decade or so because of the huge campaigns engendered by a phase of motorway constructions, inner-city clearances and gas pipelines. That has gone. A sharp distinction arose between *research* and *rescue*. A research excavation, digging to answer questions about the past, digging where an excavation may seem desirable but is in no way essential, is now very expensive indeed. It has long passed out of the scope of almost all archaeological societies, even if the digging force is prepared to labour unpaid. The few purely research excavations are more or less exclusively by universities or professional bodies that can obtain substantial academic grants. Conversely, the predominant rescue excavations—they range from the very large to the very small, a two-day, two-trench operation —arise all the time as more and more components of the detectable past are protected by law, but are then threatened with damage or obliteration by normal development, and must be investigated and recorded. Because they involve the staff of archaeological units or professional contracting teams, rescue works are also very expensive. Funding, whether from central and local government or from the developers themselves, exists. Largely because most rescue excavations arise at short notice, what does *not* always exist is everything else: the time, the leisure and devoted expertise to convert all the results into a synthetic narrative, a book for the informed general public, or an endless series of spaces (museum store-rooms) in which to house everything so expensively disinterred.

Looking back over the last ten years, a period in which there has been very little change from the position outlined above, one might distinguish between the practice and the results of archaeology in Cornwall and Scilly. The practice is actually in better shape than in many other parts of Highland or Atlantic Britain. The Cornwall Archaeological Society exists, is stable, has lectures and outings, runs a Young Archaeologist element, is more than solvent, has no competitors west of the Tamar and continues to publish *Cornwall Archaeology*—even if the journal's main function, as with almost all such archaeological society annuals, is to house long technical reports from the backlog of (mainly rescue) digs by CAU/HEU or other bodies, their publication being funded from English Heritage. The large archaeological unit (which nearly everyone still thinks of, and calls, 'CAU') must dispassionately be regarded as a howling success. It has grown almost exponentially from the Cornwall Committee for Rescue Archaeology's 1975 team of two and budget of £8,500 to a very substantial component of the County Council's structure, its funding is drawn as much from external national sources and statutory authorities as from the council tax payer, its function has become to monitor and manage almost every physical activity in Cornwall likely to affect the known built or potential heritage, and it publishes extensively and promptly. A full catalogue is beyond the scope of this paper but one could single out the great two-part *Survey* of Bodmin Moor (in booksellers' language, a 'bow-wave, ground-breaking' accomplishment), specific reports on sites like St Michael's Mount or most of Cornwall's estuaries, and a string of *ad hoc* reports arising from another task, overseeing any work affecting medieval churches and churchyards. A major current responsibility, combining industrial archaeology with fieldwork and documented history, is preparation of all the papers required to submit a bid for designation as a World Heritage Site covering the principal mining areas, mining settlements and mineral tramways over much of Cornwall.

If we turn to results, it is now far from clear what the public wants. Could anyone, using the data garnered over the last half-century, write a new *Archaeology of Cornwall and Scilly*? I very much doubt it, unless it was 'dumbed down' almost to what might be termed 'Noddy-language'. A full appreciation would occupy two volumes, cost nearly £100, and be unintelligible to many in the street. By the time it was finished and published, major revisions might well be required. Is the alternative to think of books couched at a median level, i.e. accurate, factual, professionally written by the few archaeologists who can write directly for an informed public without any obsession about critical colleagues? And might one prefer, as a policy, to target special periods (Neolithic Cornwall; Cornwall's Medieval Castles), sub-regions (The Archaeology of the Lizard Peninsula), and even individual sites or monuments? Would people dwelling east of Helston pay on any scale for a work confined to the Lizard?

Does this apparent bottleneck, between the flourishing practice of archaeology in Cornwall and the disseminating of what is being found and what it implies about our past, matter? Perhaps not yet, on any great scale; but it may come to do so, and one can already see manifestations that may require correction. The political misuse of archaeology reached new depths in pre-war Nazi Germany, and on lesser scales has not been unknown after 1950. In Cornwall (which does not stand alone in this respect) there is frequent confusion between a concept labelled 'the Celts, Celtic', originally and essentially a linguistic term, and the gradual assumption since post-Roman times of a regional, supposedly ethnic if not ethno-political, identity labelled 'Cornwall, the Cornish'. Harmless enough, for instance, was the recent competition for a tall cross to be erected near the Tamar, implying 'Welcome to Cornwall' or even 'You Are Now Entering A Separate Cornwall'. Describing the shortlisted designs, including the winning one, as 'Celtic' is, however, far more problematic, as it is when applied to many of the comparatively late tall stone crosses common in East Cornwall. Much less harmless are the assumptions constantly voiced in letters to the *Western Morning News* and other Cornish papers that a particular, separate identity of Cornwall—let alone the mélange of its population past and present—can be vouchsafed from what is known about Britain in the Early Iron Age, or earlier. Often tempted to correct some of the wilder claims, pro-Cornish or anti-Cornish, but always refraining from doing so, I point out that no known archaeology in Britain can answer questions of this kind. Yet whose fault is it that they are asked in the first place?

TINTAGEL

If one had to select a single case study from the last decade, that of Tintagel would best present the state of Cornish archaeological endeavours. The principal feature of Tintagel, really a site-complex, is the (almost) Island and the remains on the adjoining headland, linked and secondary being the nearby Norman parish church of St Materiana in its progressively extended churchyard. One could point to three levels of perception. There is no prehistoric occupation, but something existed here in late Roman times, possibly a tax-gathering station. From the fifth to eighth centuries AD the Island, with mainland defences, was used periodically as a coastal citadel, distinguished by importation of large quantities of pottery vessels and containers from the east Mediterranean and North Africa, on a scale that suggests both trade in streamed tin and occupation by the equivalent of regional kings. A chapel appeared on the Island around AD 1000. Apparently prompted by Geoffrey of Monmouth's invention of Tintagel as a seat of 'Gorlois', an imaginary Cornish ruler, and the conception by trickery of 'Arthur', a bizarre stone-walled castle was built on the Island and headland by Richard, Earl of Cornwall, from about 1230. Strategically

pointless, the castle fell in to disuse and ruins, the site being sometimes
employed as a prison. It remained, and it still is, the property of the
Duchy of Cornwall and by the late 1920s had been placed in the
care of HM Office of Works, today after numerous changes of title
represented by English Heritage. Extensive excavations of the Island,
1933 to 1938, led to and promoted an interpretation of the place as a
Celtic monastery. Not until the 1970s was this idea challenged and
abandoned as being manifestly wrong.

That compressed account is what archaeology and history tell
us. Modern Tintagel, a depressed settlement since the end of slate
quarrying, has to live on tourism; and tourism has to centre on the link,
started by Geoffrey of Monmouth and then re-kindled by Tennyson,
Swinburne, Hardy and others, with a non-historical King Arthur and
the entire Arthurian panoply. This second perception constitutes
people's living. A *third* perception, partly kindled by dissemination of
recent results from archaeology, forms part of the assertion of Cornish
identity. It is at least possible that pre-Geoffrey, before the 1120s, the
relevant legends here were of King Mark, Tristan and Iseult; that the

TINTAGELL CASTLE, CORNWALL.

1. Tintagel depicted in J. Britton and E. W. Brayley's, 1831 volume Cornwall
Illustrated in a Series of Views. *They commented: 'The accompanying print
conveys some idea of the situation in which a fortress was erected at a remote
date, and which became the place of residence and retreat of some of the Earls
of Cornwall. It is traditionally said to have belonged to Prince* (sic) *Arthur.*

post-Roman occupants were the regional kings of *Dumnonia*, a region that by 700 included and distinguished *Cornubia*, Cornwall; and that in these and other respects Tintagel is a primary emotional focus of what became medieval Cornwall. The rash of unsightly notices and signs with 'English Heritage' causes genuine offence and distress and the recent expunging of the first word probably aroused more applause than condemnation.

In the late 1980s the Institute of Cornish Studies, obtaining substantial grants, re-examined and catalogued thousands of finds from Tintagel, conducted a visitor survey for the Duchy of Cornwall, and helped to arrange further small-scale excavations by CAU and an English Heritage unit; the Island was at last properly surveyed by the Royal Commission on the Historical Monuments of England. *Cornish Studies* 16 (1988), a special issue of 'Tintagel Papers', promptly reported the developments. In 1990 and 1991, CAU and the Institute jointly conducted excavations at Tintagel churchyard, handsomely funded by Mobil North Sea Limited; an extensive programme for schools was run alongside this, and the two project reports were circulated internationally (thousands of each as far afield as Greenland and Japan!). This campaign confirmed that the churchyard has been the Citadel's associated Christian cemetery since about AD 500, and also unearthed north of the parish church the foundations of its unknown tenth- to eleventh-century predecessor. From the mid-1990s, work on the Island recommenced, the aim being to identify the nature of the numerous post-Roman buildings, and also to confirm the post-Roman date of the mainland-side 'Great Ditch'; all this was entrusted to the University of Glasgow, supported by CAU throughout. The position in AD 2002, as we pause to draw breath, is that entirely new proposals for the investigation and presentation of Tintagel island —which is, in the long term, geologically threatened—are being digested and considered by all the appropriate authorities.

Questions of course arise. What part did, or could, the amateur archaeological following in Cornwall play in this? The answer is none, because we are faced with exacting work in a highly specialist area; the Institute was able to participate because it then had a considerable archaeological capacity and was at the same time involved with creating a Sites and Monuments Record of Scilly and with several years of productive fieldwork arising from the electrification of the Islands. How many of the results have percolated through to the general public? This is hard to assess, and has barely affected the second, legendary and commercial, presentation of Tintagel as a tourist attraction; but the new findings and interpretations were all made available in my 1993 commissioned book *Tintagel: Arthur and Archaeology*

(Batsford/English Heritage), a revised version of which will have to appear in a year or so. In the academic world, of course, a long string of appropriate reports has consolidated Tintagel's status as a site of international importance. Do the results support, confuse or in any way deny Cornish claims to separate identity retrojected into pre-Norman times? To the historian this has to be a non-question because we cannot know, and can only infer within limits, the political, ethnic and linguistic natures of the site's various occupants. A fairly safe inference is that before the eighth century the Island was one of several potential 'royal' seats, that its external contacts were extraordinary, its wealth-potential obvious, its Christian affiliations very early, and that Geoffrey of Monmouth replaced one set of, alas irrecoverable, legends with his own Arthurian obsession. Lastly, is this an illustration of the future, or of one future, of Cornish archaeology? As far as anyone can guess, inevitably so. Archaeology has been prodded into becoming Big Business, intertwined with commerce and tourism. Tintagel is simply our Tower of London, our Stonehenge. That does not preclude the ongoing and intensively professional work of CAU, and occasional university participation. It is very different from the 1950s.

BIBLIOGRAPHIC NOTE FOR SOCIAL HISTORIANS

The much-needed account of archaeology in Cornwall and Scilly, from Dr William Borlaise in the 1750s up to at least 1950, has yet to be written. The decades from *c.*1930 to 1960 are analysed in 'The Fiftieth Anniversary of the West Cornwall Field Club', *Cornish Archaeology* 24, 1985, pp. 5–14; a general conspexus of progress and results, by periods, constitutes the Silver Jubilee volume of *Cornish Archaeology* 25, 1986. The last two papers in this deal with 'The Historical Heritage: Present and Future Attitudes' and 'The Next Quarter-Century'. Detailed *Annual Reports*, from 1st, 1975–6, to 10th, 1984–85, of the Cornwall Committee for Rescue Archaeology (CCRA), were deposited in all the main Cornish libraries; these ceased after 1985 when the CCRA committee and workforce became the Cornwall Archaeological Unit. All the minutes and progress reports of CAU will have been deposited with Cornwall Record Office. The long and, for Cornwall, highly remunerative involvement of the Institute of Cornish Studies with archaeology, in partnership with CCRA and CAU, and *per se*, is manifest in numerous papers in *Cornish Studies*, first series, 1 to 16, and in various numbered *Special Reports*. The main project in Scilly is described in Jeanette Ratcliffe, *The Archaeology of Scilly: An Assessment of the Resource and Recommendations for its Future* (CAU, Truro, 1988), and J. Ratcliffe *et al.*, *Lighting up the Past in Scilly* (ICS and CAU, Truro, 1991). Since 1993, CAU has issued a handsome annual *Archaeology Alive*, with (for example) no. 8 covering 1999–2000, which summarizes virtually all archaeological work in a preceding year. Progressive changes in British archaeology since the 1950s—the restricted field for the amateur societies, the research/rescue distinction, the alarming backlogs in publication and storage of finds, and the burdens of legislation—are discussed in national books, journals and conference proceedings. Cornwall, however, not having experienced motorway construction and major historic inner-city redevelopments, is seldom mentioned.

LOOKING FORWARD TO LOOKING BACK: THE STUDY OF MEDIEVAL HISTORY IN CORNWALL

Allen Buckley

INTRODUCTION

Medieval Cornwall is sufficiently remote from us for it to have acquired a rose-coloured and romantic aspect. Its remoteness also affords the people and society of that time the appearance of being fundamentally different from us and from our society. Yet, most of the important institutions of modern British society can trace their origins back to that time. Many of our venerable higher educational establishments, our ecclesiastical structures, our religious and political ideologies, our local and national governance, our ideas on national identity, culture and language, have their roots in the events of the thirteenth to sixteenth centuries.

With this is in mind it seems appropriate to assess and evaluate what work is currently taking place in the field of medieval Cornish history. This article will begin by reflecting on what we mean by the 'medieval'. It then sets out some of the content, methods and data typical of recent work in Cornish medieval history. The bulk of the contribution sets out to identify what light studies of medieval history can shed on a number of questions historians and others might ask about the Cornish past. Finally, it asks what can be done to encourage closer cooperation between scholars, to provide help with specific tasks, and to open up the vast and relatively untouched collections of documents in the various archives in Cornwall and up-country?

THE MEDIEVAL CONTEXT

For historians, the very word 'medieval' is problematic and eludes precise definition. It is misleading for a variety of reasons to describe the centuries between the departure of the Romans (*c.*430 AD) and the Battle of Bosworth (1485) as the Middle Ages or the medieval period. Nowadays, the historical periods associated with such terms as feudalism, the Renaissance and the Reformation are viewed as less precise than a few generations ago, and it would be a rash historian indeed who sought to fix any of these time-honoured and sometimes misleading words with any kind of precision. The great changes which took place in Europe during the fifteenth century and continued until after the deadly religious wars of the first half of the seventeenth century were not merely the death throes of an obsolete system of thought, faith and government, they were a continuation of processes which had been ongoing for centuries before that time. The Renaissance or rebirth of the ideas, philosophy and science of the Greeks and other ancient civilizations did not suddenly happen, and the release of the manuscripts from ancient libraries was not an 'event' so much as a protracted process, the results of which were still being appreciated and acted upon by such thinkers as Isaac Newton at the end of the seventeenth century. The same can be said of over-tight definitions of medieval feudalism and the Reformation, not to mention the wide-ranging influence of the Humanists of the early sixteenth century.

The remoteness of the medieval and Tudor periods has made the study of them daunting. The nature of the original manuscript material, written as it is in Late Latin, Old French and Middle to Early Modern English, has precluded all but the very determined from using it. Consequently, recourse is frequently (or mostly) to published work when studying the medieval and early modern periods. Another difficulty has been the location of the manuscript material, spread as it is in archives all over the country. The Duchy records are largely in London, as are almost all of the central government records, such as the Exchequer Accounts, and the Close and Patent Rolls. The further we go back the thinner the spread of manuscript material and the less continuous it is. Specific information on particular subjects also gets patchier as we move back in history. This has inevitably led to in-depth, detailed studies of spectacularly small aspects of medieval history. These may be academically intriguing and useful, but they are often of limited interest to those who want to know how medieval society in Cornwall actually worked. However, in Cornwall during the second half of the twentieth century we were fortunate to have had such scholars as Leslie Douch, Peter Hull, Oliver Padel, W.M.M. Picken,

P.A.S. Pool and Charles Thomas. All of them have successfully examined aspects of Cornwall's medieval history and produced results that have proved useful to academics and interested amateurs alike.[1]

More recently, the work of these scholars has been extended in other directions. The diverse areas of Cornish medieval history research in the 1990s included research by Joanna Mattingly on late medieval ecclesiastical structure and by Paul Cockerham on memorial inscriptions and monuments. Brian Murdoch has expanded our knowledge of Cornish literature, while Nicholas Orme has deepened our awareness of the Cornish medieval church. David Harvey has reflected on issues of identity, authority and territorialization in the medieval period, with particular reference to West Cornwall. James Whetter has written on thirteenth- and fifteenth-century Cornish socio-economic history and on such characters as Sir Henry Bodrugan. Maryanne Kowaleski has assessed the economic importance of the late medieval expansion in Cornish fisheries and my own studies have attempted to reconstruct the world of late medieval tinners and tinworks. Christine North has examined the will and inventory of Edward Arundell, based on the Arundell Papers, and Ronald Waldron examined the work and influence of John Trevisa.[2] This by no means covers all the ongoing work, but it does serve to remind us of the variety of effort within the parameters of what we call the medieval period.

There is not merely heterogeneity in subject matter, for there are also wide differences in approach and aims. For example, Picken's study of pre-Conquest church deeds for Cornwall involves a close study of single aspects of previously studied documents.[3] General conclusions are not always drawn, for his intention was to correct previous inaccuracies and to ensure that the individual facts, no matter how obscure or individually insignificant, were accurate. He helped to lay an essential foundation for all historians seeking to build general theories on proven facts. At the other end of the scale, scholars like Harvey make use of concepts and theories that may be unfamiliar to the average local or medieval historian, using examples from Cornwall to test wider generalizations.[4]

A growing methodological diversity has perhaps been encouraged by the opening up of new archival sources. The increasing volume of recently acquired relevant records in the Cornwall Record Office (CRO) supplements a limited and variable series of collections there and in such archives as the Courtney Library at the County Museum. The purchase of the Arundell Collection by the CRO in the early 1990s, and its subsequent cataloguing by Oliver Padel and Lucy McCann, furnished a major source of information on the workings and relationships of medieval Cornwall. The continuous series of records on landholdings for specific manors has given opportunity for close analysis on such subjects as the nature and variety of tenant–landlord relationships, the developing pattern of surname use and other aspects of the intricate workings of the post-feudal manorial system in Cornwall. The detailed analysis of a large part of these records by Padel and Fox has opened up a hitherto barely touched aspect of Cornish history. Probably not since the time of Charles Henderson has such a monumental task been undertaken in the study of medieval Cornwall.[5]

RECONSTRUCTING MEDIEVAL CORNWALL

But how far does this growing corpus of work on the medieval history of Cornwall take us in answering the principal questions most historians ask? First, what did Cornish people do? What was their everyday life in the medieval period? Second, how did they earn their living? What were the economic and social structures of medieval Cornwall? Third, what did they believe? What attitudes did they hold and what identities did they construct for themselves? With all these questions we also need to ask how far the situation in Cornwall varied from other places and place Cornwall into its comparative perspective.

The context for studying everyday life in Cornwall has recently become much clearer. Undoubtedly, the most significant modern contribution to the study of Cornwall during its medieval period has been the cataloguing and study of the Arundell Collection of manorial records. Lucy McCann and Oliver Padel's enormous task was followed by Harold Fox and Oliver Padel's book on *The Cornish Lands of the Arundells of Lanherne, Fourteenth to Sixteenth Centuries*. The enormous body of extracts will prove a most valuable addition to the material available to those studying the period. The explanations given in the introduction are not merely invaluable to the layman, but also furnish the somewhat better-informed historian with a clearer understanding of how the manorial system worked in Cornwall. Even among some historians there persists the belief that a manor was essentially a manor house. However, one of the first points made in defining a manor is to show that it was a landed estate without necessarily having a 'manor house'. Connerton is given as an example of one of the largest manorial estates in Cornwall, but one that probably did not have a central residence for its holder or owner. Tenements are defined as part of a manorial estate, and the relationships and allegiances owed by the tenants are dealt with. Types of tenants, free or conventionary, are discussed with Cornish examples from the Arundell records, and expressions like 'suit of court', 'socage' and 'knight's service' are explained, as are the implications of 'homage' and 'relief'. The importance to conventionary tenements of such things as 'entry fines' and the paying of 'common suit' are clarified. Fox and Padel explain the host of special expressions for particular and peculiar arrangements in the manorial system, and examples are cited from the records.[6]

One of the benefits of the Fox and Padel study is the help it gives in understanding how such things as the manorial system developed long after the medieval period ended. Social, economic and constitutional changes all had a bearing on the many changes and modifications within the system, but vestiges of the medieval landlord–tenant relationship are still seen down to our own time. Moreover, in the periods of great industrial turmoil of the seventeenth to nineteenth centuries the manorial system, established by the eleventh century and modified continuously ever since, was crucial to social developments and relationships in Cornwall. This discussion of the manorial system, which was at the very centre of all social, economic and hierarchical life in Cornwall over many centuries, is among the most interesting, informative and satisfying available. It really is a *tour de force*.[7]

An example of the valuable contribution the Arundell Collection has made to our understanding of Cornwall is the opportunity taken to extend Padel's study of the development of Cornish surnames.[8] The many examples of patronymic (familial) and toponymic (place-name) surnames given are used to illustrate the extent of the surname types used in late medieval to early modern West Cornwall. The discussion on the whys and wherefores of 'three-part' names (i.e. 'John Thomme Harry' and 'John Petit Predannek') is certainly thought-provoking if inconclusive. Some of these included two-part surnames, as in John Thomas Davy, Randulph Hicke (Richard) Edward and Richard Thomas Rawlyn (Ralph). These examples indicate that John son of Thomas son of David is intended, and likewise with the others. We are, however, cautioned against believing that this is an unbreakable rule: further work needs to be done! At other times the final element is a place-name. It has long been acknowledged that John Thomas Tresidder may have meant John, son of Thomas Tresidder, and that the third element probably referred to either the present or former residence of the person mentioned or his father. This section of the introduction opens up the discussion to allow for various explanations. Certainly, the fluidity of surnames at the time is amply demonstrated.

In dealing with types of surname (place-names, patronymic, descriptive [nicknames] and occupational), Fox and Padel give an interesting breakdown. Of 795 surnames in total, 362 are place names, 149 are patronymic, 89 are descriptive and 60 refer to occupations. Of the total 135 cannot be easily classified. The authors hasten to comment that these figures are highly misleading taken in isolation, and there clearly now needs to be more comparative work.[9] But their analysis certainly reinforces the view that surnames were fixed relatively late in Cornwall, as in Wales, and that toponymic names were more common in the earlier period. Their work also allows for some general conclusions on surname fluidity and the locality of particular usage. Particular light is shed on the use of Cornish words in surnames (other than Cornish place-names). It is indicated (although not conclusively) that greater Cornish language use in rural West Cornwall, as opposed to urban centres, ports and the extreme east of the county, can be detected in Cornish words used in occupational surnames. Examples are given: Trehar (tailor), Gweader (weaver) and Goff and Angoff or Angove (smith). They also point out that 'nicknames' are not frequent in the records used, but among those which are, we find Pengwyn (whitehead), Scovern (ear or big ears), Byan, Vyan, Vean (little/small) and Hire (tall). Given the relative frequency with which the Cornish word for English or Saxon appears in place-names (Coswinsawsen, Bejawsa, etc), it is surprising that few examples are found in surnames.[10]

The use of 'alias' to indicate the fluidity of surnames continued well into the eighteenth century of course, and the references to Pascoe Kerne of Tresylian[11] concern the same family as 'Richard Kearne alias Tresillian', who in March 1593 leased Trevenson (Illogan) from John Angove, including 'tolle tynne and tynne works'.[12] The Tehidy Accounts contain several examples from the first half of the eighteenth century of men using an alias (or former family surname) to supplement their presently used surname. Henry John alias Sparnon of Gwinear, the founder of Dolcoath Mine, is mentioned in connection with leasing North and South Entral tenements (Camborne) from Tehidy Manor, on 16 January 1723/24.[13] Henry John used the same alias on a mining lease agreement with Tehidy Manor dated 1720, for a sett on Entral side of the Red River, below Brea village. Other examples from the Tehidy Accounts are William Richards alias Daniell, for a tinwork at Tolskithy (Illogan), dated 16 July 16 1723,[14] and Thomas Roberts alias Bodruggo, for tin produced at Tolskithy, 30 April 1723.[15]

The Arundell records throw unexpected light on the John family of Gwinear, for there are several references to link them to 'Henry John alias Sparnon of Gwinear'. In 1549 they show that Thomas Spernam held Coswinsawsen in Gwinear, and in the same manor of Roseworthy were several members of the John family at Coswinsawsen and Roseworthy, including one James John.[16] In 1563 the Survey of the Earl of Oxford's Land, under Coswinsawsen, gives Thomasine

John, daughter of James John, and the next entry mentions one 'Spernam', whom the authors link with the aforementioned Thomas.[17] Coswinsawsen borders Camborne parish, and less than a mile away is Dolcoath and Entral, where Henry moved to from Gwinear less than 150 years later, taking over and developing the most productive and important mine in the history of Cornwall.

The Arundell documents also add to our knowledge of the ways in which Cornish people earned their living in former centuries. A glance at the index reveals dozens of mentions of aspects of the medieval tin industry, and they form a useful supplement to other records from that time. An example of this is the case of blowing houses or mills. There are seven references to them in Arundell, stretching from 1499 to 1571, and these lay between the parishes of Lanivet in the east and Sithney in the west. Up to three blowing houses (mills) were in Lanivet parish, one at Rosehill (Manor of Bodwannick), one at Reperry, where there was also a stamping mill, and another near St Bennets Chapel, which also had a stamps. In 1509 and again in 1571 there are mentions of blowing houses at Nancetrisick in Sithney (Manor of Prospidnick). In 1499 two blowing houses lay at Kennal in Stithians (Manor of Kennal), and in 1549, 1552 and 1563 there was a blowing house operating at Roseworthy in Gwinear, in one of the busiest tin mining and streaming districts of the late medieval period.[18]

The study of the tin industry in the period covered by Arundell has been my own area of special interest for over twenty years. For the most part I have used records such as SC2 and E101 from the Public Record Office, and Additional Manuscript 24746 of the British Library. These have been supplemented by a wide variety of other records, many of which have overlapped in an incidental way with those sources most obviously concerned with the tin industry. Such sources as churchwardens' accounts, subsidy rolls, military surveys and tinners lists have all helped to 'put meat on the bones' of my tinners and their works. Over several years Oliver Padel helped me identify and locate many of the tinworkings difficult to place. Conversely, the multitude of obscure and almost extinct place-names referred to in the tinbounds registrations supplemented Padel's own data, a fact which he generously acknowledged in his definitive *Cornish Place-Name Elements* (1985).[19]

My examination of the Additional Manuscript 24746 material, supplemented by other sources, has located nearly 300 tinworks for the period 1497 to 1520. Analysis enables us to determine with a fair degree of accuracy the type of tinwork recorded, of either stream work, for alluvial tin, or a lode mine, of either openwork ('coffin' or 'beam') or shaft and level mine. The records I have examined cover the three largest Stannary districts of Penwith-Kerrier, Blackmore and Fowey-more. The records have been most extensive for the most westerly Stannary of Penwith-Kerrier, and it is there that I have concentrated my research for the last two decades, only venturing further east for special studies or to compare data for analysis. The principal exception to this has been the transcription and study of the *Bailiff of Blackmoor* by Thomas Beare (1586). Among the many fascinating facts about the tinners and their industry of the late medieval to early Tudor period has been the variety of social and economic classes involved in the actual ownership and operation of the tinworks. It has been possible to identify in a general way very many of these people, so that five types of tinner emerge quite clearly from those obscure times. The farmer, working the moor at the edge of his agricultural holding, appears to make up between a third and two-fifths of all tinners; the full-time tinner, the skilled worker, was probably involved in almost all the tinworks above or below ground; the spalier or wage earner stood in for the gentry and entrepreneurs and worked their dole; the gentry invested in the larger stream works and almost all the lode workings, whether openwork or underground; and, finally, the entrepreneur spread his interests widely across the Stannaries. Some of the entrepreneurs, like John Benyll (Bevyll), who held doles in six stream works in Marazion, Ludgvan, St Hilary and Towednack, as well as a mine in Marazion, had extensive portfolios. Two entrepreneurs in Foweymore Stannary held shares in eleven and fourteen tinworks, respectively. In Penwith-Kerrier Stannary some 36 entrepreneurs have been identified, who were involved in 130 tinworks, which was 69 per cent of the 186 tinworks identified. Also in Penwith-Kerrier, two knights and five gentry were involved in the more expensively operated lode mines. It need hardly be said that using such records as subsidy rolls, military surveys and churchwardens' accounts can considerably enhance our knowledge of these men. Arundell will undoubtedly add still more to what we know of them and their industry.[20]

Moving beyond mining, Maryanne Kowaleski's article 'The Expansion of the South-Western Fisheries in Late Medieval England' is a straightforward study in economic history, examining the records of the industry from the late fourteenth century to the early sixteenth century.[21] She points out that the contribution made by the expanding fishing industry in Cornwall and Devon to the economy was extremely significant, although largely unnoticed by economic historians. She traces the rising number of fishermen, boats devoted to fishing and the quantities of fish exported, as opposed to those caught for domestic consumption. One of the points Kowaleski makes is that at the port of Exeter over the 150 years covered by her survey the number of ships carrying fish trebled and the number of fish cargoes and importers doubled. It is significant that the proportion of those reliant on the fish industry in Cornwall in that period is even greater than in Devon. In most Cornish ports over a third of sea-borne trade was in fish, with St Ives, Penzance, Looe and Marazion having between 40 and 60 per cent involvement in fish exporting every year. Kowaleski uses a wide variety of material sources for her research, most of which has been published before, but she has used it to produce results which appear to demonstrate the growth and importance of a late medieval Cornish industry in a new way.

What did people in medieval Cornwall believe? Ronald Waldron's article in the *Journal of the Royal Institution of Cornwall* on John Trevisa is a reminder of the abiding interest in influential Cornishmen of the fourteenth century.[22] Waldron analyses an important Cornishman's attitudes to a host of contemporary issues, at a time, we must remember, of tremendous changes and controversies in this country and on the continent. In doing this he illustrates how closely educated Cornishmen of the time identified with England. His references to the success of John Cornwall and Richard Pencrych in influencing educational trends in England demonstrate his pride in his own countrymen, and his consciousness of the Cornish role in the English cultural-educational scene of the time. Waldron's work on Trevisa reminds us that as early as the fourteenth century some Cornishmen could identify themselves as both Cornish and English, possessing a sense of group identity that is strongly suggestive of modern 'nested' spatial identities in Cornwall. His fascinating study emphasizes the importance of these Cornishmen in helping shape the religious, cultural and linguistic attitudes at the higher levels of English society. Trevisa is shown to have been a blunt-speaking and critical translator of such enormous medieval works as the *Polychronicon* (a history of the world to 1360) by Ranulph Higden, and *De Proprietatibus Rerum* (a medieval encyclopedia) by Bartholomew Glanville.

Living at the time of Chaucer and Wycliff, when politics and religion could be dangerous subjects, when Lollards' influence was growing among the higher echelons of society, and when the storm clouds were gathering over all those suspected of heresy, Trevisa (like Chaucer) appeared to know when to speak and when, diplomatically, to withdraw. Both men had powerful patrons to protect them. Trevisa's religious views were certainly more radical than those of many Lollards and were potentially dangerous. It is of interest that maps drawn by historians to show the spread of Lollardy through England indicate nothing much in the extreme south-west and Cornwall. Given Trevisa's views and the progressive attitudes of such men as Cornwall and

Pencrych, might it not make an interesting piece of research to estimate the extent of Lollardy west of Exeter?

In contrast with Waldron is the work of David Harvey. His articles deal with issues of hagiography, identity, territory and landscape in West Cornwall, and a variety of related subjects, some of which are concerned with Cornwall and some with historical theory in general. His approach is necessarily heavy on analysis and theoretical concepts of how we understand history, and lighter on answering such simple questions as who did what, when, how and why?[23] Harvey's use of Athelstan's charter of St Buryan (AD 943) and other documents to demonstrate the need for continuity and the appeal to tradition and the past in establishing ownership and authority is interesting, even though the ideas and conclusions are not especially new or original. The value of such work as carried out by Harvey lies in the way that he contextualizes Cornwall. Like other places, Cornwall was subject to a process of territorialization as 'elite', Anglo-Norman influence promoted a certain view of territory, reflected in an emerging parochial framework. Nevertheless, this interacted with 'Celtic Cornish forces and arrangements' in a dialogue that produced a distinct territorial template in Cornwall.[24]

Our understanding of the religious world view of Cornish people in the late fifteenth century and on the verge of the Protestant Reformation has been greatly enhanced over the past decade or so. Prominent in this sphere has been Joanna Mattingly's work on saints' cults and gilds in the sixteenth century and her interpretation of the St Neot stained glass windows, together with her insight into the possible role of the Helston shoemakers' gild in helping to precipitate the 1549 rebellion.[25] The St Neot work, in particular, has gone a considerable way towards allowing us to get inside the very different religious 'mind-set' of the late medieval (and Tudor) Cornish man or woman.[26]

FUTURE DIRECTIONS?

What further directions can research into Cornish medieval history take? One possibility lies in more cross-analysis, linking the often overly specialized, discrete studies with other topics and themes. For example, what does surname analysis tell us about early patterns of migration? And how far do the names of tin bounds in the sixteenth century reveal the historical geography of the Cornish language at this crucial period of change?

An important motive for the establishment in 2001 of a seminar group to share information on medieval Cornish studies was the apparent 'interest overlap' which several of us had noted. Whilst searching for information on the stained glass windows of St Neot Church, Joanna Mattingly enquired about the local subscribers' names, which appear on some of the windows. This led to a search of the Stannary records to discover if those named men had made surplus money (which paid for the windows) from the tin industry. Once this was established with a fair degree of certainty, other records were used to flesh out those named individuals. The tinbound registrations were supplemented by the 1522 military survey, the 1524 and 1545 subsidy rolls and the tinners lists of the 1530s. This holistic approach meant we were, in effect, including every aspect of the lives of those late medieval St Neot parishioners. The tinner was involved in church refurbishment; he was a local tax-payer with determinable wealth; he was registered for military service and his military equipment was recorded. A search of parish registers and churchwardens' accounts (assuming they exist for St Neot) might tell us something of the man's marital status, number of children, local positions of responsibility or authority, whether he contributed to the poor of the parish or was, at times, a recipient of parish charity. Manorial records (if they are extant for the appropriate landholdings) could tell us even more about this man and his social and economic position and relationships. From this it is apparent that an interest in the finance and organization of stain glass windows can intrude into every aspect of St Neot life. An interest in the late medieval tin industry at St Neot can inform us of a wide range of facts about the subjects of our study, enhancing in every way our view of the background to the industry and the economic and social imperatives involved.[27]

Another feature of the renewed interest in Cornwall's history is the *Victoria County History (VCH)* project. The two areas of study chosen to kick-start the project—the locally based examination (led currently by Joanna Mattingly) of the fishing communities of Mousehole, Newlyn and their Mount's Bay locality, and the academic study of Cornwall's religious history by Nicholas Orme—appear to be ideal for exploiting the renaissance of interest in Cornwall's past. Together with the pre-1700 history seminar group, under the auspices of the Institute of Cornish Studies, the *VCH* project could see us move forward in a more cooperative way as we pursue our individual areas of study into Cornwall's past. The great variety of subjects researched and the several different approaches to research that have been noted here need not militate against working together. For the people we are looking back at and the events and institutions we are examining are all directly related and very frequently, as with the churchmen and tinners of St Neot, they are the same people.

Bernard Deacon, a self-confessed modernist, has made a series of suggestions on how the study of medieval Cornish history might move forward.[28] He highlights the need for comparative work to set Cornish studies into a European, Celtic and Anglo-Cornish context. He sees the movements of Bretons into and out of Cornwall during the late medieval to early modern period as a rich source of potentially fruitful study. The reasons for the noticeably high influx of Bretons into Cornwall at certain times and their exodus at others, he believes, should be examined in detail, taking into account wage and demographic changes and also varying mortality rates in Cornwall during the fifteenth and sixteenth centuries. Political changes in Brittany and religious changes in this country between the last decades of the fifteenth century and the middle of the sixteenth century also undoubtedly had a bearing on Breton migration patterns, so that their study could throw much-needed light on what was happening in Cornwall at that turbulent time.

Other suggestions are not difficult to make. There has been little research on the role of women in the medieval and Tudor period. Nobody has taken up Hatcher's proposition that late medieval Cornwall was a particularly diversified economy to look at its overall economic history at other early periods.[29] Similarly, there has been a dearth of detailed work on the political institutions of these centuries other than the Church, or the inter-relationship between wider processes, political events and socio-economic structures.[30] In general, there remains a reluctance to generalize and to make connections. We need more syntheses, such as that provided by Fox and Padel or by Nicholas Orme in his Introduction to *The Saints of Cornwall*.[31] These might serve to open up the period to the non-specialist and create a dialogue between the medievalist and other historians, particularly those who during the last decade or so have been responsible for driving forward new approaches to the study of Cornish history.

Given the wide variety of areas being studied, the large number of individuals involved and the enormous body of virtually untouched manuscript material available, the future of medieval Cornish history should be assured. However, if we are really to see progress in the field, it seems that moves like the *Victoria County History* project and the Institute of Cornish Studies seminar group should be supplemented by a more general movement to involve and encourage all those with an interest in Cornish history. How can this be done? Perhaps more use can be made of the media, for it is through the letters pages of the local press that we have become aware of the deep-rooted interest in certain areas of Cornish history. The arguments to and fro over what did or did not happen in 1549 remind us of the depth of genuine interest, but also of the fundamental ignorance of so many of the facts of the story. Local newspapers have an abiding interest in Cornish history, and there must be ways to promote the results of serious historical study, and to educate both Cornish people and newcomers about Cornwall's fascinating history and outstanding achievements. In promoting interest in accurate and well-researched Cornish history, we can help serious-minded people to separate history from the plethora of shallow and largely inaccurate heritage material which threatens to submerge the Duchy in an ocean of brochures and meaningless memorabilia. In the next few years we have a great opportunity to expand and deepen the study of Cornish history, for if we seek out ways to encourage more involvement and more thorough research, we will also be aiding all those currently involved, for every new participant is a potential source of new ideas, and new approaches to old problems, and their enthusiasm will encourage us to keep searching for that elusive fact, obscure explanation or wider context.

NOTES AND REFERENCES
1. 'Essays 1947–91', in W.M.M. Picken, *A Medieval Cornish Miscellany,* ed. O.J. Padel, Chichester, 2000; P.A.S. Pool, 'The Tithings of Cornwall', *Journal of the Royal Institution of Cornwall (JRIC)*, 1981; P.A.S. Pool, 'The Penheleg Manuscript', *JRIC*, 1960; O.J. Padel, *Cornish Place-Name Elements,* London, 1985a; O.J. Padel, 'Cornish Surnames in 1327', *Nomina* 9, 1985b; O.J. Paldel, 'From Cornish Place-Names to Surnames in Cornwall', *Journal of Cornwall Family History Society*, 1985c; A.C. Thomas, *Christian Antiquities of the Parish of Camborne*, Camborne, 1967; A.C. Thomas, *Christian Celts: Messages and Images*, Stroud, 1998; H.L. Douch, 'Household Accounts at Lanherne', *JRIC*, 1953; P.H. Hull, *The Caption of Seisen of the Duchy of Cornwall 1337,* 1971; *Cartulary of St Michael's Mount, Cornwall,* 1962.

2. J. Mattingly, 'The Medieval Parish Gilds of Cornwall', *JRIC*, 1986–90; J. Mattingly, 'A Tin Miner and Bal Maiden', *JRIC*, 2001; B. Murdoch, *Cornish Literature,* Cambridge, 1993; N. Orme (ed.), *English Church Dedications: With a Survey of Cornwall and Devon,* Exeter, 1996; N. Orme, *Unity and Variety: A History of the Church in Devon and Cornwall,* Exeter, 1991; P. Cockerham, 'Models of Memorialisation: Cornwall, Ireland and Brittany Compared', in Philip Payton (ed.), *Cornish Studies: Nine,* Exeter, 2001; D. Harvey, articles in *Landscape History,* 1997; *Journal of Historical Geography,* 2000; *International Journal of Heritage Studies,* 2001; J. Whetter , *Cornwall in the 13th Century,* St Austell, 1998; J. Whetter, *The Bodrugans,* St Austell, 1995; M. Kowaleski, 'The Expansion of South-Western Fisheries in Late Medieval England', *Economic History Review,* LIII,3 2000, pp. 429–54; R. Waldron 'The Mind of John Trevisa', *JRIC,* 2001; C. North, 'The Will and Inventory of Edward Arundell of Treveliew and Lanherne 1539–86', *JRIC,* 2001; J.A. Buckley, *Tudor Tin Bounds,* Redruth, 1987; J.A. Buckley, 'Who were the Tinners?', *Journal of the Trevithick Society,* 1997.

3. Picken, 2000.

4. Harvey, 1997.
5. H.S.A. Fox and O.J. Padel, *The Cornish Lands of the Arundells of Lanherne Fourteenth to Sixteenth Centuries*, Exeter, 2000. This work supplements and complements the earlier work by John Hatcher on Duchy of Cornwall manors: see John Hatcher, *Rural Economy and Society in the Duchy of Cornwall 1300–1500*, Cambridge, 1970.
6. Fox and Padel, 2000, pp. lii–lxvii.
7. Fox and Padel, 2000, pp. lii–lxvii; ci–cxxiii.
8. Padel, 1985a, pp. 81–7.
9. For example, comparing this with the findings of David Postles, *The Surnames of Devon*, Oxford, 1995.
10. Fox and Padel, 2000, pp. cxxiv–cxlvii.
11. Fox and Padel, 2000, p. cxxiv.
12. HB 5/165, Royal Institution of Cornwall, Truro.
13. Tehidy Accts 57b, p. 12; Cornwall Record Office.
14. Tehidy Accts 57b, p. 10.
15. Tehidy Accts 57b, p. 16.
16. Fox and Padel, 2000, pp. 58, 159.
17. Fox and Padel, 2000, p. 169.
18. Fox and Padel, 2000, pp. 116, 123, 150, 160, 168, 201, 205.
19. Padel, 1985b, p. ix.
20. Thomas Beare, *The Bailiff of Blackmoor 1586,* ed. J.A.Buckley, 1994, Additional manuscript 24746, British Library. For an accessible introduction to medieval metal mining that uses archaeological evidence to flesh out the historical documents see also Sandy Gerrard, *The Early British Tin Industry*, Stroud, 2000.
21. Kowaleski, 2000; see also Maryanne Kowaleski, *The Havener's Accounts of the Earldom and Duchy of Cornwall, 1287–1356*, Exeter, 2002.
22. Waldron, 2001.
23. Harvey, 1997; Harvey, 2000; Harvey, 2001.
24. Harvey, 1997.
25. Joanna Mattingly, 'Stories in the Glass-Reconstructing the St Neot Pre-Reformation Glazing Scheme', *JRIC*, 2000, pp. 9–55.
26. Robert Whiting, *The Blind Devotion of the People: Popular Religion and the English Reformation,* Cambridge, 1989.
27. Mattingly, 2001, p. 96.
28. Bernard Deacon, 'Researching the Medieval and Early Modern Periods', *Cornish History Network Newsletter* 12, 2001, pp. 8–11.
29. see Hatcher, 1970.
30. For an exception see Ian Arthurson, 'Fear and Loathing in West Cornwall: Seven New Letters on the 1548 Rising', *JRIC,* 2000, pp. 69–96.
31. Nicholas Orme, *The Saints of Cornwall*, Oxford, 2000.

RE-DISCOVERING DIFFERENCE: THE RECENT HISTORIOGRAPHY OF EARLY MODERN CORNWALL

Mark Stoyle

INTRODUCTION

Over the past ten years, Cornish historical studies have enjoyed what can only be described as a renaissance. Nowhere has this been more apparent than in the field of early modern history, where the standard works which have dominated interpretations of the period for upwards of half a century (most notably Mary Coate's great study of the Civil War and A.L. Rowse's masterpiece, *Tudor Cornwall*[1]) are fast beginning to recede into history themselves as their findings are built upon, refined and—in several important respects—overturned by a host of new books and articles. What can account for this sudden upsurge of historical writing on Tudor and Stuart Cornwall? At the local level, the phenomenon clearly owes much to the dynamism of the staff and students of the Institute of Cornish Studies and to the rebirth of the present series, *Cornish Studies*. At the national level, the explosion of interest in 'British history'—which has fuelled the growing realization that 'archipelagic approaches' may be applied to the history of Cornwall, just as they have been applied to the histories of Ireland, Scotland and Wales—has also played a vital role. Yet among the rising generation of scholars, some possess no particular connection with the Institute, while others—doggedly 'Kernowsceptic' —remain to be convinced that Cornish history is anything more than a sub-division of English local history. The new wave of writing on early modern Cornwall is the product of many different perspectives, in other words, rather than the creation of a single faction or school. This paper sets out to review some of the most important contributions which have been made to this fast-expanding field over the course of the past decade. It concentrates, in particular, on accounts which stress Cornish 'difference' and on the violent episodes which today, as for centuries before, stand at the very heart of the debate over Cornwall's early modern history: the Tudor rebellions of 1497 and 1548–9, and the Civil War of 1642–6.

ECONOMY, SOCIETY AND CULTURE

Despite what has been said already, it would be misleading to claim that the story of the past ten years has been one of rapid advance on every front. Economic history has long been in the doldrums among scholars of early modern Britain as a whole, and this fact is reflected in the field of Cornish Studies, as it is elsewhere. Few new studies of the economy of sixteenth- and seventeenth-century Cornwall have emerged over the past decade to supplement the earlier monographs by economic historians like Lewis, Hatcher and Whetter—and there is little sign that this situation is about to improve, although Whetter's book is once again in print.[2] A handful of significant pieces have admittedly appeared: Todd Gray's book on harvest failure, for example, Graham Haslam's two articles on the Duchy of Cornwall and Sandy Gerrard's overview of the early modern Cornish tin industry.[3] In addition, David Cullum's unpublished Ph.D. thesis provides a valuable portrait of society and economy in seventeenth-century West Cornwall and affords some intriguing insights into the peculiarly 'closed' nature of local society. Cullum's observation that 'strangers' buried at Madron between 1600 and 1650 were more likely to be denizens of foreign countries than they were to be English is especially worthy of note.[4] Yet, these exceptions aside, the overall picture is one of stasis.

By contrast, cultural studies of early modern Cornwall are booming—and particular attention has been paid over the last ten years to literary themes. Brian Murdoch's major monograph on Cornish literature was published in 1993, while other recent books and articles have touched, *inter alia*, on the theme of tyranny in the sixteenth-century saint's play *Beunans Meriasek*; on the attitude of Shakespeare and other Tudor and Stuart playwrights to the Cornish; on the recusant scholar Nicholas Roscarrock's *Lives of the Saints*; and on the antecedents of Nicholas Boson's Late Cornish folk-tale, *John of Chyanhor*.[5] Two substantial studies of the Cornish gentry class have also appeared, both of which devote a considerable amount of attention to the cultural outlook of Cornwall's early modern governors.[6] The history of the Late Cornish language is thriving too. Andrew Hawke has recently published an edition of a long-lost

English–Cornish vocabulary (probably compiled in Cornwall at some time between 1575 and 1650) which not only provides a number of previously unrecorded Cornish words but also hints at the existence of 'an antiquarian interest in Cornish in Wales during the seventeenth century',[7] while the dramatic discovery of a substantial section of what appears to be a hitherto unknown sixteenth-century miracle play (*Beunans Ke*) promises more excitement for the future. Meanwhile, Matthew Spriggs has written a tantalizing account of his quest for a cache of documents written in Cornish which may yet await discovery: the sermon-notes compiled by the Reverend Joseph Sherwood of St Erth in *circa* 1680. In this article—one of the shrewdest and most enjoyable pieces to have been published on early modern Cornwall in recent years—Spriggs not only shows how much still remains to be discovered about the history of the Late Cornish language and its speakers, but also provides a model example of how future work in this direction should proceed.[8]

Nor have cultural approaches to the history of early modern Cornwall over the past decade been restricted to the analysis of traditional documents alone. Two recent articles by Paul Cockerham have considered the early modern funerary monuments of Cornwall as *Volkskunst*, or folk art, and have analysed the nature, chronological range and geographical distribution of these intriguing survivals in stone. One of the most important findings to have emerged from his work is that the people of early modern Cornwall displayed 'a passion for physical memorialization' which was highly unusual, if not unique, in Tudor and Stuart Britain.[9] At the same time, Cockerham shows that the Cornish clung to outmoded styles of memorial inscription and design 'long after . . . [they] had been abandoned elsewhere': a fact which undoubtedly helps to explain the 'amazingly conservative' appearance of contemporary Cornish church monuments on which Pevsner and others have commented.[10] So distinctive were the products of the local funerary workshops—in particular the slate monuments which were turned out in such large numbers during the seventeenth century—that Cockerham argues that these memorials should be included among the contemporary signifiers of Cornish cultural difference.[11]

Yet matters are less straightforward than they at first appear, for, as Cockerham freely admits, 'the inhabitants of that most "Cornish" of regions, Penwith', erected considerably fewer memorials than did their neighbours elsewhere. There is a puzzle here, one which Cockerham attempts to solve by claiming that the 'topographical and ethnic self-containment' of the West Cornish 'did away with the need for such didactic status symbols'.[12] There may well be some truth in this;

alternatively, one might suggest that, in a region where few below the level of the gentry could read English, there was little point in erecting costly inscribed monuments to proclaim the virtues of the dead. Whatever the case, Cockerham's pioneering research has underlined the valuable contribution which these not-so-mute stones can make to the study of Cornwall's early modern past.

REBELLION

While hitherto neglected topics continue to be opened up, the traditional scholarly interest in the Cornish rebellions of the Tudor period shows no sign of abating. On the contrary, there has been a flood of new writing on this subject over the past decade. Thus Ian Arthurson has provided a fresh discussion of the insurrections of 1497: a discussion which suggests that Yorkist sympathizers among the local gentry may have helped to engineer the two revolts which took place against Henry VII in West Cornwall.[13] Philip Payton—building on the earlier work of A.L. Rowse and J.A. Buckley—has put forward a very different thesis: that the rebellion of May 1497 was fuelled by Cornish resistance to the intruding power of the English state and by deep-seated popular hostility to the King's attempts to 'dilute local privileges and usages'.[14] Elsewhere, Payton has cited evidence to show that a bitter sense of resentment continued to fester against Henry VII in Cornwall long after the rebels had been defeated.[15] Payton's central thesis—that a concern for Cornish identity helped to underpin the disturbances of 1497—has been variously received, with some scholars, such as John Chynoweth, denying it and others, including myself, offering support.[16]

This debate pales into insignificance compared with that which has raged over the subsequent Cornish rebellions of 1548–9. Of the many recent books and articles which have discussed the mid-Tudor insurrections, perhaps the most idiosyncratic in its approach to the risings has been Robert Whiting's monograph on the popular reception of the Reformation in the South-West. Whiting not only strove to play down what many earlier writers had taken for granted—the importance of religious conservatism in motivating the rebels—but he also challenged the traditional view that the Prayer Book Rebellion of 1549 had been 'representative of regional opinion'. Instead, Whiting argued that religious indifference had been rife throughout the mid-Tudor South-West, and that the Devon and Cornish men who had taken part in the rising had formed 'a relatively unimpressive percentage of the two counties' approximately 200,000 inhabitants'.[17] This latter claim is hard to accept. Of the approximately 200,000 people who dwelt in the South-West in 1549, around half would have been women. Of the remaining 100,000 male inhabitants, between a half and two-thirds would have been either too old or too young to have fought. The force of between 6,000 and 10,000 men which the rebels eventually managed to raise thus represented somewhere between 12 per cent and 25 per cent of the region's total population of 40–50,000 adult males: a staggering success by contemporary standards.

Whiting's claim that the Prayer Book rebels did not represent majority opinion in Cornwall is clearly implausible, then, but his scepticism about the traditional view of the insurrection 'as a purely religious revolt' is now shared by many other scholars.[18] Having said this, most of the detailed work carried out on the Cornish rebellions over the last ten years has tended to confirm the importance of religious traditionalism in motivating the insurrectionists. Ian Arthurson has recently published an important collection of documents relating to the western commotion of 1548 which reveal that Dr Roger Tongue—an 'outspoken reformer' with close court connections—was sent into the Meneage in the aftermath of the rising to preach to local people in St Keverne church: clear evidence of the Edwardian regime's belief that the initial outbreak of rebellion there had been the product of deep-seated religious conservatism.[19] Whiting's own discovery that the rood at Stratton church, which had been removed in accordance with royal orders in 1548, was re-erected during the rebellion of the following year, provides further evidence of the insurgents' attachment to the traditional faith.[20] And Joanna Mattingly has recently made the intriguing suggestion that a craft gild established by a group of local men in Helston may have been set up on 15 June 1549, just days after the Prayer Book Rebellion began. If this date is correct, then the men's action must surely be assumed to have reflected their hope that such local gilds—which had been abolished by the Crown in 1547—would shortly be restored across the realm.[21] More generally, Howard Colvin and Paul Cockerham have argued that the sheer volume of building work carried out on Cornish and Devon churches during Henry VIII's reign tends to undermine Whiting's argument that local attachment to traditional Catholicism was weak.[22]

As the battle over the religious issue has continued to rage, so an increasing amount of research has begun to be carried out into the other contributory causes of the Cornish rebellions of 1548–9. Here, Helen Speight has offered an especially valuable series of insights. In her meticulously researched Ph.D. thesis—a piece of work which deserves to be much more widely known—Speight has demonstrated the existence of a crisis in local government between 1547 and 1549: a crisis which was partially caused by the appointment of a number of 'ephemeral', lesser gentry figures to the Cornish magistrates' bench. As local respect for the JPs plummeted, she suggests, and as factional rivalries between the established, religiously conservative gentlemen and their *arriviste*, religiously conformist rivals intensified, so the forces of law and order in the South-West became increasingly paralysed: leading to a situation in which disorder, once it had started, would be difficult if not impossible to contain.[23] While Speight has stressed the weakness of local government, other historians have stressed the role of Cornish 'difference'. Both Philip Payton and I have argued that there was a specifically Cornish dimension to the risings of 1548 and 1549, and that those Cornishmen who joined the rebel hosts were motivated, at least in part, by a desire to protect traditional 'Cornishness' from what they perceived as English cultural aggression.[24] Some consideration has also been given to the lasting consequences of the rebel defeat; in my own new book, *West Britons*, I suggest that by causing a link between the Cornish tongue and sedition to become established in the minds of the ruling elite, the 1549 rebels may inadvertently have helped to seal the fate of the language.[25]

CIVIL WAR

Turning from the convulsions of the 1540s to those of the 1640s, we find that the issues of religion, gentry factionalism and Cornish identity have again been at the forefront of recent debate. All three subjects were touched upon in Mary Coate's standard history of the Civil War in Cornwall, but over the last ten years a great deal of new work has appeared. The most detailed discussion of local religious divisions on the eve of the Civil War will now be found in Anne Duffin's monograph *Faction and Faith* (1996): the first substantial book to appear on seventeenth-century Cornish politics for over half a century. Like Coate before her, Duffin has been keen to stress the existence of strong currents of zealously Protestant feeling among the greater gentry families of early Stuart Cornwall; her book contains a great deal of valuable information about the ideas and attitudes of upper-class Cornish Puritans.[26] At the same time Duffin has argued that, among the ordinary Cornish people, religious conservatism remained strong and that the vociferous popular royalism which was so evident in Cornwall during the Civil War was partially 'underpinned by a desire to preserve the established church' from Puritan despoilment: a conclusion which enjoys unanimous support among other recent scholars of the period.[27]

It is Duffin, too, who has provided an updated account of factional rivalry among the Cornish gentry during the decades which preceded the Civil War.[28] She convincingly demonstrates that, although 'there were many competing influences' on individual Cornish gentlemen during the 1620s and 1630s, it was religious differences which did most to define the opposing factions—and most to determine the eventual choice of sides in 1642.[29] One of the most important differences between the view of mid-seventeenth-century Cornwall which was previously put forward by Coate and that which has more recently been advanced by Duffin is that, whereas the former laid considerable stress on notions of Cornish distinctiveness, the latter has been at pains to play such notions down. In the preface to her book, Duffin observes that, while many of the interests of the Cornish gentry had 'a specifically Cornish focus', the 'principal issues which . . . concerned Cornish gentlemen in this period' were precisely the same as those which concerned gentlemen in other parts of the realm. Ramming the point home, she later remarks that the 'Celtic heritage' of early Stuart Cornwall 'should not be over-emphasised, particularly for the gentry'.[30] The main thrust of Duffin's argument—that the greater gentry were the most thoroughly 'Anglicized' inhabitants of early Stuart Cornwall—is undoubtedly correct, but even among this class there were some who remained fiercely proud of their Cornishness as late as the 1680s.[31] Below the level of the gentry governors, moreover, awareness of Cornish 'difference' was still very widespread on the eve of the Civil War, particularly among the Cornish-speaking population in the far west—and recent interpretations have suggested that this fact is of crucial significance in explaining the events of 1642–6.[32]

Musing on the nature of the English Civil War in 1996, John Pocock—the godfather of the new 'British history'—observed that 'this is a war in which it is possible to know something about the common soldier's point of view, and I could wish to know more about what . . . [the King's] Welsh and Cornish regiments thought they were doing and who they thought they were'.[33] Much of my own writing over the course of the past decade has been designed to address these same questions, and to explain why the ordinary people of Wales and Cornwall should have adhered to the Royalist cause so much more stoutly than their English neighbours did. In my first book, *Loyalty and Locality* (1994), a study of popular allegiance in Devon during the Civil War, I put forward the argument that the intensity of Welsh and Cornish Royalism might have sprung from the same basic root: 'a deep religious conservatism, fostered by isolation and racial difference'.[34] In a series of later articles, I explored the issue of wartime allegiance in more depth, and suggested that the ordinary people of Wales and Cornwall might have eventually come out for the King, rather than for Parliament, 'because, while Charles I was seen as the King of Great Britain, the defender of the rights and privileges of all his subject peoples, the Parliamentarians were associated with a narrowly English interest'.[35] In *West Britons* (2002), I attempted to bring all of these ideas together in a study which argued that issues of identity and ethnicity had lain at the very heart of Cornwall's experiences during the Civil War (and, indeed, of Cornwall's early modern history as a whole).[36]

How have these arguments been received? One or two ultra-conservative historians have responded with extreme scepticism. S.K. Roberts, for example, has alleged that *Loyalty and Locality* 'promotes notions of ethnicity as factors in wartime allegiance on the thinnest of evidence'.[37] Yet this dismissive attitude is untypical, and the argument that there was an ethnic dimension to the Civil War in Cornwall—and, indeed, in Wales—has now begun to penetrate the historiographical mainstream.[38] In a recent survey of early Stuart England, Derek Hirst has indicated his support for the view that the Civil War in Cornwall and Wales had possessed 'racial undertones', and urged his readers to remember that 'the British problem was not confined to Scotland and Ireland'.[39] Andy Wood has made similar points and has suggested that 'godly' Parliamentarians regarded the Welsh and Cornish as second-class citizens who—'just like English Catholics'—were inhabitants of '[the] English Empire, but . . . only partial members of it'.[40] Among specialists in Cornish history, too, the thesis that Cornwall's unique war-time experiences had reflected its unique cultural identity has attracted considerable support. Joanna Mattingly, for example, has recently suggested that a hitherto unnoticed 'campaign of iconoclasm' carried out by Roundhead soldiers in Cornwall between 1651 and 1653 had been both 'religious and anti-Cornish in [its] motivation'.[41] More generally, the argument—first put forward by Philip Payton—that Cornwall's behaviour during the Civil War had mirrored its behaviour in 1497 and 1549 is also beginning to make headway.[42] The most up-to-date edition of Antony Fletcher's classic textbook on Tudor rebellions acknowledges that 'Cornwall was a culture to itself with a recurrent pattern of independent behaviour from the fifteenth century to the Civil War'.[43]

CONCLUSION

So much for the developments of the past ten years. Where might studies of early modern Cornwall go from here? To assume that accounts which stress the role of Cornish difference will continue to enjoy the generally favourable response which they have met with so far would probably be unwise. As books and articles which challenge the traditional, Anglocentric view of Cornwall's past become—in the words of one recent writer—'increasingly fashionable',[44] so they run the risk of attaining the status of a new orthodoxy: one which is vulnerable to attack in its turn. The Kernowsceptic backlash may be just around the corner, in other words, and if such a backlash does, in the end, materialize, it is not difficult to guess what its primary objectives will be: to thrust the historiography of early modern Cornwall firmly back into the box labelled 'English local history', and to nail down the lid. My own opinion is that such efforts are doomed to failure: that—to change the metaphor slightly—this particular genie is now out of the bottle for good. Even so, there can be little doubt that the publication of accounts of Cornwall's early modern history which are informed by a considered scepticism about notions of Cornish difference would strengthen the field as a whole. To descend from the general to the specific, which are the particular areas upon which future research might most profitably concentrate? Bernard Deacon's recent call for more attention to be paid to cultural divisions *within* Tudor and Stuart Cornwall should undoubtedly be heeded.[45] Above all, though, it is the history of the established Church in Cornwall between the Reformation and the Civil War which seems, to me at least, to be in most urgent need of re-assessment.[46] Several scholars have stressed the deep conservatism of that Church.[47] But what, exactly, did this 'conservatism' consist of? What was the precise nature of the accommodation which the local clergy made with traditional Cornish culture? To what extent did the beliefs and practices of Cornish 'Anglicans' differ from those of their English neighbours? And how far would it be fair to characterize the established Church in Cornwall as a central pillar of contemporary Cornish identity? These are surely among the most important questions with which students of early modern Cornwall must wrestle during the next decade of Cornish Studies.

NOTES AND REFERENCES

1. M. Coate, *Cornwall in the Great Civil War and Interregnum, 1642–60*, Oxford, 1933; and A.L. Rowse, *Tudor Cornwall: Portrait of a Society*, London, 1941. Almost as influential in shaping twentieth-century views of early modern Cornwall was F. Rose-Troup, *The Western Rebellion of 1549*, London, 1913.

2. G.R. Lewis, *The Stannaries: A Study of the Medieval Tin Miners of Cornwall and Devon*, London, 1908; J. Hatcher, *Rural Economy and Society in the Duchy of Cornwall, 1300–1500*, Cambridge, 1970; J. Whetter, *Cornwall in the Seventeenth Century: An Economic Survey of Kernow*, Padstow 1974, republished St Austell, 2002.

3. T. Gray (ed.), *Harvest Failure in Devon and Cornwall: The Book of Orders and the Corn Surveys of 1623 and 1630–31*, Redruth, 1992; G. Haslam, 'The Elizabethan Duchy of Cornwall: An Estate in Stasis' and 'Jacobean

Phoenix: The Duchy of Cornwall in the Principates of Henry Frederick and Charles', in R.W. Hoyle (ed.), *The Estates of the English Crown, 1558–1640*, Cambridge, 1992, pp. 88–111 and 263–96; and S. Gerrard, 'The Tin Industry in Sixteenth and Seventeenth Century Cornwall', in R. Kain and W. Ravenhill (eds), *Historical Atlas of South West England*, Exeter, 1999, pp. 330–7. There is also a certain amount of discussion of socio-economic issues in A. Duffin, *Faction and Faith: Politics and Religion of the Cornish Gentry before the Civil War*, Exeter, 1996, chapter 1.

4. D.H. Cullum, 'Society and Economy in West Cornwall, 1588–1705', unpublished Ph.D. thesis, University of Exeter, 1994, p. 41.

5. B. Murdoch, *Cornish Literature*, Cambridge, 1993; P. Payton, 'A Concealed Envy Against the English: A Note on the Aftermath of the 1497 Rebellions in Cornwall', in Philip Payton (ed.), *Cornish Studies: One*, Exeter, 1993, pp. 9–12; L. Olsen, 'Tyranny in *Beunans Meriasek*', in Philip Payton (ed.), *Cornish Studies: Five*, Exeter, 1997, pp. 52–9; A. Kent, 'Art Thou of Cornish Crew?: Shakespeare, Henry V and Cornish Identity', in Philip Payton (ed.), *Cornish Studies: Four*, Exeter, 1996a, pp. 7–25; M. Stoyle, *West Britons: Cornish Identities and the Early Modern British State*, Exeter, 2002, pp. 36–40; N. Orme (ed.), *Nicholas Roscarrock's Lives of the Saints: Cornwall and Devon*, Exeter, 1992; B. Murdoch, 'Is John of Chyanhor really a Cornish Ruodlieb?' in Payton (ed.), 1996a, pp. 45–63.

6. J. Chynoweth, 'The Gentry of Tudor Cornwall', unpublished Ph.D. thesis, University of Exeter, 1994, especially pp. 90–112, 155–74, 201–20; and Duffin, 1996.

7. A. Hawke, 'A Rediscovered Cornish–English Vocabulary', in Philip Payton (ed.), *Cornish Studies: Nine*, Exeter, 2001, pp. 83–104, especially pp. 86 and 96.

8. M. Spriggs, 'The Reverend Joseph Sherwood: A Cornish Language Will o' the Wisp?' in Philip Payton (ed.), *Cornish Studies: Six*, Exeter, 1998, pp. 46–61.

9. P. Cockerham, 'On My Grave a Marble Stone: Early Modern Cornish Memorialization', in Philip Payton (ed.), *Cornish Studies: Eight*, Exeter, 2000, pp. 9–39; and P. Cockerham, 'Models of Memoralization: Cornwall, Ireland and Brittany Compared', in Payton (ed.), 2001, pp. 45–82, especially p. 46.

10. Cockerham, 2001, p. 57; and N. Pevsner, *The Buildings of England: Cornwall*, London, 1951, p. 21.

11. Cockerham, 2000, p. 30; and Cockerham, 2001, p. 46.

12. Cockerham, 2000, pp. 26–28, 31; and Cockerham, 2001, p. 69.

13. I. Arthurson, *The Perkin Warbeck Conspiracy, 1491–99*, Stroud, 1994, especially pp. 162–4, 168, 182.

14. P. Payton, *The Making of Modern Cornwall: Historical Experience and the Persistence of 'Difference'*, Redruth, 1992, pp. 54–5.

15. Payton, 1993, pp. 4–13.

16. See Chynoweth, 1994, pp. 27–8; and M. Stoyle, 'Cornish Rebellions, 1497–1648', *History Today* 47.5, May 1997, pp. 23–5.

17. R. Whiting, *The Blind Devotion of the People: Popular Religion and the English Reformation*, Cambridge, 1991, especially pp. 34–8, 268.

18. See, for example, H.M. Speight, 'Local Government and Politics in Devon and Cornwall, 1509–49, with Special Reference to the South-Western Rebellion of 1549', unpublished Ph.D. thesis, Sussex University, 1991, p. 2.

19. I. Arthurson, 'Fear and Loathing in West Cornwall: Seven New Letters on the 1548 Rising', *Journal of the Royal Institution of Cornwall*, 2000, pp. 68–96.

20. Whiting, 1991, p. 76.

21. J. Mattingly, 'The Helston Shoemaker's Gild and a Possible Connection with the 1549 Rebellion', in Payton (ed.), 1998, pp. 23–45, especially pp. 26–9, 30–7.

22. H. Colvin, 'Church Building in Devon in the Sixteenth Century', in *Essays in English Architectural History*, London, 1999, p. 45; and Cockerham, 2000, p. 13.

23. Speight, 1991, especially pp. 80, 84, 90, 94–5, 136–9, 144–5, 196.

24. Payton, 1992, pp. 57–60; P. Payton, *Cornwall*, Fowey, 1996b, pp. 137–142; Stoyle, 1997, p. 26; and M. Stoyle, 'The Dissidence of Despair: Rebellion and Identity in Early Modern Cornwall', *Journal of British Studies* 38.4, October 1999, pp. 436–8.

25. Stoyle, 2000, pp. 45–9.

26. Duffin, 1996, especially chapter 2.

27. Duffin, 1996, p. 212. See also A.C. Miller, 'Joseph Jane's Account of Cornwall during the Civil War', *English Historical Review* 90, 1975, p. 98; Payton, 1992, p. 62; and M. Stoyle, *Loyalty and Locality: Popular Allegiance in Devon during the English Civil War*, Exeter, 1994, pp. 237–8.

28. For earlier accounts, see J. Stucley, *Sir Bevill Grenvile and his Times, 1596–1643*, Chichester, 1983; and R. Cust, 'The Forced Loan and English Politics, 1626–28', unpublished Ph.D. thesis, University of London, 1984, especially pp. 314–28, 352, 401–3.

29. Duffin, 1996, p. 212.

30. Duffin, 1996, pp. xiv, 2.

31. For example, William Scawen of Molenick; see Stoyle, 2002, chapter 7.

32. See, for example, M. Stoyle, 'Pagans or Paragons?: Images of the Cornish during the English Civil War', *English Historical Review* 111.441, April 1996, pp. 299–323; and Payton, 1996b, pp. 155–66.

33. J.G.A. Pocock, 'The Atlantic Archipelago and the War of the Three Kingdoms', in B. Bradshaw and J. Morrill (eds), *The British Problem c. 1534–1707: State Formation in the Atlantic Archipelago*, London, 1996, p. 181.

34. Stoyle, 1994, p. 239.

35. Stoyle, 1996, p. 322. See also M. Stoyle, 'Sir Richard Grenville's Creatures: The New Cornish Tertia, 1644–46, in Payton (ed.), 1996a, pp. 26–44; M. Stoyle, 'Caricaturing Cymru: Images of the Welsh in the London Press, 1642–46', in D. Dunn (ed.), *War and Society in Medieval and Early Modern Britain*, Liverpool, 2000, pp. 162–79; and M. Stoyle, 'English

Nationalism, Celtic Particularism and the English Civil War', *Historical Journal*, 43.4, 2000, pp. 1113–28.

36. Stoyle, 2002.

37. S.K. Roberts, review of *Loyalty and Locality*, in *Southern History* 19, 1997, p. 157.

38. See, for example, A. Hughes, *The Causes of the English Civil War*, 2nd edn, London, 1998, p. 51; J. Pocock, 'The New British History in Atlantic Perspective: An Antipodean Commentary', *American Historical Review* 104.2, April 1999, p. 495; J. Barratt, *Cavaliers: The Royalist Army at War, 1642–46*, Stroud, 2000, pp. 98, 110; and L. Bowen, 'The Most Base, Peasantly, Perfidious People in the World: Popular Representations of Wales and the Welsh during the Civil Wars and Interregnum', seminar paper, 2001. I am most grateful to Lloyd Bowen for sending me a copy of this important paper, which is soon to be published.

39. D. Hirst, *England in Conflict, 1603–1660: Kingdom, Community, Commonwealth*, London, 1999, p. 200.

40. A. Wood, *Riot, Rebellion and Popular Politics in Early Modern England*, Basingstoke, 2002, p. 133.

41. J. Mattingly, 'Stories in the Glass: Reconstructing the St Neot Pre-Reformation Glazing Scheme', *Journal of the Royal Institution of Cornwall*, 2000, p. 9.

42. P. Payton, 'The Cornish Rebellions', *Cornish Nation (Kenethel Gernewek)*, 1973, p. 81; and Payton, 1992, pp. 61–3.

43. A. Fletcher and D. MacCulloch, *Tudor Rebellions*, 4th edn, London, 1997, p. 120.

44. Arthurson, 2000, p. 74.

45. B. Deacon, 'In Search of the Missing Turn: The Spatial Dimension and Cornish Studies', in Payton (ed.), 2000, pp. 213–30.

46. Many valuable studies which explore *aspects* of church history in Cornwall between *c*.1540 and 1642 already exist, of course. Among the most important of these are Rose-Troup, 1913, especially chapters 1–5; Rowse, 1941, especially chapter 13; I. Cassidy, 'The Episcopate of William Cotton, Bishop of Exeter, 1588–1621', unpublished D.Phil. thesis, University of Oxford, 1963, especially pp. 50, 90; J.A. Vage, 'The Diocese of Exeter, 1519–1646: A Study of Church Government in the Age of the Reformation', unpublished Ph.D. thesis, University of Cambridge, 1991; J. Barry, 'The Seventeenth and Eighteenth Centuries', in N. Orme (ed.), *Unity and Variety: A History of the Church in Devon and Cornwall*, Exeter, 1991; Whiting, 1991; and Duffin, 1996, especially chapter 2. What is needed now, I would argue, is a study which draws on the perspectives offered by these writers *and* on the new 'British historiography' in order to construct an updated overview of the history of the Church in Cornwall over the period as a whole.

47. See, for example, Coate, 1933, p. 327; A. Fletcher, *The Outbreak of the English Civil War*, London, 1981, p. 311; and Stoyle, 1994, pp. 37–8.

INDUSTRIAL CELTS?
CORNISH IDENTITY IN THE AGE OF
TECHNOLOGICAL PROWESS

Philip Payton

INTRODUCTION

In an editorial in December 2001, the *Guardian* newspaper reflected the ignorance of many in Britain and beyond, feigning surprise at Cornwall's 'century of industrial (yes, industrial) decay'. Like many of its readers, no doubt, the *Guardian* was more comfortable with its image of Cornwall as 'a magic place, steeped in history and pre-history, both Arthurian and Wagnerian', although it was shrewd enough to recognize that 'Cornwall's fortune is also its curse. Few of the summer visitors who wonder at its wild beauty or wander through its pictur-esque streets and lanes realise that it also England's [*sic*] poorest county.'[1]

In proffering these comments, the *Guardian* had touched upon many of the paradoxes of modern Cornwall, identifying both the contrast (and conflict) between Cornwall's past (and present) as an industrial region and the commonplace imagery of 'magic' and 'Arthur', *and* the role of popularly held touristic constructions of Cornwall in obscuring that industrial experience and its deleterious aftermath still felt today. In so doing, the newspaper had also touched the raw nerve of identity, not only pointing to the potential for disparity between internal (Cornish) and external (tourist) visions of Cornwall but hinting too at wider debates about the exact location of Cornish identity. Here the *Guardian* had engaged, albeit un-wittingly, in one of the key dialogues of the 'New Cornish Studies'. For, amongst other things, New Cornish Studies has attempted to situate analysis of Cornwall's industrial experience within the new academic understanding of the inherent diversity of British industrialization, while it has also tried to probe the contradictions (if contradictions they be) between the apparently competing constructions of Cornwall as an (English?) industrial region and as a Celtic rural idyll.

THE PIONEER OF DEEP MINING AND STEAM PUMPING TECHNOLOGY

The publication of A.K. Hamilton Jenkin's *The Cornish Miner* in 1927 was the first in a string of twentieth-century books illuminating (and celebrating) Cornwall's industrial history, followed in 1953 by John Rowe's classic academic study *Cornwall in the Age of the Industrial Revolution* and in the 1960s by D.B. Barton's proliferation of titles, notably *A History of Copper Mining in Cornwall and Devon*, *A History of Tin Mining and Smelting in Cornwall* and *The Cornish Beam Engine*. Numerous supporting volumes, such as Cyril Noall's trilogy (*Botallack, Levant, Geevor*), W.H. Pascoe's *The History of the Cornish Copper Company* and John Keast's *The King of Mid-Cornwall* appeared throughout 1960s, 1970s and 1980s, while titles such as Jim Lewis's *A Richly Yielding Piece of Ground: The Story of Fowey Consols Mine* in 1997 and Clive Carter's *Cornish Engineering 1801-2001* in 2001 evidenced the continuing popularity of the *genre* up to the Millennium and beyond.[2] Indeed, several of Barton's books had been republished during the 1980s, while a new edition of John Rowe's volume appeared in 1993, including new, additional material that had not been published back in 1953. To this was added the scholarly activity of the Trevithick Society, including its respected *Journal*, and in 2000 Anthony Burton's's new biography *Richard Trevithick: Giant of Steam* was presented to the Cornish and wider British reading publics.[3] Summarizing such work, in 1987 Roger Burt, long an academic devotee of Cornish mining history, had concluded confidently that:

> Cornwall was the most important metal mining county in the United Kingdom. It probably had the longest history of continuous production and a total value of output that dwarfed its nearest rivals. Together with associated districts just east of the Tamar, it produced nearly all of the country's tin and arsenic and most of its copper . . . [T]he county . . . became a leader in the early stages of British industrialisation. During the eighteenth and early nineteenth centuries Cornwall pioneered deep mining and steam pumping technology and its miners and managers were eagerly welcomed in mining districts throughout the world.[4]

And yet, despite this sustained rhetoric and the solid empirical research that underpinned it, the message that Cornwall was one of the birthplaces and nurseries of the Industrial Revolution appeared only occasionally to penetrate the wider academic consciousness of scholars interested in the economic history and geography of the British Isles. At best, Cornwall was merely a sideshow in a more important Industrial Revolution located principally in the Midlands and North of England, in South Wales, and in Central Scotland. Maxine Berg's brief and dismissive treatment of the Cornish industrial experience in her otherwise exhaustive and monumental study of *The Age of Manufactures*, published in 1985, exemplifies the point: 'in the middle of the nineteenth century mining suddenly declined and the region was rapidly transformed into a holiday resort'.[5] Eric Richards, too, saw Cornwall as on the 'margin' of British industrialization, pointing to an incipient de-industrialization after 1815,[6] a view echoed in more extreme form by Stephen Fisher and Michael Havinden who contended that 'From being a leading region in 1700–1720, the South West [Cornwall and Devon] has experienced a long relative decline in national significance over the late eighteenth and the nineteenth centuries'.[7]

Significantly, this interpretation was fed by a sketchy knowledge of Cornish mining history which wholly failed to understand that Gwennap was indeed 'the richest square mile on earth' for a period in the early nineteenth century, with Consolidated and United Mines in the 1830s involving capital investment of tens of thousands of pounds and placing them amongst the largest enterprises in the world at that time. It was also centred on an undue emphasis on the Devon experience, where the fortunes of the serge industry were read uncritically as being symptomatic of the peninsula as a whole. Thus in the late eighteenth and early nineteenth centuries, it was alleged, 'The Southwestern economy continued to expand slowly but the stagnation of the Devon serge industry heralded the beginnings of de-industrialisation'.[8] It might have been so for Devon, but for Cornwall it presaged half a century and more of sustained expansion, placing Cornwall at the forefront of technological advance and underpinning an enhanced sense of Cornish identity based on industrial prowess, the progenitor of the 'myth of Cousin Jack'—the belief (encouraged by the Cornish themselves) that Cornishmen the world over were innately qualified above all others as skilled hard-rock miners.

However, even as Fisher and Havinden were in 1991 crafting their unpromising picture of 'regional' economic activity, so in other regions historians, geographers and others were beginning to offer more penetrating insights into the fortunes of British regional industrial development and the fashioning of regional industrial identities. Indeed, as early as the mid and late 1980s a new wave of economic historians, historical geographers and political scientists had argued that industrialization in the British Isles had promoted regional differentiation rather than national homogeneity. In contrast to the earlier generation of scholars that had assumed cultural, social and political uniformity in Britain as a 'natural' outcome of the industrial experience, these new writers concluded that industrialization both perpetuated and reinforced regional 'difference'. Indeed, commentators such as Jack Langton, Pat Hudson and Derek Urwin argued that the Industrial Revolution gave new meaning to regional identities, the often highly specialized and distinctive forms of industrial activity that had emerged becoming defining cultural icons. As Dai Smith, champion of the socio-economic and cultural history of industrial South Wales, put it: 'there was an explosion into industrial pre-eminence of regions *as* regions'.[9] In Cornwall, glasses were raised to 'fish, tin and copper', while in South Wales it was coal, in Clydeside it was shipbuilding, and so on. In the North of England in particular, the regional 'difference' that had characterized the medieval period and had posed such problems for the assertion of Tudor rule was 're-invented' in the industrial era. An urban civic pride was everywhere apparent, on the one hand presenting 'the North' as possessing uniform cultural traits (in contradistinction to the metropolitan South) but also pointing to an intricate relationship of 'northern' sub-cultures from the Midlands to the Tyne.

Significantly, Hugh Kearney in his ground-breaking 1989 volume *The British Isles: A History of Four Nations* argued that nineteenth-century Cornwall was both integral and exceptional to this 'northern' pattern: integral in that Cornwall exhibited economic and social be-haviour akin to that of the northern sub-cultures but exceptional in that Cornwall was neither in nor of the North.[10] The experience of Cornwall had more in common with the North than the South of which it was ostensibly a part, but in the final analysis Cornwall was unique. As Sidney Pollard put it, Cornwall was an early and highly distinctive region of industrializing Britain:

> it was tin and copper mining and smelting which formed the basis of one of the most advanced engineering centres in the world to the 1840s, and of a complex industrial society exhibiting early developments of banking and risk-sharing to deal with the particular needs of local industry as well as a remarkable attempt to cartelize copper in the 1790s.[11]

Pollard was writing in 1981 but it was not until a decade later that Cornish historians began to respond in earnest to his (and other) academic perspectives. By the early 1990s there was a desire not only to react to the stimuli of Pollard, Urwin, Smith, Kearney and the others to present Cornwall unequivocally as one of the major and distinctive industrial regions of Britain, but also to engage head-on with the issue of Cornish identity in the industrial period. Here, in contrast to Kearney and others who saw Cornish identity as merely a variant of typical 'northern' sub-cultures, there was a new insistence that nineteenth-century Cornish identity was intrinsically 'ethnic', exhibiting at certain points a behaviour and consciousness distinct from that of 'England'. This view first received explicit explanation in my 1992 book *The Making of Modern Cornwall* (itself based upon a slightly earlier Ph.D. thesis at the University of Plymouth) but was the subject of more thorough-going debate in Bernard Deacon's 2001 doctoral thesis 'The Reformulation of Territorial Identity: Cornwall in the Late Eighteenth and Nineteenth Centuries'.[12]

CORNUBIA TRIUMPHANT?

Intended as a clarion call for then newly emergent New Cornish Studies, *The Making of Modern Cornwall* was a conscious attempt to respond to the new British historiography proposed by Kearney and others but also to employ social theory with the aim of locating Cornwall firmly within the pattern of European sub-state territories identified by political scientists such as Rokkan and Urwin. Here the relationship between 'centre' and 'periphery' within the state was seen as all-important in both perpetuating territorial distinctiveness and accounting for the deleterious socio-economic conditions often experienced by such territories, not least in the modern era where (according to Urwin) '[c]ontemporary regional economic problems are the consequence of an economic specialization compounded after 1918 by far-reaching structural industrial change'.[13] Relating this approach to Cornwall, it was argued that Cornwall's 'difference' had endured because of (rather than despite) its historical experience, drawing upon Sidney Tarrow's model of phases of peripherality to explain that experience.[14]

Tarrow admitted the antiquity of the peripheral condition, postulating an 'older peripheralism' of territorial and cultural isolation that had emerged in response to the state-building activities of the medieval and Renaissance eras. Geographically remote from the centre of such states, and with a modicum of constitutional accommodation to reconcile it to ultimate external control and to formalize and secure that control, a peripheral territory was to a considerable degree insulated from the state. To this was added peripheral distinctions in language, religion, habit, and perhaps socio-economic organization, creating a significant cultural divide from the centre. However, as Tarrow intimated, this territorial and cultural isolation was at length disturbed by the new forces of industrialization. This heralded what Tarrow dubbed a 'second peripheralism', in which industrialization brought in its wake economic and social marginality, a result of a peripheral territory's typically imperfect or over-specialized experience of industrialization, manifest in a lack of industrial diversification and consequent de-industrialization, emigration, depopulation, and structural decay.

It was argued in *The Making of Modern Cornwall* that Tarrow's model was applicable to Cornwall. There had indeed been an 'older peripheralism' of territorial and cultural isolation but there was also a 'second peripheralism' of economic and social marginality resulting from Cornwall's experience of industrialization. Cornwall's industrialization was deeply paradoxical. It placed Cornwall for a time at the cutting edge of technological advance, informing an assertive Cornish identity based on industrial prowess, and had allowed Cornwall to perform as an independent actor in the Industrial Revolution— at least in the late eighteenth century and the first half of the nineteenth. However, as Richards had intimated but not quite understood, this independent action was largely outside the networks of British industrial linkage (notwithstanding the early Cornish foray into South Wales smelting and into international mining markets), with Cornwall never achieving the 'critical mass' of other industrial areas and, crucially, failing to diversify to meet the challenge of structural change. In other words, Cornwall's industrialization remained imperfect, over-specialized and incomplete, this flawed experience disguised by Cornwall's apparent technological triumphs and denied by those who—ultimately—continued to throw good money after bad to try to keep mining afloat.

Indeed, huge structural changes did overtake the Cornish economy, reducing it both relatively and absolutely from its erstwhile position as the international centre of deep hard-rock mining and associated steam engineering to only a minor component of British and global industrial activity. Attempts at diversification into clothes manufacture, horticulture, china clay production (really another kind of mining) and tourism seemed small fry compared to the glory days of 'the richest square mile'. In any case, many of the new jobs created called for unskilled, low-paid and often female labour, while the skilled Cornish workforce (the miners) was by now largely overseas, with well-paid jobs in South Africa or Michigan enabling money to be sent home to Cornwall, keeping destitution from the doors of many Cornish families and providing that veneer of prosperity evident in Redruth and elsewhere. Returning emigrants, some well-off after their successes on the mining frontiers of the globe and fired with the entrepreneurial zeal of the New World, helped Cornwall to devise an economic coping strategy in the aftermath of the mining collapse, putting funds and energy into attempts at diversification. A brief upturn in mining itself in 1908 hinted at better days ahead, creating a new mood of hope in Cornwall amidst the prevailing 'dependency culture'. But the optimism was illusory, the coping strategy producing at best a 'remission' (as Ronald Perry has called it) in the 'paralysis' that marked 'second peripheralism' in its matured manifestation and which by the 1920s brought real suffering to Cornwall and its people as they wrestled with the effects of economic and social marginality.[15] Moreover, Cornwall's experience of de-industrialization prefigured major structural changes within the wider British economy, the emphasis moving towards financial and other service sector activities, locating much new wealth creation thereafter in London and the South-East as the old industrial regions one by one began their long decline.

The Making of Modern Cornwall put the case for the centre–periphery model but it also argued strongly that the experience of industrialization had had a profound impact upon Cornish identity. 'Second peripheralism' itself had the effect of perpetuating 'difference' into the modern period, while the dramatic and all-encompassing nature of Cornish mining at its zenith, with its distinctive characteristics and its dominating presence in the landscape quite literally from the Tamar to Land's End, touched the lives of almost all. In such circumstances, Cornwall built its distinctive identity as an industrial region in the manner suggested by Smith, Langton and others. But in so doing, it also perpetuated an 'ethnic' awareness of collective self from the earlier period of 'older peripheralism', blending an existing and profound sense of 'Cornishness' into new institutions and activities (from Methodism to male voice choirs) and investing them with deep 'Cornish' meaning: 'This [industrial] sense of identity generated a considerable pride, sometimes a feeling of superiority, in being Cornish which—although born of the eighteenth and nineteenth centuries—was in many respects in keeping with the earlier Cornish identity based on geographical isolation, political accommodation, and Celtic culture'.[16] Although ostensibly 'in England', Cornwall's position remained ambiguous, the Cornish on occasions asserting an identity that was deliberately oppositional to England and Englishness, with observers from outside almost routinely commenting on Cornwall's 'un-English' quality. In 1861, for example, the *Chambers Journal* thought Cornwall

'one of the most un-English of English counties', while even in distant
Moonta in far-away South Australia the local mine directors were
prepared to discuss 'Cornish nationality' and its effect upon the
solidarity of their workforce.[17]

DOLCOATH COPPER MINE, CAMBORNE, CORNWALL.

2. Dolcoath mine in 1831, the epitome—for many Cornish people—of
Cornish industrial prowess and technological advance.

'CORNWALL THE BRAVE AND TRULY GREAT'

In effect, *The Making of Modern Cornwall* was a preliminary attempt
to contextualize the Cornish industrial experience within a wider
explanation of Cornwall's history, and to set that experience within
broader models of regional economic specialization and cultural and
political differentiation. It fell to Bernard Deacon to take the analysis
further, producing an array of new insights and furnishing a subtler,
more nuanced understanding of the complex, shifting strands of
territorial identity in late-eighteenth- and nineteenth-century Cornwall.
Writing in Ella Westland's important collection *Cornwall: The Cultural
Construction of Place*, published in 1997, Deacon observed that:

> The converging work of some economic historians and
> economic geographers helps to contextualise Cornwall, one of
> Europe's early industrial regions. Langton (1984) and Hudson

(1989, 1992) argue that industrialisation produced distinct place identities as economic specialisation increased the differences between places at the same time that they were being inserted into an emerging global economy. Industrial regions thus gave rise to cultural regions. However, this approach emphasises material structures over discourses and images of regions, the economic over the cultural. To balance this I therefore combine this model of industrial regions with the work of Paasi (1986, 1991) who brings together material factors and discursive representations in a model of regional identity formation which stresses the role of insiders and outsiders in the construction of identities and that of social institutions in the reproduction of those identities over time.[18]

In the same article, Deacon argued that in the nineteenth century working-class reaction to rapid economic change combined with a proactive middle-class pride in Cornwall's industrial prowess to produce a vigorous and assertive Cornish identity. This, in turn, was reproduced in 'county' institutions, in newspapers, in novels, and in chapels, the workplace and the home. In subsequent years, Deacon developed these ideas further, culminating in 2001 in his doctoral thesis 'The Reformulation of Territorial Identity: Cornwall in the Late Eighteenth and Nineteenth Centuries'. Echoing his and others' earlier work, he argued in the thesis that 'new symbols of distinctiveness' in Cornwall in the early nineteenth century cohered around an ideology of 'industrial civilisation'. This reflected Cornwall's status as an 'industrial region' but 'the new co-existed with the old, as other symbols of identity that looked back to Cornwall's pre-industrial era were grafted onto a sense of regional pride bestowed by industrialisation'.[19] 'Cornishness' thus constructed was a 'nested identity', one that co-existed with other identities (Englishness, British-ness) at other scales, but one that was given legitimacy, content and meaning by eighteenth- and nineteenth-century Cornish historians who had created an 'ethnic history' in which the Cornish were differentiated from their neighbours. Thus, as Deacon notes, Borlase, writing in 1796, considered that from the time that Athelstan set the Tamar as the Cornish border 'we are to consider Cornwall under the Saxon yoke ... [T]he Cornish Britons maintained a perpetual struggle against the Saxons for the full space of 500 years.'[20] Similarly, Drew in 1824 considered Athelstan's intervention 'both fatal and final to the independence of the Cornish. This, amidst all the struggles that Corn-wall made to preserve her liberty untainted, and that her enemies made to rob her of that inestimable jewel, this was the era of the first subjugation of the Cornish by the English.'[21]

Deacon also considers the roles of the Cornish upper and middle classes (including that distinctively Cornish component of the latter, the mine captains) as agents of identity formation in the period. He goes on to compare Cornwall with other industrial regions and, observes that while in some respects the Cornish experience was similar to that of other places, in others it was not. Indeed, one marked difference was that Cornish industrialization was not accompanied by substantial in-migration from other regions. Instead, it was characterized by significant intra-Cornwall flows of people, a process that consolidated a sense of Cornish territorial identity in the mid-nineteenth century, while between 1841 and 1861 Cornwall had a higher proportion of native-born than any English county. Moreover, in the first half of the nineteenth century at least, Cornish industrialization had produced 'a social compromise that crystallized a proto-industrial society'. Here, '[r]elatively independent communities lived and worked in a network of "dispersed paternalism", reflecting both Cornwall's settlement geography and the persistence of an "economy of makeshifts" that cushioned communities from the full rigours of market relations'.[22] This social compromise, Deacon contends, helps to explain both the resistance in Cornwall in the early nineteenth century to what he terms 'class narratives' and the ready embrace of Methodism by the Cornish people. Methodism, he suggests, fitted the structures of late-eighteenth-century Cornish society, producing a revivalist, cottage 'folk-religion'.

By the 1840s, however, Cornwall's proto-industrial character was already beginning to break down, with 'traditional' forms starting to fragment and with Methodism already assuming a more public nonconformist identity. This was a period of modernization, in which Cornwall began to look more like other industrial regions, but by the 1870s de-industrialization had already begun to take effect, producing new divergences and differentiations. By this time, however, the distinctive Cornish identity born of industrialization was firmly entrenched. It exhibited a continuing ethnic dimension, distinguishing it from the industrial regions of England, but it existed alongside the dominant discourses of Englishness and Britishness, together with an emerging narrative of 'Celticity', to create multi-layered, overlapping categories of identity. This, as Deacon shows, sometimes produced complex responses, such as that penned by Francis Harvey in South Africa in the 1860s when an emigrant 'exile' from his native Hayle. Here, paradoxically, he objected to the sneering metropolitan suggestions that Cornwall was 'not of England' while at the same time appealing to possible representations of Cornwall that did indeed differentiate it from England:

> it is a fact that in Cockneydom, and may be elsewhere, where other blunderers have grown up, Cornwall the brave and truly great, has been of mere slander called 'West Barbary' and 'not of England'; well be it so, Cornishmen can well afford to smile at all this slang and stupid malignity; may be, Cornwall may justly be proud, as being in all her history, in her internal priceless worth, and in the glorious elements with which she has served and aided, and honoured every valuable interest of the nation; of being in truth, if 'not of' yet superior by far to England, if really 'not of it'.[23]

However, as Deacon observes, such sentiment did not easily trans- late into political aspirations as the Home Rule All Round debate emerged in the later nineteenth century. As one Cornishman explained in 1881, 'Cornish people were very happy to be united to England, and they did not wish for Home Rule'.[24] For, as Deacon himself explains:

> by the 1880s, Cornish men at least were uniting around a narrative of shared origins, contemporary economic distinctiveness and Celtic imaginings. A distinct regional consciousness had been re-forged over the years of industrialisation. Yet, ethnic consciousness was rendered opaque and hesitant by a parallel narrative of Englishness. The regional identity did not, at this time, produce a national identity. The latter was made difficult by the 'space of possibilities' that surrounded the Cornish identity. The absence of a distinct cultural institution as, in Wales, the Welsh language, or formal institutions as, in Scotland, separate ecclesiastical or legal structures, meant that there was relatively little around which national imaginings could cohere. In contrast, the consensus was that Cornwall was an English county, albeit a distinct one, and this was to remain the dominant image right through the twentieth century.[25]

Of course, we may object that as the assertive Cornish identity based on industrial prowess became less credible as Cornwall progres- sively de-industrialzsed, and as some opinion leaders reacted to the enormity of the situation in which they found themselves by attempting to locate Cornwall more assuredly within a 'Celtic national identity' (in the process advocating language revival and the creation of new

'Celtic' institutions), so the position described by Deacon became less certain. However, we can agree with Deacon that the real achievement of the last decade in the actual study of the Cornish industrial experience is that 'Those years [the industrial period] ought no longer to be viewed as an embarrassing void between the Cornish identity of the late medieval period and the re-discovered Cornish identity of the twentieth century'.[26] But are there other achievements? To what extent, we are entitled to ask, has the Payton–Deacon nexus managed to penetrate the wider debate on industrial identities in the 'Celtic lands' and, specifically, to what extent has the case of Cornwall influenced discussion of the 'industrial Celt'?

'THE ENGINEER AND THE CELTIC FRINGE'

In one sense, despite ten year's effort, it is still early days, not least because Deacon's recently completed Ph.D. is not yet published. However, notwithstanding the popular success with the reading public of Burton's *Richard Trevithick* (or indeed of E.V. Thompson's novels, many of them set in Cornwall in the industrial period), the academic world itself has been slow to wake up to the possibilities of considering Cornwall in its discussion of the 'industrial Celt'. For example, Christopher Harvie's entertaining and provocative paper 'Larry Doyle and Captain MacWhirr: The Engineer and the Celtic Fringe', delivered at the 'Cymru a'r Cymry 2000/Wales and the Welsh 2000' conference at Aberystwyth and subsequently published in a book of the same name, devoted just three words to Cornwall—one being 'Cornwall', the others 'Richard Trevithick'.[27] In a wide-ranging survey encompassing Ireland, Scotland and Wales, together with glimpses of their global impacts, there was no room apparently for the Cornish beam engine, for Cornish innovations in high pressure steam or locomotion or hard-rock mining, or for the Cornish role in the development of the international mining economy.

Nor was there room for insights drawn from the Cornish experience to help illustrate the themes of paradox and contradiction pursued by Harvie. Indeed, some of Harvie's themes were highly relevant to the Cornish experience, especially the apparent contrast or even conflict between nineteenth- and even twentieth-century images of 'the Celt' (essentially rural and technologically backward) and the 'industrial' (basically urban and progressive). Such stereotypes originated in English prejudice but were also co-opted by at least some of the 'Celtic' peoples themselves. On the one hand, Protestant Ulster folk and Scottish Lowlanders were apt to look down upon their 'backward' compatriots in southern Ireland and the Highlands, eschewing notions of their own 'Celticity' and preferring to sign up to myths of Anglo-Saxon origin. On the other hand, Celtic nationalists, with their particular blend of Romantic and Revivalist ideology, willingly adopted constructions in which 'the Celts' were a rural and anti-materialist people in marked contrast to their dull, consumerist English neighbours. In 1882 Matthew Arnold (Cornish on his mother's side) could depict Ulster, in contradistinction in his view to rural, Celtic-Catholic Ireland, as a progressive 'Protestant north' where Anglo-Saxon civilization, economic as well as cultural, existed in 'full force'.[28] As recently as the 1940s and 1950s the writer Hugh Shearman could, according to Gillian McIntosh, present 'readers with an image of [industrial] Northern Ireland as a centre of culture and progression and modernity'.[29] But for Eamon de Valera, architect of Irish independence, rurality was idyllic, not backward:

> That Ireland which we dreamed of would be the home of a people who valued material wealth only as a basis of right living, of a people who were satisfied with frugal comfort and devoted their leisure to things of the spirit; a land whose countryside would be bright and cosy homesteads, whose fields and villages would be joyous with the sounds of industry [*sic*: he means hard work], the romping of sturdy children, the contests of athletic youths, the laughter of comely maidens; whose firesides would be forums of the wisdom of serene old age.[30]

Language (in this case, Irish) was central to such a vision. So it was in Wales, where images of Wales, and thus Welsh national sentiment, were built increasingly around an assumed link between rurality and the Welsh language. D.J. Davies, then Plaid Cymru's agriculture spokesman, wrote in 1937 that 'Placing the people back on the land is not only appropriate but is essential if the Welsh nation is to live . . . a nation with its roots in the country and the soil'.[31] In the following year, Saunders Lewis could insist that the urban south of his country must 'for the sake of the moral health of Wales and for the moral and physical welfare of its population . . . be de-industrialised'.[32] Such a view crept into Welsh historiography, Gwyn 'Cairo' Williams observing, for example, that 'To the people of Cardiganshire the glow of the furnaces of Dowlais, which they could see in the night sky from their hilltops, symbolised a kind of hell'.[33] But Gwyn Alf Williams fretted at the way in which narratives of Welsh history depicted the industrialization of South Wales as somehow 'unnatural', and he complained at the manner in which the English-speaking majority of the urbanized coalfields were so often 'written out' of that history.[34]

His objections prompted the academic intervention of Dai Smith, who not only attempted the rehabilitation of South Wales in Welsh historiography but shed new light on the complexities and contradictions of modern Welsh identity, emphasizing spatial dimensions as well as cultural: 'The quintessential nature of Welshness this [twentieth] century is that of divided sensibility . . . The borders of "Wales" are mapped out differently in the diversity of the Welsh mind; and yet they still overlap.'[35]

By the time Christopher Harvie was speaking at Aberystwyth in 2000, such a view, if not yet commonplace, was at least gaining wider currency and attracting widespread discussion. The notion of the 'industrial Celt' tumbled out of such debate, acknowledging the tensions and oppositions sketched above but also noting that 'industrialization' was in fact, like it or not, a central component of the modern 'Celtic' experience. A glance at Cornwall's history would have revealed an exemplar but few cared to look that way. If they had, they would have viewed debates about identity formation and re-formation in the eras of industrialization and de-industrialization, of Revivalist predictions and contrasting images of pre-industrial, industrial and indeed post-industrial Cornwall.

Harvie, pondering the negative aspects of 'the post-industrial politics of the former menials of the steam engine', saw in the violent contemporary history of Northern Ireland the worst examples of such negativity, inferring that Ulster's experience today could become that of other parts of the 'North Atlantic *littoral*' tomorrow and intimating that the province's relatively early de-industrialization might be part of the explanation for this: 'Was it Ulster's fate to reach this stage somewhat faster than elsewhere?'.[36] If he had looked at Cornwall, he would not have found violence but he would have discovered deleterious post-industrial socio-economic conditions that disadvantaged local people in employment, health and especially housing where many were trapped in the low-wage/high house price nexus. He would have found one of the poorest regions in the European Union and disquietingly high levels of powerlessness and frustration, vented occasionally in outbursts such as John Angarrack's *Breaking the Chains*.[37] Just as Cornwall and the Cornish were the all-too-often invisible examples of the 'industrial Celt', so they were too of the 'post-industrial Celt'.

Be that as it may, one of the few external commentators to observe the comparative importance for other 'Celtic' areas of recent work on Cornish identity re-formation is Máiréad Nic Craith who, picking up on the complexities and paradoxes of the Cornish situation, notes that in Northern Ireland 'an exploration of the Celtic dimension

illustrates that the heritage of the Region is often shared and sometimes divided',[38] with socio-economic change mirrored in changes in
cultural identities. James Vernon, too, has acknowledged recent work
in Cornwall on Cornish identities, though he is somewhat dismissive of
it as 'the determined efforts of a new generation of Cornish nationalist
historians', his own efforts signally failing to note or understand the
significance of the industrial era in moulding Cornish identity. But it
has been left to Amy Hale to offer a more explicit illustration of the
importance of Cornwall and the Cornish in understanding modern
constructions of Celticity. Writing in Harvey *et al.*'s collection *Celtic
Geographies*, published in 2002, she compared 'differing moral
geographies' of the Cornish landscape with the aim of juxtaposing
two contrasting, sometimes conflicting and occasionally complementary imaginings of 'Celtic Cornwall': that of the indigenous 'ethnic
Cornish' and that of outsiders drawn to Cornwall in search of 'Celtic
spirituality'. Although the 'ethnic Cornish' construction might include
powerful Revivalist elements, including the familiar aspects of rurality
and language, sharing too with 'Celtic spiritualists' an enthusiasm for
ancient standing stones and holy wells, it was also located firmly within
the realms of the 'industrial Celt'. As Hale explained:

> Many [ethnic] Cornish view the remains of Cornwall's
> industrial past—such as abandoned tin mines, and to a lesser
> degree the debris left from clay mining known as 'tips'—as
> icons of Cornishness of which they are proud . . . Although
> today the abandoned mines are not icons of the Celtic revival
> in Cornwall in the same way that the Cornish language and
> the annual gathering of Cornish bards known as the Gorseth
> may be, there is no doubt that the remains of native industry
> are embraced by revivalists and underscore a Cornish sense of
> ethnic difference—a difference that is often expressed within
> the discourse of Celticity.[39]

Moreover, '[t]hese industrial areas are recognised as part of the
Cornish heartland, and have acquired great symbolic value by virtue
of their importance in Cornish cultural and economic development.
The discarded mine stacks are emblematic of a past Celtic vitality,
almost as sacred to some Cornish people as the megalithic monuments.'[40] Here identification of the 'industrial Celt' is explicit, showing
how, despite the ostensibly oppositional nature of 'Celt' and
'industrial', the relationship between the two has been renegotiated in
post-industrial Cornwall to create a new synthesis (almost symbiosis)
within a renewed discourse of 'Celticity'. Significantly, although this

renegotiation became overt in the twentieth century, especially since 1945, it seeds were sown (as Deacon has argued convincingly) in the industrial period itself, hinting that oppositional barriers were not as impervious as people then and now have imagined. This renegotiation has also, of course, been noticed by academic commentators (in Cornwall at least), informing their analyses of modern Cornish identities.

'IMAGINING THE FISHING'

But if, with one or two exceptions, these analyses have yet to impact fully upon the wider examinations of 'industrial Celtic' identities, then one must observe too that even within Cornwall there is still much work to do. In his recent article 'Imagining the Fishing', Deacon turns his attention to the fishing communities of West Cornwall, looking afresh at the Newlyn School of painters and examining the motives of those outside artists drawn to the Penwith peninsula in the late nineteenth and twentieth centuries.[41] In so doing, he reminds us of the School's importance in constructing a particular 'imagining' of the fishing communities, a construction which, despite the modernization that had attended the fishing industry, was essentially 'non-industrial' in its depiction of Newlyn and environs. Indeed, we may observe that largely as a result of this depiction the fishing communities and their industry have been subtly removed from the dominant 'mino-centric' (to use the phrase coined by Sharron Schwartz) view of industrial Cornwall, a process encouraged by the Cornish themselves (with their view of mining as central to industrial identity) but pursued strongly by outside artists who 'co-opted' the fishing communities for their own designs.

And if we have allowed our own 'imaginings' of those fishing communities to be coloured by those artists, so we have been complicit in writing fishing out of the history of nineteenth-century Cornwall, or at least confining it to the margins and the footnotes. Of course, there have been important studies by local historians such as Cyril Noall, John Corin and Tony Pawlyn, while the imminent *Victoria County History* project promises to focus in part on Newlyn and Mount's Bay. But, in probing the identity of nineteenth-century Cornwall, we have in our generalization that 'Cornwall was mining, and mining was Cornwall' failed to consider fully the place of fishing communities— both in the overall complexity of Cornish territorial identity (the Cornish arms sports a miner *and* a fisherman) and, crucially, in the place-specific identities of particular parts of Cornwall. Recent commentaries by Bernard Deacon, Sharron Shwartz, Ronald Perry and others, while noting the importance of Cornwall-wide generalizations, have also called for intra-Cornwall comparisons and micro-scale studies. Cornwall's fishing communities lend themselves to such an approach, not least from the perspective of Cornish identity—or identities. After all, it was in the fishing communities of the far-west that the Cornish language lingered longest, informing the dialects of English as they developed, and tied-in with a folk culture which to some degree is with us still but is under-researched and imperfectly understood.

But if the fishing communities have not received the attention they deserve, then the same may be said of Cornwall's maritime history as a whole. Again, one may point to a number of particular contributions, from wreck and rescue to smuggling and trading, but there is as yet no over-arching narrative of Cornwall's maritime history, let alone specific consideration of the importance of the maritime experience to Cornish identity—except, perhaps, in the context of emigration. This is in marked contrast to neighbouring Devon and to the Channel Islands, where comprehensive surveys exist already, although the preliminary work by the late Stephen Fisher in marshalling a team of specialists to conduct such a project may yet bear fruit. The opening of the National Maritime Museum at Falmouth must be surely an important stimulus to the study of maritime Cornwall, while the sophistication that has been achieved thus far in the study of industrial Cornwall demands further consideration of the maritime dimension in the late eighteenth and nineteenth centuries if this progress is to be maintained. Perhaps there is even room for Cornish Studies to trail-blaze the notion of the 'maritime Celt', building upon Barry Cunliffe's 2001 volume *Facing the Ocean: The Atlantic and its Peoples* and returning again to E.G. Bowen's 1969 book *Saints, Seaways and Settlements in the Celtic Lands* —albeit with the benefit of modern perspectives and recent scholarship.

CONCLUSION

Be that as it may, there are rich pickings for those who would wish to look again at the identity (or identities) of industrial Cornwall. For example, the 'mino-centric' and male-oriented nature of much of modern Cornish culture (everything from rugby football to male voice choirs), and the scholarship that has addressed it, has until very recently excluded explicit considerations of gender, though Cornish Studies as a discipline has moved firmly of late to address that imbalance. That said, feminist perspectives are in their infancy and, with relatively few Cornish Studies practitioners actively engaged, 'tokenism' and 'lip-service' remain a real danger.

Equally, post-industrial Cornwall, with its curious hybrid and synthetic identities, is a 'keenly lode' for Cornish researchers, no longer perhaps the marginal tale of a marginal place and people but rather an exemplar of the wider malaise of the 'North Atlantic *littoral*' identified by Christopher Harvie. Here Cornwall may have that wide comparative relevance that we seek, not only in providing traces of the anomic culture postulated by Harvie but in engaging more directly in consideration of the changing discourses of 'Celticity' in the transition from industrial to post-industrial society. For all the objections of linguistic conservatives, the term 'Celtic' now has widespread and diverse currency. As Edward J. Cowan has noted, 'For good or ill the Celtic label is now well established and no amount of flytings between archaeologists, linguists and historians will change that fact'. Although Cowan exhibited a healthy, critical scepticism of 'the Celtic craze of the later twentieth century . . . [with its] clamjamfry of nonsense that is now popularly deemed to constitute part of Celtic heritage', he was also shrewd and wise enough to acknowledge that if the twentieth century was thus 'the Celtic century', then in the twenty-first this all-pervasive 'Celticity' was a phenomenon 'which craves the attention of scholarly investigation rather than the arrogance of academic dismissal'.[42] In Cornwall, this is a view that has already won adherents, where the case for examining the transition from industrial to post-industrial society within changing discourses of Celticity is already well made but where there remains much to be done if Cornwall is to continue to capture and maintain the attention of scholars elsewhere in the Celtic world and beyond.

NOTES AND REFERENCES

1. *Guardian*, 15 December 2001.
2. A.K. Hamilton Jenkin, *The Cornish Miner*, London, 1927, republished Newton Abbot, 1923; John Rowe, *Cornwall in the Age of the Industrial Revolution*, Liverpool, 1953, republished St Austell, 1993; D.B. Barton, *A History of Copper Mining in Cornwall and Devon*, Truro, 1968; D.B. Barton, *A History of Tin Mining and Smelting in Cornwall*, Truro, 1965, republished Exeter, 1989; D.B. Barton, *The Cornish Beam Engine*, Truro, 1969, republished Exeter, 1989; Cyril Noall, *Botallack*, Truro, 1972; Cyril Noall, *Levant: The Mine Beneath the Sea*, Truro, 1970; Cyril Noall, *Geevor*, Penzance, 1983; W.H. Pascoe, *The History of the Cornish Copper Company*, Redruth, n.d. *c.* 1982; John Keast, *The King of Mid-Cornwall: The Life of Joseph Thomas Treffry, 1782–1850*, Redruth, 1982; Jim Lewis, *A Richly Yielding Piece of Ground: The Story of Fowey Consols Mine*, St Austell, 1997; Clive Carter, *Cornish Engineering 1801–2001: Two Centuries of Industrial Excellence in Camborne*, Camborne, 2001.
3. Richard Burton, *Richard Trevithick: Giant of Steam*, London, 2000.
4. Roger Burt, with Peter Waite and Ray Burnley, *Cornish Mines*, Exeter, 1987, p. ix.

5. Maxine Berg, *The Age of Manufacturers 1700–1820*, London, 1983, p. 125.
6. Eric Richards, 'Margins of the Industrial Revolution', in Patrick O'Brien and Roland Quinault (eds), *The Industrial Revolution and British Society*, Cambridge, 1993.
7. Stephen Fisher and Michael Havinden. 'The Long-Term Evolution of the Economy of South West England from Autonomy to Dependence', in M.A. Havinden, J. Queniart and J. Stanyer (eds), *Centre and Periphery: Cornwall and Devon Compared*, Exeter, 1991, p. 76.
8. Fisher and Havinden, 1991, p. 80.
9. Dai Smith, *Wales! Wales?*, London, 1984, p. 17.
10. Hugh Kearney, *The British Isles: A History of Four Nations*, Cambridge, 1989.
11. Sidney Pollard, *Peaceful Conquest: The Industrialisation of the British Isles, 1760–1970*, Oxford, 1981, p. 14.
12. Philip Payton, *The Making of Modern Cornwall: Historical Experience and the Persistence of 'Difference'*, Redruth, 1992; Bernard Deacon, 'The Reformation of Territorial Identity: Cornwall in the late Eighteenth and Nineteenth Centuries', unpublished Ph.D. thesis, Open University, 2001.
13. Stein Rokkan and Derek W. Unwin (eds), *The Politics of Territorial Identity: Studies in European Regionalism*, London, 1982, p. 37.
14. Sidney Tarrow, *Between Centre and Periphery: Grassroots Politicians in Italy and France*, New Haven, 1977.
15. Ronald Perry, *Cornish History Network Newsletter*.
16. Payton, 1992, p. 92.
17. *Chambers Journal*, 17 February 1861; Philip Payton, *The Cornish Miner in Australia: Cousin Jack Down Under*, Redruth, 1984, p. 99.
18. Bernard Deacon, '"The Hollow Jarring of the Distant Steam Engine": Images of Cornwall between West Barbary and Delectable Duchy', in Ella Westland (ed.), *Cornwall: The Cultural Construction of Peace*, Penzance, 1997, p. 7.
19. Deacon, 2001, p. 5.
20. William Borlase, *Antiquities Historical and Monumental of the County of Cornwall*, London, 1754 and 1769, pp. 42–4.
21. Forescue Hitchins and Samuel Drew, *The History of Cornwall*, Helston, 1824, p. 725.
22. Deacon, 2001, p. 6.
23. Francis Harvey, *Autobiography of Zethar: St Phillockias, Cornu-waille, England*, Durban, 1867, p. 29.
24. *West Briton*, 1881.
25. Deacon, 2001, pp. 331–2.
26. Deacon, 2001, pp. 337.
27. Christopher Harvie, 'Larry Doyle and Captain MacWhirr: The Engineer and the Celtic Fringe', in Geraint H. Jenkins (ed.), *Cymru a'r Cymry 2000: Wales and the Welsh 2000*, Aberystwyth, 2001, p. 126.
28. Cited in James Loughlin, *Ulster Unionism and British National Identity Since 1885*, London, 1995, p. 24.

29. Cited in Gilliam McIntosh, *The Force of Culture: Unionist Identities in Twentieth-Century Ireland*, Cork, 1999.
30. Cited in Michael O'Henry, 'Institutions for the Promotion of Indigenious Music: The Case for Ireland's *Comhaltas Ceoltoiri Eirann*' *Ethnomusicology* 33.1, 1992, p. 69.
31. Cited in Smith, 1984, p. 105.
32. Cited in Smith, 1984, p. 105.
33. Gwyn Williams, *The Land Remembers: A View of Wales*, London, 1977, p. 185.
34. See Geraint H. Jenkins, *The People's Historian: Professor Gwyn A. Williams, 1925–1995*, Aberystwyth, 1996, p. 7.
35. Smith, 1984, p. 168.
36. Harvie, 2001, p. 140.
37. John Angarrack, *Breaking the Chains*, Camborne, 1999.
38. Máiréad Nic Craith, *Plural Identities: Singular Narratives—The Case of Northern Ireland*, Oxford, 2002, p. 92.
39. Amy Hale, 'Whose Celtic Cornwall? The Ethnic Cornish Meet Celtic Spirituality', in David C. Harvey Rhys Jones, Neil McInroy and Christine Milligan (eds), *Celtic Geographies: Old Culture, New Times*, London, 2002, p. 164.
40. Hale, 2002, p. 164.
41. Bernard Deacon, 'Imagining the Fishing: Artists and Fishermen in Late Nineteenth Century Cornwall', *Rural History* 12.2, 2001, pp. 159–78.
42. Edward J. Cowan, 'The Invention of Celtic Scotland', in E.J. Cowan and R. Edward McDonald (eds), *Alba: Celtic Scotland in the Medieval Era*, East Linton, 2000, p. 23.

CORNISH MIGRATION STUDIES: AN EPISTEMOLOGICAL AND PARADIGMATIC CRITIQUE

Sharron P. Schwartz[1]

INTRODUCTION

Migration has, without a doubt, become a central plank in the platform upon which the 'new Cornish historiography' has been constructed. Barely a year goes by without the publication of a new book or article somewhere in the world that reveals more about the epic story of Cornish migration.[2] For Cornwall was, according to demographer Dudley Baines, one of the leading migration regions in England and Wales, losing in the last quarter of the nineteenth century 118,500 people: a figure representing over 40 per cent of its young adult males and over 25 per cent of its young adult females. These percentages, when analysed within the broader context of England and Wales, make it possible that gross emigration could have included about 20 per cent of the male Cornish-born population in each ten-year period from 1861 to 1900 and about 10 per cent of the female. This would make the Cornish male by far the largest group of native emigrants to leave the shores of England and Wales and the Cornish female a close second. These figures are all the more remarkable given that Cornwall's population never exceeded half a million in the century after 1815—so remarkable, in fact, that Dudley Baines has concluded that Cornwall was 'probably an emigration region comparable with any in Europe'.[3]

The reasons for the degree of emigration from Cornwall, according to Baines, are not difficult to find—being 'obviously connected with the decline of copper and tin mining after the crisis of

1866'. Between 1860 and 1870 Cornwall was the only 'English' county where there were more lifetime male emigrants than lifetime internal migrants. Cornish miners were, he notes, more likely to emigrate than to move to other parts of Britain. Indeed, Cornwall lost (net of returns) over 44 per cent of the male population between the ages of 15 and 24 overseas, as compared with just under 30 per cent to other parts of England and Wales. Yet, he also states that even during this period it is unlikely that more than half of the Cornish emigrants had been dependent on mining. This presumably means that Cornish emigration *would have been substantial without the miners* and comparable to that from Devon.[4]

Here Baines makes an incredibly important point, for the majority of studies of Cornish migration have tended to be particularly 'mino-centric', to coin a phrase. Although mining, either directly or indirectly, accounted for much of Cornish migration, dwelling on the migration brought about by the mining industry has obscured the occupational diversity of demographic flows, particularly of agricultural movement, which was quite significant in the early nineteenth century as Payton has highlighted.[5] Added to this, in spite of work by Payton, Deacon and Schwartz which clearly shows that migration from Cornwall commenced well before mining decline in the late nineteenth century, common consensus persists in connecting Cornish migration to a crisis in the mining industry from the mid-1860s onwards.[6] And these are only two of a number of factors that problematize an approach to the subject of migration from Cornwall.

Noting the lack of a conceptual framework that adequately explains the complex nature of Cornish migration, this paper examines the subject from new perspectives offering theories recently developed in the context of Third World labour migration to more advanced nations. Firstly, it contrasts and then challenges the traditional dichotomy of a vibrant Cornish diaspora and a moribund homeland by introducing the concept of a dynamic, fluid, transnational migrant circuit which captures complex migration interactions spanning multiple settings. Secondly, it compares the conventional neo-classical interpretation of individual decision-making with a paradigm of collective decision-making by families or communities that involves risk-diversification. Thirdly, the role of women, largely omitted or peripheralized in narratives of Cornish migration, is revised and the gender imbalance in current migration literature addressed. Fourthly, the paper questions the negative treatment of remittance-use postulated by Cornish historians and offers a more positive approach, where remittances help to regenerate and diversify an economy affected by the collapse of mining. Fifthly, it modifies the conventional pessimistic treatment of return migrants by offering insights into the positive effects of social remittances and human capital introduced to sending communities by return migrants. Finally, it suggests the need to move away from 'mino-centric' and homogenous approaches to Cornish migration and highlights the need for quantitative evidence examining demographic flows at various spatial levels.

MIGRATION MODELS

One of the main problems in international migration studies has been the development of an all-embracing model that might adequately explore the complexity of factors prompting migration decisions.[7] Migration studies is not a specific social science discipline, but rather an interdisciplinary field of studies that uses some aspects of the theory and methodology of numerous disciplines, ranging from economics, political science, sociology and anthropology to demography, geography and of course history, reflecting the fact that the migratory process itself cannot be compartmentalized into specific components, but is driven by myriad factors affecting an individual's life. Confusingly, each social science has a range of paradigms with differing theoretical frameworks, methodology, research logic and research objectives. Little wonder, then, that there has been a failure to adopt a generally agreed upon body of theory and methods in migration studies in general, let alone within Cornish Studies.

Indeed, Deacon has highlighted the deficiencies of its conceptual framework: 'While the basic story . . . has been covered, although often on an almost entirely anecdotal and micro-level, there have been few attempts to view this as part of a global network of Cornish emigration or to place it in its wider context'.[8] Payton, too, has noted the need to move away from consideration of the impact of the Cornish overseas towards a more 'Coru-centric' overview in which the changing nature of emigration over time could be seen in proper perspective. He stresses the need to set a new research agenda 'which might emphasize synthesis (the drawing together of hitherto compartmentalised strands) as well as identifying specific socio-economic phenomena such as "emigration culture", "emigration trade", and "dependency culture"'.[9] So far, the key models that attempt to explain Cornish migration have been those offered by Burke and Payton.

Burke states that Cornish migration was far more complex than simple push–pull factors suggest, and notes the lack of a general theory of migration beyond the broadest generality. Although she argues against viewing Cornish workers, particularly miners, as coerced labour, she offers little more than setting the Cornish migration experience firmly within a neo-Marxist paradigm of capitalist exploitation. According to this hypothesis, Cornish labour migrants became, in effect, pawns at the whim of a global capitalist market that shifted constantly as the demands for labour waxed and waned in tune with the rise and decline of various metalliferous mining regions: 'a segment of the labour force that could be flexibly deployed wherever there was a need for labour to enable commodity production to expand'.[10]

Payton seeks reasons for the extraordinary extent of Cornish migration, and he argued initially—in his important work, *The Making of Modern Cornwall*—that one of the chief reasons was that Cornwall's economy was fatally flawed. Overspecialized, incomplete and imperfect, founded mainly on mining and associated industries, it could not survive the mining decline of the late nineteenth century, becoming one of the first regions at the forefront of the Industrial Revolution in Britain to de-industrialize. A period of economic and social marginalization ensued, argued Payton, ushering in what he has termed the era of 'second peripheralism' of which the 'great migration' was the most visible attribute.[11] According to his hypothesis (and like Burke's, it presents a neo-Marxist perspective), Cornwall had passed from being a key industrial region to one on the periphery as the centre of economic gravity in Britain shifted to the South East of England, leaving Cornwall in crisis.

However, the work of economic historian Pat Hudson, a proponent of the industrial systems perspective, offers another possible and less pessimistic explanation for the migration of Cornish labour. According to her, the organization of work and work practice prevalent in successfully expanding industrial regions often comes to influence the methods of an entire sector.[12] This would help to explain the migration in the very early nineteenth century of thousands of Cornish miners and associated tradesmen particularly to Latin America: they were travelling from a dynamic thrusting industrial region that was renowned for its development of hard-rock mining and steam technology. Highly sought after, they took the work practices of the Cornish mining industry world-wide over the succeeding decades.

Yet, it is incontrovertible that by the latter stages of the nineteenth century the centre of economic gravity had radically shifted so that Cornwall was no longer a transmitter of capital, skills and technology, but rather a receiver of them. Capital, ideas and innovative methods of production in mining and engineering were increasingly introduced to Cornwall, often by returning migrants, from new metalliferous mining areas overseas, so that by the 1920s Cornwall had even ceased to be a major labour-sending region. The same was true of other branches of industry—food processing, hotel management, dynamite manufacture, quarrying, shipbuilding and agriculture.[13]

Here, Frank Thistlethwaite's model of the stages of labour migration can provide a useful paradigm to explain the migration of Cornish labour. For in order to understand what factors could have contributed to this remarkable turn-around, we might turn our attention to the dissemination of technology through the migration of technicians—an aspect of migration history that Thistlethwaite noted in 1960 as deserving of a great deal of further study. He states that British industrial leadership, capital, commerce and trade routes combined to encourage an unprecedented emigration of British technicians across the world, who provided the essential *cadre* of skills. This included not just the British colonies that were keen to attract immigrant able-bodied labour, but also the informal empire: the countries not a part of the British Empire but nonetheless within the sphere of British political, economic and cultural influence. He notes the case of Cornish miners, whom he argues 'provided the first, aristocratic generation of mine captains in the lead, tin and copper mines not only of Illinois and Michigan, but of Bolivia, the Rand, Broken Hill, sometimes moving from continent to continent in pursuit of their esoteric craft'.[14]

In the Thistlethwaite model here are three essential stages of migration: firstly the migration of the creative innovators who introduced new technologies; secondly, and following rapidly behind, the hundreds of skilled operatives who usually settled into communities, some for only a short time before returning to their place of origin, or moving on to another region; and finally, the phase when the skilled operatives and innovators are no longer required, superseded by native and/or cheaper labour. When this occurs, according to Thistlethwaite, only those in managerial posts remain and the migration of technicians comes to an end.[15] This does not necessarily conflict with Payton's perspective; in fact it adds another complementary explanation for Cornish labour migration. At the same time (in the mid-nineteenth century) that Cornwall was losing its drive and dynamism which Hudson states characterized thrusting industrial regions, so the Cornish overseas found themselves competing with and being slowly replaced by native labour.

THE 'DIASPORA' DICHOTOMY

One of the key problems to beset Cornish migration studies has been the use of a vibrant Cornish diaspora on the one hand and a stricken Cornish homeland on the other, rather than a dynamic paradigm of a transmigrant circuit connected to transnational communities in which out-migration, onward movement, return migration and repeat migration interact with each other.[16] Here one might question the use of the term 'diaspora', which is perhaps inappropriate to describe the Cornish migration experience and has probably contributed to the unduly pessimistic interpretations of Cornwall's 'Great Migration'. Indeed, Hamilton Jenkin and other notable writers of Cornish migration saw the movement of people from Cornwall as inextricably linked to mining decline. The language is evocative: Hamilton Jenkin talks of the 'exodus' and 'severed connections' while his contemporary Baring Gould comments on the engine houses 'abandoned' by miners who had gone abroad.[17]

Although the traditional meaning of 'diaspora' taken from the Greek, 'to sow over', was associated with migration and colonization with trade, commercial and cultural linkages, in modern parlance, as Robin Cohen has noted, it conjures up something quite different. Diaspora today evokes thoughts of crisis, enforced exile, political upheaval and loss, a collective tragedy that has beset ethnic groups such as the Jews, Gypsies, Armenians or Palestinians.[18] Perhaps, therefore, the term 'diaspora' is best reserved for a specific kind of transnational tie involving expulsion or involuntary exile, based on a lost or imagined homeland that is still to be established.[19] Consequently, there has arisen a tendency to polarize interpretations of the Cornish migration experience: the non-migrant who remained in Cornwall and those who left—the 'exiles'.

The danger of this polarized perspective is that it inevitably leads to viewing the emigrant as lost to the 'homeland', an exile who had rejected his or her native community for a new and better environment. More importantly, this often involved the migrant severing links with his or her sending community in the process. Indeed, Hamilton Jenkin is aware of the 'Cornwalls beyond Cornwall', but he sees such communities as operating independently of Cornwall itself. In his seminal work, *The Cornish Miner*, the two worlds manifest similar behaviours, beliefs and ways of life, yet function separately, while A.L. Rowse in uncharacteristically emotive prose in his *A Cornish Childhood* talks of 'home[s] broken up' and the 'tragedy' of men flocking off to South Africa.[20] This antithesis in interpretation has been superbly captured by Payton: 'we have striven to celebrate the triumphs, to admire the stoicism of our ancestors . . . on the other [hand] we have mourned the scattering of the Cornish, the dereliction and depopulation of Cornwall itself'.[21]

Indeed, a vast empirical edifice has been built around the experiences of 'Cousin Jack' communities overseas—the term taken to mean all Cornish male migrants but which is mainly associated with emigrant Cornish miners—the filio-pietism of which contrasts with the relatively sparse and invariably bleak discourses of those who remained.

Here the deficiencies in Cornish migration literature become apparent. Previous work has dwelt almost exclusively on demographic flows rather than on migration structures and the interdependence of place of origin and destination. For it is important to remember that migration not only informs us of the society to which people migrate, but also the society from whence they migrated, and crucially the interaction connecting the two, in the networks of migration promotion.[22] The third of these points in particular—the socio-economic effects of the global interactions between sending and receiving communities—has been overlooked or lost within the polarized paradigm offered in Cornish migration discourses.

However, replacing the static concept of diaspora with the fluid, multi-faceted notion of transnationalism allows us to explore more fully the complexity of the Cornish migration phenomenon. Migrants do not necessarily lose touch with their sending communities, as many Third World studies have shown. Several factors, including the ease of travel and communication, the role that migrants can play in sending-country economies and political futures of sending countries, heighten the intensity and durability of modern transnational communities, within which migrants remain involved in the affairs of their sending communities.[23] Connections between sending and receiving countries grow stronger, as transmigrants and their society of origin forge a dense web of transnational relations that unites them in a continuous transterritorial social formation.[24] Thus emerges a 'transnational public sphere'.[25]

Habermas, in his theory of 'communicative action', defines a public sphere as a space where citizens come together to debate their common affairs, contest meanings and negotiate claims.[26] Public spheres may disintegrate if migrants sever their homeland ties and completely assimilate into their host communities, or they can develop into a transnational collectivity where both migrants and non-migrants come together periodically to articulate collective claims. Cornish observers have long recognized the transnational nature of migration. 'If we took into account the Cornish and their children outside', the Cornish MP Leonard Courtney told the Midland Cornish Society in 1900, 'there is really a greater Cornwall outside than inside.' The editor of the *West Briton*, reporting the speech, added that 'the Cornish outside become more Cornish than the Cornish themselves'.[27] 'Few individuals or institutions in Cornwall were not touched by the effects of the "Great Migration"', notes Payton. Towards the end of the nineteenth century, he argues, 'a discernible Cornish "international identity" emerged . . . one that was voiced in many parts of the globe through insistent declarations of loyalty to Cornwall from "Cornish Associations" . . . and which was exhibited at many levels—most notably in the press'.[28]

This flowering of an international Cornish consciousness can be interpreted as evidence of a transnational collectivity. Although Payton is aware of its existence, his interpretation veers towards pessimism, focusing on the negative effects of a dependency culture, mourning the scattering of the Cornish and the dereliction of Cornwall itself in the wake of mining failure. He does not consider the potential benefits of a developing transnational collectivity, which can be viewed, not just as a vehicle to mobilize financial remittances for communities back home, but also as an arena for the dissemination of *social remittances*. This migration-driven form of cultural diffusion encompasses new ideas, behaviours and identities that flow from receiving to sending country communities.[29]

But Payton is not alone in this interpretation. Rowse mentions in some detail the links that bound the mining villages near St Austell to the urban centres of South Africa—Maritzburg, Johannesburg, Kimberley, Cape Town. He notes the regular comings and goings of the migrants, the receipt of letters, postcards and books, the remittances sent home to wives, the exchange of newspapers and journals and the rise of Cornish associations and societies in the Transvaal—'people knew what was going on in South Africa rather better than what was happening "up the country" '.[30] This is clear evidence of a transnational collectivity, with people raising families across borders and emigrants remaining interested and closely connected with the affairs of their sending communities.

As the recent work of social network theorists such as Monica Boyd, Peggy Levitt and Graeme Hugo has highlighted, where dense migration networks develop and the flow of people, capital and goods become so widespread and the impact of migration so informative, migrants *and* non-migrants alike participate in the transnational nature of life.[31] So it was, then, that even those Cornish who had never ventured overseas viewed America and South Africa as almost 'the parish next door' in the late nineteenth and early twentieth centuries. Indeed, by the late nineteenth century Cornish migration was so diffuse that transnational communities sometimes spanned multiple settings. Hence the interest among a group of Cornish immigrant miners in Butte, Montana, of a strike among miners in the Johannesburg gold mines, South Africa, where many had previously worked, or had family connections.[32]

3. *A Cornish emigration poster from the late 1830s, providing important*
information for individuals and families contemplating their futures.
Reproduced courtesy of the Royal Institution of Cornwall.

CASH OR CULTURE? MIGRATION DECISIONS REVIEWED
A second problem is an undue reliance upon models of individualistic
decision-making driven by expectations of higher incomes. A strong
economic rationale has been identified by Roger Burt and Sandra
Kippen for the overseas migration of the Cornish in the nineteenth
century, particularly of miners: alternative employment in Cornwall
was poorly paid. Their hard-rock skills and knowledge were largely
non-transferable and in limited demand in the rest of the United
Kingdom. Importantly, the labour market for their highly specialized

occupation had become a global one early in the nineteenth century: this aided their migration overseas. Overseas, the Cornish could expect to earn two to three times more as miners, and perhaps ten times more as supervisors of native labour. Even taking into account the probability of a shorter working life because of the hazards of mining, economic logic favoured emigration overseas as the best strategy.[33] However, Burt and Kippen downplay the social factors that underpin migration decisions, for migration decisions are not driven by purely economic factors. For, as Boyd and Hugo have stressed, there is a need to move away from 'atomistic' neo-classical interpretations, where migrants are assumed to act in a totally individual manner, towards a collective decision-making process where broader macro-structural forces as well as those forces operating on the individual can be taken into account.

In Burt and Kippen's treatment of nineteenth-century migration decisions by Cornish miners, little consideration is given to the possibility of collective strategies in which members of a family or community are sent out to acquire social or entrepreneurial skills, as well as capital, which will enable the sending group(s) to survive and grow. In addition to the work of social network theorists such as Boyd and Hugo, work by proponents of the new economics of labour migration has emphasized that out-migration, onward migration and return migration may be interlinked, part of a conscious strategy of risk diversification and capital accumulation by households and communities.[34]

Oded Stark, more than anyone else, has done much to revise attitudes on migration by viewing it within the context of the household. The decision to sanction and finance the migration of an individual (or individuals) by either a family or a community has been interpreted as a form of insurance, of risk diversification of income sources—the head of the household or community spreading the risk by financing the migration of a few rather than risking the failure of an entire group.[35] Households, therefore, self-finance new production methods in order to overcome market failures in a self-enforcing, mutually interdependent, contractual arrangement between the family and the individual migrant. And in Cornwall's case, the lost labour effect was negligible, for as Ronald Perry has argued, with the failure of Cornwall's mining industry the migration of miners removed a redundant labour force.[36] A risk diversification strategy was hinted at by Damaris Rose in her article on household structure and subsistence in the mining communities of late-nineteenth-century Cornwall. But like Mark Brayshay (who analysed the effect of mining decline and migration on three Cornish communities) she adopts the traditional, pessimistic view of migration on the family: 'During the period of most severe industrial decline, there were . . . severe limitations on the possibility of entire families emigrating in order to keep the family going as an economic unit. Families fragmented, literally, in order to survive.'[37]

There is enormous diversity in migration processes and simplistic models such as the push–pull hypothesis are deficient in explaining who moved, why they chose to migrate, or why they migrated when they did. The extreme selectivity of who moved confirms the importance of asking questions about why some individuals of families became migrants while others remained in their localities, even in apparently similar circumstances. This raises the question of rational decision-making, with differences in the characteristics of individuals or their families influencing their responses to migration, as highlighted by Stephan Goetz.[38] This would be to some degree dependent on certain exogenous factors, such as access to information and migration networks. Those households or communities well-connected to kin and communities overseas are more likely to have access to superior information and would therefore have the greatest propensity to migrate. This perspective highlights the dynamics of social or personal networks based on family and households, a reminder that migration is as much a social product as an economic one, but nevertheless one that is an outcome of many factors that cross-cut each other.

In much Cornish migration literature the importance of the family's role and its significance in shaping migration decisions has not been elucidated. This seems a remarkable oversight, as the family is historically the quintessential unit of economic organization. In this instance, the family can be taken to extend beyond the nuclear family to encompass blood relations and in some instances members of close-knit communities related through marriage only, or long-term residents of families to whom there is no blood tie. As Hugo explains, as families attempted to survive in difficult circumstances, or even in order to improve their circumstances, they have traditionally opted for particular mobility strategies which maximized resources whilst minimizing risks.[39] And this leads on to the next important point of examination: the role of women in the migration decision and process.

WHATEVER HAPPENED TO 'COUSIN JENNY'?

The polarity of Cornish migration studies is emphasized yet again in the discussion of women. Firstly, women are usually assumed to migrate as part of a family unit. The majority of narratives of the Cornish overseas have tended to focus on mining settlements, in which

'Cousin Jenny', the female equivalent of 'Cousin Jack', has not received the attention bestowed upon her male counterpart. In recent years historians have begun to increase our awareness of the role of gender in mining communities. As E.P. Thompson famously rescued the working-class man from 'the enormous condescension of posterity',[40] so scholars of gender in the United States and Canada have highlighted the fact that the lives and contribution of women in mining communities can no longer be ignored, downplayed or disregarded as a secondary field of study.[41]

Traditionally, mining settlements have been perceived to be quintessentially patriarchal, with women largely cast as either shadowy or sensational figures who existed on the margins of those societies, for example as prostitutes, or as passive bystanders: the wives, sisters or mothers of miners. Documenting women's activities in the mining communities is considerably more difficult because of their invisibility. By and large, they did not fit into any of the categories devised by traditional historians: they did not venture underground, were not firemen, bankers, members of law enforcement agencies or political parties. Women are usually assumed to be economically inactive and as migrants were often not given an occupation in official statistics. This is because much of their work within both sending and receiving communities took place in the invisible economic sector—it was unpaid labour. Yet, there were women who ran businesses such as boarding houses, shops and schools, while some were even prospectors and miners in their own right, as the work of Susan Zanjani has shown. Those who migrated from an agricultural background to open up the wheat-lands of Northern America, South Africa and Australia were every bit as much pioneers as their men-folk. As Baines has shown, although Cornish women were less likely than men to migrate across international borders, they still accounted for significant demographic flows nationally: to other parts of England and Wales where, as Deacon has noted, they found employment in occupations such as domestic service.[42]

However intangible Cornish women's contribution to the 'Great Migration' is perceived to be, their importance has to be acknowledged. For as Janet Finn has argued in her work on the mining communities of Butte, Montana, and Chuquicamata, Chile, 'just as mining men wrested copper from the ground, women extracted and forged the resources of community from the raw materials at hand'.[43] Therefore, in crafting the everyday—baking, story-telling, helping in places of worship, with Cornish cultural events and kindergartens— women were upholding values and imperatives that were central to the continuation of Cornish customs and traditions overseas. Moreover, it was often women who maintained a vital link through letters home to family and friends in sending communities.

Secondly, and conversely, if Cornish women remained in their sending communities, they are cast as passive participants in the migration decision: it is the men who migrate and the women who wait.[44] Indeed, Gillian Burke, who first raised the question of gender in the Cornish metal mining industry,[45] has surprisingly little to say on the subject of gender and migration. Questioning why more women did not emigrate, she concludes rather tentatively that they probably did not want to but that the main reason was likely to have been economic.[46] Yet, family strategies involving remittances are often linked to gender roles and cultural values and have important demographic consequences such as delayed family formation and consequent effects on fertility rates.

In patriarchal societies, household strategies that do not involve the migration of women may not be made on the basis of economic rationality, but on the assumption, for example, that males are the breadwinners and females are dependent on them as mothers, spouses and daughters.[47] Indeed, Schwartz has noted that in late-nineteenth-century Cornwall the ideology of separate spheres took on an increasing importance and women's socio-economic role was redefined within strict parameters of accepted mores of femininity.[48] This in turn has important implications for residential patterns and household arrangements. Some sending communities with a high percentage of male migrants take on a more 'matrifocal' nature.[49] With absent fathers and husbands there are likely to be less traditional 'nuclear families' and more extended families: for example, sisters and their families cohabiting or daughters and their children moving back to reside with parents.[50]

However, in much Cornish migration literature one gains the impression that these women were somehow deeply impoverished by the departure of their men-folk. Jenkin even goes so far as to comment that the women at home 'were in some cases demoralised by the weekly drafts', but he does not qualify this statement with any evidence.[51] Dependent on their husbands' remittance cheques, they are left behind to head often large families. Yet, no one seems to have considered how liberating it might have been for women to be freed from long cycles of pregnancy and breast-feeding. As the heads of households, women assumed the role of decision-makers able to decide how to manage the sums of money that arrived via bankers' drafts, amounts that they were not accustomed to receive in Cornwall and that offered financial security for perhaps the first time. Many were doubtless empowered by this new-found freedom.

Moreover, although the migration pattern common from the mid-nineteenth century was that of the lone male 'bird of passage' (as opposed to the 'folk migrations' to the British colonies of the first half of the nineteenth century), this does not indicate the lack of female involvement in migration strategies. For viewing the family as collectively seeking to overcome economic constraints does not preclude female involvement. From this perspective, although women do not migrate in the same numbers as men, they are still active participants in the decision to sanction the migration of one or more family members and therefore intimately involved in the whole process.[52] Studies of migration must, like those of industrialization, be multifaceted and analysed through the lens of gender ideology. This highlights the need for more empirical research to examine how issues of gender might have historically impinged on the migration decision. Without a doubt, the time is long overdue for 'Cousin Jenny' to take her place along side that of 'Cousin Jack' in Cornish migration studies.

'GETTING BY AND MAKING DO'? THE IMPACT OF 'MIGRAPOUNDS'

Cornish migration studies have not moved much beyond the neo-classical model postulated by Michael Todaro. This concludes that the effects of international emigration on communities are largely negative, as higher living standards are achieved through the inflow of money from abroad rather than from economic expansion at home.[53] In Todaro's model this undermines the prospects for economic growth and is widely thought to reinforce a pattern of community dependence.[54] However, many early researchers either ignored or downplayed the role of remittances and, unduly influenced by the dependency theory, lacked a theoretical rationale that took account of complex migration development interactions. Negative income-multiplier effects are implicitly assumed for out-migration, generating a downward spiral of cumulative causation, as the departure of people reduce demand for local goods and services, leading to further business failures and outward movement. Deacon and Payton have also argued that the trauma of economic failure was reflected in an equally profound social and cultural transformation, a loss of the self-confidence and assertiveness that was once associated with mining ascendancy.[55]

Strangely enough, when remittances sent home are considered, the possibility of positive income-multiplier effects is ignored. Deacon and Payton recognize the size of the inflow of remittances and calculate that as much as £1 million a year—enough to keep an eighth of the Cornish population in basic standards of comfort—was flowing into

Cornwall around 1900 from the Transvaal alone.[56] However, the inflow of 'migrapounds' is assumed by some commentators to have been largely wasted, particularly by women, frittered away on mindless consumerism—pianos, furniture and clothing epitomized by the ostentatious ladies' ostrich feather hats that turned local chapels 'into a tournament of fashion'.[57] Yet an uneasy dichotomy is detectable, for a direct contrast to the 'mad spending' scenario is the 'miserly saving' response.[58] This has been picked up by Deacon, who argues that the decline of Cornwall's mining industry from the mid-nineteenth century marked for many what he describes as the inception of a poverty-ridden, drab existence of 'getting-by' and 'making-do': 'Cornish people were forced to come to terms with a declining industrial base. Under-employment and economic insecurity led to a culture of "making-do" as heroism in the face of grinding day to day hardship became a social virtue.'[59]

John Rowe also argues that emigration only solved or ameliorated individual problems and he argues that it actually increased social distress in some areas for families that had to live on meagre or irregular remittances, creating social inequality.[60] Pessimistic accounts such as these have more recently led historians like Gillian Burke, for example, to pass a damning verdict of the socio-economic effects of migration on Cornwall, even though, as she admits, more work has yet to be done on the interaction between migrants and their native communities. According to her, 'the consequences within Cornwall of this diaspora were almost wholly bad'.[61]

This negative treatment of the impact of remittance use upon sending communities is not, of course, a monopoly of Cornish writers. Many modern surveys of international migration and remittance use from Third World countries to advanced industrial nations have likewise concluded that foreign earnings are spent mainly on non-productive commodities—food, clothing, consumer goods, and housing. They note the divisive effect of migration on some communities, because not only does it spawn a dependency culture, but it also improves the material well-being of particular families without leading to sustainable economic growth within migrant communities.[62]

Moreover, poorer households face barriers to international migration in the form of high costs and inadequate information. As Oded Stark, J. Edward Taylor and Shlomo Yitzhaki have hypothesised, migration initially entails high costs and risks that are exceptionally high in the case of international migration. Therefore, the usual pattern sees the wealthier go first and begin to remit.[63] This tends initially to widen income inequalities, as poorer households with less opportunity to participate in income-generating activities at home have more of an incentive to send family members overseas yet are unable to do so. However, once access to migrant labour markets becomes diffused across the sending community households and migration networks develop, Douglas Massey, Luin Goldring and Jorge Durand have argued that the unequal effects of remittances is reversed.[64]

Remittances, therefore, need not be viewed pessimistically.[65] A growing number of researchers contend that financial remittances may, in certain circumstances, be a positive element, setting in motion a development dynamic by lessening constraints upon production and investment in sending regions.[66] Remittances from international labour migration free up financial and risk constraints on local production and can then play an important role in the promotion of economic growth and development. The economic scales balance out in time, as negative lost-labour effects are counter-balanced by positive investment within migrant households that yield new sources of income. Crucially, income and employment multipliers from remittances are fairly high and many of the indirect benefits are not just enjoyed by the migrant households themselves, but are shared with others in the community who provide them with goods and services which would be absent without international migration. In the new economics of labour migration therefore, emigration plus financial remittances may increase productivity in the sending communities by encouraging risk-averse households to undertake potentially productive investment: in other words, by enhancing, rather than reducing, the entrepreneurial culture.[67] These positive effects are more likely if the economic structure permits diversification, and if the financial infrastructure is capable of channelling small inflows of savings into business investment.[68]

The example of remittance use in Cornwall, referred to earlier, stressed the frivolous or at least expenditure 'to get by'. Expenditure upon ostrich feathers and pianos also implied a high leakage of money outside Cornwall with no benefit upon the local economy. But even here there would surely have been a favourable effect through the margins that went into the pockets of local milliners and shop-keepers. It seems probable, however, that the bulk of the money spent on consumption would go on basic necessities which would mean that a greater proportion stayed in the hands of local producers.

Remittances can in some cases allow communities to overcome capital constraints in the financing of places of worship, schools, housing and municipal improvements, including public parks, street lighting, sewerage systems, health centres and libraries. Demand for materials to build such community infrastructure stimulates the growth of local industries such as quarries, foundries and brick-works.

Schwartz and Parker demonstrated this with respect to Lanner, and Perry and Schwartz do likewise in their study of late Victorian Redruth.[69] Moreover, as Perry's studies have suggested, nineteenth-century Cornwall had both the social and economic infrastructure and the sophisticated banking system to cope with remittance-led development and the potential for economic diversification.[70]

THE 'RITE' OF RETURN

Next we focus on return migration, which has inexplicably been largely disregarded in migration literature and, therefore, lacks the depth of studies and theoretical models that have been applied to other areas of demography. Yet Baines has estimated that during the late nineteenth and early twentieth centuries almost a third of all European migrants returned to their areas of origin.[71] Three distinct phases of scholarship in return migration can be defined. The first focused on the push–pull factors of migration in the context of industrialization, which at least made some allowances for counter-flows of those who returned to their areas of origin.[72] The next phase interpreted return migration through the core–periphery model, where emigrants move from the under-developed peripheral regions to core industrial areas. Within this conceptual framework, return migration was seen as a form of feedback from receiving to sending communities which has certain effects upon the latter.[73] The third and most recent approach is currently being developed. This new model sees return migration as being a fundamental part of the migration cycle, not an endgame, but rather another phase in a dynamic, fluid circuit. Viewed within the context of globalization, areas of origin and destination are bound together in transnational spaces by migrants who construct and maintain simultaneous and multi-stranded relations that span multiple borders.[74]

However, before progressing further it is necessary to clarify the precise meaning of 'return migration', which by definition has been taken to mean a process involving the movement to one's country or area of origin either temporarily or for long periods, after a significant period in another country or region.[75] One of the key debates raised by Bovenkerk and Gmelch focuses around whether return migration is an admission of failure or represents some degree of success.[76] This is extremely difficult to generalize and Lewis has noted that migration selectivity must play a key role in studies concerned with measuring the impact of migration in both sending and receiving communities.[77] But the selectivity process itself is fraught with problems, for not enough is known about it, or its impacts upon sending communities.[78] It is problematic purely because it is multidimensional, but according to

Ammassari and Black it is possible to distinguish between two categories of migrants—skilled and unskilled—and to analyse which of the two manifest the greatest propensity to return.[79] For the latter, migration often represents a survival strategy with the migrants exercising little choice other than to migrate. The former group (the skilled migrants) is more predisposed to view migration as an advancement strategy and opportunity for upward social mobility.[80]

But do migrants leave their communities determined to return? An initial survey of Cornish migrant letters has been useful in helping to determine the intention of migrants, but they might not always be truthful, with some containing inflated accounts of migrant life or unduly discouraging views by jaundiced, unsuccessful immigrants, and should be treated with a degree of caution.[81] It seems reasonable to suggest that not all migrants set out with the intention of permanent settlement. Numerous Cornish migrants appear to have left with the intention of working away from home for a period of a few years in order to make enough money to return in a more secure financial position. Those connected to the mining industry, for example, were often recruited on short-term fixed contracts aided by occupational specificity. Yet if the original intention of migrants is more often than not assumed to have been one of permanent migration, then some scholars have argued that those who returned to their native communities have to be classed as failures. But Piore turns this supposition on its head by radically suggesting that if most migration is intended to be temporary, then staying represents a change of plans, perhaps suggesting that it is the failures that do not return to their native communities.[82]

For Gmelch the reality lies somewhere between these two extreme positions: return migrants are probably not great successes or great failures. The highly successful migrants are reluctant to return to their place of origin as they have little desire to forfeit a secure well-paid job and lifestyle, nor do they wish to be financially obligated to family or kin members upon their return. The most unsuccessful migrants seldom return as they would not want their failure to be exposed and more importantly they have not the financial wherewithal or resources to return.[83] Crucially, when considering return migration it is important to bear in mind that migration patterns from any one region may change over time, from migration representing advancement, to survival strategies or vice versa, which would in turn effect the decision to return. For as Ewa Morawska points out, the character of the migrations between the receiving and the sending communities affecting return migration are not a constant but a variable affected by the economic, social and political developments occurring in the country of departure and the country of arrival.[84]

Another important consideration is what effect(s) return migrants have on the socio-economic, political and cultural life of sending regions. In much mainstream literature, returning migrants are not viewed as bringing with them critical new industrial skills that would benefit their sending communities.[85] Moreover, when migrants do return, any cultural assimilation that did occur in their sojourn abroad is assumed to discourage them from performing traditional forms of labour (for example as farm hands or cleaners), occupations now seen as beneath them. Kraljic found that Croatian return migrants from the United States became extremely dissatisfied with their former home and longed to return to America. Yet paradoxically, just as Croatia was no longer home America was not either, which created a group of people who did not truly fit in anywhere.[86] Return migration viewed from this perspective is wholly divisive.

But is this verdict of return migration far too pessimistic? Research by Schwartz and Perry has identified many instances of Cornish returning migrants bringing with them financial capital used to buy farms, housing and small shops. While this has been criticized by some writers as being investment in non-productive commodities, Christian Dustmann and Oliver Kirchkamp have found that more than half of returning migrants are economically active after return and that most of them engage in entrepreneurial activities.[87] Many return migrants set up businesses, expanding commercial activity and services that might well prove to be more productive than writers such as André Lebon have recognized.

But perhaps even more significant is the less tangible human and social capital return migrants bring with them, which promotes changes in their native communities. Human capital is defined as the ideas, behaviour, skills and education acquired through migration. Social capital involves the network of more or less institutionalized relationships that are built up both among migrants and between sending and receiving communities. Although these human and social remittances are clearly more difficult to evaluate than financial flows, this does not mean that they are necessarily less important. For as Levitt reminds us, cultural flows around the world are not just spread by institutions and regimes such as governments: 'Ordinary people are also cultural creators and carriers. Migrants bring back the values and practices they have been exposed to and add these social remittances to the repertoire, both expanding and transforming it.'[88]

One of the chief agents for the dissemination of social remittances is the return migrant. Often possessed of innovative methods of problem-solving, new political ideas, increased business acumen, or valuable new skills, these migrants inject a dynamism that would have been absent without international migration. Return migrants making visits to family members, or religious or fraternal institutions, or for marriage purposes, are vital in the maintenance of social networks as they embody information and resources about receiving communities, and sustain kinship and community obligations across time and space, leading to more migration.[89]

Yet, in Cornish Studies return migration has, by and large, been treated as synonymous with failure. Instances of this equation of return migration and failure permeate Gillian Burke's pioneering study of the Cornish diaspora.[90] The first is the home-coming of Cornwall's greatest son, engineer Richard Trevithick, from Latin America in 1827. He received a hero's welcome, but is found to be penniless. The second alludes to a favourite dramatic device of late Victorian Cornish novelists, epitomised by Harris's story *Cousin Jacky*. This work of fiction depicts a miner's return from Chile to his native village, only to find himself a stranger, his old home in ruins, his kinfolk dead and his sweetheart vanished, representing those Cornish who were in effect displaced people due to their emigration. As with Kraljic's Croatian return migrants, the fictitious Cousin Jacky was reluctantly once more 'forced' into 'exile'.[91]

The third set of return migrants that Burke identified come from the *Report of the Health of Cornish Miners* in 1904, where nearly two-thirds of the deaths occurred among men who had come back from overseas suffering from a lung disease known as miners' phthisis.[92] There is no doubting the suffering of many return migrants, but according to Baines nearly 40 per cent of English migrants between 1860 and 1914 came back.[93] If so many Cornish miners returned in a pitiful condition, we can only echo his question about European migration in general: 'if so many failed, why did countless others follow in their footsteps?'. Yet, in terms of the economic logic upon which the theories of Cornish historians depend, a reasonable proportion of successful return migrants might seem necessary to sustain and encourage migration flows.

Conventional Cornish analyses of the migration process have always emphasized the loss of human and social skills through out-migration, but have not recognized gains through return migration. However, work by Rossler, Schwartz and Perry has highlighted the role of migrants who returned to Cornwall with significant financial, social and human capital. Hörst Rossler mentions the improved skills of stonemasons who returned from America to Constantine to re-invigorate the local quarry industry.[94] Numerous examples can be found of Cornish return migrants playing key roles in economic, political, cultural and religious life, in particular helping to diversify an economy stricken by mining decline and launching Cornwall on its new economic trajectory as a tourist resort.[95] Yet, more work has to be done on how ideas and practices taken from Cornwall are transformed in host countries and then transmitted back to Cornwall resulting in the emergence of new cultural products that challenge the lives of those who stay behind.

THE CHANGING NATURE OF CORNISH MIGRATION FLOW

Finally, it is well to remember the point that Morawska makes: migration is a variable affected by the economic, social and political developments occurring in the country of departure and the country of arrival.[96] During long periods of time migration patterns from any one region may change, from migration representing advancement, to survival strategies or vice versa. The 'Great Migration' from Cornwall spanned a century from 1815 and was by no means a homogenous phenomenon.

Agriculture has long been treated as the Cinderella of the economic order in Cornish Studies. This is perhaps reflected in migration literature too, for apart from the work of Philip Payton and Margaret James Korany,[97] there has been scant analysis of migration from areas such as North Cornwall, where farming was an important industry and the Bible Christian sect provided a strong rationale for emigration. Moreover, these emigration flows, principally to North America, represented a different type of migration from the 'bird of passage' scenario often equated with mining migration. Comprised of a significant number of yeoman farmers seeking to escape a combination of factors from dislike of the status quo, high tithes and rents on farms with marginal soils, and religious freedom, these migration flows were early, occurring in the 1830s and 1840s.[98] They were also characterized by family groups who intended to settle permanently elsewhere. Unlike assisted emigration to Australia and New Zealand, these flows often involved those with the financial wherewithal to raise sufficient capital to emigrate. A survey of migrants from the Redruth Registration District surprisingly revealed that farmers and agriculturists accounted for almost half of the migration to the United States of America from the mining parishes of Camborne, Redruth and Illogan before 1850.[99] Clearly, the migration of those from agricultural backgrounds deserves much greater scrutiny, although it is of course also the case that occupational boundaries were by no means certain in those times, 'copper miners' also becoming 'agicultural labourers' on many occasions.

In the case of mining-related migration, one could argue that in

To Sail the First of April,
1841,

FOR QUEBEC,

The fine fast sailing, British-built, Copper
bolted BARQUE

VITTORIA,

650 Tons Burthen,

Mosey Simpson, Commander,

LYING AT MALPUS, IN TRURO RIVER,

Has very superior accommodation for Steerage and Cabin Passengers.

The Commander having been many years in the North American Trade,
can give much valuable information regarding the Colonies, to any that may
feel disposed to take a passage in the said ship.

Apply to the CAPTAIN on board,

Mrs. SIMPSON, at the Seven Stars Inn, Truro,

Or to the Owner, NICHOLAS MITCHELL, Malpus.

Dated, February 13th, 1841.

E. HEARD, PRINTER, BOOKBINDER, &c., BOSCAWEN-STREET, TRURO.

4. *On the eve of the 'Hungry Forties', a poster advertizes passages to Quebec.*
Reprinted courtesy of the Royal Institution of Cornwall.

the first half of the nineteenth century a sojourn abroad was viewed as
an advancement strategy, as indeed it was among the stonemasons of
Constantine.[100] However, in the late nineteenth century the declining
industrial opportunities at home meant that risk diversification or
survival strategies were increasingly resorted to which often involved a
period spent overseas as a labour migrant. Importantly, these migrants
travelled along dense transnational migration networks that had been

in place for many years. By the early twentieth century migration had seemingly become a part of the Cornish psyche. However, at the same time the Cornish overseas had begun to be superseded by native labour and by the early 1900s numbers began to fall, the third stage in Thistlethwaite's model—the phase when the skilled operatives and innovators are no longer required, and are superseded by native and/or cheaper labour. Eventually, by the inter-war period only those in managerial or highly skilled posts remained overseas. The migration of technicians had largely come to an end and, as outlined by Payton, Cornwall suffered economically as a consequence of not being able to resort to migration, magnifying the socio-economic paralysis which was a defining characteristic of the 'second peripheralism'.[101]

Quite apart from the theoretical deficiencies in Cornish migration studies there is clearly the need for more quantitative evidence, as apart from Baines's calculations for the late nineteenth century we are not sure how many people migrated, where they went, or how many returned. The reason for this lack of knowledge is that the Cornish are ethnically invisible in official statistics that record them as either 'English' or 'British'. To solve this problem, an academic research project—the Cornish Global Migration Programme, of which the author was formerly director—has been set up to assemble a database of Cornish migrants. This will allow us to calculate, among other things, year and parish of departure, occupation, migration destination, further moves and returns to Cornwall. Research has begun to reveal that *vis-à-vis* the timing, parish of departure, occupation and destination of migrants, migration was not a homogenous process but exhibited huge differences across Cornwall extending to parochial level, indicating vastly different migration flows from places only a few miles apart. The factors responsible for such spatial differences indicate the need for finer-mesh local studies.

CONCLUSION

Reviewing the theoretical approaches from many disciplines, one begins to appreciate that analyses need to take account of *both* individual motives *and* the structural factors that influence migration decisions. While economic models isolate economic decision-making and therefore do not analyse the political and social contexts that influence migration decisions, structuralist analyses overstate the political-economic contexts that determine migration decisions and overlook migrants' agency. Within migration studies there are, therefore, a number of theories that attempt to conceptualize causal processes at different levels of analysis—the individual, the household, the national and the international. It is important to realize that these cannot be taken as being inherently incompatible. In some circumstances it would be possible for individuals to maximize income whilst families or communities engage in minimizing risk, while the context in which both decisions operate are the same—the result of structural forces operating at national and international levels. Moreover, as this paper has shown, differing and not necessarily conflicting models may be used to explain migration flows at various periods in Cornwall's history.

A corpus of excellent work has been built around the immigrant Cornish experience, but it is now time to adopt a fresh epistemological approach. In order to do this there is a need to transcend the polarized positions offered in much conventional literature where migration is deemed a triumph in overseas communities but a tragedy for those at home, where only the failures dared return to eke out a living on handouts from abroad. Migration must be viewed as a variable, complex life decision influenced not only by macrostructural and microstructural forces both regional, national and international, but cross-cut in myriad ways, for example by issues of gender, religion, class and occupational specificity. Only by analysing Cornish migration through a prism of transnationalism can we capture the mechanisms by which complex migration interactions shaped cultural, political, social and economic life in sending and receiving communities. And only then can we begin to appreciate the continuing ramifications of the 'Great Migration' on the modern Cornish, *both* at home and overseas.

NOTES AND REFERENCES

1. I gratefully acknowledge the help, advice and inspiration of Ronald Perry, who has worked with me over the past four years and has aided my doctoral research on transnationality, labour migration and economic theories in innumerable and invaluable ways.
2. Some examples include: A.C. Todd, *The Cornish Miner in America*, Truro, 1967; A.L. Rowse, *The Cornish in America*, Redruth, 1967; J. Rowe, *The Hard Rock Men: Cornish Immigrants and the North American Mining Frontier*, Liverpool, 1973; A.C. Todd, *The Search for Silver: Cornish Miners in Mexico 1824–1947*, Padstow, 1977; G.B. Dickason, *Cornish Immigrants to South Africa*, Cape Town, 1978; J. Faull, *Cornish Heritage: A Miner's Story*, Adelaide, 1979 and *The Cornish in Australia*, Melbourne, 1983; Philip Payton, *The Cornish Miner in Australia: Cousin Jack Down Under*, Redruth, 1984 and *The Cornish Overseas*, Fowey, 1999a; Pat Lay, *One and All: Cornish in New South Wales*, Qeanbeyan, 1999; Richard Dawe, *Cornish Pioneers in South Africa: Gold, Diamonds, Copper and Blood*, St Austell, 1998.
3. Dudley Baines, *Migration in a Mature Economy and Internal Migration in England and Wales, 1861–1900*, Cambridge, 1985, p. 159.

4. Baines, 1985, p. 159.
5. Philip Payton, ' "Reforming Thirties" and "Hungry Forties": The Genesis of Cornwall's Emigration Trade', in Philip Payton (ed.), *Cornish Studies: Four*, Exeter, 1996, pp. 107–27.
6. Payton, 1996; Bernard Deacon, 'Proto-Industrialisation and Potatoes: a Revised Narrative for Nineteenth Century Cornwall', in Philip Payton (ed.), *Cornish Studies: Five*, Exeter, 1997, pp. 64–84; Sharron Schwartz, 'Migration to the USA, 1815–1930: Preliminary Comparative Demographics for the Redruth and St Austell Registration Districts', *Cornish History Network Newsletter* 6, 1999a; Sharron Schwartz, 'The Making of a Myth: Cornish Miners in the New World in the Early Nineteenth Century', in Philip Payton (ed.), *Cornish Studies: Nine*, Exeter, 2001, pp. 105–26; Sharron Schwartz, 'Exporting the Industrial Revolution: The Migration of Cornish Mining Technology to Latin America in the Early Nineteenth Century', in Heidi Slettedahl Machpherson and Will Kaufman (eds), *New Perspectives in Translantic Studies*, New York, 2002, pp. 143–58.
7. S. Castles, 'International Migration and the Global Agenda: Reflections on the 1998 UN Technical Symposium', *International Migration* 37.1, 1999, pp. 5–19.
8. Bernard Deacon, 'Cornish Emigration', unpublished paper, n.d. *c*.1993, p. 17.
9. Philip Payton, 'Cornish Emigration in Response to Changes in the International Copper Market in the 1860s', in Philip Payton (ed.), *Cornish Studies: Three*, Exeter, 1995, pp. 60–82.
10. Gillian Burke, 'The Cornish Diaspora of the Nineteenth Century', in Shula Marks and Peter Richardson (eds), *International Labour Migration: Historical Perspectives*, London, 1984, pp. 57–75.
11. See Philip Payton, *The Making of Modern Cornwall: Historical Experience and the Persistence of 'Difference'*, Redruth, 1992, p. 114.
12. Pat Hudson (ed.), *Regions and Industries: A Perspective on the Industrial Revolution in Britain*, Cambridge, 1989, p. 23.
13. Ronald Perry, 'The Making of Modern Cornwall, 1800–2000: A Geo-Economic Perspective', in this volume.
14. F. Thistlewaite, 'Migration from Europe Overseas in the Nineteenth and Twentieth Centuries', in J. Vecoli and S.M. Sinke (eds), *A Century of European Migrations, 1830–1930*, Urbana, 1991, p. 30.
15. Thistlewaite, 1991, p. 30.
16. Transnationalism can be broadly defined as binding social groups across 'international' borders in the name of ethnic, racial, religious, linguistic, locality or nation-state of origin, class, gender, or any other factor. For more on transnationalism see D. Mato, 'On Global and Local Agents and the Social Making of Transnational Identities and Related Agendas in "Latin America", *Identities* 4.2 1997, pp. 167–212.
17. A.K. Hamilton Jenkin, *The Cornish Miner*, reprinted Newton Abbot, 1972, p. 303; S. Baring-Gould, *A Book of the West: Cornwall*, London, 1981, pp. 65–6.

18. R. Cohen, *Global Diasporas: An Introduction*, London, 1997, pp. ix–x.

19. R. Cohen, 'Diasporas and the Nation-State: From Victims to Challengers', *International Affairs 72, 1996, pp. 507–20.*

20. Hamilton Jenkin, 1972, pp. 307, 328, 331; A.L. Rowse, *A Cornish Childhood*, Redruth, 1998, pp. 23, 34.

21. Payton, 1999, p. 17.

22. Michael Wintle: 'Push-Factors in Emigration: The Case of the Province of Zeeland in the Nineteenth Century', *Population Studies*, 46, 1992, pp. 5230–37.

23. Nancy Foner, 'What's New about Transnationalism? New York Immigrants Today and at the Turn of the Century', paper presented at 'Transnational Communities and the Political Economy of New York in the 1990s Conference', The New School for Social Research, February 1997; M. Wyman, *Round Trip to America*, Ithaca, NY, 1993; Peggy Levitt, 'Social Remittances: Migration Driven Local-Level Forms of Cultural Diffusion', *International Migration Review* 32.4, 1998, pp. 926–48.

24. L.E. Guarnizo, 'The Emergence of a Transnational Social Formation and the Mirage of Return Migration among Dominican Transmigrants', *Identities—Global Studies in Culture and Power* 4.2, 1997, pp. 281–322.

25. Y. Soysal, 'Changing Parameters of Citizenship and Claims-Making: Organised Islam in Europen Public Spheres', *Theory and Society* 26, 1997, pp. 509–27.

26. Jurgen Habermas, *The Theory of Communicative Action*, Vol. 1(2), Boston, 1984.

27. *West Briton*, 20 February 1900.

28. Payton, 1992, p. 112.

29. Levitt, 1998.

30. Rowse, 1998, pp. 34–5.

31. M. Boyd, 'Family and Personal Networks in International Migration: Recent Developments and New Agendas', *International Migration Review* 23.3, 1989, pp. 638–70, p. 639; G. Hugo, 'Migration and the Family', *Family: Challenges for the Future*, United Nations Publications E.95.IV.4, New York, 1996, pp. 335–78; Peggy Levitt, 'Transnational Communities—Some Preliminary Thoughts and Further Questions', abstract from *World on the Move* 5.1, 2000, http://www.ssc.msu.edu/~intermig/wom/v5no1/levitt.htm, 13 November 2002.

32. *Cornishman*, 24 July 1913.

33. Roger Burt and Sandra Kippen, 'Rational Choice and a Lifetime in Metal Mining: Employment Decisions by Nineteenth Century Cornish Miners', *International Review of Social History* 46, 2001, pp. 45–75.

34. J. Hoddinott, 'A Model of Migration and Remittances applied to Western Kenya', *Oxford Economic Papers*, new series 46.3, 1994, pp. 459–76, and D.S. Massey and K.E. Espinosa, 'What's Driving Mexico–U.S. Migration? A Theoretical, Empirical, and Policy Analysis', *American Journal of Sociology* 102, 1997, pp. 939–99.

35. Oded Stark, *The Migration of Labor*, Cambridge, 1991.

36. Ronald Perry, 'Cornwall's Mining Collapse Revisited: An Empirical Study of Economic Re-adjustment in Late-Victorian and Edwardian Cornwall', *The Cornish Historian*, 2001, http:/www.ex.chn/cmcr0108.pdf, 12 December 2001.

37. Damaris Rose, 'Home Ownership, Subsistence and Historical Change: The Mining District of West Cornwall in the Late Nineteenth Century', in N. Thrift and P. Williams (eds), *Class and Space: The Making of an Urban Society*, London, 1987, p. 112; M. Brayshay, 'Depopulation and Changing Household Structure in the Mining Communities of West Cornwall, 1851–71', *Local Population Studies* 25, 1980.

38. S.J. Goetz, 'Migration and Local Labor Markets', *The Web Book of Regional Sciences*, Regional Research Institute, West Virginia University, http://www.rri.wvu.edu/WebBook/Goetz/Migx2.htm, 14 November 2001.

39. Hugo, 1996, pp. 335–78.

40. E.P. Thompson, *The Making of the English Working Class*, London, 1980.

41. See Paula Petrik, *No Step Backward: Women and Family on the Rocky Mountain Mining Frontier, Helena, Montana, 1865–1900*, Helena, 1987; Jeremy Mouat, *Roaring Days: Rossland's Mines and the History of British Columbia*, Vancouver, 1995; Mary Murphy, *Mining Cultures: Men, Women and Leisure in Butte, 1914–1941*, Urbana, 1997; Susan Zanjani, *A Mine of Her Own: Women Prospectors in the American West, 1850–1950*, Nebraska, 1997; Elizabeth Jameson, *All that Glitters: Class, Conflict and Community in Cripple Creek*, Urbana, 1998; Laurie Mercer 'Class, Gender, and Power in the Mining Communities of the Americas', *Labour/Le Travail 44*, 1999, pp. 205–15.

42. Bernard Deacon, 'A Forgotten Migration Stream: The Cornish Movement to England and Wales in the Nineteenth Century', in Philip Payton (ed.), *Cornish Studies: Six*, Exeter, 1998, pp. 96–117. See also Philip Payton, *The Cornish Farmer in Australia*, Redruth, 1987 for lists of lone female migrants to South Australia.

43. J.L. Finn, *Tracing the Veins: Of Copper, Culture and Community from Butte to Chuquicamata*, Berkeley, 1998, p. 168.

44. This phrase has been taken from a work of that name by Caroline B. Brettell, *Men Who Migrate, Women Who Wait: Population and History in a Portuguese Parish*, Princeton, 1986.

45. Gillian Burke, 'The Decline of the Independent Bâl Maiden', in Angela John (ed.), *Unequal Opportunities*, Blackwell, 1986.

46. See Gillian Burke, 'The Cornish Miner and the Cornish Mining Industry 1870–1921', unpublished Ph.D. thesis, University of London, 1981.

47. See M. Schmink, 'Women and Urban Industrial Development in Brazil', in J. Nash and H. Safa (eds), *Women and Change in Latin America*, South Hadley, 1986, pp. 136–64.

48. Sharron Schwartz, 'In Defence of Customary Rights: Labouring Women's Experience of Industralization in Cornwall, c1750–1870', in Philip Payton (ed.), *Cornish Studies: Seven*, Exeter, 1999b, pp. 8–31; 'No

Place for a Woman: Gender at Work in Cornwall's Metalliferous Mining Industry', in Philip Payton (ed.), *Cornish Studies: Eight*, Exeter, 2000, pp. 69–96.

49. Census returns for the ecclesiastical parish of Lanner in 1891 show that one-eighth of homes were headed by married women whose husbands were absent: Sharron Schwartz and Roger Parker, *Lanner: A Cornish Mining Parish*, Tiverton, 1998, p. 163.

50. Sometimes the taking in of lodgers for financial purposes results in marital infidelity and illegitimacy. How the community views this very much dependent on its collective values and ideas of what constitutes immorality.

51. Hamilton Jenkin, 1927, p. 330.

52. In some instances females might have been forced to migrate, as being in a subordinate position in their native economy has meant that they have been prone to unemployment and therefore more subject to migration in periods of economic readjustment.

53. J.E. Taylor, J. Arango, G. Hugo, A. Kouaouci, D.S. Massey and A. Pellegrino, 'International Migration and Community Development', *Population Index* 62.3, Fall 1996, pp. 397–418.

54. Michael P. Todaro, 'A Model of Labor Migration and Urban Development in Less Developed Countries', *American Economic Review*, 59, 1969, pp. 138–49.

55. Bernard Deacon and Philip Payton, 'Reinventing Cornwall', in Philip Payton (ed.), *Cornish Studies: One*, Exeter, 1993a, p. 68.

56. Deacon and Payton, 1993, p. 66.

57. Schwartz and Parker, 1998, p. 157.

58. Schwartz and Parker, 1998, p. 157, quoting St Day Headmaster, Richard Blewett.

59. Bernard Deacon, 'And Shall Trelawny Die? The Cornish Identity', in Philip Payton (ed.), *Cornwall Since the War: The Contemporary History of a European Region*, Redruth, 1993b, p. 205.

60. John Rowe, *Cornwall in the Age of the Industrial Revolution*, St Austell, 1993, p. 321.

61. Burke, 1981, pp. 450–1.

62. A. Lebon, 'Les Envois de Fonds des Migrants et Leur Utilisation', *International Migration* 22.4, 1984, pp. 281–333; Jorge Durand and Douglas S. Massey, 'Mexican Migration to the United States: A Critical Review', *Latin American Research Review*, 27, 1992, pp. 3–42; Guarnizo, 1997, pp. 281–322; B. Barham and S. Boucher, 'Migration, Remittances and Inequality: Estimating the Net Effects of Migration on Income Distribution', *Journal of Development Economics* 55.2, 1998, pp. 307–31.

63. O. Stark, J.E. Taylor, and S. Yitzhaki, 'Migration, Remittances in Inequality: A Sensitivity Analysis Using the Extended Gini Index', Journal of Development Economics, 28, 1988, pp. 309–22.

64. D.S. Massey, L.P. Goldring and J. Durand, 'Continuities in Transnational Migration: An Analysis of 19 Mexican Communities', *American Journal of Sociology 99*, 1994, pp. 1492–533.

65. Taylor *et al.*, 1996; J.E. Taylor, 'The New Economics of Labour Migration and the Role of Remittances in the Migration Process', *International Migration* 37.1, 1999, pp. 63–88.
66. S. Djajic, 'Emigration and Welfare in an Economy with Foreign Capital,' *Journal of Development Economics* 56.2, 1998, pp. 433–45.
67. Taylor, 1999.
68. Taylor *et al.*, 1996.
69. Schwartz and Parker, 1998, pp. 159–60; Ronald Perry and Sharron Schwartz, 'James Hicks: Architect of Regeneration in Victorian Redruth', *Journal of the Royal Institution of Cornwall*, II, IV, 2001, pp. 64–77.
70. Perry, 2001.
71. Dudley Baines, 'European Emigration, 1815–1930: Looking at the Emigration Decision Again', *Economic History Review* 47.3, 1994, pp. 530–1.
72. E.S. Lee, 'A Theory of Migration', *Demography* 3.1, 1966, pp. 47–57.
73. A. Portes and J. Walton, *Class and the International System*, New York, 1981.
74. N. Glick-Schiller, L. Basch and C. Szanton-Blanc (eds), *Toward a Transnational Perspective on Migration*, New York, 1992.
75. Savina Ammassari and Richard Black, 'Harnessing the Potential of Migration and Return to Promote Development: Applying Concepts to West Africa', *Sussex Working Papers*, Sussex Centre for Migration Research, July 2001, http://ww.sussex.ac.uk/Units/SCMR/working_papers/mwp3.pdf, 14 November 2002.
76. See for example F. Bovenkerk, *The Sociology of Return Migration: A Bibliographic Essay*, Publications of the Research Group on European Migration Problems 20, The Hague, 1974, and G. Gmelch, 'Return Migration', *Annual Review of Anthropology* 9, 1980, pp. 135–59.
77. See G.J. Lewis, *Human Migration. A Geographical Perspective*, London, 1982.
78. See R. King, *Return Migration and Regional Economic Problems*, London, 1986.
79. Ammassari and Black, 2001, p. 12.
80. See for example the case of successful return migrants to Jamaica. E. Thomas-Hope, 'Return Migration to Jamaica and its Development Potential', *International Migration* 37.1, 1999, pp. 183–207.
81. A collection of migrant letters is held by the Cornish Global Migration Programme, an academic research project supported by the Institute of Cornish Studies, currently located at the Murdoch House Adult Education Centre, Redruth.
82. M.J. Piore, *Birds of Passage: Migrant Labour in Industrial Societies*, Cambridge, 1979, p. 50.
83. Gmelch, 1980, pp. 135–59.
84. Ewa Morawska, 'Return Migration: Theoretical and Research Agendas', in R.J. Vecoli and S.M. Sinke, *A Century of European Migrations, 1830–1930*, Chicago, 1991, p. 278.

85. Lebon, 1984, pp. 281–333.
86. F. Kraljic, 'Round Trip to Croatia, 1900–1914', in R.J. Vecoli and S.M.A. Sinke (eds), *A Century of European Migrations, 1830–1930*, Chicago, 1991, p. 414.
87. C. Dustmann and O. Kirchkamp, 'The Optimal Migration Duration and Activity Choice after Re-Migration', Institute for the Study of Labor, Mannheim University, 2001, http://www.sfb504.uni-mannheim.de/~oliver/rmig.pdf, 14 November 2001.
88. Peggy Levitt, *The Transnational Villagers*, Berkeley, 2001, p. 55.
89. See R. Ballard, 'The Political Economy of Migration: Pakistan, Britain and the Middle East', in J. Eades (ed.), *Migrant Workers and the Social Order*, London, 1987, pp. 17–41.
90. Burke, 1984.
91. J. Henry Harris, *The Luck of Wheal Vor and Other Stories*, Truro, 1901, pp. 85–91.
92. Burke, 1984.
93. Baines, 1994, p. 535.
94. Hörst Rossler, 'Constantine Stonemasons in Search of Work Abroad, 1870–1900', in Philip Payton (ed.), *Cornish Studies: Two*, Exeter, 1994, pp. 48–82.
95. Ronald Perry, 'Silvanus Trevail and the Development of Modern Tourism in Cornwall', *Journal of the Royal Institution of Cornwall* 3.2, 1999, pp. 33–43; Perry and Schwartz, 2001; Sharron Schwartz, 'Cornish Migration to Latin America: A Transnational Perspective', unpublished Ph.D. thesis, University of Exeter, 2002.
96. Morawska, 1991, p. 278.
97. Margaret James-Korany, '"Blue Books" as Sources for Cornish Emigration History', in Payton (ed.), 1993a, pp. 31–45.
98. See Payton, 1995.
99. Schwartz, 1999a.
100. Rossler, 1994.
101. Payton, 1992, p. 167.

THE MAKING OF MODERN CORNWALL, 1800–2000: A GEO-ECONOMIC PERSPECTIVE

Ronald Perry[1]

INTRODUCTION

During the past decade, writers in the field of Cornish Studies have constructed paradigms of modern Cornish history which both enhance and revise Hamilton Jenkin's rich, folkloric narratives and John Rowe's classic account of the rise and fall of the 'Copper Kingdom'.[2] Prime movers in this are Philip Payton and Bernard Deacon,[3] and this article is a commentary upon, and a critique of, their work, informed by some important recent studies by Sharron Schwartz and empirical research by the present author. Payton's interpretation involves phases of core–periphery dependency between Cornwall and the British state. After an 'older peripheralism' of cultural and territorial isolation during medieval and Renaissance times, Cornwall enters a 'second peripheralism' as a leading industrial region—'Cornubia triumphant'. This, however, is inherently unsustainable because of over-specialization upon mining and is followed by de-industrialization and inertia—'the great paralysis'—which lasts until the mid-twentieth century. Up to this point, Payton adapts existing models, but he then introduces an original concept, a 'third peripheralism' of branch-factory and immigration-led dependency which continues until the present day.

Deacon's originality lies in his combination of an industrial-regions perspective with a stage theory of regional identity formation: as a pioneer industrial region, Cornwall escapes from dependency upon the British state long enough to develop a distinct regional culture, but not long enough to reach the critical demographic mass or large central place needed to provide the basis for self-generating growth as a fully-fledged industrial region. In the model of regional identity formation adapted by Deacon, two of the four stages are mainly socio-cultural: self-awareness of a separate identity and creation of distinct regional badges of identity. But two have economic overtones, namely the construction of regional institutions and the recognition of the region's territorial integrity by the central state. The far-reaching and imaginative interpretations of Payton and Deacon encompass a whole range of political, cultural and social, as well as spatial and economic issues, stretching back in time to medieval Cornwall. This article, however, focuses upon geo-economic aspects and covers the period from the late eighteenth century to the present day, offering a different perspective, through the use of a path-dependent model in which economic options in one period result from events and decisions in previous periods.[4] It concentrates in particular on spatial strategies and Cornwall's place as an important component in a global economy.

FROM THE NAPOLEONIC WARS TO THE COPPER CRASH

For Jenkin and Rowe, the critical events of the nineteenth century were the Copper Crash of the 1860s, followed by mass emigration. Payton and Deacon, however, have shifted the turning point, as far as migration was concerned, back in time to the 1830s and 1840s. Payton has identified a 'culture of migration' at that time in non-mining areas such as the Lizard Peninsula and North Cornwall,[5] while Deacon has emphasized that, even when Cornish mining output was reaching a historical peak in the 1850s, the Cornish propensity to migrate was higher than that of any English region.[6]

In this article, such movement is seen as part of a wider process of capitalist development—the institutionalization of financial, entrepreneurial, technological and labour mobility in a global trading circuit. Labour migration is treated, therefore, as a dependent variable, following prior movement of capital, technology and management. As a result, Cornwall's economic watershed is moved still further back in time to a series of entrepreneurial initiatives in the late eighteenth and early nineteenth centuries.

At the beginning of the nineteenth century, Roger Burt has claimed, in contradiction to Deacon's thesis, Cornwall's 'backward and forward linkages with advanced engineering supplying and processing industries created the critical mass necessary for sustained growth'.[7] But in this case why did such an advanced, vertically integrated industrial region fail to diversify and expand? The answer, it is suggested, lies in the historical contingency of its economic structure. Industrial

prowess largely relied upon leadership in methods of extracting
a non-renewable resource which was subject to increasing costs as
adventurers dug deeper and deeper for progressively poorer lodes.
Lack of timber and coal also put Cornwall at a competitive dis-
advantage in the development of down-stream activities in metal
processing and manufacturing. And diversification into non-mining
sectors such as tourism, which had begun in a small way during the
Napoleonic Wars, required better links to central England. Over the
next few decades Cornish adventurers met, or tried to meet, these
challenges by a number of initiatives: diffusion of superior technological, entrepreneurial, managerial and artisanal skills to less
developed regions; transfer of capital and entrepreneurship to a more
promising site for metal processing; and an attempt to build a direct
railway link to London.

Schwartz has described how the installation of high-pressure steam
engines by Richard Trevithick in the silver mines of Peru in 1818 paved
the way for the diffusion of Cornish, and British, capital, technology
and enterprise to Latin America. The commercial dynasties of
Cornwall—the Williams, Vivians, Foxes, Harveys, among others—
financed Latin American mining companies in the 1820s, exported
mining machinery from their foundries and sent out engineers,
managers, agents and artisans who ran the mines, installed and maintained the equipment, and traded as importers and exporters of a wide
range of merchandise.[8] And this transfer of tangible and intangible
capital later spread to many parts of the globe: for instance they
opened safety fuse factories in France, the USA, Australia and
Canada.[9]

Now, although this study concentrates upon geo-economic forces,
the part played in this transfer of capital and technology by centralist
strategies must be recognized. As Schwartz has shown,[10] the political
aim of investment in Latin America (encouraged by the young
Disraeli) was to counter French, Spanish and Portuguese influence. For
Latin America was not virgin mining territory like parts of North
America or Australia, but had been developed for centuries under
Spanish and Portuguese rule and then fallen into decay through years
of internal conflict. And most of the British companies sent out to
exploit Latin American resources as part of this capitalist strategy
were London-based. Nonetheless, the inner economic dynamism was
Cornish. Cornwall's adventurers, engineers and miners were not acting
as mere peripheral functionaries but were pioneers of an independent,
industrially advanced region which was transferring its superior equipment and knowledge to a less technically developed area.

In the promotion of down-stream metal processing and

manufacturing, however, Cornish adventurers followed a different pathway. An oligopoly of South Wales-based smelters held the whip hand in fixing the price of metallic ores, because the supply was highly inelastic in the short term since capital invested in mining was literally 'sunk capital' and production could not be turned on and off like a tap. Accordingly, Cornish adventurers—again including the Vivians, Foxes and Williams—transferred capital and entrepreneurial skills to Glamorgan and Monmouth, where some of them played an important role in local commercial and political affairs as JPs, MPs, high sheriffs and lord mayors.[11] Other traders followed suit: a merchant from north-east Cornwall prospered as a ship's chandler and ship broker in Cardiff, where his son became Lord Mayor.[12] Where capital and enterprise went, artisans and labourers followed, and South Wales became one of the prime targets for Cornish emigrants, as Deacon has shown.[13] An influential Quaker family, the Foxes of Falmouth, exemplified Cornwall's role in a two-way vertical and horizontal integration. They despatched coal and pig iron from their collieries and foundries in South Wales (often using their own ships) to Portreath on the north coast of Cornwall, a harbour in which they had a financial interest, and thence by mineral railway, in which they also had shares, to their Cornish mines and foundries. On the return journey, using the same route, they shipped ore from their Cornish mines to their South Wales smelters.

Again, this type of capital, technology and labour transfer did not fit a model of core–periphery dependency, nor did it conform to an industrial regions model in which an advanced region diffuses its superior technical knowledge and expertise to a less developed one. It represented movement from one independent, specialized industrial region to another. But, in the long run, it was the South Wales economy which was the beneficiary of this transfer in terms of population and industrial diversification. As Deacon has shown,[14] two-way trade between Cornwall and South Wales quadrupled during the first half of the nineteenth century, but whereas, in 1801, Cornwall's population was two-thirds larger than that of Monmouth and Glamorgan combined, by 1861 it was a third smaller. The population of Cornwall's ports, some 10,000–15,000 by the end of the nineteenth century, was dwarfed by comparison with Cardiff which had grown from 2,000 to 164,000 and Swansea from 10,000 to 95,000. And while in 1851 the proportion of the Cornish male labour force in Cornish metal mines was greater than that of Welsh male workers in Welsh coal mines, the percentage of Cornish workers engaged in metal processing, manufacturing and engineering was markedly smaller—indeed it was actually below the average for Britain as a whole.

In addition to the transfer of capital, technology and skilled labour to Latin America and South Wales, a third spatial strategy, in which Cornish entrepreneurs, including the Foxes, were involved, was to construct a direct inland rail link to Exeter. Falmouth's strategic location and large natural anchorage positioned it to play a leading role as a port of first and last call for admiralty and trading vessels as well as in the export of modern industrialism to the New World. In the mid-1820s, at the height of the Latin American investment boom, its streets were thronged with mine agents, engineers, traders and miners awaiting embarkation. But the arrival of steam power threatened this locational advantage as ships steamed up the channel to railheads nearer London instead of calling at Falmouth for orders or to pick up or unload packets and passengers.

Local adventurers and landowners, including Lord Falmouth, the Foxes and another important Quaker banking family, the Tweedys, swiftly reacted to this challenge and called public meetings, attended by the landed gentry and bourgeoisie of Cornwall, to raise finance for a fast and direct railway across the spine of Cornwall and west Devon to reach a line that was being built from London to Exeter. At one meeting Sir William Hussey Vivian, hero of Waterloo and local MP, warned the assembly that 'if Plymouth got a line before Falmouth, the former would supersede the latter', whereas if Falmouth won the railway race it would remain 'the port of London'.[15]

Once more this initiative does not conform unambiguously to one or other of the theoretical models considered so far. Its promoters were prime movers in an outward-looking maritime economy, but were they also seeking to involve Cornwall in a core–periphery dependency upon London? Paradoxically, however, the very enthusiasm of Cornish entrepreneurs for overseas trade with a developing global mining economy defeated efforts to finance a Falmouth—Exeter line. West Cornwall mining adventurers, for whom cheaper sea transport was perfectly satisfactory for the carriage of metal ores, coal or timber, saw no sense in risking large sums of money (£14,000 a mile was mentioned) to build a line across a commercial wilderness to a region with which they had few trading links. The optimistic mid-Cornwall entrepreneur Joseph Treffry, who thought a line could be constructed for £3,000 a mile, favoured a south coast route via Plymouth.[16] North Cornwall merchants wanted a link via Padstow to Ireland. Accordingly, the leading Falmothians, seeing they had no chance of a direct line across Cornwall, switched their support to the south coast route but still found themselves competing against another Falmouth group who persisted in trying to raise funds for the direct line. The wider British public, having burnt their fingers in the railway mania of the 1840s, were loth to invest. It was not until 1863 that the railway arrived at Falmouth, fifteen years after it reached Plymouth, and even then it was only a branch line of the main route from Plymouth to Penzance.[17]

But it was not really the lateness of the arrival of the railways that held Cornwall back. For, despite Sir Hussey Vivian's rhetoric, Plymouth had already superseded Falmouth. Devonport had expanded greatly as a naval base during the Napoleonic Wars and Plymouth as a chemical-processing centre for the manufacture of starch, sugar, alkalis and soap.[18] Even before the railway arrived there in 1848, Plymouth possessed an industrial and commercial agglomeration of the kind that Cornwall never achieved and also became, as one of the two government emigration depots, an important link in Cornish labour movement, dominant in East Cornwall and a conduit for long-distant migration for most major Cornish towns.[19] Plymouth already presented a formidable barrier to commercial development further west.

FROM THE COPPER CRASH TO THE GREAT WAR

For the period that followed the Copper Crash of the 1860s, the dominant narrative has been one of decline and inertia, both among Cornish historians— Rowe's 'end of the Copper Kingdom', Symons's 'death throes of an industry', and Payton's 'great paralysis'—and among historians of Britain and Europe. Berg and Pollard, for instance, compressed the period into a brief transition from advanced industrial region to holiday resort.[20] According to Payton, 'technological supremacy soon gave way to early de-industrialisation as the Cornish economy was unable to diversify in response to rapid economic change'.[21] In Deacon's view, an 'Indian summer' in the 1850s boom in mining led only to a 'limited diversification' which was 'insufficient to weather the restructuring of the 1870s to 1890s . . . As a result, Cornwall's mid-century modernisation was arrested in mid-development.'[22] Cornish people, Deacon and Payton have argued, were traumatized by the diminution of their industrial prowess, and imbued with 'fatalism and even hopelessness . . . a carefulness with money and an even more inward-looking, austere attitude to life . . . a culture of poverty and dependency'.[23] By the early 1900s, Payton concluded, Cornwall was 'a far cry from that vibrant, self-confident, innovative land that had existed only a half century or so before'.[24]

This article has contended that it was the very responsiveness of earlier Cornish entrepreneurial actions—export of up-stream technology to the New World, transfer of down-stream technology to South Wales—combined with failure to avoid a rail route reinforcing Plymouth as a regional naval base and industrial port, that prevented the kind of diversification and modernization that Payton and Deacon referred to. Moreover, their Cornwall-centred approach overlooks the fact that their criticism of the sluggish performance of many Cornish mining entrepreneurs matched those made in the later nineteenth century in other pioneering British industrial regions where the dominant sector had reached a mature stage of development and was encountering mounting foreign competition: in ship-building in the north-east of England, textiles in the north-west, slate quarrying in North Wales and smelting in South Wales.[25] In the mid-1800s these entrepreneurs had been elevated to the status of folk heroes. Later in the century they were accused of an aversion to risk-taking, a reluctance to invest in up-to-date equipment, an unwillingness to adopt new methods, a willingness to allow workers to control their own operations, and compared unfavourably with stereotypes of scientific Germans and dynamic Americans who were challenging Britain's industrial leadership.[26] Justification for such behaviour, however, was always the same in Cornwall and elsewhere: by keeping down the overhead costs of capital, maintenance and labour supervision, entrepreneurs could ride out increasingly lengthy downturns in a progressively more volatile global market where external competition was intensifying. Not just in Cornwall, but in many pioneering industrial regions, artisanal forms of industrial organization survived which could not compete with new capital-intensive structures over- seas where machines were preferred to men as more reliable and productive.

Moreover, entrepreneurial response was not as lethargic as the Payton and Deacon narrative suggests. Many foundries closed down, but a similar number of men were taken on by a newer generation of engineers who diversified their marketing to Cornish-owned or Cornish-managed mines abroad, or to the expanding local china clay industry, and switched from steam to pneumatic and electrical power[27] or moved into boat-building, or explosives manufacture. Meanwhile, the Cornish china clay industry was expanding at a rapid rate. In its early development, outsiders had made the running. Cookworthy, a Plymouth chemist, had opened a pit in Cornwall to supply his pottery, later transferred to Bristol, and he was followed by such famous porcelain producers as Wedgewood, Spode and Minton. This seemed a straightforward case of core–periphery vertical integration, with central manufacturers controlling supplies of Cornish clay. But by the mid-1800s ownership had passed to local merchants: not, however, to the Williams, Foxes, Vivians or Bolithos, who had a finger in nearly every industrial and commercial pie, but to a new group of mid Cornwall adventurers—farmers, shopkeepers, blacksmiths, saddlers and coal merchants. Historians of the clay industry, while noting these developments, do not, in my opinion, explain them satisfactorily.[28] The result was, however, that the china clay industry offered a new sector in which Cornwall conformed to a model of independent, specialized industrial region, not one of core–periphery dependency. Between 1858 and 1912, Cornish china clay production rose twelve-fold, a massive increase that was accomplished by a complete reorientation of marketing, from dependency upon Midlands potteries towards world-wide use as a filler for textiles, paper, chemicals and pharmaceutical products, with three-quarters exported overseas. On the supply side, substantial improvements in labour productivity took place through the use of pipelines and railways. Redundant steam pumps from local mines were introduced and a technological spillover occurred from Cornish mining academies, as mining engineers adapted new methods of processing and filtration.[29]

NON-MINING DIVERSIFICATION AND THE REMOVAL OF SUPPLY-SIDE CONSTRAINTS[30]

In other developing sectors of the Cornish economy, however, core–periphery dependency was growing. For rapid economic and demographic expansion was occurring in other British regions, and a rising urban middle class was demanding goods and services that had previously been the preserve of the rich: dairy produce, high quality meat, fresh fish, early potatoes, fruit, vegetables and flowers, seaside holidays and retirement havens far from the mounting pollution and congestion of the big cities. In the provision of all these items, Cornwall offered climatic, topographical and locational advantages, but first of all supply-side constraints had to be removed—the environmental blight of mining operations and poor rail access to central England.[31] As these impediments were removed and rail links were improved, marginal land was cleared (sometimes using redundant mine labour), scientific agriculture and modern dairying methods were introduced, agricultural output in Cornwall rose at a faster pace than in Devon or Somerset, and market gardening expanded, particularly in the Scillies, around Penzance and in the Tamar valley. A chain of hotels, villas and terraced lodgings sprang up around the coast and, as the Great Western Railway (GWR) launched its 'Cornish Riviera' campaign, employment in hotel and catering activities increased by over 50 per cent in the first decade of the twentieth century.

MODERNIZING BOURGEOISIE, EXTERNALLY TRAINED PROFESSIONALS AND ARTISANAL PRAGMATISM

While Deacon has argued that mining collapse arrested the modernization of the Cornish economy and robbed Cornwall of a middle class which might have challenged the landed gentry,[32] the suggestion here is that a 'modernizing bourgeoisie' evolved which responded to changes in external demand and the removal of supply-side constraints.[33] This comprised capitalist aristocrats, together with 'older money' who had made fortunes in mining, smelting and banking and 'newer money' from an upwardly mobile petty bourgeoisie. The 'older money' had by now acquired landed estates, were educated at English public schools and universities, and were, for the most part, pillars of the Anglican Church and the Tory Party. They occupied positions of power and prestige as high sheriffs, deputy lieutenants, justices of the peace, members of Parliament, county aldermen or councillors, presidents of literary and scientific institutes and masters of fox hounds.

In an earlier age they might have retreated to their country houses but the coming of the railways, the telegraph and the telephone enabled them to live on their estates yet participate in business, not as mere sleeping partners but as active directors of banks, railways, mines, smelters, hotel companies and food processing companies. They worked closely with members of the new monied classes, who were often sons of yeomen farmers or small traders who had been drawn by their political or religious affiliations, as well as their interests as important rate-payers, into positions of local power as bastions of the Liberal Party and the Nonconformist Church and as county and district councillors.[34]

But if a modernizing bourgeoisie played a useful part in diversification, it could not provide the innovatory and technical expertise required in such a large array of non-mining sectors as dairy farming, horticulture, explosives manufacture, ship-building, electrical and pneumatic equipment and tourism.[35] Unlike the inventor-adventurers of old, leading an army of 'practical mechanics' who constantly adapted existing skills to new situations, the new generation of entrepreneurs had to import managerial and technical skills and knowledge and lean heavily upon the marketing expertise of the GWR. In introducing a new class of externally-trained technicians and managers, however, they ran up against resistance from artisanal pragmatism, particularly in food processing and fishing. Building modern food processing factories and engaging outside agricultural experts was one thing; getting farmers to deliver standard quantities and qualities of eggs, milk and pigs at regular intervals was quite another. Eventually, however, these difficulties were ironed out.[36] But in fishing, as Deacon has noted, fishermen reversed the general trend towards more capital-intensive methods by reverting from seine fishing, financed by merchants like the Bolithos and the Foxes, to small-scale, labour-intensive drift fishing,[37] and did not combine, as they did in Scotland, to finance large steam drifters. Yet in Newlyn they had earlier raised a large sum of money to modernize their harbour, and Newlyn became the premier fish-landing port in Cornwall and the South-West of Britain.[38] Willingness to invest in port facilities, but not in large-scale fishing, suggests a determination to continue a small-scale, family-oriented way of life.[39]

REMITTANCES, RETURN MIGRANTS AND THE REVERSAL OF INFORMATIONAL FLOWS

Elsewhere in this issue of *Cornish Studies*, Sharron Schwartz has discussed the unbalanced way in which Cornish historians have treated the economic impact of outward and return migrants,[40] and only a few points need to be made here. Paradoxically, while writers stress the negative income and employment multiplier effects of outward migration upon the local economy, when migrants pump money back into the economy via remittances these too are treated negatively. Thus Deacon and Payton, while estimating that remittances *c.*1900 would keep one-eighth of the population at a minimum standard of existence, concluded that this created a 'culture of dependency'.[41] Yet, as Schwartz and Perry have shown, remittances at this time were used productively to finance smallholdings, mines, quarries, house building and the construction of educational and religious institutions. Similarly, while Burke focused upon return migration as an admission of failure,[42] Schwartz and Perry have instanced many cases where it was a sign of success. Migrants came back not only with financial capital but also with valuable human capital in the form of commercial acumen and technical skills they had acquired elsewhere, and they played a useful role in revitalizing public life and injecting capital and entre-preneurial energy into mining, quarrying, the manufacture of explosives and tourism.[43] Informational flows had reversed and Corn-wall was a net importer of technology in many fields.

'HEMMED IN AS WE ARE . . .'

Some influential voices, however, seemed to be rejecting Cornwall's role as an independent, specialized, outward-looking industrial region in favour of trade with England. 'Hemmed in as we are by the sea on three sides and the Three Towns on the fourth', complained E.G. Heard, Editor of the *West Briton* and an acknowledged authority on local industry and commerce, Cornwall had 'no facilities for increasing business'.[44] The 'Three Towns' were Devonport, Stonehouse and Plymouth, which had coalesced into an agglomeration of nearly 200,000 people, a dozen times greater than any Cornish town. And the Editor

of the *Western Morning News*, Plymouth-based but a regular contributor to the proceedings of the Royal Cornwall Polytechnic Society
at Falmouth, called Plymouth 'the metropolis of Cornwall'.[45]

While Deacon has attributed Cornwall's failure to attain a critical
mass to a lack of industrial diversification,[46] the rise of Plymouth
illustrates how dominant centres could develop through trade as well as
industry. But Cornwall also failed to develop commercially, its trading
ports remained tiny and its holiday resorts were small. Newquay, rising
star of the tourist trade and the only specialist holiday centre, barely
reached a population of 4,000 by the Edwardian era, whereas Torquay
had risen from a fishing village to a town of 34,000. Plymouth's
dominance as a port of first and last call for ocean liners brought some
prosperity to Devon's tourist trade, but little to Cornwall's. By 1912,
some 200 liners a year were disembarking nearly 14,000 passengers at
Plymouth, but while some stayed to visit 'Pilgrim' sites and others set
off on a Great Western train to London and the Midlands, few turned
west into Cornwall.[47]

To sum up the economic experiences of the 1870—1914 period,
they once more did not fit a single explanatory model. Diversification
into non-mining goods and services for the markets of central England
introduced core–periphery dependency, with a marked increase in
technological and managerial dependency. On the other hand, infusion
of financial and human capital by return migrants involved a new form
of reliance, not upon central England but upon formerly peripheral
regions overseas which were rapidly developing into core regions in
their own right. In complete contrast, export-based activities in mining
and china clay refining fitted an industrial regions model, institutionalized by the formation of a stock exchange to channel Cornish capital
into mining ventures abroad[48] and by the building of shipping fleets by
Cornish entrepreneurs.[49]

CORNWALL 1900–1950: INSTABILITY AND
CORE–PERIPHERY DEPENDENCY

In the opening years of the twentieth century, Cornwall's entrepreneurs seemed to be setting the territory on the road to recovery.[50]
Agriculture, horticulture, food processing, china clay production,
engineering, high explosives manufacture, ship-repairing and tourism
were all doing well, and even mining, after closing down almost completely in the dying years of the nineteenth century, enjoyed a brief
remission as tin prices trebled, and sales of by-products such as
bitumen and arsenic boomed.[51] Remittances from bread-winners
abroad were flowing in.[52] Depopulation was reverting into re-
population, albeit only marginally, and employment was climbing back

to earlier levels, although more for females than males. Productivity was increasing in mining, clay-working and farming. These successes, however, resulted from a fortuitous juxtaposition of favourable internal and external circumstances: a release of supply-side constraints, through the decline of mining, upon goods and services in which Cornwall enjoyed a comparative advantage, and for which coincidentally external demand was rising.

Economic independence, however, was becoming increasingly eroded. A branch-factory, branch-office economy, which Payton characterized as a key component of his 'third peripheralism', was already becoming more and more apparent. For mergers and monopolies were in the air throughout Britain and abroad: a GWR–LSWR duopoly controlled rail access, an oligopoly of London financiers acquired the entire Cornish banking network,[53] and local agents for other financial services such as insurance worked for head offices up-country. In 1899 only Truro had a branch of a multiple retailer; by 1910 there was at least one in each of the ten largest Cornish towns.[54] The biggest food processing factory was sold to a Wiltshire company, the two largest high explosives works were under-cut until they sold out to a giant chemical combine, and, although Cornish adventurers opened safety fuse factories in Germany, Austria and Hungary before the First World War, these too were acquired soon after the war ended by the chemical giant which became Imperial Chemical Industries. The leading Cornish shipping line was also sold to the P and O.[55]

During the inter-war years, the reproduction rate of new indigenous enterprises was very low. Even within the same economic sector, however, entrepreneurial performance varied widely. An engineering firm in Camborne, a ship-repairers in Falmouth and a china clay refiner in St Austell not merely weathered the economic perturbations, but greatly expanded their workforce to several thousand apiece.[56] In tourism, while some resorts like Newquay enthusiastically joined forces with the GWR, which once again took the lead in holiday promotions, others, like Penzance, were so laggardly that the General Manager of the GWR suggested that the only solution was to blow them up with dynamite and start again.[57] In contrast, Plymouth launched an extensive building programme to develop its facilities for tourists and retirees that surpassed the efforts of Cornish resorts, assisted by the GWR which siphoned off tourists from across the ocean and diverted them to central England.[58] Payton and Thornton have argued that the GWR helped to construct a powerful Cornish-Celtic identity in the years up to 1939,[59] but, as Alan Bennett has suggested, the railway company's main concern was to persuade

American and colonial visitors, who arrived in their thousands in
Plymouth, to ignore Cornwall and set off immediately for the heart
of 'Anglo-Saxon England', to London and 'Shakespeare land'.[60]
Plymouth, as always, imposed a barrier of intervening opportunity to
Cornish development and the GWR's exploitation of Cornish Celticity
was an early example of the use of the Cornish heritage to promote a
centralist Paddington-inspired strategy.

In the early 1950s, the Cornish economy was enjoying one of
its periodic 'Indian summers'—or false dawns—as nearly all sectors
worked flat out to meet the global needs of post-war reconstruction.
Once again, however, this conjunction of favourable circumstances
faded as other places recovered and modernized, reducing demand for
Cornish products.[61] The experience of the first half of the century,
however, failed once more to fit a single developmental model. Core–
periphery dependency had been greatly reinforced by increasing
external control, first of private and then of public sector institutions
through nationalization policies for electricity, gas and water supply.
While farmers and fishermen retained a *de jure* independence, they
were *de facto* increasingly the prisoners of central government policy.
On the other hand, some important elements of the independent,
industrial, export-oriented economy remained—and thrived—in
engineering, ship-repairing and china clay processing.

THE INSTITUTIONALIZATION OF CORE-PERIPHERY DEPENDENCY

In the 1960s, for the first time, a set of economic policies was devised
for outlying regions. Hitherto, apart from the injection, mainly for
strategic reasons, of some factories, Cornwall had been ignored
by central policy-makers, whose attention had focused upon massive
structural problems in the old industrial areas of Scotland, Wales and
northern England. However, as part of a preoccupation with faster
economic growth, regional economists in Britain and many other parts
of Europe equipped themselves with a new mental map which divided
the world into dynamic and thrusting central regions which were held
back by congestion and labour shortages, and which contrasted with
lagging, under-utilized peripheries. To solve both sets of problems,
large tracts of outer Britain, including Cornwall, were granted regional
aid on a massive scale, factories were persuaded to move to these
outlying areas and regional growth points were identified which would
be large enough to attract high-technology industry from the centre
and stem the brain-drain of workers from the periphery. Transport and
communication links, chiefly roads, were improved.[62]

In its early stages, this institutionalization of Cornwall's core–

periphery status had favourable effects upon the quantity, if not the quality, of local employment. The number of jobs in the manufacturing sector went up by more than 50 per cent between the 1960s and the mid-1970s, although two-thirds of them were in branch factories, employing lesser-skilled operatives, controlled by headquarters outside Cornwall, which retained the better-paid opportunities in marketing, research and development and administration. Most of Cornwall's growth in manufacturing employment occurred in what were five out of the UK's bottom six earning sectors, in which technology and products were coming to the end of their useful lives. (The sixth low-paying sector, food and drink processing, was already well established.) This was not a specifically Cornish experience, but one of the paradoxes of central government strategy for Cornwall was that, while one decentralization policy subsidised low-paying manufacturing firms to move in, other 'decentralization' policies were actually moving higher-paid work in public utilities and services out of Cornwall to so-called 'regional centres' in Plymouth, Taunton, Exeter or Bristol. For Cornwall, 'decentralization' often meant centralization.

Plymouth, by far the biggest agglomeration in the South-West of Britain, was an obvious choice for a regional growth point, but although it contained a relatively large share of manufacturing employment by regional standards, this was heavily skewed towards the naval dockyards with little spin-off into local high-technology growth of the kind that regional centres were supposed to provide. It was also deficient, even by South-West standards, in the vital and rapidly growing financial services sector. And it continued to fulfil the role of a barrier to economic growth in Cornwall. Far from initiating a 'tidal flow of high technology development across the Tamar', as one of Cornwall's development officers hoped, its net effect was to drain higher-level employment out of Cornwall, to 'regional' offices in Plymouth.[63]

Another main economic propellant was a wave of car-borne, self-catering campers, caravanners and chalet-dwellers which rose from under a million per annum in the immediate post-war years to over three million a year by the mid-1970s. In terms of full-time equivalent jobs, which is how many regional planners assessed the impact of tourism, it was probably as important as manufacturing growth, but the work was part-time, semi-skilled and lower-paid. Nevertheless the combined effect of employment expansion in manufacturing, engineering, tourism, china clay processing and a slight resurgence in mining was accompanied by a demographic turnaround from depopulation to repopulation, leading one regional economist to conclude that the 'rural periphery' of Cornwall was merging into the

prosperous core-region of the South-East.[64] And as if to confirm this
assertion, the South West Economic Planning Council published
its strategy, optimistically entitled *A Region with a Future*, in which
a broad swathe of prosperity spread from somewhere north of
Gloucester all the way to Truro and beyond.[65]

These visions faded, however, after the oil-price crisis of the
mid-1970s, as the inflow of firms from a rapidly shrinking British
manufacturing sector dried up and many of the factories that had come
to Cornwall shut down. More significantly, locally owned companies
that had survived and expanded through earlier crises were swallowed
up by British or international corporations, and their workforces were
often reduced to a fraction of their former size. The death knell of the
old, independent, export-based industrial structure of Cornwall was
finally sounded in the closing years of the twentieth century when the
last tin mine (South Crofty) shut down and china clay processing was
absorbed by a continental group.

FROM INDUSTRY-LED TO IMMIGRATION-LED GROWTH

And yet demographic and employment growth continued. Between
1961 and 2001 the Cornish population increased by nearly a half,
entirely because of in-migration since its rather elderly indigenous
population was dwindling. Contrary to popular opinion, however, two-
thirds or more of this inflow was composed of working-age people with
their dependants, and the economic consequences of this were spelt out
as early as 1974 in a report by the present author as 'imported unemployment'.[66] An inflow of the elderly or the non-working well-to-do
might generate an extra twenty or so jobs for every hundred incomers,
but an influx which included a substantial number of job seekers, while
generating some employment, in the service sector, would also lead to
a net increase in unemployment. This conclusion was disputed by the
Department of Employment, which sent a team of researchers to
Cornwall who later confirmed the existence of 'imported unemployment',[67] which has persisted despite the best efforts of dozens of local,
regional and state agencies to create more jobs.

Probably of equal or greater long-term importance, although more
difficult to quantify, was the effect of repopulation upon
entrepreneurial performance. Some local planners treated it
optimistically as an injection of 'dynamic graduates' who would
galvanize a remote backwater into action.[68] But a major survey by
Perry, Dean and Brown challenged the assumption of dynamism.[69]
They recorded a clear-cut division between in-migrants and the
indigenous population in terms of educational attainment, home
ownership and job status. The incomers scored more highly on all

counts and indeed occupied a large proportion of the upper-level jobs in industry, commerce, local government, education and health services. But rather than acting as a revitalizing force, they were, if not seeking a life of leisure, at least opting for a more leisurely lifestyle. Memories of vacations in Cornwall, together with a professed desire to quit the competitive 'rat race' of big-city life, were strong motivating forces for their move to Cornwall. These findings were reinforced by later surveys, one of which focused upon tourist operators, a large proportion of whom were newcomers with no knowledge or experience of the industry but with pleasant memories as consumers, rather than producers, of holidays.[70] Other surveys, directed by Malcolm Williams, traced a downward socio-economic path of incomers through time, and contrasted it with the upward mobility of younger Cornish migrants to the 'escalator' region of southern England.[71]

SUMMARY AND CONCLUSIONS
This article offers an interpretation which does not fit comfortably into an over-arching theory involving phases of core–periphery dependency, nor into a simple reversion from industrialization to de-industrialization. Whereas Payton and Deacon attributed decline to a lack of entrepreneurial responsiveness to changing economic conditions after the Copper Crash, the contention here is that it was the very swiftness of an earlier response that had already led to a slowing down in demographic and industrial growth. For this reason, this article starts by shifting a critical turning point in Cornish economic history back in time from the Copper Crash and ensuing crisis migration of the 1870s to spatial strategies from the early 1800s. Groups of adventurers diffused their superior technological and managerial skills to underdeveloped regions overseas, transferred capital and enterprise to a more promising site for metal processing in South Wales, and attempted to retain and enhance Falmouth's link with London by financing a direct railway line. However, because the railway link that was finally built passed through Plymouth, it opened up intervening opportunities for commercial and tourist development in South Devon as well as reinforcing Plymouth's regional importance as a naval base and industrial, chemical-processing port and emigration depot. Where capital, technology and enterprise went, labour followed, and the combined effect of these entrepreneurial actions was to institutionalize labour mobility.

In terms of theoretical modelling, the first of these spatial strategies conformed to an independent export-oriented industrial regions perspective, where areas escaped for a time from the hegemony of London. The second, however, involved vertical and horizontal integration between two independent, export-oriented industrial regions, with the Cornish mining economy becoming a supplier of raw materials, of diminishing importance, to South Wales. And the third strategy, the projected Falmouth–London link, is open to opposing theoretical interpretations. It can be seen as an attempt to reinforce a core–periphery dependency upon London, or to maintain Falmouth as a key link in an outward-looking, global maritime economy. Whatever their theoretical implications, however, the combined economic outcome of these actions—export of up-stream technology, transfer of down-stream processes, institutionalization of mobility, reinforcement of Plymouth's regional influence—was to block progress towards the attainment of a critical demographic mass.

Whereas Deacon has placed the 'Indian summer' of the merchant bourgeoisie in the 1850s, this paper postulates a whole series of 'Indian Summers'—or false dawns—in the early 1900s, the 1950s, and even the early 1970s. Late Victorian and Edwardian Cornwall has been characterized by Deacon and Payton by a failure to diversify and to modernize, an entrepreneurial climate of getting-by and making-do, and a culture of dependency upon an inflow of remittances from bread-winners abroad, with return migrants treated as liabilities rather than assets. This article stresses the importance of non-mining diversification and the appearance of a 'modernizing bourgeoisie', which met a rising demand for goods and services in which Cornwall offered geographic, climatic or topographic advantages that had previously been constrained by the predominance of mining. But they lacked the expertise to provide product and process innovation and new methods of management and marketing across a wide range of activities, and had to bring in externally trained professional managers and technicians. This article also highlights the positive multiplier effects of remittances and the role played by return migrants in bringing back both financial and human capital in the shape of knowledge of new methods and technologies.

Once again, these experiences do not fit a single theoretical model. Diversification into non-mining activities reinforced a core–periphery dependency upon markets in central England. In contrast, export-oriented expansion in china clay and engineering conformed to the independent industrial region model. Although the twentieth century opened with a confluence of favourable internal and external circumstances, this contingent prosperity was constrained by an irreversible loss of local entrepreneurial control. Railway and banking networks, shipping lines, shops, food processing factories and high explosives works passed into outside hands, a process continued by the nationalization of public utilities in the 1940s and the hegemony of centralist policies in farming and fishing. Already, from the early 1900s, Cornwall was experiencing the branch-factory, branch-office dependency that Payton saw as characterizing his 'third peripheralism' from the 1960s. While these experiences were part of a wider British pattern, and while some important locally owned firms expanded, economic diversification had gone hand in hand with spatial fragmentation. Cornwall, *c.*1950, was a mosaic of economic specialisms, its small-firm, small-town structure impeding the development of non-traded interdependencies that propelled economic growth. Meanwhile, Plymouth posed a growing barrier of intervening opportunities and—aided and abetted by the GWR—siphoned off transatlantic visitors to central England.

The latter part of the twentieth century witnessed the demise of large components of the independent export-base economy and the institutionalization of core–periphery dependency through centralist policies of regional aid. A turnaround from depopulation to re-population occurred, propelled first by industry-led, policy-inspired development and then by immigration-led growth. But while population rose by nearly 50 per cent and employment also increased, 'imported unemployment' also grew through an inflow of working-age migrants. Although better educated and of higher job status, these incomers, because of their preference for a more leisurely lifestyle, failed to galvanize the economy and—in the longer term—moved down the employment ladder, in contrast to the upwardly mobile Cornish out-migration to the 'escalator' region of southern England. Cornwall remained a low-earning, high unemployment peripheral region and the award of 'Objective 1' status by the European Union confirmed the failure of over three decades of regional policy.

ECONOMIC DEVELOPMENT AND REGIONAL IDENTITY
What light does this survey throw upon the formation of Cornwall's regional identity, a major focus of the new Cornish historiography? The history of the period, it has been argued here, is not one of a succession of different phases of peripherality, but rather of a lengthy and uneven transition, interrupted by a number of 'Indian summers' or false dawns, from an advanced, economically independent, export-oriented industrial region to core–peripheral dependency, externally controlled and internally run by outsiders. Yet, despite this, Cornwall has developed two of the four stages of regional identity formation in the model used by Deacon: self-awareness of a unique distinctiveness, and construction of badges of linguistic, historical and cultural 'difference'. Cornwall's period of industrial pre-eminence, as Deacon has shown, lasted long enough to add an awareness of industrial

heritage to a Celtic past. The *Cornish Studies* series has been of importance in strengthening these processes.

But what of the other two stages: formation of strong regional institutions and recognition of a regional distinctiveness by the central state? As far as the construction of Cornwall-wide institutions is concerned, the entrepreneurial contribution has been disappointing. Initiatives before the Copper Crash— transfer of capital, technology and skills to the New World and to South Wales—institutionalized international economic mobility, not internal cohesion. And the failure of Cornish adventurers to see the significance of a direct railway to Exeter encouraged the growth of Plymouth as an ever-increasing barrier of intervening opportunity between Cornwall and central England that, along with mining failure, prevented the attainment of critical mass. A lack of commercial as well as industrial growth is seen here as the defining problem in Cornwall's retarded development.

As a result, the internal economic diversification that followed the Copper Crash, however welcome it was, created a mosaic of economic specialisms and local occupational loyalties. This not only led to technological dependency upon other regions, but hindered attempts to create unity of effort. The history of entrepreneurial endeavours was one of missed opportunities to construct Cornwall-wide commercial and industrial associations. But here the Anglicization of leading members of the 'modernizing bourgeoisie' was of importance. As argued elsewhere, although some of them supported early Cornish cultural associations, they were essentially 'English establishment antiquarians'. They kept their cultural and their business life in separate compartments and were reluctant to respond to patriotic requests to form Cornwall-wide consortia.[72]

As for external recognition of Cornwall's regional distinctiveness, centrally directed regional policy-making has been based on function, not territory or culture. While increasingly paying lip-service to 'Cornishness' to help market Cornish products and services, central planners use statistical indicators of economic performance such as employment and earnings to define spatial boundaries and ignore differences of language, history or culture. The result has been a proliferation of agencies (typically forty to fifty in number) which administer a variety of functional policies—rural development, tourist promotion, industrial revival, urban regeneration—in overlapping areas from a number of 'regional centres', most of them outside Cornwall. In this process the crushing superiority of Plymouth's informational networks, its 'regional' television channels, its university, its central government 'sub-regional' offices and its mixed public and private sector quangos, masked Cornwall's economic characteristics in a 'South-West' or combined Devon and Cornwall 'peninsula' format. Cornwall was statistically invisible. Of course, the proposed Cornish Assembly would be a first step towards a solution for this problem.[73]

A SERIOUS IMBALANCE IN ECONOMIC RESEARCH
Finally, a significant imbalance in research into the economic history of modern Cornwall must be noted. An unduly Cornwall-centred and mining-biased focus has neglected extra-Cornwall influences, for example the growing significance of Plymouth as a barrier to Cornish commercial development. A preoccupation with mining's rise and fall has also meant a paucity of archival work on intra-Cornwall differences in other sectors. When it is considered that, for well over a century, first farming, then china clay processing, then tourism have over-shadowed mining in terms of employment and incomes, the relative lack of research on the economic history of the claylands, agricultural districts and holiday resorts is regrettable. A mining-centred approach has also contributed to a marked gender bias, and much work remains to be done on the female contribution to the economic development of Cornwall, including the activities of female entrepreneurs known to have existed in such sectors as banking, brewing, food processing, china clay, clothing manufacture, ship-building and tourism.[74]

Another reason for this imbalance is an orientation towards socio-cultural and political issues, concerned with the formation of the modern Cornish identity. These necessarily involve Cornwall-wide generalizations since the quest for a distinct identity goes hand-in-glove with the search for greater autonomy for Cornwall as a region. This article does not challenge the need for such generalizations: on the contrary, it supports them as an essential counterweight to a mass of action plans and strategic programmes which subsume Cornwall within wider 'regions' like the 'West Country' or the 'South-West'. But does it help to foreground Cornwall-wide cultural generalizations which neglect extra-Cornwall economic influences and understate intra-Cornwall economic differences? The aim should surely be to valorize the Cornish 'difference', not to essentialize it.

NOTES AND REFERENCES
1. For the development of the issues presented in this article, the author is greatly indebted to discussions with Alan Bennett, Bernard Deacon, John Probert, Sharron Schwartz, Andrew Symons and Peter Wills, and also to seminars conducted by Amy Hale and Philip Payton.
2. A.K. Hamilton Jenkin, *Cornwall and its People*, London, 1945; John Rowe, *Cornwall in the Age of the Industrial Revolution*, 1953, repr. St Austell, 1993.

3. Philip Payton, *The Making of Modern Cornwall*, Redruth, 1992; Philip Payton, 'Territory and Identity', in Philip Payton (ed.), *Cornwall Since the War*, Redruth, 1993a, pp. 224–53; Philip Payton, ' "Reforming Thirties" and "Hungry Forties": The Genesis of Cornwall's Emigration Trade', in Philip Payton (ed.), *Cornish Studies: Four*, Exeter, 1996, pp. 107–27; Philip Payton, 'Re-inventing Celtic Australia', in Amy Hale and Philip Payton (eds), *New Directions in Celtic Studies*, Exeter, 2000, pp. 108–25; Bernard Deacon, 'And Shall Trelawny Die? The Cornish Identity', in Payton (ed.), 1993a, pp. 200–23; Bernard Deacon, 'Proto-regionalisation: The Case of Cornwall', *Journal of Regional and Local Studies*, 2000, pp. 27–41; Bernard Deacon, 'The Jarring of the Distant Steam Engine', in Ella Westland (ed.), *Cornwall: The Cultural Construction of Place*, Penzance, 1997, pp. 7–21; Bernard Deacon, 'A Forgotten Migration Stream: The Cornish Movement to England and Wales in the Nineteenth Century', in Philip Payton (ed.), *Cornish Studies: Six*, Exeter, 1998, pp. 96–117; Bernard Deacon and Philip Payton, 'Re-inventing Cornwall: Culture Change on the European Periphery', in Philip Payton (ed.), *Cornish Studies: One*, Exeter 1993b, pp. 80–96.

4. For discussions of these issues see Chris Freeman and Luc Soete, *The Economics of Industrial Innovation*, London, 1997, pp. 43–8; J.L. Anderson, *Explaining Long-term Economic Change*, Cambridge, 1995, pp. 59–60; Jack J. Vromen, *Economic Evolution*, London, 1995, pp. 212–13; Michael Storper, 'The Resurgence of Regional Economics', *European Urban and Regional Studies*, 1995, pp. 191–221; John Adams, 'Institutions and Economic Development', in Marc C. Tool (ed.), *Institutional Economics: Theory, Method, Policy*, Boston, 1993, pp. 270–82; for a treatment from a relevant Irish perspective see Bryan Fynes and Sean Ennis, *Competing From the Periphery*, Dublin, 1997; Peader Kirkby, *The Celtic Tiger in Distress*, New York, 2002.

5. Payton, 1996.

6. Deacon, 2000.

7. Roger Burt, 'Proto-industralisation and Stages of Growth in the Metal Mining Industries', *Journal of European Economic History* 27, 1998, p. 103. For an example of an industrial regions approach, see Pat Hudson, *The Industrial Revolution*, London, 1992 and *Regions and Industries*, Cambridge, 1989.

8. Sharron Schwartz, 'The Making of a Myth: Cornish Miners in the New World in the Early Nineteenth Century', in Philip Payton (ed.), *Cornish Studies: Nine*, Exeter, 2001, pp. 105–27; 'Exporting the Industrial Revolution: The Migration of Cornish Mining Technology to Latin America, 1812–48', in Heidi Slettedahl Macpherson and Will Kaufman (eds), *New Perspectives in Transatlantic Studies*, New York, 2002, pp. 143–58.

9. *Bickford Smith and Company Limited*, Tuckingmill, 1932; John E. Eelsworth, *The Ensign–Bickford Company and the Safety Fuse Industry in America*, Chicago, 1936.

10. Schwartz, 2001.

11. J.R. Harris, *The Copper King*, Liverpool, 1964; Ronald Rees, *South Wales and the Copper Trade*, Cardiff, 2000.
12. Michael and Vernon Cory, *The English Corys*, Dorset, 1995, pp. 41–2.
13. Deacon, 1998; I am indebted to Bernard Deacon for much of the empirical comparisons between Cornwall and South Wales.
14. Deacon, 1998.
15. Sir Hussey Vivian, quoted in R.L. Brett, *Barclay Fox's Journal*, London, 1865, p. 11.
16. Edward Osler, *History of the Cornwall Railway, 1855–1848*, repr. Weston-Super-Mare, 1982.
17. Other political and geo-economic issues were also involved. The Tories and the GWR backed the coastal line, the Liberals and the LSWR supported the central line via Padstow for sea connections to Ireland. See E.T. MacDermott, *History of the Great Western Railway*, London, 1964; O.S. Nock, *The GWR in the Nineteenth Century*, London, 1962; David St John Thomas, *The West Country*, Newton Abbot, 1981.
18. Crispen Gill, *Plymouth, a New History*, Devon, 1966.
19. I am indebted to Andrew Symons and Bernard Deacon for information on Plymouth as an emigration depot.
20. Rowe, 1993; John C. Symons, *The Death Throes of an Industry: Cornish Mining 1885–1915*, Worcester, 1999; Payton, 1992; Maxine Berg, *The Age of Manufacturers*, London, 1994; Sidney Pollard, *Peaceful Conquest*, Oxford, 1981.
21. Payton, 2000, p. 113.
22. Deacon, 1997, pp. 77–8.
23. Deacon and Payton, 1993, p. 68.
24. Payton, 1992, p. 114.
25. William Lazonick, 'The Cotton Industry', pp. 18–51, and Edward Lorenz and Frank Wilkinson, 'The Ship-Building Industry', pp. 109–34, both in Bernard Elbaum and William Lazonick, *The Decline of the British Economy*, Oxford, 1986; Alun John Richards, *Slate Quarrying in Wales*, Llanryst, 1995; Harris, 1964.
26. Walter E. Houghton, *The Victorian Frame of Mind*, Yale, 1957; P.L. Payne, *British Entrepreneurship in the Nineteenth Century*, London, 1985; Elbaum and Lazonick, 1986; D.H. Aldcroft, 'The Entrepreneur and the British Economy, 1870–1914', *Economic History Review*, 1964, pp. 113–34.
27. Among them were the Holman brothers (who exported seven-eighths of their output), Bartle, Stephens and Pryor, all from the Camborne–Redruth area, Troy of Helston and the Charlestown Foundry near St Austell, which was greatly enlarged by the Martyns, a clay-producing family. For a fuller discussion see Ronald Perry, 'Cornwall's Mining Collapse Revisited', *Cornish History*, 2001.
28. For a discussion of these issues, see Ronald Perry, *Clayland Leaders 1850–1914*, forthcoming 2002.
29. Productivity improvements in clay production is one of the lacunae in the economic history of the industry. See Jos. M. Coon, 'The China Clay

Industry', *Royal Cornwall Polytechnic Society (RCPS)*, 1927, pp. 56–68; Jos. M. Coon, 'Granite and China Clay', *RCPS*, 1929, pp. 282–300; Kenneth Hudson, *The History of English China Clays*, Newton Abbot, n.d.; Philip Varcoe, *China Clay: The Early Years*, St Austell, 1978; R.M. Barton, *A History of the China-Clay Industry*, Truro, 1996.

30. For a fuller discussion of the issues in the following section, see Ronald Perry and Sharron Schwartz, 'James Hicks, Architect of Regeneration in Victorian Redruth', *Journal of the Royal Institution of Cornwall (JRIC)*, 2001 and 2002.

31. For agriculture see 'The Conditions and Products of Cornwall', *West Briton*, 16 April 1868; for tourism see E. Whitfield Crofts, *Tourist's Companion to West Cornwall*, Penzance, 1877.

32. Deacon, 1997.

33. For discussion of members of this group, see Schwartz and Perry, 2001.

34. Perry, 2001.

35. Perry, 1999.

36. *West Briton*, 2 September 1915.

37. Bernard Deacon, 'Imagining the Fishing: Artists and Fishermen in Late Nineteenth Century Cornwall', *Rural History* 12.2, 2001, pp. 159–78.

38. Helped by loans from Bolitho's Bank and led by their remarkable vicar, the Revd Wladislaw Lach-Szryma, antiquarian and modernizer. See John Corin, *Fishermen's Conflict*, Newton Abbot, 1988.

39. However, cheaper coal was one advantage that east coast owners enjoyed.

40. Sharron P. Schwartz, 'Cornish Migration Studies: An Epistemological and Paradigmatic Critique', in this volume.

41. Deacon and Payton, 1993.

42. Gilliam Burke, 'The Cornish Miner and the Cornish Mining Industry', unpublished Ph.D. thesis, University of London, 1981.

43. Sharron Schwartz and Ronald Perry, 'The Return of Cousin Jack', *Cornish Historian*, 2002; Ronald Perry and Sharron Schwartz, 2001, pp. 64–77; Ronald Perry, 'Silvanus Trevail and the Development of Modern Tourism in Cornwall', *JRIC* 1999, pp. 33–43.

44. *West Briton*, 20 March 1890.

45. R.N. Worth, *History of Plymouth*, 1890, p. 339.

46. Deacon, 1997.

47. J.V. Somers-Cocks, 'The Great Western Railway and the Development of Devon and Cornwall', *Devon and Cornwall Notes and Queries*, 1987, pp. 9–22; G. Kinch, 'Railways and the Balance of Trade in Victorian Devon', *Devon and Cornwall Notes and Queries*, 1988, pp. 85–8.

48. Perry, 2001, forthcoming 2002.

49. K.J. O'Donoghue and H.S. Appleyard, *Hain of St Ives*, Kendal, 1986.

50. Ronald Perry, 'A Remission in the Great Paralysis?' *Cornish History Network Newsletter*, 1997, pp. 1–2.

51. Symons, 1999.

52. Deacon and Payton, 1993, pp. 80–86.

53. Perry, forthcoming 2002.

54. Andrew Alexander and Gareth Shaw, 'Retail Trading, 1850–1939', in

Roger Kain and William Ravenhill, *Historical Atlas of South West England*, Exeter, 1999, pp. 462–71.

55. O'Donoghue and Appleyard, 1986, p. 11.
56. Ronald Perry, 'Cornwall Circa 1950', in Payton (ed.), 1993a, pp. 22–47.
57. John Murray (ed.), *A Preliminary Survey of Devon and Cornwall*, Exeter, 1947, pp. 239–42; Sir Felix Pole, in *Tre, Pol, and Pen*, London, 1928.
58. Murray, 1947, pp. 221–2 and 236.
59. Philip Payton and Paul Thornton, 'The Great Western Railway and the Cornish-Celtic Revival', in Philip Payton (ed.), *Cornish Studies: Three*, 1995, pp. 83–103.
60. Alan Bennett, *The Great Western Railway in West Cornwall*, Cheltenham, 1995.
61. Ronald Perry, 'Economic Change and Opposition Policies', in Payton (ed.), 1993a.
62. For a fuller discussion of regional policy in peripheral maritime areas with particular reference to Cornwall, see Ronald Perry, Ken Dean and Bryan Brown, *Counterurbanisation*, Norwich, 1986.
63. For a more detailed discussion see R. Perry, 'The Role of the Small Manufacturing Business in Cornwall's Economic Development', *South West Papers in Geography*, Exeter, 1982.
64. Derek Spooner, 'Industrial Movement, Rural Areas and Regional Policy', *Regional Development and Planning Conference*, Budapest, 1973, p. 147.
65. South West Economic Planning Council, *A Region With a Future*, Bristol, 1967, and *Strategic Settlement Plan*, Bristol, 1973.
66. Ronald Perry, *The Employment Situation in Cornwall*, Redruth, 1974.
67. Robert McNabb, *Unemployment in West Cornwall*, Bristol, 1979.
68. Bernard Deacon, Andrew George and Ronald Perry, *Cornwall at the Crossroads*, Redruth, 1988.
69. Ronald Perry *et al.*, 1986.
70. Gareth Shaw, Alan Williams and J. Greenwood, *Tourism and the Economy of Cornwall*, Exeter, 1987.
71. Malcolm Williams and Tony Chapman, 'Cornwall, Poverty and In-Migration', in Philip Payton (ed.), *Cornish Studies: Six*, Exeter, 1998; See also Peter Wills, 'Cornish Regional Development', in Payton (ed.), 1998, pp. 143–62.
72. Ronald Perry, 'Celtic Revival and Economic Development in Edwardian Cornwall', in Philip Payton (ed.), *Cornish Studies: Five*, Exeter, 1997, pp. 100–12.
73. Cornish Constitutional Convention, *Governance for Cornwall in the 21st Century*, Truro, 2002; Philip Payton, *A Vision of Cornwall*, Fowey, 2002, especially chapter 8.
74. For two attempts to redress the balance see Sharron Schwartz, 'No Place For a Woman: Gender at Work in Cornwall's Metalliferous mining Industry', and Ronald Perry, 'The Bread Winners: Gender, Locality and Diversity in Late Victorian and Edwardian Cornwall', in Philip Payton (ed.), *Cornish Studies: Eight*, Exeter, 2000, pp. 69–96 and 115–27.

PARTY, PERSONALITY AND PLACE: RESEARCHING THE POLITICS OF MODERN CORNWALL

Garry Tregidga

INTRODUCTION

One of the central features of Cornish Studies over the past decade has been a growing interest in political issues. Topics ranging from Cornish electioneering at the end of the eighteenth century to the rise of anti-metropolitanism in the last century have been studied by a wide variety of scholars. The first part of this article will explore the role of the Institute of Cornish Studies in providing an interdisciplinary framework as this process developed in the early 1990s. By bringing together a variety of perspectives, not least through the second series of *Cornish Studies*, it has been possible to consider the wider implications of research in the new field of Cornish political studies. Consideration will then be given to the principal areas of interest over the past ten years, noting various changes of interpretation and pointing to the recognition of anti-metropolitanism as the core dynamic of the region's distinctive political culture. Indeed, the article will then conclude on the point that it is this ethno-regionalist factor, in both a historical and a contemporary context, which is likely to witness still further research over the next ten years as Cornwall attempts to meet the challenge of the new constitutional reorganization that is currently developing throughout the United Kingdom.

ESTABLISHING FRAMEWORKS

Philip Payton's 1994 article on Cornwall's radical tradition provides a useful starting point for exploring the emergence and development of

Cornish political studies. Recognizing the growing interest in Cornish politics at that time, ranging from Edwin Jaggard's consideration of the continuity and change debate in the nineteenth century to the work of scholars looking at issues of alignment and mobilization after 1900, Payton constructed a concise synthesis of ongoing research. He emphasized the remarkable survival of Cornish radicalism from the Age of Reform in the nineteenth century to the eve of the Second World War. Not only did this explain the failure of the Labour Party in Cornwall, it also indicated 'an intimate relationship between a distinctive Cornish political culture and the wider Cornish identity'. Although in the long term it was the Conservatives who, paradoxically, became the main beneficiary of this process, it was significant that the Liberal Party was able to survive the so-called Age of Alignment after the First World War as a major force in Cornwall. Payton added that this reflected the Liberal Party's ability 'to project itself as both the plausible radical alternative to the Conservatives and as the "Cornish party" '. It was well-placed to exploit the trend towards anti-metropolitanism after the Second World War, even 'co-opting where electorally appropriate the rhetoric and even policies of Cornish nationalism'.[1]

The result was the creation of a unifying or core narrative that could explain the events of the nineteenth and twentieth centuries. In the absence of a specific political research unit, on the lines, for example, of the Institute of Welsh Politics at Aberystwyth, such an interdisciplinary perspective was valuable. Although at this time Cornwall was certainly attracting the attention of both historians and political scientists, it appears that there were different reasons for this interest. Researchers from the discipline of political science offered an early perspective. Even in the late 1970s Colin Rallings and Adrian Lee were presenting papers on Cornwall that noted both the region's distinctive electoral behaviour and the rise of anti-metropolitanism.[2] This led in 1993 to Lee's statistical survey of electoral politics in Cornwall during the post-war era. Basing his study on an application of Miller's method of assessing the statistical measure of voting deviation between one area and another, Lee compared Cornwall with other areas of the United Kingdom. He concluded that the extent of the region's diversity was directly comparable with the 'deviation' in Wales from voting behaviour in England detected by Miller. The deviation figure for Cornwall did not fall 'below the Welsh' for a single post-war election and from 1959 to 1966 was 'substantially above'. Lee added that at the local government level, '[c]ounty elections in Cornwall display the greatest variety of patterns of contestation to be found anywhere in the United Kingdom'.[3]

Lee's approach was set against the wider background of a growing interest in issues of regional diversity and centre–periphery politics. By 1970 an upsurge in support for separatist parties in Western Europe, combined with signs of a general realignment of electoral politics, appeared to undermine the conventional belief in unified and homogeneous states. This coincided with new research into the long-term relationship between the 'centre' and its 'peripheries' by academics like Stein Rokkan and Derek Urwin who pointed to the significance of state-building processes dating back to the medieval period.[4] Such ideas were central to Payton's *The Making of Modern Cornwall* in 1992. Adapting and developing Sidney Tarrow's idea of various 'phases of peripherality', he concluded that 'in each historical period the experience of Cornwall has been highly individual when compared to that of the English "centre", or indeed other areas of Britain'. The changing phase of 'second peripheralism' as a result of the effective collapse of mining in the second half of the nineteenth century was to lead to 'social and economic marginalisation' for Cornwall.[5] This phenomenon, as we shall see later, provided the basis of Payton's explanation for the survival of the Cornish Radical Tradition.

For some historians, however, there was a different motivation for studying the events of the nineteenth century. In the mid-1970s Edwin Jaggard had become very interested in local-level electoral politics as a result of his studies for a Masters degree on 'The 1841 General Election in England and Wales' at the University of Western Australia. Under the Ph.D. supervision of Professor Richard Davis at Washington University in St Louis he began to study the electoral politics of Cornwall over the period from 1760 to 1910. Just a few years earlier Davis had played a leading role in a major scholarly debate over the political power of the aristocracy in England during the years before and after the 1832 Reform Act. Davis encouraged Jaggard to study Cornwall in this context on the grounds that the region 'had plenty to offer, not least because of its pre-reform reputation. It would be a challenge to see what happened after 1832'.[6] Cornwall was, therefore, regarded by Jaggard as a case study that enabled him to 'enter debates about the working of the electoral system in England'. This interest has led to an impressive list of journal articles, which culminated in 1999 with a book entitled *Cornwall Politics in the Age of Reform, 1790–1885*.[7] Mention should also be made of the late Brian Elvins, who sadly died during 2001. He was a pioneer in the study of the political history of the region and in 1959 completed an influential M.A. thesis, which was entitled 'The Reform Movement and County Politics in Cornwall, 1809–1852'.[8] Interestingly, it appears that it was the launch of the new *Cornish Studies* series in the 1990s that encouraged him to rekindle his interest in the events of the first half of the nineteenth century. The result was that he became a regular contributor to the series with a number of informative and stimulating articles on the political developments of this early period.[9]

This example of the influence of *Cornish Studies* is a reminder that the local field of political research is constantly developing and expanding. With the series acting as a platform for the work of both historians and political scientists, a positive exchange of ideas is now possible. Jaggard, for example, is currently considering ways of engaging with the core debates initiated by New Cornish Studies as a parallel project to his current focus on the politics of small towns in England and Wales in the nineteenth century.[10] Given the inter-disciplinary nature of the work of the Institute of Cornish Studies, it is also not surprising that ideas from other academic debates, such as spatial considerations or the subjective methodology of oral history, are being used to build on the framework of Payton's core narrative. In order to explore these issues in greater detail, we must now consider some specific examples of recent work on Cornish politics in three areas: party identity; spatial diversity; and personality studies.

RECENT TRENDS IN CORNISH POLITICAL STUDIES

Issues of party identity in a Cornish context tend to be focused on the electoral experience of the Liberal Party. A good example of this approach can be seen in the work of Elvins, whose collection of articles in *Cornish Studies* traced the origins of Cornish Liberalism during the first half of the nineteenth century. In his 1998 study of Sir John Colman Rashleigh he focused on the emergence of a sustained challenge to the aristocratic establishment. He analysed the activities of Rashleigh's 'Friends of Parliamentary Reform', which was formed in 1809 with the intention of removing the defects of the notorious rotten borough system. Elvins pointed to the long-term significance of this move by stressing that Rashleigh, along with his 'group of like-minded friends, broke the existing mould of politics in Cornwall, laying the foundation for Liberal supremacy, and establishing a tradition which lasted into the twentieth century and which exhibited a revival in the recent 1997 General Election, with four of Cornwall's five MPs being Liberal Democrats'.[11] In subsequent articles Elvins went on to discuss both the contribution of the Lemon family interest and the emergence of the *West Briton* newspaper in the context of early Liberal politics.

The focus on Cornish Liberalism is perhaps even more evident with regard to studies of the twentieth century. Over the past decade there has been a natural tendency to concentrate on this party, given its ability to survive as a major force following Cornwall's apparently unique experience during the Age of Alignment. Sustained by their continuing links with Methodism and the relative weakness of local trade unionism, the Liberals remained the obvious alternative to the Conservatives and the natural heirs of the Cornish Radical Tradition. The triumphs of 1923 and 1929, when the Liberals completely monopolized Cornwall's parliamentary representation, pointed to the electoral vitality of the party at the grass-roots. Indeed, it was no wonder that some contemporary observers remarked that Cornwall in the 1920s was the 'last refuge of Liberalism'.[12] For Payton, this was a product of the 'paralysis that had afflicted Cornish society and economy'. De-industrialization in the era of 'second peripheralism' prevented the development of Labour and left the Liberal/Methodist nexus 'fossilized' after 1918 'as the only viable radical alternative to the Conservatives and, indeed, as the "party of Cornwall"'.[13]

This theme has been continued through my own research into Cornish politics.[14] By seeking to place the experience of Cornwall within wider debates surrounding the dramatic decline of the Liberal Party after the First World War, I have attempted to move away from the conventional focus on urban Britain to the neglected world of rural politics. A constructive model for this approach has been provided by Rokkan's views on the formation and consolidation of core political cleavages.[15] This interpretation was based on the political history of Scandinavia, where socialist parties, the New Left, had established an early supremacy at the state level through support in urban and industrial areas. In peripheral areas, however, an inherent combination of regionalist, rural and religious discontent offered a more secure environment for the Liberals and other parties of the Old Left. When applied to Cornwall, this model helps to explain the survival of traditional politics in the first half of the twentieth century. Even in 1945, when Labour formed its first majority government at Westminster, the Liberals still came second in Cornwall in terms of their overall share of the popular vote.[16] By building on this hard core of support, the Liberals were able to stage an early recovery in the Duchy during the late 1950s. Victories by Peter Bessell and John Pardoe in the 1960s were followed by the triumph of David Penhaligon in the following decade, and these events arguably created a cultural and historical context for the dominance of the Liberal Democrats in the parliamentary elections of 1997 and 2001.

Recent work, however, has started to highlight the need for detailed studies of the other principal parties. For the twentieth century, this is certainly the case with the Labour Party. My article in *Cornish Studies: Seven* suggested that Cornwall, far from being a political backwater for socialism, was briefly at the forefront in the rise of socialism during the period immediately after the First World War. Labour's share of the vote in West Cornwall in 1918 was actually higher than in many industrial areas of Britain destined to become Labour strongholds.[17] In order to fully understand the nature of Cornwall's Radical Tradition, it is essential that researchers look in greater detail at the paradoxical history of Cornish socialism. One might add that we also need to look at the changing fortunes of the Conservative Party. Despite the academic interest in issues relating to the survival of Liberalism, the practical reality is that the Conservatives were the dominant force in Cornish politics from 1931 until their disastrous setback in 1997. Besides, such an approach will also enable scholars to redefine the position of the Liberals within the context of Cornish politics as a whole. The sweeping Liberal landslides of the 1920s make it tempting to interpret that party's subsequent survival as a Cornwall-wide phenomenon. In reality, however, the Labour Party had emerged by 1945 as the main alternative to the Conservatives in the West Cornwall constituencies of Truro, Camborne and St Ives. Only in Bodmin and North Cornwall did the Liberals remain ahead of Labour during the dark days of defeat in the early 1950s. The revival of the latter part of that decade was shared more with Devon border seats like Torrington and North Devon than with West Cornwall, which might lead us to apply the term of 'Tamar Liberalism' rather than 'Cornish Liberalism'. Indeed, it was only with David Penhaligon's historic breakthrough at Truro in 1974 that the Liberals started to break the mould of West Cornwall politics.[18]

This reference to spatial diversity brings us to the issue of place in political research. Bernard Deacon in *Cornish Studies: Eight* pointed out that 'the Cornish Studies researcher must stay alert to processes that operate at different scales: the global, the Cornish and the local'. Such an approach would go beyond the usual tendency of concentrating on Cornwall as a single entity and provide a framework for exploring the interconnections between 'these different scales'.[19] Although there has been no formal application of the spatial turn to studies of Cornish politics, it appears that researchers in this area are already operating at different levels. For the nineteenth century we can point to Jaggard's recognition of the need to give equal consideration to the mining, fishing and agricultural parts of the region. Ignoring the tendency to focus on the cultural and economic predominance of mining, his *Cornwall Politics in the Age of Reform* pointed to intra-Cornwall differences between the county divisions of East and West. The political implications were significant. Rural issues were much more to the fore in East Cornwall, with the farmers developing a reputation as an independent force and challenging the official

Conservative candidate and his gentry supporters in 1852. The subsequent victory of the agricultural candidate in this election came over thirty years before C.A.V. Conybeare's popular victory over the middle-class establishment in Camborne.[20] Similarly, David Thomson's recent study of municipal politics in Truro in the 1830s is a reminder of the need to investigate developments at the micro level. His consideration of the theme of civic pride placed Truro within the context of comparative work on borough politics in West Yorkshire.[21]

Analytical work on the twentieth century is also incorporating the role of space. It was mentioned earlier that the Liberal Party fared better in the rural divisions of East Cornwall after the 1920s than in the industrial communities further west. My own research on this subject suggests that this reflected the failure of the Labour Party to establish a secure base from which it could expand into the rural hinterland of the region. A model for this process can be seen in Wales, where Labour first established a core base in the mining valleys of the south before expanding into the remoter parts of the principality.[22] This was not really an option for the Cornish Labour movement, a result of the failure of what Treve Crago describes as the period of 'proto-alignment' in the years immediately after the First World War.[23] After Labour's temporary breakthrough in 1918 the party's progress in West Cornwall was more gradual and this enabled the Tamar Liberals to survive on the rump of the Radical tradition until their first post-1945 revival. In that sense we must link internal spatial diversity to economic factors if we are to explain the politics of the periphery. Yet we also need to consider the global aspects of the Cornish experience. This was addressed in a recent article by Payton who focused upon the transplantation of the Cornish Radical Tradition to South Australia in the late nineteenth and early twentieth centuries. The Liberal/Nonconformist nexus, as in Cornwall, played a critical role in shaping progressive politics, leading eventually to a distinctly Cornish image for the state's United Labor Party. Payton concluded that there are clear 'parallels between the Cornish and South Australian experiences', with the apparent paralysis of Cornish politics being echoed by the eventual ' "fossilization" of the Cornish-Methodist-mining influence in the Labor Party in the inter-war period'.[24]

Finally, we must consider the need for studies of individuals associated with Cornish politics. Both Elvins and Jaggard have provided useful biographies of personalities from the nineteenth century, in particular the historical significance, as was mentioned earlier, of Sir John Colman Rashleigh's contribution to early Liberal politics and the recent edited collection of the 1868 election papers of Arthur Pendarves Vivian.[25] Yet there is a clear case for more scholarly research into the lives of other influential politicians who have been able to shape the history of Cornish politics. Payton's brief sketch of Isaac Foot in *The Making of Modern Cornwall* nicely captures the appeal of an individual who so clearly personified the distinctive nature of Cornish politics.[26] Foot was also more than just a product of his times. His ability to articulate the moral politics of the Old Left might well have been the critical factor in ensuring the continuance of the Cornish Radical Tradition. Detailed studies of such charismatic individuals should be encouraged in order to build a more complete picture. Moreover, a consideration of personalities, rather than just the conventional focus on statistical evidence, would surely assist Cornish political studies in appealing to a wider audience.

Personality studies should not be restricted to the leading figures in society. The ongoing research associated with the Cornish Audio Visual Archive (CAVA) project offers the potential of investigating this subject at a variety of levels. Although the remit of CAVA now covers all aspects of the historical and contemporary life of Cornwall and the Cornish, this multimedia research programme actually grew out of an idea that simply envisaged the use of oral history as a method of studying the region's political culture in the twentieth century. Researchers associated with CAVA are now beginning to offer fresh perspectives on a range of issues, notably Crago in his ongoing reappraisal of the political dimension to the Celto-Cornish Revival and Kayleigh Milden with regard to the historic relationship between Methodism and politics.[27] Oral history can be applied in different ways. In the first place, it offers the potential of providing extra data on the local level, thereby supplementing more conventional sources of information and enabling scholars to investigate such topics as family voting patterns and wider cultural influences through reference to individual life histories. Yet talking about the past with those who participated in it, even created it, is also a means of exploring the everyday dynamics of Cornish political life. Electoral behaviour is not necessarily a rational process. By exploring the subjective dimension of micro-politics we can further enhance our understanding of the party identity and spatial diversity issues outlined earlier.

EXPLORING THE POLITICS OF ANTI-METROPOLITANISM

So far the principal concern of this paper has been a consideration of Cornwall's political culture as a whole. Yet the ethno-regionalist dimension to local electoral behaviour deserves special consideration. On a superficial level this statement might seem surprising. Whilst a nationalist movement, Mebyon Kernow (Sons of Cornwall), was created in 1951, its electoral record over the past few decades has hardly been impressive in comparison with its more successful counterparts in Scotland and Wales. Deacon's 1983 study of the electoral impact of Cornish nationalism noted that its best vote in a parliamentary election was a mere 4.02 per cent, which was achieved by Colin Murley at St Ives in 1979. The author concluded that once Mebyon Kernow was seen as an insignificant force in Westminster elections its potential was further undermined by a voting system that 'positively encourages tactical voting'.[28] Recent challenges to the London-based parties have shown no sign of a breakthrough for Mebyon Kernow at the parliamentary level. Setbacks in 1983 meant that the party did not contest any further elections until 1997 when its four candidates polled an average vote of 0.83 per cent followed in 2001 by a modest increase to just 2.14 per cent for its three nominees.

Some observers, however, have pointed to other ways of analysing the politics of Cornish nationalism. Payton and Lee have pointed out that the mere existence of Mebyon Kernow 'was in itself enough to mark the political experience of Cornwall off from that of English counties and to suggest the existence of an autonomous political culture in which the articulation of separate identity and a sense of anti-metropolitanism was of underlying significance'.[29] This was clearly evident in the 1960s when leading members of the London-based parties joined Mebyon Kernow, which at that stage was more a pressure group than a party, to demonstrate their support for its political aspirations, notably David Mudd for the Conservatives and Cornwall's two Liberal MPs, Peter Bessell and John Pardoe.[30] An anti-metropolitan agenda continues to be advocated by groups and individuals across the political spectrum. In December 2001 the Cornish Constitutional Convention was able to present a petition of 50,000 signatures in favour of a regional assembly for Cornwall, a move that was also publicly supported by the Duchy's four Liberal Democrat MPs and a variety of councillors and public figures. Mebyon Kernow itself has occasionally been able to win a respectable level of support outside of Westminster elections, notably 10,205 votes (5.9 per cent or nearly 10 per cent of the total Cornish vote) in the European parliamentary constituency of Cornwall and Plymouth and in recent years an even higher mean vote of 12.1 per cent per candidate in the 2001 county council elections.[31] With nominal representation on four out of the six district councils, one might add that the failure to adopt a specific election strategy based on the immediate objective of building a strong base in local government has been a critical factor in preventing the nationalists from making a breakthrough. A forthcoming study of Mebyon Kernow and the wider politics of Cornish nationalism

MEBYON KERNOW

VOTE

| TRURAN | X |

LIB·LAB·TORY HAVE HAD THEIR DAY
VOTE MEBYON KERNOW THE CORNISHWAY
PARLIAMENTARY ELECTION 1979
THURSDAY MAY 3rd

PLEASE DISPLAY THIS IN YOUR WINDOW

Published by Neil Plummer, Blythe, New Road, Stythyans.
Printed by Penzance Priniers, 48 Causewayhead, Penzance.

5.   A Mebyon Kernow poster from the 1979 General Election campaign.

will offer another opportunity of reassessing this distinctive aspect of
Cornish political studies.[32]

In academic research the Revivalist background to Cornish
nationalism has been given greater consideration in recent years. My
own work in this area suggests that we need to go back before the
Second World War in order to trace the historical development of
anti-metropolitanism. Although accepting the essentially antiquarian
nature of the early Celtic Revival, my article in *Cornish Studies: Five*
indicated that during the Edwardian period some leading members

of the Liberal Party were already using Celtic imagery for political purposes and starting to echo their Welsh counterparts by developing a Cornish agenda that would embrace the local disestablishment of the Anglican Church and the creation of a regional assembly for Cornwall.[33] This was followed two years later by a consideration of the links between the Celtic Revival and the inter-war Cornish Labour movement. In the 1930s Labour politicians like A.L. Rowse, parliamentary candidate for Penryn and Falmouth, made a conscious effort to establish the concept of community socialism within Cornwall's political culture. The changing nature of the Celto-Cornish movement meant that younger Revivalists were willing to develop their ideas within the context of a specific form of 'Cornish socialism'.[34] Indeed, ongoing research by Crago is indicating a wider politicization of the Cornish cultural movement at this time than has been previously recognized.[35] One might add that we also need to go beyond the Cornish movement itself in order to fully understand the impact of the Celtic Revival in the twentieth century. The political career of Peter Bessell is a good example. It appears that Bessell was the first post-war political figure to give any serious thought to Cornish nationalism and his support for an ethno-regionalist agenda was evident several years before he joined Mebyon Kernow. What is also significant is that the interest shown by Bessell and his party colleagues in 'Cornish' issues suggests that the 'Tamar' factor was not preventing the Bodmin Liberal association from developing policies in a Cornwall-wide framework.[36] Once again, this is a reminder of the historical significance of anti-metropolitan politics in the region.

Yet we also require new research into the politics of contemporary Cornwall. The work of the Cornish Constitutional Convention is taking place against the background of wider constitutional change throughout the United Kingdom, with the Scottish Parliament and Assemblies for Wales, Northern Ireland and London likely to be followed by the creation of elected regional authorities in parts of England. Contemporary perspectives on Cornwall's place in this new regional order are now starting to emerge. Payton's latest study places the debate on the region's future in this devolutionary context, noting that the potential of institutional regeneration offered by the new Combined Universities in Cornwall campus at Tremough would be further enhanced through the creation of a Cornish Assembly. He added that this extension of institutional reform offers the prospect of 'a strong voice for Cornwall in the emerging Britain of the regions and within Europe'.[37] Bernard Deacon has recently addressed other issues relating to the current process of regionalization. Focusing on the alternative government model of a seven-county South-West region, he identified the role of policy-makers at this level in articulating a new regional discourse that effectively excluded the imagery and political claims of other scales in community identification.[38] This new research is to be welcomed. The agenda of Cornish political studies embraces both historical and contemporary issues. Given the continuing interest in centre–periphery politics, which is evident through the present focus on such issues as the impact of European integration and globalization on peripheral identities, it is appropriate that Cornwall is used as a case study by those scholars wishing to enter wider British and European debates.[39]

CONCLUSION
The research culture that has developed around the Institute of Cornish Studies over the past few years is currently creating new opportunities for researchers engaged in the broad area of Cornish political studies. Building on the core narrative outlined earlier, scholars have explored such areas as the rise and survival of the Liberal Party and the implications of spatial diversity. This work should now be extended to incorporate the history of other political parties and the role of individuals within the electoral process. The renewed interest in contemporary politics comes at a critical time in the constitutional development of the United Kingdom. In order to explore these issues we can use a range of quantitative and qualitative approaches, with the statistical emphasis of political scientists now being complemented by the use of oral history by CAVA. Indeed, a useful model might be that of the Institute of Welsh Politics, which conducted life evidence interviews with politicians, pressure group officials and other leading personalities as part of its study of the devolution process in Wales.[40] The South-West of Britain, as the Rt Hon. Charles Kennedy MP remarked, 'is not populated by homogenous country dwellers with identical aspirations and political beliefs, but by a rather more diverse people'.[41] It is now the task of Cornish political studies to build on this recognition of diverse political cultures by encouraging further academic research on the subject in the years ahead.

NOTES AND REFERENCES
1. Philip Payton, 'Labour Failure and Liberal Tenacity: Radical Politics and Cornish Political Culture, 1880–1939', in Philip Payton (ed.), *Cornish Studies: Two*, Exeter, 1994, pp. 83–95.
2. Colin Rallings and Adrian Lee, 'Cornwall: The "Celtic Fringe" in English Politics', unpublished paper.
3. Adrian Lee, 'Political Parties and Elections', in Philip Payton (ed.),

Cornwall Since the War: The Contemporary History of a European Region, Redruth, 1993a, pp. 253–71.

4. Stein Rokkan, *Citizens, Elections, Parties: Approaches to the Comparative Study of the Processes of Development*, Oslo, 1970; Sidney Tarrow, *Between Centre and Periphery: Grassroots Politicians in Italy and France*, Yale, 1977; Stein Rokkan and Derek Urwin, *The Politics of Territorial Identity: Studies in European Regionalism*, London, 1982.

5. Philip Payton, *The Making of Modern Cornwall: Historical Experience and the Persistence of 'Difference'*, Redruth, 1992.

6. Email communication with Edwin Jaggard, 27 May 2002; Edwin Jaggard, 'Patrons, Principles and Parties: Cornwall Politics, 1760–1910', unpublished Ph.D. thesis, St Louis, 1980.

7. Examples include Edwin Jaggard, 'The Parliamentary Reform Movement in Cornwall, 1805–1826', *Parliamentary History* 2, 1983, pp. 113–29; Edwin Jaggard, 'Liberals and Conservatives in West Cornwall, 1832–1868', in Philip Payton (ed.), *Cornish Studies: One*, Exeter, 1993b, pp. 14–30; Edwin Jaggard, *Cornwall Politics in the Age of Reform, 1790–1885*, Cambridge, 1999.

8. Brian Elvins, 'Aspects of Parliamentary Representation in Cornwall before the Reform Bill', B.A. dissertation, University of Birmingham, 1957; Brian Elvins, 'The Reform Movement and County Politics in Cornwall, 1809–52', M.A. dissertation, University of Birmingham, 1959.

9. Brian Elvins, 'Cornwall's Unsung Political Hero: Sir John Colman Rashleigh (1772–1847)', in Philip Payton (ed.), *Cornish Studies: Six* Exeter, 1998, pp. 81–96; Brian Elvins, 'The Lemon Family Interest in Cornish Politics', in Philip Payton (ed.), *Cornish Studies: Seven*, Exeter, 1999, pp. 49–74; Brian Elvins, 'Cornwall's Newspaper War: The Political Rivalry between the *Royal Cornwall Gazette* and the *West Briton*, 1810–1831', in Philip Payton (ed.), *Cornish Studies: Nine*, Exeter, 2001, pp. 145–73.

10. Email communication with Edwin Jaggard, 27 May 2002.

11. Elvins, 1998, p. 81.

12. *Cornish Guardian*, 6 June 1929.

13. Payton, 1992, p. 156; Payton, 1994, pp. 89–93.

14. Garry Tregidga, 'The Survival of Cornish Liberalism, 1918–45' *Journal of the Royal Institution of Cornwall*, 1992, pp. 211–32; Garry Tregidga, *The Liberal Party in South-West Britain since 1918: Political Decline, Dormancy and Rebirth*, Exeter, 2000a.

15. Rokkan, 1970, pp. 72–144.

16. Tregidga, 1992, p. 211.

17. Garry Tregidga, 'Socialism and the Old Left: The Labour Party in Cornwall during the Inter-War Period', in Payton (ed.), 1999, pp. 74–94.

18. Election results derived from F.W.S. Craig (ed.), *British Parliamentary Election Results 1950–1970*, Chichester, 1971; see also Tregidga, 2000a, p. 21.

19. Bernard Deacon, 'In Search of the Missing "Turn": The Spatial

Dimension and Cornish Studies', in Philip Payton (ed.), *Cornish Studies: Eight*, 2000, Exeter, pp. 213–30.

20. Jaggard, 1999, pp. 11 and 146.
21. David Thomson, 'Civic Pride in Truro in the Early Nineteenth Century', *Cornish History*, http:www.ex.ac.uk/chn/journal.
22. Tregidga, 1999a, p. 79.
23. Treve Crago, ' "Play the Game as Men Play It": Women in Politics during the Era of the "Cornish Proto-Alignment" 1918–1922' in Payton (ed.), 2000, pp. 147–60.
24. Philip Payton, ' "Vote Labor, and Rid South Australia of a Danger to the Purity of Our Race": The Cornish Radical Tradition in South Australia, 1900–1939', in Payton (ed.), 2001, pp. 173–203.
25. Edwin Jaggard, *Liberalism in West Cornwall: The 1868 Election Papers of A. Pendarves Vivian, MP,* Exeter, 2000.
26. Payton, 1992, p. 157.
27. Treve Crago, 'Mad Celts or Proto Nationalists?: An "Unofficial" Reappraisal of the 20th century Cornish Celtic Revival', unpublished paper given to the 3rd Public History Conference, Rushkin College, Oxford, 2002; Kayleigh Milden and Garry Tregidga, 'Reflections on Rescorla: A Study of Micro-peripheral Identity', *Cornish History*, http: www.ex.ac.uk/chn/journal.
28. Bernard Deacon, 'The Electoral Impact of Cornish Nationalism', in Cathal O Luain (ed.), *For a Celtic Future: A Tribute to Alan Heusaff,* Dublin, 1983, p. 244.
29. Payton, 1992, p. 203; Adrian Lee, 'Cornwall: Aspects of Regionalism and Nationalism', unpublished paper presented to Workshop of Nationalist and Regionalist Movements in Western Europe, University of Strathclyde, p. 1.
30. Payton, 1992, pp. 228–31.
31. Garry Tregidga, 'Devolution for the Duchy: The Liberal Party and the Nationalist Movement in Cornwall', *Journal of Liberal Democrat History* 22, Spring 1999b, p. 22; Mebyon Kernow election statistics calculated by Bernard Deacon.
32. Bernard Deacon, Dick Cole, Treve Crago and Garry Tregidga, *Mebyon Kernow and Cornish Nationalism: The Concise History,* forthcoming.
33. Garry Tregidga, 'The Politics of the Celto-Cornish Revival, 1886–1939', in Philip Payton (ed.), *Cornish Studies: Five*, Exeter, 1997, pp. 125–50.
34. Tregidga, 199a, p. 88.
35. Treve Crago, 'Highlighting the Social Dynamics of Oral History (An Investigation into the Changing Senses of Identity Occurring within Cornish Communities between the World Wars)', unpublished paper given to the 24th International Congress of Genealogical and Heraldic Sciences, Besancon, 2000.
36. Garry Tregidga, "Bodmin Man": Peter Bessell and Cornish Politics in the 1950s and 1960s' in Payton (ed.), 2000b, pp. 161–81.
37. Philip Payton, *A Vision of Cornwall,* Fowey, 2002, p. 207.
38. Bernard Deacon, 'Building the Region: Culture and Territory in the South

West of England', *Everyday Cultures Working Paper Series*, No. 3, Milton Keynes, 2002.

39. For examples of current work in this area see 29th ECPR Joint Sessions of workshops on 'Centres and Peripheries in a Changing World', Grenoble, April 2001, http: www.essex.ac.uk/ecpr/jointsessions/grenoble/papers.
40. For further information see http://www.aber.ac.uk.interpol/sgc-iwp/IWP.
41. Charles Kennedy, 'Foreword', in Tregidga, 2000a, p. xi.

BRIAN ELVINS AND NINETEENTH-CENTURY CORNISH ELECTORAL POLITICS

Edwin Jaggard

INTRODUCTION

The untimely death of Brian Elvins in 2001 deprived Cornwall of one its most active political historians, a scholar whose publications during the previous decade had contributed enormously to the elucidation of nineteenth-century Cornish politics. Much of this recent work had appeared in *Cornish Studies* and, as Garry Tredidga suggests elsewhere in this volume, it is almost as if the launch of the new series in 1993 had spurred him to return to the academic interests that he had nurtured more than thirty years before. At any rate, Brian Elvins must be counted as one of those responsible for the flowering of Cornish political studies, and in an edition devoted to a review of the development of Cornish Studies during the last ten years or so it seems appropriate to mark his contribution.

'THE REFORM MOVEMENT AND COUNTY POLITICS'

In 1980 I visited Pelyn near Lostwithiel, home of the Kendall family for many generations, to talk to the late Nicholas Kendall, who responded to one of my many questions by mentioning that there had long been 'bad blood' between his family and the Carew Poles of Antony. This particular conversation was invaluable for two reasons: firstly I realized that the repercussions of the 1852 East Cornwall election when Nicholas Kendall (1800–78) defeated William Pole Carew, arousing tremendous bitterness in the process, may have lingered on into the late twentieth century; secondly the latter-day Kendall referred to the 'Carey' Poles, ending the mystery of the 'Mr Carey' (William Pole Carew) whom I had read about in mid-nineteenth-century political correspondence.

The lunch at Pelyn, my understanding of the confusing events in East Cornwall politics in 1851–2, and the fact that I was actually living in Cornwall in 1980, arose partly because of the late Brian Elvins and his 1959 M.A. thesis 'The Reform Movement and County Politics in Cornwall 1809–52'. In particular it was this thesis, which I first encountered in Perth, Western Australia, and then read in St Louis, Missouri, that became the springboard for my later academic career. So how and why did this unlikely confluence of events unfold? And how much do I owe to Brian Elvins's perceptive analysis of what he had defined as 'county politics'?

How and why? In 1977, having completed an M.A. in British history at the University of Western Australia, I began thinking about enrolling in a Ph.D., somewhere, sometime soon. During research for the M.A. I had made use of the writings of four historians, all of whom for various reasons had an impact on my view of British electoral politics. Richard Davis (Buckinghamshire), T.J. Nossiter (Northumberland and Durham) and R.J. Olney (Lincolnshire) had completed nineteenth-century local political studies and all, to some degree, had engaged with the arguments of the American D.C. Moore. Moore's conclusions about the complex origins of the 1832 Reform Act, as well as his certitude concerning the politics of deference and their electoral significance, provided a starting point for my own ideas, and since the politics of so few counties had been analysed I decided to research another county in order to test recent generalizations?

Hidden away in Moore's bibliography in *The Politics of Deference* was a reference to Brian Elvins's 1959 M.A. thesis, so here was a possibility, a county where some work had been done already, albeit on a relatively narrow topic, and therefore where there were likely to be extensive collections of family papers. However, before this choice could be finalized I had to find an overseas university whose history department contained at least one member willing to supervise such a project, and which also offered financial aid to foreign students, because I would be accompanied by my wife and two daughters. Contact with Richard Davis quickly convinced me that Washington University in St Louis would be my destination, because Davis himself was excited by the project, and as he pointed out, both Jack Hexter and Derek Hirst in the same department, would encourage my 'political case study' perspective. Furthermore, Davis thought Cornwall would be a good choice for someone who wished to complete a Ph.D. as quickly as possible. As he rightly pointed out, Cornwall was an extremely distinctive territory and shared a boundary with only one county; therefore most family and political relationships would be essentially local.

Arriving in St Louis in August 1978 I found the coursework requirements left me some time for preliminary work on the Ph.D. Besides, I had to develop a thesis proposal. Naturally, therefore, I ordered a copy of Elvins's thesis, and when it arrived I was delighted to find how rich a collection of political papers was held in the Cornwall Record Office, although at that time I was not aware how little had survived from those identified with Cornish Liberalism post-1832. At this point Elvins became my guide, introducing me to all the twists and turns in county politics, particularly before 1832. Here was one of the most regularly quoted unpublished M.A. theses, a mine of information, although pursuing different objectives from mine.

It soon became obvious too that despite the detail of Elvin's thesis (the informative endnotes to each chapter revealed as much if not more than the text), there was plenty of room for me to develop my own arguments about borough as well as county politics. What made this possible was that in the late 1950s when the thesis was being written, apart from Gash's *Politics in the Age of Peel*, the amount of analysis of post-1832 electoral politics was relatively minor. Therefore Elvins had little opportunity to test his Cornish evidence against broader generalizations, nor could he compare developments in Cornwall with those elsewhere, for example in Buckinghamshire. Consequently, the result was an informative narrative, interspersed with analysis of the key players' motives and viewpoints. Twenty years later opportunities were there to use the same and additional material in different ways.

Nevertheless, Elvins introduced me to 'county politics', together with the Cornish aristocracy and gentry, so I read and re-read the thesis. By the time I left St Louis in September 1979 the outline of events to 1852 was clear. Moreover I knew who the Liberal and Conservative power-brokers were, and their allies, just as I could identify the ideological issues separating them. Perhaps of equal importance was the potential to use the thesis as a comprehensive biographical dictionary of the aristocracy, gentry, and more prosperous farmers. Thanks to Elvins, and Veronica Chesher's 1957 B. Litt. dissertation on the Rashleigh, Enys and Basset families, when I arrived in Truro I knew what I was looking for.

During the ensuing thirteen hectic months of research and writing, I attempted to make contact with Elvins, but received no response. I was excited to find some additional material, most notably correspondence between Colman Rashleigh, co-leader of the Cornish reformers with Rev. Robert Walker, and his relative Thomas Holt White.

This revealed new aspects of Rashleigh's personal networks, and his reformist principles. I also had the opportunity to examine the post-1815 farmer–reformer alliance, the beginning point of the farmers' political gyrations during the next sixty years—always governed by blatant self-interest. Where Elvins led I did not necessarily follow, but I always carefully considered his path.

It would not be true to say that his thesis was a constant presence during this period, because although I was examining Cornwall electoral politics between 1760 and 1910, including the boroughs, the focus of his research was no more than a minor part of mine. Even so I vividly recall comparing my judgements of issues and personalities with his. And whether they were similar or different, I was always grateful for the reference point. Yet in some ways it was a relief to break free after 1852, to explore county politics on my own, particularly with the insights gained from the Jolliffe and Pendarves Vivian Mss which together brought me to 1885.

THE ELVINS CONTRIBUTION
The uniqueness of Brian Elvins's contribution to the study of nineteenth-century British electoral politics is easy to identify. Before 1960 relatively few historians had shown much interest in the topic, with the most notable exception being Norman Gash (mentioned previously), who developed a powerful, if one-sided argument about the continuity of electoral politics pre- and post-1832. Certainly the genesis of parliamentary reform at Westminster had been examined by G.S. Veitch and many others, and there had been several studies of the Whig party in the late eighteenth and early nineteenth centuries. However, no-one had produced a sustained analysis of electoral politics in a single county, with the first Reform Act being the fulcrum. Like Gash, Elvins was not particularly interested in the 'high' politics of Westminster; more important for him were the expressions of political opinion in the provinces.

The thesis was innovative and ground-breaking in a number of ways: the discovery of a sustained and ultimately successful county-based reform movement led by Colman Rashleigh, the Rev. Robert Walker, and a small group of lesser gentry; partially uncovering the support given by the yeomen and tenant farmers to the reformers; the successful challenge to the once-powerful Tory hegemony in Cornwall, eventually resulting in the creation of a powerful Liberal Party whose opponents could never make a sustained challenge to their growing dominance; the undoubted importance of reform, repeal of the Corn Laws, religious issues and other questions of the day at various elections; and a persistent and powerful localism.

Elvins's thesis is probably unique because it is so wide-ranging. Ostensibly its boundaries were quite narrow—the reform movement in county politics between 1809 and 1852. However anyone who has consulted the 350-odd foolscap pages (far more than the requirements for a modern day Ph.D.) soon realizes that Elvins examined a range of topics interlinked with his principal focus. Furthermore, several of these were integral to later studies of electoral politics in Great Britain.

First and foremost his analysis of Cornwall's sustained and powerful movement for parliamentary reform was original, and very important. The genesis of reform at Westminister was relatively well documented in the late 1950s, but developments outside, apart from the short-lived political unions, were relatively unknown. Elvins began filling the gap, starting in 1805 and tracing the question of parliamentary reform and the Cornish reformers through to the 1830s. Yet he also realized how these developments had to be placed in context. How, for example, did the reformers win support for their arguments? He discovered both 'county meetings' and the press were employed, therefore both needed to be analysed. The establishment and ongoing rivalry between the *West Briton* (Whig-Liberal) and *Royal Cornwall Gazette* (Tory) underpinned Elvins's account of the reform movement, revealing how both political 'parties' argued their cases. The same was true of county meetings, forums skilfully used by the reformers to widen their support and popularize the question.

The politics of the 1825–26 county elections are almost a self-contained case study, skilfully reconstructed by Elvins to reveal all the personal and ideological nuances at play. Moreover, he places the elections within the context of the broader issues preoccupying many elsewhere in Britain—Catholic emancipation, and the abolition of slavery being two examples. The elections reveal Elvins at his best, mastering an extensive range of sources to present an analysis notable for its informative detail. And there was much more: the fundamental constitutional issues at stake in Catholic emancipation, making this the necessary precursor to parliamentary reform, led Elvins to examine the two as part of a continuing process of debate. Before, most historians had recognized the importance of the annual registrations of voters and party organization post-1832. In Cornwall the intricacies of each were exposed, as was the self-interest of East Cornwall's farmers from the 1830s to the 1850s. Professor Travis Crosby's *English Farmers and Politics of Protection* (1977) reveals how indebted he was to Elvins's pioneering research into farmers' political activism.

For Elvins, electoral politics were multi-dimensional. Outcomes were the product of myriad forces and influences, all of which he successfully set himself to include in his analysis. In addition there was a Namier-like intensity to his determination to identify almost every active participant in county electoral politics. The assumption behind this was that family or business relationships frequently had political consequences, so they needed to be understood. For this reason the endnotes of each chapter bulged with additional biographical and other details, enriching the thesis enormously. The almost loving attention to such intricacies is revealed in the explanation why Edward Pendarves, a Whig-Reformer candidate in the 1826 county election, was supported by the well-known Tory William Rashleigh:

> The relationship between Pendarves and Rashleigh came from the Stackhouse family. Pendarves was the second son of John Stackhouse, the younger son of Rev. W. Stackhouse DD. Rector of St Erme. W. Rashleigh's mother was the Rev. W. Stackhouse's younger daughter while the eldest son, William Stackhouse had married Mary daughter of Jonathan Rashleigh, William Rashleigh's grandfather. Finally, W. Rashleigh himself had married Rachel the daughter of William Stackhouse. Thus while William Rashleigh had a Stackhouse for a mother, his wife, a Stackhouse, had a Rashleigh for a mother.

Pendarves, Colman Rashleigh and the Rev. Robert Walker were particularly prominent in the thesis, but biographical details are provided on more than 120 individuals, aristocracy, gentry, farmers, newspaper proprietors, miners and others!

By the end of 1980, thesis written, Ph.D. awarded, I was back in Perth ready to begin publishing what I had discovered. Predictably, because I felt far more confident writing about county politics, when my two 'breakthrough' articles appeared in 1983, one was on the parliamentary reform movement in Cornwall from 1805 to 1826, the other on county electoral politics 1826–32. This was very much the ground covered by Elvins; however, my objective was to use material in my thesis to enter debates about the particularity of county reform movements, and the role of ultra-Tories in supporting parliamentary reform in 1830–31. The Elvins influence lingered on.

This was not the end of the story. In the following years when I regularly consulted my battered copy of his thesis, I admired Elvins's ability to uncover the details of county politics, to provide so much material for so many historians seeking local examples to prove their points: various writers for *The History of Parliament*, D.C. Moore, Travis Crosby, Frank O'Gorman—the list is long and impressive, emphasizing how highly original and valuable much of the contents were. Unfortunately, Elvins never had the opportunity to publish in the 1960s. Yet I continually wondered whether he would suddenly reappear, confronting us with new evidence from sources unknown or unavailable to others.

He did so, in the 1990s. Having retired from school teaching, he apparently decided to re-immerse himself in Cornish county politics. At first, when he began publishing sections of the thesis he seemed reluctant to alter his original work. Gradually this changed as he realized his research could now be placed within a much broader historiographical framework. In a sense the study of British electoral politics since 1959 had caught up to and passed Elvins, so his new challenge was to address this, to re-assert himself. Before he died, while retaining his trademark love of detail, and lengthy endnotes, he was in the process of the successful transformation of his thesis into a series of articles.

CONCLUSION
By now my indebtedness to Brian Elvins should be obvious. He was someone whose thoroughness provided the foundation for a ground-breaking historical study going far beyond straightforward narrative. He also exemplified many of the hallmarks of a good historian—his research was scholarly, he had the rare ability to incorporate into his analyses material from an extensive range of sources, he wrote clearly, and his enjoyment of his subject was obvious. He remains *the* authority on Cornish county politics between 1800 and 1850, but he was much more besides, for he also understood the political, social, economic and family networks of Cornwall's landed society, and their political significance. For many reasons Brian Elvins's unique contribution to Cornwall's history deserves to be acknowledged.

'IN SOME STATE . . .':
A DECADE OF THE LITERATURE AND
LITERARY STUDIES OF CORNWALL

Alan M. Kent

INTRODUCTION: DUALITY AND DEVELOPMENT

This article seeks to review critically the development of both literature in Cornwall and literary criticism about Cornwall over the past ten years. The reflections offered here are drawn from my own experiences both as a practising writer and as an academic interested in the literary culture of these islands and where that culture has intersected and merged with others. The route-map to my current position is outlined in my study *The Literature of Cornwall: Continuity, Identity, Difference 1000–2000* (2000), where I conclude that in order for the literary imagining of Cornwall to be revitalized, writers must end the lament for what is lost and seek new ways of 'de-revivalizing' the literature.[1] This ongoing exploration is informed by an engagement in literary studies in a newly configured Britain, which we may term the 'Anglo-Celtic archipelago'.[2] This discourse comes at a point in Cornwall's political and economic history when European Union Objective 1 funding has been secured and a high proportion of the population (apparently some 50,000) are lobbying for devolved political status.[3]

This broadly 'cultural materialist' contextual framework for understanding the literature of Cornwall is also located in the paradigm of post-colonial theory,[4] and takes the position that the Celtic territories of this archipelago were the initial colonial territories of the English nation-state, and that this relationship is still in negotiation and is being re-imagined. Cornwall, therefore, still has an unresolved duality of place when compared to other Anglo-Celtic territories. Paradoxically, this duality of place over successive centuries has actually led to the 'uniqueness', not to mention the sometimes strange brilliance of writing from Cornwall. Conversely, attempts to resolve this duality—indeed to sweep it away completely—have been central in terms of the writing of many poets, novelists, dramatists and observers of the literature produced about Cornwall and Cornish culture. In this article I argue that this duality has put literature and identity politics in Cornwall 'in some state': confused and sometimes unfocused, but also vibrant, contemporary and dynamic. I also argue that due to a merging set of cultural, political, technological and academic factors, for the first time a 'Cornish literary studies' is now 'real'. Before explaining the rise and growth of literary studies in Cornwall, it is perhaps necessary to document—albeit cursorily in an article of this size—a consideration of some of the texts presently of interest.

LITERATURE IN CORNWALL AT THE MILLENNIUM: AN OVERVIEW

The historical romantic novel of Cornwall, recently given thorough examination by Westland,[5] and which I additionally suggested may have its roots both in the 'extraordinary artificiality' of nineteenth-century Anglo-Cornish fiction[6] and in a lineage leading from Joseph Hocking through Daphne du Maurier to Winston Graham,[7] has continued its apparent rather radical politicization and awareness of Cornish identity outside the conventional constructions of mining and maritime culture. We must be guarded, therefore, against knocking too easily the apparent inauthentic nature of such narratives, when for popular readerships inside and outside of Cornwall they remain convincing imaginings. One of historical romance's principal practitioners, E.V. Thompson, has continued to shape the *genre*. Though works like *Winds of Fortune* (2000)[8]—set around St Michael's Mount—do repeat the formula established with his earlier novels,[9] *Seek a New Dawn* (2001)[10] hailed a new direction, as Thompson seems to draw upon much of the Cornish scholarship written by Payton and others on mining and agriculture in South Australia,[11] and indeed the new mobile and pied ethnic identity of the Cornish in the global context. Meanwhile Winston Graham, subject to considerable re-assessment in the past ten years,[12] also published the 'final' novel of his Poldark saga: *Bella Poldark* (2002),[13] which with its heightened sense of Cornish ethnic identity matched popular conscience. In some ways a new direction, in others a return to subject matter already popular in the 'pulp Methodism' of Silas and Joseph Hocking, Dennis Russell meanwhile set his historical saga *Carew* (2000) during the Civil War, offering a biographical novel about the life of Alexander Carew.[14]

Outside of historical romance, the Anglo-Cornish novel appeared to be in ascension during the early half of the 1990s,[15] but seemingly reached stasis in the latter part of the decade. Although those writers who had made an impact in the early part of the decade were still writing, the difficulty faced was the old problem: that the readership base for the realist, contemporary novel was not well enough established for publishers and therefore writers to develop the form. This particular difficulty is still not resolved, and at present the publishers of the hegemonic 'centre' appear reluctant to take the same kind of chance as say with younger and new writing from Ireland, Scotland and elsewhere.[16] There remains this crucial piece of cultural manoeuvring to ensure the 'centre' does take notice; otherwise the realist narratives so seemingly demanded will not be written. One exception is John Branfield's *A Breath of Fresh Air* (2001)[17] with its theme of greed, taking for its starting point the Newlyn School paintings of Stanhope Forbes, Harold Harvey and Laura Knight collected by the novel's protagonist Roger Trevail. Branfield, whose major contribution to children's literature of Cornwall is documented elsewhere,[18] is one of the few novelists of Anglo-Cornish willing to engage with the contemporary fashionability of the West Cornwall art scene. From a cultural materialist position we might argue that such a text would predictably emerge with the prominance of both the Newlyn School and the Tate St Ives in the marketing of Cornwall, but nevertheless it is a fine novel. One Anglo-Cornish novelist who had not really visited Cornish subject matter in fiction since *Birthstone* (1980)[19] was D.M. Thomas, whose novel *Charlotte: The Final Journey of Jane Eyre*, (2000)[20] re-examined the links of the Brontës with Cornwall, actually the subject of a earlier critical study by Hill.[21] The other significant prose work has been the publication of Jack Clemo's novel *The Clay Kiln* (2000). It is set in the china clay mining region of mid-Cornwall during the years 1938–9. Just like Clemo's other two published novels—*Wilding Graft* (1948) and *The Shadowed Bed* (1986)[22]—the tone is typical early Clemo, the novelist still stamping his very particular vision of Cornwall onto readers at the end of the twentieth century:

> The pit was full of that harsh melancholy which makes this area of Cornwall so repellant to the casual tourist. A latent ferocity breathed forth from the mouldering hollows of rocks, as from a skeleton. The crags jutting in all directions, impassive to the play of moonbeams and shadow, might have been gravestones.[23]

Methuen, one of Clemo's early publishers, collected together an anthology of the St Eval-born Anglo-Cornish playwright Nick Darke, including the Cornish-themed plays *The King of Prussia* (about the lives of famed smugglers Harry and John Carter of Prussia Cove) and *Ting Tang Mine.*[24] Darke's skills as a dramatist are manifested in both his dialogue, which is full of brusque and direct Cornish humour, integrated into realistic Cornu-English speech, and his ability to maintain the pace of often epic stories. Nowhere is this better seen than in his 1999 play *The Riot*, which dramatizes the Newlyn fishermen's dispute over Sunday observance. Here, the dialogue is stark and powerful:

> Billy: Make im swear an oath.
> Tack: Oo's e with now?
> Billy: Primitive Methodists.
> Tack: E left em after e broke a circuit preacher's back.
> Billy: Wesleyans?
> Tack: They chucked 'im out when e demolished the chapel up
>   Trevarrack.
> Billy: Bible Christians.
> Tack: Bible Christians took im on.
> Billy: Bible Christian oath.
> Tack: E won't break that.[25]

Darke's ongoing association with the Kneehigh Theatre Company has proved particularly productive. His subject matter is often maritime and mining culture in Cornwall, culled mainly from the eighteenth, nineteenth and early twentieth centuries, perhaps principally because it is when he sees a fully operational Anglo-Celtic Cornish culture operating on the European and global levels. It will be interesting to see if, as Darke's drama progresses, he integrates more post-war and millennial themes.

Cornu-English writing has been able to progress via use of the monologue as short story, developed by Simon Parker in his ground-breaking *A Star on the Mizzen* (1997)[26]—which looked, like Darke, at the Newlyn fishermen who in 1896 refused to go to sea on Sundays —and my own *Dreaming in Cornish* (1998),[27] a fictionalized version of the meeting between the Mousehole-based Cornish language scholar John Keigwin and the pioneer of Celtic Studies, Edward Lhuyd. However, there is still much work which remains in the popular domain—in magazines, newspapers, on BBC Radio Cornwall and in Gorseth competitions—of the 'dialect-in-aspic' type 'tyin'-the-dunkey-up-on-the-carn' narratives which often denegrate the vitality of lived

Cornu-English speech, and fail to notice emergent hybridizations, new words and grammars which inform the real experience of many Cornish people.

One such writer dealing with the difficulty of this delicate re-negotiation between retension and comedy, not to mention the seriousness and progression of the form, is the Redruth-based poet Les Merton. In his poem 'Arfurr', the reader sees Merton juggling the self-confident identity of a very manly Cornish 'King Arthur' with humour. The effect, however, considerably develops Cornu-English poetry:

> Eee wuz fo-wur fut nothun,
>   eed go ta a do un sey,
> 'Who wuz tha tallust bloke
>   furr I cum un.'[28]

As a publisher, Merton began to develop his own Palores (Chough) Publications list, developing the sophisticated poetry magazine *Poetry Cornwall/Barhonyeth Kernow*[29] and publishing Cornu-centric poets such as Diana Manning, Jenny Hamlett and Peter Hollywood.[30] Merton's difficulty, though, is whether the stapled A3 booklet is actually a regression to the 'rusty staple' low-scale production values enshrined in post-war Cornish publications.[31] Likewise the iconography of Palores was drawn straight out of an earlier, outmoded symbol of the pre-Second World War Cornish revival which had struggled on into the late twentieth century.[32] That said, both Merton's and Palores's scope is ambitious.

Poetry in both Cornish and in English continued throughout the period, with Tim Saunders's collected poems in Cornish from 1974 to 1999, *The High Tide* (1999),[33] becoming the benchmark volume in that language, both in terms of the standard of poetry and the production values of the publication. Poetry in Cornish continued to be circulated in the relatively safe cultural zone of the Cornish-language maga-zines,[34] but new poets such as the St Ives-based Mick Paynter have at last started to move the genre beyond Cornish nationalism and lament in poems which considered African-American heroes, heresy or the life of Primo Levi.[35] Certainly, poetry in Cornish was, as one might expect, having a good deal more success than fiction. Despite the efforts of writers such as Michael Palmer in novels such as *Dyvroans* (1998),[36] poetry in Cornish was at least in 'bite-sized' pieces and, with appro-priate translations both in publications and at readings, could be handled by broadly non-Cornish-speaking audiences. Indeed, it might even be argued that for such audiences, poetry in Cornish was 'exotic', but it did not have to come with the difficulties of learning the language: it was often Celtic enough.

My own Anglo-Cornish poetry, in particular in *The Hensbarrow Homilies* (2002),[37] has steered in a direction away from its early engagement with nationalism, to a more formally rigorous exploration of issues of identity both in Cornwall and in North America, juxtaposing non-standard English language with standard to enable the reader to come to conclusions over 'difference', and also to work through the cultural negotiations which have to take place in Cornwall's 'duality' to understand the ironies and difficulties of being Cornish in the twentieth and twenty-first centuries. Interestingly, Anglo-Cornish poetry was also beginning to form a crucial part of the events and entertainments at Cornish Gatherings across the globe,[38] perhaps demonstrating, as we shall see later in this article, a merging of the indigenous Cornish poets and those of the diaspora to form a new union of rethought 'states', which voiced these minority and yet pluralist identities, local histories and global communalism, alongside ethnic and cultural nationalism. Such Gatherings and the resultant literature celebrated within them— ranging perhaps from Robert Stephen Hawker and John Harris,[39] to Newton G. Thomas and W.F. Skyhawk,[40] effectively continuing the crisis in the idea of single nations as communities. McKinney was also demonstrating the historical cross-cultural sharing of lyrics and Cornu-English verse in his work on the the Grass Valley Carol Choir.[41] Outside of the main genres of literature in Cornwall, other interesting hybridizations were also taking place. The magazine of 'ancient sites and sacred sites in Cornwall', *Meyn Mamvro*, recorded neo-Pagan ritual invocations in the Cornish language, linking a number of cross-cultural movements and social trends, ranging from the solar eclipse of 1999 to 'Celtic' tourism in general:

Gwethiggy an West
Nearthow an Durrow
Teithy howlsethas
An moar brauz
Awonow ha goverow
Fentidniow downe
An glawe
Thera nye goz creia
Re an durrow goz breis beaw.

[Guardians of the West
Powers of water
Place of sunset

The great sea
Rivers and streams
Deep wells
The rain
I call you
By the waters of your living womb.][42]

In such a way barriers between using one or the other of the two
operational languages in the territory were also being strategically
demolished, demonstrating a new cooperation and that the kind of
one-dimensional 'Celtic' culture dreamed of by some revivalists was in
effect only ever a pipe dream. There was in a growing understanding by
activists and writers that Cornwall was no Brittany or Wales, nor ever
could be, and that the 'gaze' afforded on them had to end. I have
already provided an initial survey of the significant development of
indigenous film in Cornwall in my 2000 study,[43] but one text worth
mentioning here is the gritty film-noir *Hwerow Hweg/Bitter Sweet*
(2002) directed by Antal Kovacs.[44] The 90-minute film was the first
ever shot entirely in Cornish, but it is debatable what impact the text
will have beyond the relatively small circle of active Cornish speakers,
despite its subtitling in English. That said, the ambition of this project
does mark a growing confidence in Cornish film-making in Cornish
language, which hitherto had only really been witnessed in Wales with
Welsh-language film.[45] The establishment of the Objective 1-linked
Cornwall Film Fund in 2001 should assist future writing and film
production.

THE SHAPING OF CORNU-CENTRIC LITERARY
STUDIES

Until the development of New Cornish Studies in the early 1990s, there
had been few serious attempts to document the literary history of
the territory. In terms of literature written in Cornish, J.E. Caerwyn
Williams's oft-quoted 1971 study *Literature in Celtic Countries* in effect
continued the Irish, Welsh and Scottish dominance,[46] not to say
dismissiveness towards smaller territories such as Cornwall and the Isle
of Man, established as far back as Magnus Maclean's 1902 work *The
Literature of the Celts*.[47] Though written some seventy years apart,
their ideological agenda were identical. As I have argued elsewhere,
Cornwall's literature did not fit the established Celtic model, nor
apparently was there enough of it to say anything substantial.[48] That
said, literary scholarship had a pedigree in Irish, Welsh and Scottish
writing, of the kind that never existed in Cornwall. This, coupled with
the lack of any mechanisms of higher education, certainly prevented

internal scholars from taking it upon themselves to deal with the enormity of the problem.

This changed when the Institute of Cornish Studies began work on 1 October 1972, under the direction of Professor Charles Thomas, its initial aim being to provide 'a focus for, and the co-ordination and encouragement of, all forms of research in Cornwall'.[49] Certainly the first run of the journal of *Cornish Studies/Studhyansow Kernewek* from 1973 to 1987 allowed for some initial investigation into literature (albeit mainly medieval) from Cornwall. Among the kinds of articles emerging during this period were examinations of 'The Cornish Dialect and English Literature', bibliographies of Cornish language and drama,[50] 'The Cornish Writings of the Boson Family',[51] exegetical notes on some passages in *Beunans Meriasek*,[52] a socio-linguistic survey of English in Cornwall, 'A Lost Manuscript of the Cornish Ordinalia?',[53] 'The Manuscripts of the Cornish Passion Poem'[54] and 'Peter of Cornwall and Launceston';[55] other themes of the journal generally took an archaeological, linguistic and natural science direction. Some scholars have been critical of this first run of *Cornish Studies* for its apparent scant consideration of other themes,[56] although this criticism is perhaps unfair. The articles themselves are generally of high quality. Clearly scholars of this period were working within a particular paradigm, and this said, many of those who were shaping Cornish literary studies were active within the journal's pages—Charles Thomas himself, K.C. Phillipps, Oliver Padel, Andrew Hawke and Myrna Combellack.[57]

Outside the Institute of Cornish Studies, other important literary scholarship was also being completed. When the second series of the ground-breaking literary and arts magazine *The Cornish Review* ended,[58] its editor Denys Val Baker (author as well of the classic study of St Ives, *Britain's Art Colony by the Sea* [1959][59]) effectively became the voice of Anglo-Cornish literary criticism throughout the 1970s with his influential work *The Timeless Land: The Creative Spirit in Cornwall* (1973), which sought to explain how Charles Dickens, Thomas Hardy, D.H. Lawrence, Virginia Woolf, Howard Spring, Daphne du Maurier, Jack Clemo, A.L. Rowse and Charles Causley had been influenced by Cornwall's 'difference'[60]—a concept that was interestingly to reappear modified in both Payton's and Kent's later works.[61] A similar work followed in 1980 in *The Spirit of Cornwall*, where Val Baker considered 'The Poet's Eye View' ranging from Hardy and John Harris through to Frances Bellerby and W.S. Graham; 'The Novelist's View', where he considers many significant novelists, ranging from Alistair Crowley to Charles Lee; and 'The Stuff of Drama', where the Cornish-language dramatic tradition is examined, with Val Baker quoting from both Andrew Boorde and Richard Carew.[62]

Cornish literature itself was to have its first major chronicler as well during the 1970s, in the form of Peter Berresford Ellis. Ellis, whose pan-Celtic credentials had already been established,[63] took it upon himself to write as comprehensive an examination of Cornish literature as was possible at this point, covering not only the major works of the canon (*Ordinalia, Beunans Meriasek, The Creacion of the World*) but also contemporary writing in Cornish. This was significant, since the work suggested not only a model for coping with the Cornish tradition (one explained by successive rise, retreat, revival, corresponding to moves in wider European and British culture) but also a continuum to the present. Therefore, in the work *The Cornish Language and its Literature* (1974)[64] Ellis is as comfortable in dealing with the Old Cornish Vocabulary and the Bodmin Manumissions as he is with the emergent Cornish-language poets such as N.J.A. Williams and Tim Saunders. Ellis's work has various flaws (ironed out in successive scholarship), and yet it remained until at least the 1990s, the sole comprehensive companion to writing in Cornish. Other works at this time were more tangential to literary scholarship, but nevertheless commented on the tradition. The *Ordinalia* itself came in for its first comprehensive study from Jane Bakere's doctoral work during the late 1970s. Her *The Cornish Ordinalia: A Critical Study* (1980) is still the standard work on the three plays.[65] Meanwhile, individual studies of both Cornish and Anglo-Cornish literature continued on a piecemeal basis, in magazines such as *Old Cornwall: The Journal of the Old Cornwall Societies, An Baner Kernewek/The Cornish Banner* and *Cornish Life.*[66]

By the turn of the 1980s, however, it was clear that new observers as well as new writers were beginning to push back the boundaries of literary scholarship. The social, political and economic crisis which had been brewing in post-war Cornwall,[67] together with a re-assertion of contemporary Cornish identity,[68] was to be reflected in not only a rise of more overtly political writers,[69] but also a crisis in Cornish literary studies too.[70] This appeared to be sudden but in fact was drawn from a catalogue of 'problems' relating to how the literary establishment, both from the tradition of English literature and and that of wider Celtic literature, was going to deal with Cornwall. Cornwall was difficult, since it did not fit the Celtic scholarship's wider notion of the 'Celtic' nation state model, but paradoxically it did not fit the English model either. Interestingly, however, territories such as Cornwall were not the only areas in literary studies undergoing massive reform. Feminism, cultural materialism, post-colonial studies had started to remove long-perceived views of not only British culture but wider world literary studies as well.[71] By the end of the 1980s, the perceived difficulties of Cornwall being 'hard to pin down' had in reality been turned around. Cornwall's marginality in both the English literary tradition and in wider Celtic scholarship was no longer a good enough descriptor of its status in the culture of these islands.

This new agenda for considering the literature of Cornwall in general as an identifiable, sustainable and significant field of research has grown steadily throughout the 1990s, paralleled by an understanding that it is impossible to understand fully the literary continuum of the territory without what M. Wynn Thomas has described in Wales as an awareness of 'corresponding cultures'.[72] In Cornwall three significant branches of literary activity are identifiable: that which is written in Cornish, that which is Anglo-Cornish and that which is written in Cornu-English (a genre that used exclusively to be labelled 'dialect'). In many senses, these strands of Cornish literary culture are mutually symbiotic—and due to Cornwall's relatively small size, they depend much on each other and their hybridizations for their sustainability.

In many senses, even the politicality of, say, contemporary writing in Cornish depends necessarily on what is being constructed in Anglo-Cornish and vice versa. This co-dependency is beginning to be realized, not only by those creating new literature but also by those commenting on and trying to understand the debate. We ignore this co-dependency at our peril, since it is this matter which goes a considerable way in explaining the term 'difference' in the literature of Cornwall. By this 'difference' I mean Cornwall's collective difference from the literature of other Celtic territories (though obviously there are some similarities with the other Brythonic territories of Brittany and Wales) but also the way in which wider 'English' literature seeks to categorize Cornwall.

A NEW AGENDA: BRINGING CORNISH LITERATURE TO GRASS

This new agenda of Cornish literary studies can be seen first in John Hurst's highly influential article 'Literature of Cornwall',[73] in which he argues that after the legacy of Arthur Quiller Couch (who died in 1944), Cornwall came to be characterized by highly individual writers—such as Charles Causley, A.L. Rowse, Jack Clemo and John Betjeman—and that it was actually difficult to conceive of (in English at least) a Cornish literary tradition. He does, however, note a sense of tradition in modern writers such as D.M. Thomas—in particular in his poetry and his 1980 novel *Birthstone*—and goes so far as to notice structural and thematic similarities in the fiction of N.R. Phillips, Myrna Combellack and myself. Hurst's powerful and indeed controversial conclusion, however, was that: 'from the time of Ordinalia to the coming of John Harris there was a literary silence over Cornwall, punctuated only occasionally by the likes of Richard Carew ... [This] does not mean the Cornish are devoid of literary gifts; only that the particular combination of circumstances was not present.'[74]

Yet by the end of the decade this position had been contested and revoked by other scholars. Maybe Hurst was thinking too solidly along an 'Anglo-Cornish' axis or indeed along 'high cultural' lines, but nevertheless Hurst's important article was to be the framing device for much of the Anglo-Cornish scholarship to follow in its wake. Alongside Hurst's article, Payton and Deacon in their 'The Ideology of Language Revival' attempted to show successive moments of ideological change and linguistic reform aligned to the revival of Cornish.[75] Though the focus was far from on Cornish literature itself, the implications for literary production were great, since (as they argued) different writers have used different versions of the language (broadly Unified, Kemmyn and Modern) to negotiate their space in contemporary literature. Allied to this was a set of thematic and structural concerns in Cornish literature, which is why (for example) the Kemmyn-based magazine *An Gannas* sets many of its stories and narratives in a fully operational apparently Celtic, medieval Cornwall,[76] and perhaps also why the Unified literary magazine *Delyow Derow/Oak Leaves*[77] uses the 'druidic' iconography of the early revival, symbolized in the Gorseth and Henry Jenner. Importantly, Payton and Deacon's article began almost unknowingly to unravel the layers of literary activity in Cornish, which had hitherto remained unstudied.

In the same year, progressing from earlier limited readings of Middle Cornish texts—often dismissed by the literary establishment as inconsequential[78]—Payton sought a political reading of *Beunans Meriasek*, showing that aspects of the play (which is usually dated as *c.*1504) were a materialist manifestation of the 1497 rebellion.[79] The ramifications of such an interpretation indicated the exciting possibilities that other apparently non-political texts in the Cornish literary canon might have subversive qualities, and that Cornish material, like that from other territories, could interestingly and productively be read against the grain. At the same time, academic enquiry also sought to understand Cornish identity throughout the centuries, which, as we shall see, had implications for literary studies. Meanwhile, throughout the 1990s the debate over the ideology of the language revival continued in articles by scholars such as Penglase, George and Williams.[80] Deacon, however, took a different stance, arguing that the debate over 'authenticity' in any kind of literary production in Cornish was actually being conducted within a limited modernist paradigm, and that the sooner those arguing over authenticity realized this, the sooner a postmodernist and inevitably more progressive literature could be produced,[81] a position which has relevance to the next development.

MURDOCH AND AFTER: CORNISH LITERATURE RE-APPRAISED

In 1993 came a highly significant breakthrough in Cornish literary studies. For the first time since Ellis's work of 1974, a scholar had attempted to document, understand and re-evaluate all of the literature produced in the Cornish language. The resultant book, *Cornish Literature* (1993), by Brian Murdoch is now regarded as the standard work on the language and its literature, and sits next to Ellis. Murdoch is a medievalist, so his criticism is strong on theology and dramaturgy. Like Hurst, he makes a telling observation on the state of literary production in Cornish: perhaps a nettle that writers in Cornish (with, as we have seen, only a few exceptions) have yet to grasp:

> In trying to evaluate the literature of revived Cornish, it is difficult to separate the concepts of nationalism (which in itself is fluid) and of elegy, the twin themes of the deserted engine house (or the lost language) and the bloody crown . . . The development of Cornish literature will depend upon new writers (and a new generation), the possibilities of enlarged readership and an agreed literary standard, as well as on the adoption of themes which are part of a broad cultural perspective, as was the case with the great works of the middle ages in Cornish.[82]

In 1996, Murdoch followed up his major work on Cornish with an article entitled 'Is John of Chyanhor Really a Cornish *Ruodlieb*?'.[83] Like his major study, this essay sought to understand literary production in Cornwall in the light of European connections, subverting our traditional understanding of Cornish speakers such as Nicholas Boson as on the margins of culture. The impact of this is significant, since it suggested that scholars in and outside Cornwall needed to rethink their observations and all too often dismissive comments on the overall marginality of literature in Cornish. In addition, in *The Dedalus Book of Medieval Literature: The Grin of the Gargoyle* (an anthology of medieval comic writing), Murdoch was affording equal status to writing about Cornwall both in Cornish (the black mass from *Beunans Meriasek*) and in English (Andrew Boorde's *Introduction to the First Boke of Knowledge*)[84] as to German, Swiss, Latin, Gaelic, Irish, Welsh, French and Italian sources. Again, in *The Cambridge Companion to*

Medieval English Theatre (1994) Murdoch offers a perceptive chapter on 'The Cornish Medieval Drama', locating it next to the York, Chester, Towneley and N-Town plays.[85]

Put another way, we see that Murdoch's dismissal of marginality and his integration of the Cornish material into such internationally used sources is essential for us to widen appreciation of works such as *Ordinalia*. The completion and publication in 1999 of Sally L. Joyce and Evelyn S. Newlyn's almost decade-long project to record and interpret Cornwall's medieval and early modern dramatic heritage as part of the University of Toronto's Records of Early English Drama project almost leaves no stone unturned and will be difficult to surpass.[86] Agan Tavas's publication finally of Nance and Smith's Unified Cornish version of *Origo Mundi* does complete the trilogy published earlier by the Cornish Language Board, yet it is hard to see its relevance given that the Cornish is not in the original spelling.[87]

ANGLO-CORNISH CRITICAL SPACE
One of the first serious attempts to document the life and work of the Anglo-Cornish poet Jack Clemo (1916–94) came in John Hurst's 'Voice From a White Silence: The Manuscripts of Jack Clemo' (1995).[88] Perhaps for the first time, a serious and detailed study of one Anglo-Cornish writer's work was made here. It was an important critical breakthrough, since it established that within Cornish Studies it was now fine for one writer to be deconstructed and explored in much more considerable detail than had been possible before. Hurst's work was an exceptional piece of scholarship, tracing Clemo's growth and the complexities of the writer's manuscripts in the University of Exeter collection.

In comparison, it was to be a further five years before anything of the like was to emerge in the *Journal of the Royal Institution of Cornwall* (2000)—paradoxically a bumper issue on writers in Newlyn featuring Crosbie Garstin, W.S. Lach-Szyrma, and also Jack Clemo[89] —a journal that since its inception featured work by Cornish activists, but had never previously included such 'literary subjects' nor indeed Anglo-Cornish literature. Fortunately, since the publication of this 'single writer'-style article, several others have followed, including Hurst's 'A Poetry of Dark Sounds: The Manuscripts of Charles Causley' and Brace's 'Cornish Identity and Landscape in the Work of Arthur Caddick'.[90] The latter article, by the cultural geographer Catherine Brace, sought interestingly to examine how in Caddick's work landscape and the geography surrounding Nancledra in West Cornwall formed a crucial metaphor for Caddick's exploration of Cornish identity. Caddick himself is one of the most interesting of poets to be re-assessed in recent years.[91] Broadly dismissive of the Cornish Revival and indeed some of the policies of Mebyon Kernow, Caddick nonetheless captures the paradox of being English but living and working in a Cornish context. Cultural geography's 'space-and-place theory' was also to find a critical outlet in Ella Westland's significant collection *Cornwall: The Cultural Construction of Place* (1997), which allowed many of those scholars already active in deconstructing various imaginings of Cornwall an opportunity to look at subjects as diverse as West Barbary, Celtic-Catholic Revivalism, the poetry of John Harris, resisting romance in the clay country, *Poldark* and Daphne du Maurier.[92]

THE CELTO-CORNISH PARADOX
As well as the Anglo-Cornish texts, the later phase of Cornish-language literary production has begun to be deconstructed. Until recently, perhaps the best work on the subject was P.A.S. Pool's *The Death of Cornish* (1982),[93] which established the core historiography, yet Matthew Spriggs sought to unravel the literary mystery of 'the Sherwood Sermons' in 'The Reverend Joseph Sherwood: A Cornish Language Will-'o-the-Wisp', while Emma Michell's 'The Myth of Objectivity: The Cornish Language and the Eighteenth-Century Antiquaries' showed how intentionally the antiquaries—both Cornish and English—sought for their own agendas an earlier death for the language than that of the real speakers and writers on the ground.[94] Allied to the agenda of the language revivalists, there has been much discussion in New Cornish Studies on what may generally be termed the 'Celto-Cornish Revival'.[95] Of course, such a discussion has significance in most areas of twentieth- and twenty-first-century Cornish Studies, but perhaps it is worth taking stock of the general conclusions that have been made and their implications for the literary ideology of Cornwall. Activists within the Cornish Gorseth appear to have wanted the Gorseth to raise literary, poetic and cultural achievement—in essence imposing perhaps misguided Brythonic mythos on Cornwall.[96] While it is true to say that literary achievement both in Cornish and in English has been raised by the Gorseth,[97] in the post-war period that achievement has been more or less static. Indeed, much energy in Cornish Studies has been devoted to showing how the Cornish Revival failed to connect with the majority of the Cornish people. When one considers the history of the literature of twentieth-century Cornwall, often it is those writers who have broadly dismissed or have disregarded the Gorseth that have been the most successful—Jack Clemo (who ironically regarded the Anglican-influenced ceremony as pagan[98]), Charles Causley and A.L. Rowse. D.M. Thomas draws rather

more on his Methodist and 'Pagan' Cornish heritage than that of the 'performance' of the Gorseth.[99] Therefore, as Celto-Cornish culture has widened, writers no longer needed either the authorization or passage of bardship to 'be Cornish'. They are also unwilling to see the Gorseth as the filtering mechanism for their work, because intrinsically (by nature of its present organization) the Gorseth is an amateur organization. Any study of the winning poems and poetry competitions both in English and in Cornish show an overt conservatism, in terms of both form and content. Indeed, many barded writers now completely eschew the ceremony entirely.[100] This is ironic, since it is these writers who have taken up Nance's call for the next generation after his 'to make Cornish walk'. However, this situation is not necessarily a bad thing. What it does demonstrate is that to be Celto-Cornish was no longer the exclusive concern of the Gorseth, as represented in television productions such as *Kernopalooza!* (1999) which merged Cornish and Cornish poetry with surfing, skating and rave culture.[101] Correspondingly, this more dynamic multiplicity of voices should make for a more enlivened and less restricted literary culture. The 'broad cultural perspective' wanted by Murdoch is much closer at hand.

Working as something of a counterpoint to all this 'lit-crit' with an exclusively Cornish perspective, Simon Trezise, in his book *The West Country as a Literary Invention: Putting Fiction in its Place* (2000),[102] examines the wider literary imagining of the south-west peninsula of Britain. It is not perhaps an easy read for many Cornish scholars, but Trezise's interest is in whether the West Country is actually a 'map of the mind' and tellingly, after considering writers with obvious Cornish connections such as Hawker and Woolf, he concedes that a specific study of literature from Cornwall is in fact necessary.[103] Of course, Trezise is right in arguing that some figures cross the boundaries of the South-West—Thomas Hardy and Sabine Baring Gould are two prominent examples.[104] What Trezise and myself agree upon is that the new interest in Cornish literary material has meant that more ambitious multidisciplinary work can be done. For example, in Richard Rastall's excellent studies of the music of early religious drama, *The Heaven Singing* (1996) and *Minstrels Playing* (2001), again Cornish medieval drama is given equivalent space to other texts, as well as a full and comprehensive analysis.[105]

GETTING IT OUT THERE: FROM SHELF TO STREET TO SCHOOLS

One of the failings of literary studies in the past was that though certain texts were known to scholars, and even those involved in the wider Cornish movement, to the general public (whether in Cornwall or not) they were not known and certainly not available. In the post-war period, one of the most curious questions in literary studies in Cornwall is why the activists of the age did not make more of the Cornish literary tradition available. We may perhaps pin this down to two factors. First of all, those activists had to work on a number of fronts to promote Cornish culture—these tended to be political, or else of the kind of pan-Celtic performance to show that Cornwall was Celtic enough to be considered in the pan-Celtic arena, an issue which as Hale has shown can be traced back to Cornwall's early pursuit of Celtic status.[106] Secondly, other Celtic territories such as Wales, Scotland, Ireland and Brittany had the kind of necessary academic and publishing infrastructure in place to facilitate a wider dissemination of their literary culture, both historical and contemporary. They were also large enough and had significant enough readerships at this point for publishers in London, Oxford and Cambridge—not to mention publishers in the United States of America, France and Germany, the latter of course a long-term centre of Celtic Studies. The risk for indigenous publishers seemed too great—the larger post-war firms such as Bradford Barton and Dyllansow Truran were more comfortable with Cornwall's sea and mining heritage, and small-scale language grammars and dictionaries, than with literature proper. For twenty books from Bradford Barton on mining, there was only one significant literary work, the D.M. Thomas edited collection *The Granite Kingdom: Poems of Cornwall* (1970).[107]

However, given the recent change in status of the make-up of the United Kingdom, as well as the increased interest in political identity and devolution rather than physical heritage, literature became a more worthy and valued part of Cornish ethos and experience, since within it could be found the passion, pride, despair and changability of the people, who in the post-war period had successively increased their own ethnic awareness. Literature and culture in the general sense could not only help the Cornish to understand themselves, but also help external observers, politicians, funders, and the wider European community to come to a better sense of who the Cornish were. This explains why it is at this point in time, and not before, that this process of exploring the Cornish literary continuum is taking place.

At the same time, in territories to which the Cornish had emigrated, notably North and South America, South Africa, Australia and New Zealand, the global Cornish community in their quest for affirmation of their own identity also sought the literature of 'home' —assisted by rapid communication via internet and email. Indeed, the revolution in communications was to be part of the reason why more of the literature of Cornwall could be disseminated across the globe.

Effectively, as elsewhere, it made both Cornish and UK publishers who had hitherto refused to recognize the significance of the work now look blinkered and suddenly out of step with the social, political and academic process.

One publisher who has recognized the changing nature of Cornwall's status is Francis Boutle. The intention of the Francis Boutle series of books on Cornish literature is to effectively 'map' the culture not only for future scholars, but also for schools and colleges, and general readerships—what successive literary scholarship has failed to do since the inception of the Cornish Revival. The anthologies have allowed wider access to material previously difficult to obtain and have been reviewed favourably. In a retrospective on the series, one newspaper described the books as 'required reading for anyone interested in Cornwall'.[108] This is a breakthrough, placing Cornish material before a 'national' audience. Prior to this, much literary criticism was still being consumed internally and like aspects of the Cornish language revival effectively 'ghettoized' in a close, non-critical community.[109]

The anthologies began with Tim Saunders's *The Wheel: An Anthology of Modern Poetry in Cornish 1850–1980* (1999),[110] a collection which at last put before readerships significant work by early-twentieth-century activists such as Henry Jenner, L.C. Duncombe Jewell, Robert Morton Nance, A.S.D. Smith and Edwin Chirgwin, but which also documented the work of writers such as Richard Gendall, J.A.N. Snell and N.J.A. Williams. This was followed closely by my own *Voices from West Barbary: An Anthology of Anglo-Cornish Poetry 1549–1928* (2000),[111] which recorded several centuries of the development of verse in or about Cornwall, making prominent not only those 'legends' of literature from Cornwall (Humphry Davy, John Harris, Robert Stephen Hawker) but also those whose voices who had been lost in the detritus of time (Charles Taylor Stephens and James Dryden Hosken, for instance). *Looking at the Mermaid: A Reader in Cornish Literature 900–1900* allowed for the first true anthology ever assembled of writing in Cornish during these dates,[112] looking not only at specific texts, but also at a range of critical and ancillary sources about Cornish and Cornish literature. As a response to numerous books which seemed to ignore the strong Cornish connections and significance to the Arthurian and allied Tristan and Yseult corpus, *Inside Merlin's Cave: A Cornish Arthurian Reader 1000–2000* placed before a readership the ongoing literary imagining of the corpus in a Cornish context.[113] The books were all written from a strongly cultural materialist critical position, as was the 2002 edition of *The Old Cornish Vocabulary*, which aimed to steer away from the usual 'Indo-European' phonological and linguistic bent of old-style Celtic Studies and aimed to present the 'literariness' of the text in its cultural, economic and political context.[114] The most recent addition to the series has been *The Dreamt Sea: An Anthology of Anglo-Cornish Poetry 1928–2000* (2002),[115] which together with *Voices from West Barbary* now forms the most comprehensive collection of Anglo-Cornish poetry assembled. Again, the volume presents major figures of the Cornish continuum alongside poets such as Maud Cherrill, Ronald Bottrall and Andrew C. Symons, whose work merits inclusion, even though they have been hitherto neglected. The collection also facilitated the inclusion of diaspora writers such as John Caddy and Brian Daldorph, both with a North American perspective. The series is coupled with an interactive educational site with teaching resources for literacy, drama and media studies from Key Stage 2 through Key Stages 3 and 4 of the British Schools' National Curriculum to Advanced Level.[116]

THE LONG ROAD AHEAD: CORNISH STATES OF MIND
Whilst literary studies about Cornwall would appear to be in a state of assent thanks to wider new negotiation of literary studies in general in Western Europe, the work of individual scholars and the vision of some publishers, this is not to say that all is rosy nor is all complete. Although changing and progressing, there is still for the moment a curious kind of cultural battle to be fought with many outside scholars, who have inherited either the English literary tradition's romanticized views of Cornwall or the wider dismissive Celtic view: a double polarization. The former is encapsulated in the way the now annual Daphne du Maurier Festival of Literature and Arts presents Cornwall and its literature, recently deconstructed by Busby and Hambly.[117] The latter is encompassed in two new significant books. Alistair Moffat's admirable *The Sea Kingdoms: The Story of Celtic Britain and Ireland* (2001) on the one hand feels it significant to include a section on Cornwall, as well as pictures of Cornish wrasslers and Padstow's Obby Oss,[118] but fails to include any literature from Cornwall at all, in a book containing several other literary texts from 'the sea kingdoms'. Likewise Brown and Stephens's important volume *Nations and Relations: Writing Across the British Isles* (2000) alludes to Cornwall in one of its chapters,[119] but fails to devote a specific chapter to the territory's literature. The long road ahead is to educate and inform scholars outside Cornwall of its literary significance.

Ironically, Brown and Stephens's book claims to examine 'the historical links between the Celtic countries of the British Isles, the complex relations between the Celtic cultures and England, the "doubleness" of literary culture in Ireland, Scotland and Wales and the challenges that face writers in a newly-configured Britain'.[120] If there is one territory, as this article has argued, that encapsulates that 'doubleness' of literary culture then it is Cornwall, so it is all the more surprising that it is not included. Happily, elsewhere Cornwall's literary culture is being integrated. Routledge's recent collection *Celtic Geographies: Old Culture, New Times* (2002) contains articles by two Cornish-based scholars, both referring to Cornwall's literary con-tinuum,[121] and John T. Koch's impressive new *Encyclopaedia of Celtic History and Culture* has detailed reference to literature from Cornwall, both in Cornish and in English.[122]

So what is there yet to achieve in Cornish literature and in literary studies about Cornwall? Gaps such as a full history of theatre (from Cornwall's important contribution to European theatre, through its authors such as Samuel Foote and Donald R. Rawe, to the unique contribution of Kneehigh's 'environmental' theatre), and perhaps even film and cinema are readily identifiable. There is much work also to complete on understanding further the relationships between medieval Cornish drama and its English and European counterparts. Fully anno-tated new translations of the original Cornish of *Ordinalia*, *Beunans Meriasek* and *The Creacion of the World* are badly needed.[123] The discovery in early 2002 of a manuscript containing a formerly 'lost' Middle Cornish play, once belonging to J.E. Caerwyn Williams, has overturned much thought about both Cornish and Cornish literature. The first part of the play is based upon the life of St Kea, while the second, Arthurian-themed section (depicting conflict with the Roman Emperor Lucius Hiberius and the clandestine relationship of Modred with Guenevere) provides yet more evidence of this connection to Cornwall, as well as secular material in Middle Cornish. Together, the play increases the corpus of Middle Cornish literature by around 20 per cent, so a revised narrative of its development is now needed.[124]

Detailed study is now urgently required of the literature of the Cornish overseas, as well as the intersection between music and poetry in the strong ballad traditions of the territory. There are still shadowy figures in Cornwall's literary past—John Pascoe of Glasney College, John Trevisa, William Hals, Joseph Sherwood and Samuel Drew—who all merit more discussion and research, like the recent re-assessment of the Hocking siblings. The literature of the last phase of Cornish in the seventeenth and eighteenth centuries really merits a new investigation, as perhaps does the whole canon of Cornish folktale.[125] Biographies and critical studies need to be written of some of the most famous Anglo-Cornish writers of the nineteenth and twentieth centuries: Mark Guy Pearse, Henry Jenner, Jack Clemo and Charles Causley.[126] Happily, some of this is beginning to happen, as witnessed in Ollard's and Jacob's biographies of A.L. Rowse, together with Payton's preliminary analysis in his recent *A Vision of Cornwall* (2002) of Rowse's complex relationship with his native Cornwall.[127] In addition, there needs to be a greater effort made by those controlling Cornish culture, marketing and tourism to preserve the literary heritage that exists physically in buildings, structures, locations and places, and to make it accessible to the Cornish and visitors alike.[128] This means more than simply naming festivals after writers associated with the territory, but a coherent strategy aiming to preserve the unique 'literary landscape' that exists.[129]

The Cornish Gorseth too needs to consider reform, to stop offering educationally outmoded practice and competitions, and to critically review its shaping of literary culture in Cornwall. Indeed, in its uncritical imitation of Welsh and Breton culture, and in its perceived exclusive association with the Anglican Church, it may have caused actual harm. That said, as anthologies such as *The Wheel* contend, the Gorseth and its associates have been crucial in redefining verse in Cornish in the twentieth century. The Cornu-English tradition is perhaps the most neglected part of the entire canon—one that has suffered from the least investment, academic enquiry and sociolinguistic study.[130] If we are truly to celebrate this rich *patois* redolent of most of the Cornish population, then this merits urgent and meticulous study for the future. In related studies, we must now consider the best way to open up this literature to students in Cornwall and elsewhere. What are the best ways of broadening the learning and teaching of Cornish literature?

Creatively, the crucial task for Cornwall will be to see if its literature can truly transcend the Tamar; it must in effect make the 'local' become international, but in so doing it must not compromise its identity and history. I wrote earlier of the duality of much writing from Celtic territories—how particular works have sustained their Celticity yet have managed to make their narratives travel and become relevant globally. Such works may comfortably be reviewed in an Irish, Scottish or Welsh canon but also fit in the wider European scene, not to mention global mass media. Writing from and about Cornwall must do this too. Once this is achieved then the 'de-revivalism' process I alluded to at the beginning will have begun. Clearly, the lament for lost 'Cornwalls' is now unfashionable and outmoded. So, though writing in Cornwall may be, to use the Cornu-English expression, 'in some state' of unrest and change, this turmoil and struggle is important. Inevitably, it will inform the heightening of consciousness and identity evident in contemporary Cornwall, and as well as reducing or at least achieving a more balanced 'duality' may even influence current political debates such as that surrounding the projected Cornish Assembly. And as a consequence of this, 'the state of mind' of writing in Cornwall will be irrevocably altered: when and how remains to be seen.

NOTES AND REFERENCES

1. A.M. Kent, *The Literature of Cornwall: Continuity, Identity, Difference 1000–2000*, Bristol, 2000, p. 283.

2. For an exploration of this concept, see S. James, *The Atlantic Celts: Ancient People or Modern Invention?*, London, 1999. For the Cornish paradox, see J. Vernon, 'Border Crossings: Cornwall and the English (Imagi)nation', in G. Cubitt (ed.), *Imagining Nations*, Manchester and New York, 1998, pp. 153–72.

3. See *Cornish World/Bys Kernowyon* 17, 1998, pp. 4–5; *Cornwall Now! and in the Future,* leaflet, Truro, 1999; *Cornish Nation* 24, 2002, p. 3. For the legal and geo-political background, see P. Laity, T. Saunders and A.M. Kent, *The Reason Why: Cornwall's Status in Constitutional and Institutional Law*, St Ives, 2001.

4. See, for example, S. Murray (ed.), *Not on Any Map: Essays on Post-coloniality and Cultural Nationalism*, Exeter, 1997.

5. E. Westland, 'The Passionate Periphery: Cornwall and Romantic Fiction', in I.A. Bell (ed.), *Peripheral Visions: Images of Nationhood in Contemporary British Fiction*, Cardiff, 1995, pp. 153–72.

6. Kent, 2000, p. 130.

7. A.M. Kent, *Pulp Methodism: The Lives and Literature of Silas, Joseph and Salome Hocking*, St Austell, 2002, pp. 160–78.

8. E.V. Thompson, *Winds of Fortune*, London, 2000.

9. See Kent, 2000, pp. 251–2.

10. E.V. Thompson, *Seek a New Dawn*, London, 2001.

11. P. Payton, *The Cornish Miner in Australia: Cousin Jack Down Under*, Redruth, 1984; P. Payton, *The Cornish Farmer in Australia*, Redruth, 1987; P. Payton, *The Cornish Overseas*, Fowey, 1999; I. Auhl, *The Story of the 'Monster Mine': The Burra Burra Mine and its Townships 1845–1877*, Adelaide, 1986; J. Selby, *South Australia's Mining Heritage*, Adelaide, 1987.

12. See Westland, 1995, pp. 165–6; N. Moody, 'Poldark Country and National Culture', in E. Westland (ed.), *Cornwall: The Cultural Construction of Place*, Penzance, 1997, pp. 129–36; Kent, 2000, pp. 246–8.

13. W. Graham, *Bella Poldark*, London, 2002. Graham had previously said the final novel was *The Twisted Sword 1815–16*, London, 1990.

14. D. Russell, *Carew*, Salcombe, 2000. Joseph and Silas Kitto Hocking set various fictions in 'glorious' moments of Cornish history, such as the Civil War. See Kent, 2002. Another 'bio-novel' concerning Robert Stephen Hawker is Jeremy Seal, *The Wreck of Sharpnose Point*, London, 2002.

15. P. Payton, *Cornwall*, Fowey, 1996, p. 285.

16. See, for example, F. Ronan, *Dixie Chicken*, London, 1994; I. Welsh,

The Acid House, London, 1995; M. Lawson, *Does the Sun Rise over Dagenham?: New Writing from London*, London, 1998.

17. J. Branfield, *A Breath of Fresh Air*, Truro, 2001.
18. A.M. Kent, ' "At the Far End of England . . .": Constructions of Cornwall in Children's Literature', *An Baner Kernewek/The Cornish Banner* 98, 1999, pp. 16–21. For comparison to an earlier Anglo-Cornish novel, see J. Branfield, *In the Country*, London, 1966.
19. D.M. Thomas, *Birthstone*, London, 1980.
20. D.M. Thomas, *Charlotte: The Final Journey of Jane Eyre*, London, 2000.
21. K. Hill, *The Brontë Sisters and Sir Humphry Davy: A Sharing of Visions*, Penzance, 1994.
22. J. Clemo, *Wilding Graft*, London, 1948 and *The Shadowed Bed*, Tring, 1986.
23. J. Clemo, *The Clay Kiln*, St Austell, 2000, p. 13.
24. N. Darke, *Plays: 1*, London, 1999.
25. N. Darke, *The Riot*, London, 1999, p. 8.
26. S. Parker, *A Star on the Mizzen*, Liskeard, 1997.
27. A.M. Kent, *Dreaming in Cornish*, Liskeard, 1998.
28. L. Merton, *Missus Laity's Tay Room*, Redruth, 2000.
29. *Poetry Cornwall / Bardhonyeth Kernow* 1, 2002.
30. J. Hamlett, *Ring Three Times for the Kitchen Maid*, Redruth, 2001; D. Manning, *I am a River*, Redruth, 2001; P. Hollywood, *Dreams that Remain*, Redruth, 2001.
31. See, for example, A.S.D. Smith, *The Story of the Cornish Language: Its Extinction and Revival*, Camborne, 1947; A.S.D. Smith, *Nebes Whethlow Ber*, Camborne, n.d.; D.R. Rawe, *Geraint: Last of the Athurians*, Padstow, 1972. *Old Cornwall* followed this format for much of the post-war period. It is a trend also followed by the Penzance-based Oakmagic publications.
32. An ideology exemplified by L. Merton (ed.), *The Spirit of a King*, Redruth, 2001.
33. T. Saunders, *The High Tide: Collected Poems in Cornish 1974–1999*, London, 1999.
34. See *An Gannas*, *Delyow Derow*, *An Garrack*, *Kernow* (1990s) and *An Balores*. *Celtic Pen* and *Celtic History Review* also provided forums for such writers.
35. M. Paynter, *Gwersyow Arta/Verses Again*, St Ives, 2001, pp. 2–3. Primo Levi (b. 1919) is an Italian writer whose most important works are his poignant memoirs of his experience in Auschwitz. See also M. Paynter, *A Crowd of Banners: Verses in Cornish*, St Ives, 2001.
36. Michael Palmer, *Dyvoroans*, Redruth, 1998.
37. A.M. Kent, *The Hensbarrow Homilies*, Penzance, 2002.
38. See, for example, J.S. Joliffe (ed.), *Programme for the 11th Gathering of Cornish Cousins September 27–30, 2001, Mineral Point, Wisconsin*, Mineral Point, 2001.
39. For examples of the work of Hawker and Harris, see A.M. Kent (ed.)

Voices from West Barbary: An Anthology of Anglo-Cornish Poetry 1549–1928, London, 2000, pp. 99–112 and pp. 125–44.

40. N.G. Thomas, *The Long Winter Ends*, New York, 1941. See Skyhawk in *The Pony Express: Stories of Pioneers and Old Trails* Vol. XXIV, No. 287, 1958, p. 11. The description of 'Gorilla Mack' the Cornishman, has interesting parallels in the work of W.H. Hudson's anthropological observations on the Cornish and in the fiction of Daphne du Maurier.

41. G. McKinney, *When Miners Sang: The Grass Valley Carol Choir*, Grass Valley, 2001.

42. *Meyn Mamvro* 43, 2000, pp. 22–3.

43. Kent, 2000, pp. 266–7.

44. *Western Morning News*, 13 March, 2002, p. 6.

45. D. Berry, *Wales and Cinema: The First Hundred Years*, Cardiff, 1996.

46. J.E.C. Williams, *Literature in Celtic Countries*, Cardiff, 1971.

47. M. Maclean, *The Literature of the Celts*, London, 1902.

48. Kent, 2000, p. 15. Similar observations are made by Brian Murdoch, *Cornish Literature, Cambridge, 1993, p. 6.*

49. Cited in P.B. Ellis, *The Cornish Language and its Literature*, London and New York, 1974, p. 193.

50. K.C. Phillipps 'The Cornish Dialect and English Literature', in C. Thomas (ed.), *Cornish Studies / Studhyansow Kernewek* 1, Redruth, 1973, pp. 53–6. For notes on Cornish language and drama bibliographies, see pp. 4 and 59.

51. O.J. Padel, 'The Cornish Writings of the Boson Family', in C. Thomas (ed.), *Cornish Studies/Studhyansow Kernewek* 3, Redruth, 1975, pp. 23–4.

52. F.A. Turk and M.M. Combellack, 'Doctoring and Diseaese in Medieval Cornwall. Exegetical Notes on Some Passages in "Beunans Meriasek" ', in C. Thomas (ed.), *Cornish Studies/Studhyansow Kernewek* 4/5, Redruth, 1976–7, pp. 56–76.

53. R. Bremann, 'A Sociolinguistic Survey of English in Cornwall' and A. Hawke 'A Lost Manuscript of the Cornish Ordinalia?', in C. Thomas (ed.), *Cornish Studies/Studhyansow Kernewek* 7, Redruth, 1979, pp. 42 and 45–60.

54. A. Hawke, 'The Manuscripts of the Cornish Passion Poem', in C. Thomas (ed.), *Cornish Studies/Studhyansow Kernewek* 9, Redruth, 1981, pp. 23–8.

55. P. Hull and R. Sharpe, 'Peter of Cornwall and Launceston', in C. Thomas (ed.), *Cornish Studies/Studhyansow Kernewek* 13, Redruth, 1985, pp. 5–51.

56. A debate considered briefly in Philip Payton (ed.), *Cornish Studies: One*, Exeter, 1993a, pp. 1–3.

57. All of these scholars have been continually active in the shaping of literature and literary studies in Cornwall. See, for example, C. Thomas, *Tintagel: Arthur and Archaeology*, London, 1993; K.C. Phillipps (ed.), *The Cornish Journal of Charles Lee*, Padstow, 1995; O. Padel (ed.), *W.M.M. Picken: A Medieval Cornish Miscellany*, Chichester, 2000, A.

Hawke, 'A Rediscovered Cornish-English Vocabulary', in P. Payton (ed.), *Cornish Studies: Nine*, Exeter, 2001, pp. 83–104; M. Combellack, *The Playing Place: A Cornish Round*, Redruth, 1989.
58. See *Cornish Review* (Series 1) and *Cornish Review* (Series 2).
59. D. Val Baker, *Britain's Art Colony by the Sea*, Bristol, 2000 (1959).
60. D. Val Baker, *The Timeless Land: The Creative Spirit in Cornwall*, Bath, 1973, p. 2.
61. P. Payton, *The Making of Modern Cornwall: Historical Experience and the Persistence of 'Difference'*, Redruth, 1992; Kent, 2000.
62. D. Val Baker, *The Spirit of Cornwall*, London, 1980, pp. 46–105.
63. For example, P.B. Ellis, *The Creed of the Celtic Revolution*, London, 1969.
64. Ellis, 1974.
65. J.A. Bakere, *The Cornish Ordinalia: A Critical Study*, Cardiff, 1980.
66. See *Old Cornwall*. This Journal of the Old Cornwall Societies has continued to feature literary articles and reviews. Of late, it has began to print more Anglo-Cornish poetry: *Old Cornwall* 12.9, 2000, p. 1. *An Baner Kernewek / The Cornish Banner* features regular literary features and reviews, shifting from an earlier strongly nationalist stance to a literary and historical quarterly. The now defunct *Cornish Scene* ran in the late 1980s and early 1990s. It featured articles on Cornish writers; for example, Sarah Foot, 'The Poet from Launceston: Charles Causley', *Cornish Scene* 3, 1988/9, pp. 18–19.
67. See Payton (ed.), *Cornwall Since the War: The Contemporary History of a European Region*, Redruth, 1993b.
68. S. Parker (ed.), *Cornwall Marches On!: Kerkedh Kernow*, Truro, 1998.
69. See the observations of D.R. Rawe, *A Prospect of Cornwall*, Chapel Amble, 1996, p. 218.
70. See A.M. Kent, 'A New Cultural Poetics', *An Baner Kernewek/The Cornish Banner* 78, 1994, p. 20; 'Smashing the Sandcastles: Realism in Contemporary Cornish fiction' in Bell (ed.), 1995, pp. 173–80.
71. A movement given useful coverage in H.W. Ludwig and L. Fietz (eds), *Poetry in the British Isles: Non-Metropolitan Perspectives*, Cardiff, 1995; M. Nic Craith (ed.), *Watching One's Tongue: Aspects of Romance and Celtic Languages*, Liverpool, 1996; G. Balakrishnan (ed.), *Mapping the Nation*, London, 1996.
72. M.W. Thomas, *Corresponding Cultures: The Two Literatures of Wales*, Cardiff, 1999.
73. J. Hurst, 'Literature in Cornwall', in Payton (ed.), 1993b, pp. 291–308.
74. Hurst, 1993, p. 307.
75. P. Payton and B. Deacon, 'The Ideology of Language Revival', in Payton (ed.), 1993b, pp. 271–90.
76. See *An Gannas*.
77. See *Delyow Derow/Oak Leaves* 1–16, 1988–96.
78. See Murdoch, 1993, p. 6. *The Cambridge History of English Literature* described *Beunans Meriasek* as 'devoid of literary merit'.
79. P. Payton, ' "A . . . Concealed Envy Against the English": A Note on the

Aftermath of the 1497 Rebellions in Cornwall', in Payton (ed.), 1993a, pp. 4–13.

80. C. Penglase, 'Authenticity in the Revival of Cornish' in P. Payton (ed.), *Cornish Studies: Two*, Exeter, 1994, pp. 96–107; K. George, 'Which Base for Revived Cornish?', in P. Payton (ed.), *Cornish Studies: Three*, Exeter, 1995, pp. 104–24; N.J.A. Williams, 'A Modern and Scholarly Cornish-English Dictionary?: Ken George's Gerlyver Kernewek Kemmyn', in P. Payton (ed.), *Cornish Studies: Nine*, Exeter, 2001, pp. 247–311.

81. B. Deacon, 'Language Revival and Language Debate: Modern and Postmodernity', in P. Payton (ed.), *Cornish Studies: Four*, Exeter, 1996, pp. 88–106.

82. Murdoch, 1993, p. 150.

83. B. Murdoch, 'Is John of Chyanhor Really a Cornish *Ruodlieb*?', in Payton (ed.), 1996, pp. 45–63.

84. B. Murdoch (ed.), *The Dedalus Book of Medieval Literature: The Grin of the Gargoyle*, Sawtry, 1995, pp. 229–32 and 201–2.

85. B. Murdoch, 'The Cornish Medieval Drama', in R. Beadle (ed.), *The Cambridge Companion to Medieval English Theatre*, Cambridge, 1994, pp. 211–9.

86. See R.C. Hays and C.E. McGee, S.L. Joyce and E.S. Newlyn (eds), *Records of Early English Drama: Dorset / Cornwall*, Toronto, 1999, pp. 369–654.

87. R.M. Nance, A.S.D. Smith, R. Chubb, R. Jenkin and G. Sandercock (eds), *The Cornish Ordinalia, First Play: Origo Mundi*, Redruth, 2001. One of the most interesting new perspectives on the end of this play is J. Hall, 'Maxmilla, the Cornish Montanist: The Final Scenes of *Origo Mundi*', in P. Payton (ed.), *Cornish Studies: Seven*, Exeter, 1999, pp. 165–92.

88. J. Hurst, 'Voice From a White Silence: The Manuscripts of Jack Clemo', in Payton (ed.), 1995, pp. 125–43.

89. See M. Perry, 'Eminent Westcountryman, Honorary Cornishman'; J. Hurst, '"The Long Friendship": Painters and Writers in Newlyn'; A.C. Symons, 'Jack Clemo's Italian Holiday', all in *Journal of the Royal Institution of Cornwall* 3, 2000, pp. 154–96.

90. J. Hurst, 'A Poetry of Dark Sounds: The Manuscripts of Charles Causley' and C. Brace, 'Cornish Identity and Landscape in the Work of Arthur Caddick', in Payton (ed.), 1999, pp. 147–64. and 130–46.

91. See Kent, 2000, p. 226. See also E. Hirth, *Never Sit Down in the Digey! The Life and Times of Arthur Caddick*, Helston, 1991.

92. Westland (ed.), 1997.

93. P.A.S. Pool, *The Death of Cornish*, Redruth, 1982.

94. M. Spriggs, 'The Reverend Joseph Sherwood: A Cornish Language Will-'o-the-Wisp' and E. Michell, 'The Myth of Objectivity: The Cornish Language and the Eighteenth-Century Antiquaries' in P. Payton (ed.), *Cornish Studies: Six*, Exeter, 1998, pp. 46–61 and 62–80.

95. See, for example, A. Hale, 'Genesis of the Celto-Cornish Revivial? L.C. Duncombe-Jewell and the Cowethas Kelto-Kernuack', R. Perry, 'Celtic

Revival and Economic Development in Edwardian Cornwall' and G. Tregidga, 'The Politics of the Celto-Cornish Revival, 1886–1939', all in P. Payton (ed.), *Cornish Studies: Five*, Exeter, 1997, pp. 100–11, 112–24 and 125–50.

96. See Kent, 2000, pp. 150–2.

97. See, for example, W.A. Morris (ed.), *Gorsedd Poems*, Redruth, n.d. There have been no sequels to this volume.

98. J. Clemo, *Confession of a Rebel*, London, 1949, pp. 88–90; *The Marriage of a Rebel*, London, 1980, pp. 139–40.

99. D.M. Thomas, *Selected Poems*, Harmondsworth, 1983, pp. 47, 49–51 and 58–9.

100. For example, R. Gendall and C. Weatherhill. Gendall is both a poet, lyricist and language scholar. Weatherhill is a successful children's novelist and the author of the important popular work *Cornish Place Names and Language*, Wilmslow, 1995, which has been central in the dissemination of Cornish language and literature to a mass readership.

101. H. Foster (dir.), *Kernopalooza!*, Plymouth, 1998. See also Kent, 2000, pp. 239–77.

102. S. Trezise, *The West Country as a Literary Invention: Putting Fiction in its Place*, Exeter, 2000. For a useful consideration of literary stereotypes, see S. Trezise, 'The Celt, the Saxon and the Cornishman: Stereotypes and Counter-Stereotypes of the Victorian Period', in P. Payton (ed.), *Cornish Studies: Eight*, Exeter, 2000, pp. 54–68.

103. Trezise, 2000, p. 240.

104. Trezise, 2000, pp. 139–208.

105. R. Rastall, *The Heaven Singing: Music in Early English Religious Drama*, Cambridge, 1996; *Minstrels Playing: Music in Early English Religious Drama II*, Cambridge, 2001.

106. Hale, 1997.

107. D.M. Thomas (ed.), *The Granite Kingdom: Poems of Cornwall*, Truro, 1970.

108. *The Guardian*, 16 March 2000, p. 11.

109. See, for example, J. Holmes (ed. and tr.), *An Dhargan a Verdhin/ The Prophecy of Merlin*, Cornwall, 1998; K. George, *Kanow Kernewek*, Cornwall, 1995; R. Edwards (ed. and tr.), *Pascon Agan Arluth/Passhyon Agan Arloedh / Kan an Passhyon/The Passion Poem/Mount Calvary*, Sutton Coldfield, 1993; K. Syed and R. Edwards, *Origo Mundi*, Sutton Coldfield, 1998.

110. T. Saunders (ed.), *The Wheel: An Anthology of Poetry in Cornish 1850– 1980*, London, 1999.

111. A.M. Kent (ed.), *Voices from West Barbary: An Anthology of Anglo-Cornish Poetry 1549–1928*, London, 2000.

112. A.M. Kent and T. Saunders (eds and trs), *Looking at the Mermaid: A Reader in Cornish Literature 900–1900*, London, 2000.

113. A. Hale, A.M. Kent and T. Saunders (eds and trs), *Inside Merlin's Cave: A Cornish Arthurian Reader 1000–2000*, London, 2000.

114. A. Hale, A.M. Kent and T. Saunders (eds and trs), *The Old Cornish Vocabulary*, London, 2002. For a context for the agenda of New Celtic Studies, see A. Hale and P. Payton (eds), *New Directions in Celtic Studies*, Exeter, 2000.
115. A.M. Kent (ed.), *The Dreamt Sea: An Anthology of Anglo-Cornish Poetry 1928–2000*, London, 2002.
116. See www.francisboutle.demon.co.uk
117. See *Festival Programme of the 6th Annual Daphne du Maurier Festival of Arts and Literature*, 2002. Of the 200 events listed, only around 10 consider Cornish-based contemporary writers or commentators. No Cornish language writers are featured. See G. Busby and Z. Hambly, 'Literary Tourism and the Daphne du Maurier Festival', in Payton (ed.), 2000, pp. 197–212.
118. A. Moffat, *The Sea Kingdoms: The Story of Celtic Britain and Ireland*, London, 2001, pp. 222–3. It does, however, note the work of John Angarrack.
119. T. Brown and R. Stephens (eds), *Nations and Relations: Writing Across the British Isles*, Cardiff, 2000, p. 6.
120. Brown and Stephens, 2000, p. 158.
121. See A. Hale, 'Whose Celtic Cornwall? The Ethnic Cornish meet Celtic Spirituality' and A.M. Kent, 'Celtic Nirvanas: Constructions of Celtic in Contemporary British Youth Culture', in D.C. Harvey, R. Jones, N. McInroy and C. Milligan (eds) *Celtic Geographies: Old Culture, New Times*, London and New York, 2002, pp. 157–70 and 208–26.
122. J.T. Koch (ed.), *The Encyclopedia of Celtic History and Culture*, Oxford, 2002.
123. P. Neuss, *The Creacion of the World: A Critical Edition and Translation*, New York and London, 1983, is excellent but presently difficult to obtain.
124. See National Library of Wales MS 23849D.
125. Scholarship is indebted to Llanerch publishers of Felinfach, Lampeter, for making available facisimile copies of the work of William Bottrell and Robert Hunt, though better newly-set editions are still required.
126. A biography of Mark Guy Pearse will soon be published. A Clemo biography is in preparation, as is a new critical study.
127. See R. Ollard, *A Man of Contradictions: A Life of A.L. Rowse*, London, 1999; V. Jacob, *Tregonissey to Trenarren: A.L. Rowse, The Cornish Years*, St Austell, 2001; P. Payton, *A Vision of Cornwall*, Fowey, 2002, chapter 5. Payton is currently working on a full-length, monograph treatment of the relationship between A.L. Rowse and Cornwall.
128. Only a cursory nod is given to the literature of Cornwall in a recent high-quality tourist publication by A. Bennett and D. Flower (eds), *The Best of Cornwall*, Bath, 2001. Only one indigenous Anglo-Cornish writer is mentioned: Arthur Quiller Couch. The West Country Tourist Board's *West Country Writers* leaflet, n.d., is equally limited.
129. Fortunately the birthplace of the Nobel Prize-winning author William Golding is now celebrated in Mount Wise, Newquay. Jack Clemo's

cottage at Goonamarris, near St Stephen-in-Brannel, was prevented from being demolished.

130. The best academic field-work enquiry was made by the Institute of Cornish Studies in the 1970s and 1980s, but little of the literature was evaluated. An exception is J. McWhorter, *The Power of Babel: A Natural History of Languages*, London, 2002, pp. 56–7.

CORNISH STUDIES AND CORNISH CULTURE(S): VALUATIONS AND DIRECTIONS

Amy Hale

INTRODUCTION

Culture is a term that is used frequently, yet it has a very wide range of meanings. In one of its earliest usages in English, 'culture' referred to processes of cultivation of animals or land. This led to what is still one of the most prevalent interpretations of the term as 'high' or 'elite' culture as the processes of cultivation became associated with human development. Thus, particular 'high' art forms became linked with 'culture'. 'Culture' was seen as something that was good, moral, and elevating of the mind. In late eighteenth-century German philosophy, the term 'culture' began to take on a more subtle meaning. Johann Herder argued that 'culture' was not monolithic or class-exclusive, but that there were distinctive cultures throughout the world, and that different cultures even existed within one society—the peasant or 'folk' culture differed from that of the ruling class. German usage was carried into English thought by the anthropologist Edward Tylor, who in 1871 defined culture as: 'That complex whole which includes knowledge, belief, art, morals, law, custom, and any other capabilities and habits acquired by man [*sic*] as a member of society'.[1] Tylor's definition has been enduring and most cultural researchers recognize 'culture' as referring to an all-encompassing, yet fluid and unbounded system involving a number of features. Therefore, it is hard to imagine a research focus in either the social sciences or the humanities that does not have culture at its centre.

Cornish Studies, by its very nature, has always been about culture, whether the research emphasis has been on archaeology, politics, history, or literature. Cornish Studies, like most 'area studies', is based on the central premise of cultural difference, and the ways in which difference is reflected and asserted in a variety of circumstances, whether that is a historical experience or the creation of a literary tradition. The original focus of Cornish Studies as it developed institutionally in the 1970s was primarily concerned with material culture (archaeology), linguistics, and history. From the early 1990s the emphasis shifted to a focus on theoretically led historical inquiry to explain continuity of identity over time. Both approaches take as a starting point the assertion that the Cornish are *culturally* distinctive, and that distinctiveness can be demonstrated in a number of inter-related arenas. Yet despite the implicit emphasis on culture within Cornish Studies, the relationship between the emerging field of Cornish Studies and the academic disciplines which focus on culture, such as cultural studies and anthropology, has been far from clear.

Within Cornwall and the development of Cornish Studies, cultural research has still barely emerged. There have been studies of Cornish language and Cornish dialect, both cultural phenomena, but not in the context of 'lived experience', as they are spoken by actual communities. There have been studies of religion, but they are primarily historical. There have been studies of material culture, but they have been archaeological. There have been studies of art, but from an art historical rather than a cultural perspective. There is no shortage of representations of Cornish culture. We have a wide variety of depictions of Cornish life throughout the centuries from a number of different types of sources. Some of these writers have aimed at objectivity, others have had a very definite and more obvious agenda in their writing. We also have a number of essays critiquing how Cornish culture has been portrayed in art, romantic literature, guidebooks and tourist attractions. What we are lacking is ethnographic studies of Cornwall that reflect a structured interaction between researcher and culture. In other words, there has been a shortage of representations of Cornwall based on field research.

Anthropologists have consistently neglected Cornwall, and Cornish subjects have only recently been considered within the scope of cultural studies. Literary and linguistic researches into Cornwall, however, have been much more developed, and since they have been well addressed elsewhere in this volume I will not cover them here. Lest it be suggested that the parameters of the above disciplines are wholly responsible for this situation, Cornish Studies historically as a field has also been reticent to fully embrace the 'cultural turn', although this is slowly changing. Here, I shall explore the reasons why

Cornwall, which should be a wonderfully rich and compelling site for cultural analysis on many levels, has been relatively neglected by the cultural disciplines. I will also examine the progress which has been made within Cornish Studies in unpacking the many complexities of the Cornish cultural landscape, past and present, and suggest areas for future research.

CORNISH CULTURE AND STUDIES OF THE PAST

Despite a lack of field-based approaches, a number of aspects of Cornish culture have been considered through historical and document-based research. These studies have been theoretically positioned to reconsider Cornish culture from a perspective of difference. Bernard Deacon has most exemplified this work with several seminal essays considering the nature of Cornish cultural identity, which he argues is based in the socio-industrial complexes of nineteenth-century Cornwall.[2] A number of other key studies reinforce this cultural paradigm by concentrating on defining features of working-class culture such as Methodism and mining. John Rule's work on Methodist culture and belief during the nineteenth century was one such approach, as is Sharron Schwartz's work on women and industry in the nineteenth century.[3] Another primary area of research into culture in Cornwall concerns artistic production, primarily literature and visual arts. Yet, there is often an ideological tension between these foci. Unlike Cornish industrial culture, some might argue, the artistic movements which flourished in Cornwall from the late nineteenth century did not reflect Cornish culture since the artists themselves (with very few exceptions) were not native to Cornwall. This perception may account for the reasons why there has been so little focus on these groups within the critical literature of Cornish Studies.

There is also a move in Cornish Studies to use material culture and older data to reveal alternative perspectives about aspects of Cornish culture in earlier periods. Paul Cockerham's work on medieval funerary monuments has provided new and interesting perspectives about relationships between Cornwall, Ireland and Brittany during the early modern period.[4] His use of material evidence as personal document is a welcome methodology. Although this research provides us with a better understanding of life in Cornwall in the past, and how Cornish culture has been perceived, represented and used, it still reflects a historiographic approach, rather than an ethnographic one. Of course, this research has provided valuable evidence about the mechanisms of culture, yet it does not systematically record the voices and opinions of living people.

CORNISH STUDIES AND ANTHROPOLOGY

There is no 'standard' ethnographic portrayal of the Cornish. In fact, there has been surprisingly little ethnographic research carried out in Cornwall. The primary exceptions are MacArthur,[5] Vink,[6] and Hale.[7] By ethnographic research I am specifically referring to research which employs qualitative methodologies, including open-ended interviews and participant observation. This obviously differs from sociological practice, which also uses interviewing but which is often primarily quantitative. In fact, much more quantitative research has been carried out in Cornwall.[8] The history and practice of anthropology in Cornwall, like much of Cornish Studies, until very recently has been driven by a focus on identity, ethnicity and difference. This, however, is a result not so much of the normative project of Cornish Studies to define a Cornish identity as it is of the way that those conducting research have historically perceived the Cornish. Cultural difference has in the past been the only justification for undertaking ethnographic research.

The history of the field of anthropology has certainly cultivated this response, and still does, albeit to a lesser degree than it has in the past. Despite the internal critiques within anthropology concerning issues of colonialism and power within anthropological fieldwork, Europeans or Americans still primarily conduct most anthropological research among non-European peoples. There is a number of reasons for this focus. First, methodologically, cultural distance is sometimes perceived to be more empirical, and therefore more reliable and valid. Second, the increase in problem-led and applied anthropology continues to encourage work in economically developing areas. Furthermore, academic trends have dictated a focus away from studying Europe, particularly Western Europe, in order to redress a perception of Eurocentric scholarship. Of course, it could be argued that Westerners studying non-Westerners actually reinforces Eurocentrism. Finally, the simple fact remains that conducting long-term fieldwork in developing areas is much more cost-effective than conducting research in developed countries.

These factors combine to provide an anthropological climate which keeps Cornwall ethnographically invisible. It is difficult to gain academic support and funding to research what are considered to be 'white people in England' by ill-informed grant-awarding bodies. There is another underlying assumption, perhaps, that literate European cultures are not in need of research, either because they are well documented already or because they can and will document themselves. This is a fallacy that, in this writer's opinion, has produced gaping holes in the ethnographic record where Western Europe, and specifically the UK, is concerned. Perhaps unwittingly, the initial thrust of current ethnographic work from the late 1980s and early 1990s, which concentrated broadly on people's perceptions of Cornish cultural difference and ethnicity, has greatly helped to establish a foundation for future research in a field which has been methodologically defined by researching difference. One would hope it has also helped to validate future study of Cornish issues.

Yet Cornwall, like other 'Celtic' areas, has occupied a particular niche in British ethnographic practice in terms of folklore studies, which were some of the earliest ethnographically led projects in Cornwall, aside from linguistic research which far predated research into 'traditional' Cornish cultural practices. In the mid to late nineteenth century, as folklore, anthropology and archaeology were emerging as separate disciplines out of antiquarianism, cultures closer to home among what was then the British Empire were perhaps thought 'too familiar' for investigation. Even the Irish, the subject of almost endless folklore studies from the late nineteenth century onwards, did not receive any significant or sustained ethnographic attention until the 1980s. This early emphasis on folklore research was formative, and helped to lay the groundwork for the later anthropological investigations into Cornish ethnicity. Folklore research, like anthropology, grew out of early discourses of race, which have now translated into discourses of ethnicity. 'Folk' (read 'primitive') provided a semantic space for cultures which exhibited difference, yet which were not distinctively racially marked, and which were considered to be a sub-set of dominant 'British' culture. That notion itself, of course, carries all sorts of ambiguities and inaccuracies, particularly when discussing Ireland.

The earliest chroniclers of Cornish life were similar to the earliest antiquarians and folklorists—they were part of yet considered themselves to be separate from the cultures they studied and wrote about, which gave them a perceived ethnographic distance that allowed their work to be read as objective portraits of Cornish life and experience. Richard Carew's 1602 *Survey of Cornwall* exemplifies this early approach.[9] Carew was resolutely Cornish, yet his perception of his relationship to the bulk of Cornish folk was separated by class and provided sufficient distance and Otherness to allow him to write about Cornish practices as though they were not also his own. This approach was perpetuated for centuries into early folklore research. It was only in the early twentieth century that native scholars could embrace their cultural position in relation to their research, but then nationalism provided a different thrust for cultural documentation throughout Europe.

In its early stages, folklore research in Cornwall was virtually indistinct from antiquarianism. The focus was on preserving 'dead' or 'dying' cultural forms. This was of course, a precursor to proto-nationalist and nationalist movements throughout Europe seeking to 'gather the fragments' to preserve and promote unique cultural expression. Until very recently folklore collecting was driven by an ethos of preservation rather than simply description. This is one reason why folklore was collected from non-dominant or 'peripheral' cultures; it was believed that modernization and the impact of dominant culture would soon eradicate practices of interest from the past. Thus, folklorists tended to concentrate their collecting efforts among the elderly of the population, thinking that this is where most of the 'traditional' knowledge would be held. Folklore was also considered to be 'anonymous' and the product of a collective cultural experience that kept it 'of the people' and out of the realms of 'art', which was believed to be the product of the individual imagination. As a result, Cornwall continues to be constructed in literature, media and popular culture either as pre-modern and as a site of 'survivals' or as a place of elite artists' colonies.

This notion of peripherality that was fostered by early folklore research in Cornwall has continued to underpin the bulk of Cornish cultural research, albeit in new and much more sophisticated ways.[10] Again, it has provided a justification and an explanation for continuing difference, particularly in relationship to the arguable perception of a dynamic centre. Mary McArthur's 1988 M.A. thesis on perceptions of Cornish ethnicity was a preliminary yet important ethnographic breakthrough. Although her research sample was comparatively small, her status as a cultural 'outsider' combined with her methodology lent a validity to her findings that not only made them useful but also provided an important research precedent for field-based methodology. Caroline Vink's 1992 work also focused on Cornish identity, using a research sample comprised entirely of ethnic activists to further understand how activists constructed their sense of ethnicity. My own research from 1998 was also a problem-led study related to identity formation, but comparing two broadly different groups— ethnic activists and those with an interest in Celtic spirituality —through interview, participant observation and ritual analysis. My primary focus was the ways in which notions of Celticity have been defined and interpreted in Cornwall over the past century. Thus, ethnographic research concerning identity issues in Cornwall has progressed from an examination of the phenomenon of Cornish identity as based in lived experience to an exploration of the sometimes competing identities constructed within a wider discourse of ethnicity.

Because the idea of a uniquely Cornish ethnicity was relatively unknown within the anthropological literature (although not in Cornwall, of course), these studies were important not only in that they helped to 'concretize' the ambiguities of ethnic experience in Cornwall for the benefit of the Cornish, but also because they contributed to wider anthropological research. However, ethnographic research has not progressed much beyond these studies. Despite the scholarly focus on identity within Cornish Studies, what is still lacking is a much longer-term, immersive, qualitative study of Cornish ethnicity that focuses specifically on non-activists, and also incorporates the perspectives of the New Cornish and hybrid Cornish ethnicities.

Nevertheless, there is some new ethnographic research being undertaken in Cornwall. For instance, University College London (UCL) has in recent years supported two ethnographic projects which were Cornwall-based. One, conducted by Patrick Laviolette, concerns attitudes to landscape and involved immersive research and participant observation.[11] UCL has also sponsored the Leskernick Project. This was also funded by the British Academy, and involved archaeological research on a Bronze Age village site on Bodmin Moor, combined with artistic installations on the site. The ethnographic component was a study of how the community conducting the research reacted to the site through creative words and images. Results and essays were then disseminated through a website.[12] The disappointment with this project is that it was completely isolated from the Cornish community around it. This was a well-funded study which was conducted over three field seasons, yet did not address any issues salient to Cornwall. Sadly, studies of this type only reinforce stereotypical perceptions of Cornwall as a romantic de-peopled landscape which produces heightened emotions. In general, research of this type is important, in that it explores how those who interpret the past understand their own relationship to the process. I suppose the disappointment for Cornish Studies is that it was a large-scale study in Cornwall that, once again, rendered the Cornish invisible.

CORNISH STUDIES AND CULTURAL STUDIES
Cultural studies approaches to Cornish culture are in the ascendant. Cultural studies as it has developed in the UK is an interesting hybrid field. Its methodology shares many features with interpretive cultural anthropology which became prevalent in the United States in the 1970s. Like interpretive anthropology, cultural studies employs a literary approach to cultural phenomena which encourages 'reading' events and practices as 'texts', which in theory reveals motives about behaviour and meaning. Cultural studies tends not to be as reliant

on ethnographic practices such as interviewing, instead favouring observation.

Within the UK, cultural studies emerged in the late 1950s from a number of frustrations with the traditional subject matters of academic inquiry. It became a force for radical leftist scholarship in that it challenged the notions of elitist British 'national' culture that were emerging, particularly those promoted by Leavisite literary criticism.[13] Writers such as Raymond Williams, Richard Hoggart and later Stuart Hall asserted a vision of a fragmented Britain, and focused their researches on working-class practices and the sub-cultures which emerged from them. This approach would initially appear to have immediate relevancy for Cornish Studies in its challenge of the status quo. However, cultural studies was developing around a discourse of class relations, predominantly with an urban focus, while the discourses underpinning Cornish Studies were those of ethnicity. Although a broad Marxist framework has certainly informed Cornish Studies in the past decade, and class distinctions have laterally become extremely relevant in academic definitions of Cornish culture, cultural studies was still predominantly concerned with varying English and urban identities. The mainstream perception of Cornwall as Romantic rural idyll would have therefore obscured it as a relevant site of inquiry.

Yet as the cultural disciplines such as anthropology and even continental sociology have continued to shift in emphasis and method, cultural studies in the UK has become informed by different theoretical approaches. The strict class focus has given way to looser, continentally influenced, Marxist considerations such as power relations, consumption patterns and hegemony, which are being more broadly applied.[14] Postmodernism, post-colonialism and post-structuralism have also been integrated into cultural studies. This has resulted in wider applications of cultural studies approaches to a range of fields, including media studies and musicology. These perspectives, particularly post-colonialism, have presented exciting frameworks for understanding a range of Cornish cultural phenomena. Nevertheless, because Cornish culture has remained ambiguous and largely invisible to cultural studies practitioners outside the immediate sphere of influence of Cornwall, there have not been any sustained efforts to develop a significant body of work utilizing this approach outside the field of literary studies, where the work of Alan M. Kent has best reflected this position.[15]

It is perhaps most logical that the predominant cultural studies work relating to Cornwall has focused on how Cornwall as a place has been constructed and consumed. This approach overlaps with cultural geography, but the emphasis of some writers on issues of power and hegemony is drawn from cultural studies. Undoubtedly the single collection which best reflects cultural studies approaches to Cornwall as a whole is the 1997 *Cornwall: The Cultural Construction of Place* edited by Ella Westland.[16] The essays here are theoretically led and blend historical inquiry with literary criticism. The overriding strategy of these essays is to analyse place as text, and look at place within text. The collection itself reveals a common tension in the study of Cornwall: the polarization between viewing Cornwall as a passive site of consumption[17] or as a dynamic site where meaning is primarily defined by its inhabitants.[18]

The cultural studies approach is probably best exemplified in *Cornwall: The Cultural Construction of Place* by Harold Birks's essay on Jamaica Inn as a tourist site.[19] Here, Birks examines notions of authority and authenticity in a space that was designed to represent a representation of an imagined Cornish experience: that of Daphne Du Maurier's 1936 novel *Jamaica Inn*. Here, Birks 'reads' the site for authority and meaning for the consumer as produced by the attraction literature and within the attraction by its displays, content and surroundings. What characterizes the cultural studies approach here is the emphasis on a semiotic approach to constructing meaning which interprets signs and signifiers, rather than on interpreting meaning through qualitative research with visitors and attraction designers. Tourist sites and tourism literature and products have been a very productive area of research for cultural studies approaches within Cornwall,[20] since the tourism industry has been so central in producing images of Cornwall that can be read as various texts and which are also germane to preoccupations of cultural studies, including consumption patterns, post-colonialism and post-structuralism. Tourist sites in Cornwall are also sites of contestation with multiple and conflicting meanings. There has also been a wealth of quantitative research concerning the tourism industry in Cornwall,[21] yet as in many other areas, qualitative research on tourism is sorely lacking.

WAYS FORWARD

In concluding this essay, I wish to come full circle to examine what the role of cultural research in Cornwall could be potentially. Since arguably the crux of Cornish Studies is culture, the field needs to embrace more fully culture in Cornwall as a subject of research. Both cultural studies and ethnographic approaches could be of value. Cornish Studies as a field, however, needs to be more supportive of ethnographic approaches. As noted, one of the primary foci of Cornish Studies since its emergence as a field has been the Cornish identity, both justifying its existence and also attempting to define its salient features. While this has certainly been an important enterprise, it can also be quite limiting, and perhaps prescriptive. Cornwall does not contain a homogenous mass of people. It never has and there are a number of hybrid Cornish identities which could profitably be researched. The Cornish themselves are not one single, easy-to-define population with a single style and consistent values. Aside from the various ethnicities residing in the peninsula, there are gender groupings, class groupings, religious groupings, industry-based groupings and sexual identities all of which overlap and combine.

Cornish Studies is arguably engaged in a normative project to locate a distinctively Cornish identity. Perhaps as a result of this focus almost nothing has ever been written looking at other groups or individuals in Cornwall. Is there a perceived danger that in promoting an ethnically diverse Cornwall or exploring cultural hybridizations, the project of Cornish Studies to promote a particular type of 'Cornishness' will become 'weakened'? In considering 'the Cornish overseas', for those who choose to focus on their Cornish inheritance, would they feel comfortable 'being Cornish' if they were also Black or Asian?[22]

There are a number of areas of focus for cultural research that should be priorities for Cornish researchers. Media and technology are two areas that impact the Cornish in a variety of ways and are becoming increasingly important in establishing transglobal identities, economies and communication. Content analysis, and research concerning consumption and attitudes to media in Cornwall could be very useful. Work on the role of the Internet in shaping perceptions of Cornwall and Cornishness has already begun, and will become more important as the Internet plays an increased role in the Cornish economy.[23] Researchers in Cornish Studies should also utilize ethnographic methods to pursue more problem-led studies with potential applications, based in lived experience. Unexplored areas include drug cultures, homelessness, and informal economies such as the black market in Cornwall. These and similar areas will provide a much fuller and more diverse picture of what the Cornish experience actually is.

Cornish Studies as a developing field over the past decade has done a great deal to promote a wider understanding of some of the basic mechanisms and features of Cornish culture. Of course, the most significant contribution has been to provide the theoretical framework for understanding and conceptualizing how various features of the culture have emerged over time. However, the growing confidence of the field and of the identity of the territory in general should now be reflected in a growing sophistication in ethnographic considerations of Cornwall. While certainly the existence of a distinctive Cornish identity still needs to be widely promoted, cultural analysis that considers

Cornish diversity, a focus on lived experience, and the inherent complexity of the population of the territory should be the work of the next generation of scholars.

NOTES AND REFERENCES

1. E. Tylor, *Primitive Culture: Research into the Development of Mythology, Philosophy, Religion, Art and Custom, London, 1871.*
2. For example, see Bernard Deacon, 'The Cornish Revival: An Analysis', unpublished manuscript, 1985; Bernard Deacon, 'And Shall Trelawny Die? The Cornish Identity', in Philip Payton (ed.), *Cornwall Since the War*, Redruth, 1993a, pp. 200–23; and Bernard Deacon, '"The Hollow Jarring of the Distant Steam Engines": Images of Cornwall between West Barbary and the Delectable Duchy', in Ella Westland (ed.), *Cornwall: The Cultural Construction of Place*, Penzance, 1997. See also Deacon's essay with Philip Payton, 'Re-inventing Cornwall: Culture Change on the Periphery', in Philip Payton (ed.), *Cornish Studies: One*, Exeter, 1993b.
3. John Rule, 'Methodism, Popular Beliefs and Village Culture in Cornwall 1800–1850', in Robert D. Storch (ed.), *Culture and Custom in Nineteenth Century England*, London, 1982, n.p., and Sharron Schwartz, 'In Defence of Customary Rights: Labouring Women's Experience of Industrialization c.1750–1870', in Philip Payton (ed.), *Cornish Studies: Seven*, Exeter, 1999, pp. 8–31.
4. P. Cockerham, ' "On my Grave a Marble Stone": Early Modern Cornish Memorialization', in Philip Payton (ed.), *Cornish Studies: Eight*, Exeter, 2000, pp. 9–39; and P. Cockerham, 'Models of Memorialization: Cornwall, Ireland and Brittany Compared', in P. Payton, (ed.), *Cornish Studies: Nine*, Exeter, 2001, pp. 45–82.
5. M. MacArthur, 'The Cornish: A Case Study in Ethnicity', unpublished M.A. thesis, University of Bristol, 1988.
6. C. Vink ' "Be Forever Cornish!": Some Observations on the Ethno-regionalist Movement in Contemporary Cornwall', in Payton (ed.), 1993b.
7. A. Hale, ' "Gathering the Fragments": Constructing Contemporary Celtic Identities in Cornwall', unpublished Ph.D. thesis, University of California, Los Angeles, 1998.
8. For excellent examples of quantitative research on Cornwall see essays in Payton (ed.), 1993a.
9. R. Carew, *The Survey of Cornwall*, ed. F.E. Halliday, London, 1953 (1602).
10. Much of the work in Cornwall relating to the centre-periphery relationship has been inspired by Philip Payton, *The Making of Modern Cornwall: Historical Experience and the Persistence of 'Difference'*, Redruth, 1992, which demonstrates the theory in a historical context.
11. P. Laviolette, 'An Iconography of Landscape Images in Cornish Art and Prose', in Philip Payton (ed.), *Cornish Studies: Seven*, Exeter, 1999.
12. http://www.ucl.ac.uk/leskernick/home.htm. See B. Bender, S. Hamilton

and C. Tilley, 'Stone Worlds, Alternative Narratives and Nested Landscapes.'

13. J. Lave, P. Duguid, N. Fernandez and E. Axel, 'Coming of Age in Birmingham: Cultural Studies and Conceptions of Subjectivity', *Annual Review of Anthropology* 21, 1992, pp. 257–82.

14. Lave *et al.*, 1992, p. 264.

15. However, Alan Kent, *The Literature of Cornwall: Continuity, Identity, Difference*, Bristol, 2000, does address contemporary media production in addition to literature from a firmly cultural materialist and Cultural Studies prospective.

16. Westland (ed.), 1997.

17. See especially H. Hughes 'A Silent Desolate Country: Images of Cornwall in Daphne Du Maurier's *Jamaica Inn*', J. Hubback 'Women, Symbolism and the Coast of Cornwall', and N. Moody 'Poldark Country and National Culture', all in Westand (ed.), 1997.

18. Especially reflected in the essays of B. Deacon '"The Hollow Jarring of Distant Steam Engines": Images of Cornwall between West Barbary and Delectable Duchy', P. Payton 'Paralysis and Revival: The Reconstruction of Celtic Catholic Cornwall 1890–1945', and A.M. Kent 'The Cornish Alps: Resisting Romance in the Clay Country', all in Westland (ed.), 1997.

19. H. Birks, 'Jamaica Inn: The Creation of Meaning on a Tourist Site', in Westland (ed.), 1997.

20. For an early Cultural Studies analysis of tourism sites in Cornwall, see J. Lowerson 'Celtic Tourism—Some Recent Magnets', in Philip Payton (ed.), *Cornish Studies: Two*, Exeter, 1994.

21. See A. Williams and G. Shaw, 'The Age of Mass Tourism', in Payton (ed.), 1993a; and P. Thornton, 'Cornwall and Changes in the Tourist Gaze', in Payton (ed.), 1993b.

22. For example, see Philip Payton, *A Vision of Cornwall*, Fowey, 2002, pp. 200–2.

23. For example, see David Crowther and Chris Carter, 'Community Identity and Cyberspace', in Philip Payton (ed.), *Cornish Studies: Nine*, Exeter, 2001.

DEFINING THE SPECTRE:
OUTLINING THE ACADEMIC POTENTIAL
OF THE 'CAVA MOVEMENT'

Treve Crago

INTRODUCTION

'A spectre is haunting the halls of the academy: the spectre of oral history.'[1] In so paraphrasing the Marxist *Manifesto*, Alessandro Portelli highlights oral history's often problematic relationship with the Italian academia. Now that this same phantom prowls the 'halls' of the Institute of Cornish Studies (ICS), the following article explains why this sometimes reviled apparition has re-materialized in Cornwall, and how it is increasingly engaging with and furthermore introducing innovative methodologies to the field of 'New Cornish Studies'.

When viewing oral history from an 'international' perspective, there is little doubt that this discipline has been problematic to traditional academics who practise a more 'conventional', conservative approach in interpreting the past. Portelli observes that, 'There seems to be a fear that once the floodgates of orality are opened, writing (and rationality along with it) will be swept out as if by a spontaneous uncontrollable mass of fluid, amorphous material'.[2] Guy Beiner of the Department of Modern Irish History at Trinity College Dublin elaborates further, noting that 'leading historians, such as A.J.P. Taylor and Hugh Trevor-Roper, have vehemently denounced the historical value of oral sources and supposedly comprehensive lists of primary sources, such as Arthur Marwick's *The Nature of History,* overlook oral sources' (the 1970 edition makes no mention of oral sources, whereas the 1981 edition includes a token gesture of two sentences).[3]

Fortunately, within the field of Cornish Studies such an outright condemnation has failed to materialize. Indeed, it is possible to go as far as to say that the remarkable resurgence of interest in oral history that has taken place throughout the length and breadth of Cornwall via the activities of the Cornish Audio Visual Archive (CAVA) probably could not have taken place without the open progressive ambiance projected by the practitioners and advocates of 'New Cornish Studies'. Whereas Beiner, within his review of oral history (appropriately entitled *Bodhaire Ui Laoire*, (feigned deafness) and its place within the contemporary Irish historiography, concedes that 'In such a conservative environment, a long time has to pass before new historical directions are accepted within the canon',[4] In marked contrast the already multidisciplinary character of Cornish Studies has allowed oral history to take its place as a central tenet of its research activities. As Philip Payton observes, 'Oral history is set to play a major part in CAVA's activities, a reflection of the increasing recognition of oral material in the repertoire of evidence available to the historian'.[5]

'FROM OLD PEOPLE AND OTHERS': A BRIEF HISTORY OF ORAL HISTORY IN CORNWALL

Just as Dr Johnson once quipped, 'all history was at first oral',[6] so within Cornwall there has always existed a rich diversity of oral tradition. Indeed, long before the advent of recording equipment, folklorists such as Robert Hunt (1807–87) were collecting stories.[7] However, it was not until just prior to the outbreak of the Second World War, with advancements in recording technology, that the idea of en-registering dialect in Cornwall was considered by the Cornish Gorsedd. The organization minutes reveal that in June 1938, at the suggestion of Edwin Chirgwin, a 'recording machine' should be purchased to record dialect 'from old people and others'. And, following enquiries made by Mrs Ashley Rowe, it was decided to raise twenty guineas for the necessary equipment. It was also decided that Major Gill of the Royal Institution of Cornwall (RIC) and Federation of Old Cornwall Societies (OCS) would assist in the project[8] (Major Gill having already made the film *The Spirit of Cornwall*[9]).

Unfortunately, although the necessary money was raised, the project never got off the ground as the outbreak of war turned people's attentions elsewhere and Major Gill died during its course. In the post-war period oral history recording was left in the hands of individuals such as Dr Roger Slack of St Ives who recorded the town's inhabitants. He was particularly interested in capturing memories of the St Ives artists, especially focusing on reminiscences concerning Alfred Wallace.[10] Other individuals recording oral history during this period included Pat Manning of the Torpoint Archives and Joe

Pengelly of the BBC. In the late 1970s and early 1980s organized community oral history projects took place funded by the Manpower Services Commission and were sponsored by Cornwall County Council in such diverse localities as Calstock, Penzance, Falmouth and Fowey. But these petered out following the demise of Manpower Services and the consequent lack of further available funding.

During this same period the Institute also became involved with oral history. As Professor Charles Thomas, former Director of the Institute, remembered in a recent interview:

> The Survey of English dialect took six localities in Cornwall. I decided that for phonetic study it was necessary to take a further 14 localities to identity informants and we had two trained researchers: David North, who had been trained at Leeds by the SED, and Adam Sharp, who is now an archaeologist, but at that stage was an English Graduate. And they were trained in recording techniques; we bought a Uher and they went out and did these. It is probably the most important piece of dialect work in Cornwall ever done.

Subsequently:

> In the course of this it was abundantly clear that when these people spoke freely, so we could get words without prompting, that there was an enormous vein of detailed reminiscence particularly dealing with farming. I remember we did Jacky Weir down at Morvah and he was brought up in what I can describe as an almost prehistoric farm. So we then amplified this. I found a Cornishman whose name alludes me [David Lance] who was working with the Imperial War Museum, which was the headquarters of the 'oral calling', enrolled him as an honorary fellow . . . sent Rosemary [Robertson], who had worked there once, up for proper training. We then put Rosemary onto family farming in West Penwith. She was fully able to do this; she recorded a vast amount of stuff, which deals with about three families. This was then transcribed.[11]

In the first series of *Cornish Studies*, the 1979 edition contained an article by Rosemary Robertson reviewing the progress of this venture. Within it she explained how in designing the project she determined the main area of historical enquiry to be 'the farm economy and practice, the daily life style and standard of living of the families, their social interactions within and beyond the household, and how these actual farms were established, expanded and passed onto the next generation'.[12] Yet, despite many hours of good-quality interview material being compiled, no further funding was made available to continue this initiative and the recordings languished unused at the Institute for many years. However, they have, with the advent of CAVA, at last been resurrected, and Sussane Wagner of the Linguistics Department of the University of Freiburg has already put the material to good use.

Following the cessation of work on the West Penwith Farming Project, for some twenty years the discipline of oral history remained unexplored at the Institute of Cornish Studies. And yet in the mean time, as is reviewed below, exciting new developments were taking place in oral history interpretation and presentation. It was not until the arrival of Garry Tregidga, when in his new role of Assistant Director of the Institute he convened meetings at County Hall in Truro, that oral history was re-launched at the Institute.

'YOU HAVE TO GO BACK': ESTABLISHING CAVA AND THE QUEST FOR INTERPRETATIVE METHODOLOGIES

Significantly, these meetings held at County Hall in 1998/99 marked the beginning of the process that would eventually culminate in the formation of CAVA. In an attempt to unravel the complexities of how it has moved from being merely an umbrella organization into also becoming a movement advocating innovative methodologies, Dr Garry Tregidga agreed to be put through the 'ordeal' of the interviewing process for the first time as an interviewee. This was an impromptu semi-structured interview that centred exclusively around the evolution of the interviewee's interest in the field of oral history rather than the more detailed but time-consuming 'life story' interviewing strategy.[13] Even so, despite attempting to confine the narrative within the domain of the past five years, in the course of this interview it was noticeable how interviewer and interviewee were leaping between 'places of memory', a term used by Alesandro Portelli to describe the erratic perceptions of time that dwell within all of our recollections. As Portelli comments, 'In memory, time becomes "place"; all the recollected past exists simultaneously in the space of the mind. Speakers therefore may tend to arrange events along paradigmatic lines of similarity rather than along syntagmatic lines of chronological sequence.'[14]

As Crago and Tregidga set about constructing and deconstructing their recent pasts, it became apparent how quickly immediate memories become 'history'. Somehow the events of a mere five years ago belonged to a far away place where their former selves haunted respective 'places of memory'.

TC: *Where did you foster this interest in oral history?*

GT: Interesting isn't it really? You have got to go back to when I was doing my Ph.D. Because when I was doing my Ph.D. I interviewed a number of people—A.L. Rowse, Baroness Seer (to name but two, I can't remember any of the others)—but it was never recorded. So I was thinking at the time that it should have been recorded not in terms of oral history per se but I thought it would be a useful aid if I put it all on tape. But when I did complete my Ph.D. I came back to Cornwall for a year from Exeter and I joined Bernard's [Bernard Deacon's] Cornish History Seminar Group. And there were one or two articles in the newsletters in about 1996, one of which was actually written by Christine North saying that there should be an oral history project and saying that there was somebody at the Cornwall Family History Society who was interested: which I assume was you?

TC: *Yes.*

GT: So isn't that strange really? I was interested back then and never knew of your existence. But your activities, which Christine North actually put in the article, got me interested to a certain extent. I was actually going to write an article in the Cornish History Seminar Group newsletter saying that there should be an oral history project. But that sort of fell by the wayside because Bernard packed up the idea of the Cornish History Seminar Group in a sense (he was to busy with various things) so I actually ending up taking it over but I never actually did write the article.[15]

When it came to the process of interpreting this short extract of interview, there was much to digest. Firstly it allowed both individuals to evaluate one another's influence upon each other, in terms of developing an interest in oral history, something that as it turned out occurred before they had even actually met! Furthermore, this section of narrative also goes some way to illustrate the broad spectrum of approaches and uses to which oral history can be applied. While at this time Tregidga's interest in the discipline was to use it merely as an additional historical source rather than as an interpretative tool, Crago was beginning to realize the potential of oral history in the more subjective process of putting the flesh on the bones in the compilation of family history.

Similarly, something that neither interviewer nor interviewee had fully appreciated before recording and analysing this interview was the important role of other 'networkers' in Cornwall such as Christine North (the former County Archivist, whose valuable 'mine of knowledge' concerning contacts was central to the success of forming CAVA). Importantly, this is a role that is still continued by Paul Brough at the Cornwall Record Office and Terry Knight at the Cornwall Centre, both of whom are integral parts of the CAVA organization. As a footnote to this particular place of memory, it should be remembered that Tregidga's taking over of the Cornish History Seminar Group and subsequent appointment at the Institute was to lead eventually to the founding of the successful Cornish History Network, with its series of annual conferences, its widely circulated *Newsletter* and innovative on-line journal, *Cornish History*. As the interview continued, so the underlying influences that lie behind the current direction of CAVA became evident.

> Well, then I came to the Institute. And one of the things that I was interested in doing was a study of Cornish politics in the twentieth century. Now oral history would have been just part of that; there would have been a structural side to it as well, so there would have been questionnaires as well as identifying other sources. But oral history would just have been part of it. So that initially was the plan. I contacted Christine North (interesting how she comes back into the picture again) saying that I was actually going to do this and she suggested that I should contact Rob Perks. So I contacted Rob Perks and went to the British Library and he was talking about the possibilities of doing other things rather than just doing politics. And strangely enough, by pure coincidence at one of the [Institute] Board meetings Geoffrey Holland suggested that we should go further than just doing a political study and that it should become a general oral history study, so that in a sense is how this idea developed.[16]

Here the narrative reveals a gradual move from the utilization of oral history in a conservative, empirical mode into an all-encompassing Cornwall-wide setting such as had been articulated in the outline of CAVA's proposed Cornish Braids project (see below). In establishing contact with Rob Perks (Secretary of the Oral History Society and

Director of the Oral History Archive at the British Library), this link opened up new possibilities to engage with ongoing methodological developments in the international oral history world, such as the work of Portelli and Passerini.[17] One question raised by visiting this particular 'place of memory' concerns the underlying motivating factors that led Tregidga to broaden his interest in oral history. While he had initially considered it to be an evolutionary process, his narrative appears to point out that he was equally responding to a commonly held perception that a more 'general' oral history project should be established, a view that was even being articulated by the Vice Chancellor of Exeter University.

The final extract of narrative is illustrative of the extent to which oral history had developed since Tregidga and Crago's initial naïve 'flirtations' with the discipline:

> The first interview I did was with Major Beer and that was Dec 1996—because I was writing this article for *Cornish Studies* which came out in the following year, so that was the first proper oral history interview that I did. And again not in terms of oral history, but I did it just to provide a record which I could use it in the sense of Frisch's more history approach because I was just using it to supplement more documents and there was precious little information on *Tyr ha Tavas,*[18] so oral history actually came into the equation. So I suppose that was the way that I was looking at it in terms of research rational. But that Birmingham conference that you went to, that changed it a lot in the way that it was perceived. And our attitudes were changing from time to time because it was being driven by a lack of funding. I managed to get some funding for you in 1999 but then of course they wouldn't give out any more funding. You know really they should have actually built on that. Well of course by this time we were thinking about this heritage lottery application and finally we have got this in and hopefully it will be successful.[19]

That the work of Michael Frisch 'seeps' into this interview reveals much about the direction in which a developing Cornish oral history movement is moving, as Frisch is eminent in the field of 'public history'.[20] Tregidga's reference to 'more history' relates to how Michael Frisch has categorized the roles of oral history into what he terms the two poles of 'more history' and 'anti history'.[21] The 'more history' approach refers to the contribution the discipline allows in the process of adding to conventional documentary sources. This is

accomplished through eyewitness accounts and the memories of inter-
viewees whose perspectives might otherwise be ignored or neglected.[22]
So perhaps in itself this process represents nothing particularly
innovative, being a continuation of what historians from all societies
world-wide have been practising for centuries, namely drawing on oral
traditions, myths and accounts, as sources of evidence.

However, through what Frisch describes as the 'anti history'
approach, oral history is revealed as having the potential to take on an
extra dimension, so as to 'touch the "real" history . . . by com-
municating with it directly'.[23] This is because within the interview
situation there is far more going on than merely recounting bland
historical narrative. The 'sensation of history' is going through a two-
way process, affecting the contemporary setting into which the
interviewee's memory re-emerges while simultaneously altering how
'the past' is then perceived by the actual interviewee. It is, without
doubt, this quest to capture 'the sensation of history' that has fuelled
recent developments in the way that oral history is approached.

In further connection with this, Tregidga's reference to 'the
Birmingham conference' refers to the Oral History Society's conference entitled 'Pleasure and Dangers in the City' which took place in
2000 and at which Crago encountered the work of Alessandro Portelli
for the first time. It was stemming from this occasion that Cornish oral
history material in effect ceased to be treated as conventional historical
data, and became a valuable interpretative source in its own right.

Portelli places a strong emphasis upon the 'distortions that oral
history creates'; for example, when he was doing an oral history of a
small working-class Italian city in the 1970s, he became puzzled when
his subjects repeatedly made factual errors or even related events that
had never happened. This was particularly evident when talking about
the death of a worker named Luigi Trastulli, who had been killed in a
clash with the police in 1949. The people that he interviewed all
insisted that the event had occurred during demonstrations in 1953. At
first this seemed like the kind of mistake that ageing memories are
prone to, confirming the reason why many historians are wary of oral
history. However, perhaps because of his background as a teacher of
American literature at the University of Rome, Portelli began to see
the errors of oral histories rather like Freudian slips, as a central part of
their meaning and their narrative strategy. Trastulli died during a
demonstration over Italy's decision to join NATO, a controversy that
had lost much of its meaning by the time Portelli did his interviews, and
the 1953 demonstrations were prompted by mass firings from local
factories, which had permanently changed the life of the population in
the area. 'I realized that memory was itself an event on which we

needed to reflect', he said in a recent interview at the University of Rome, 'Memory is not just a mirror of what has happened, it is one of the things that happens, which merits study.'[24]

Mary Marshall Clark, Director of the Oral History Research Office at Columbia University, reiterates this view, commenting: 'Alessandro Portelli's work has transformed oral history from being a kind of stepchild of history into a literary genre in its own right . . . He has allowed us to see oral histories as more than eyewitness accounts that are either true or false, and to look for themes and structures of the stories.'[25] This approach has become increasingly influential and has prompted Indiana University, for example, to change the name of its Oral History Research Centre to 'The Centre for History and Memory'.

A QUESTION OF 'COMPOSURE': APPLYING INTERPRETATIVE METHODOLOGIES TO COLLECTED CORNISH DIALOGUE

The interview quoted above, although running the risk of being ludicrously narcissistic, was included within this review to reveal something of the subtle change taking place within a section of CAVA with regard to the collected material and the way that the source material might be interpreted. Such an evolution is also evident in the style of academic papers produced during this period. For example, at the 24th International Congress of Genealogical and Heraldic Sciences, Besancon, 2000, the extracts of narrative are still being used as any other historical source.[26] In marked contrast, Crago and Tregidga's paper given in San Marino to the International Academy of Genealogy in June 2001 reveals that by then a far more interpretative approach had evolved. The following extract from this paper reveals the extent to which both individuals' research had moved towards exploring the interpretative and subjective elements of discourse:

> Their everyday conversation seemed to flow naturally from events in Cornwall to experiences in San Francisco or Johannesburg. Interestingly, this international dimension was present in the discussion of the Rescorla circle. For example, when Rundle mentioned about a local smallholding owned by Guy Udy, this led Tonkin to talk about Udy's travels in America:
>
> JT: And, of course, in the western states the cowboys and the sheep farmers didn't get on all that well . . . and one of the stories he told me, he said he was on the mountainside

with the sheep . . . and he had a sheepskin coat on he was
rather pleased with, . . . he said he seen a rider coming across
the level plain . . . and, the rider spotted him and changed
course. When that happened I went higher up still . . . He said
in the end [the rider] got tired of doing that and turned
around and went away again.

So I said, well, he could have had a message; he could have
had a letter or something like that. Didn't you want a letter
from home?

So Guy said 'well ez, I could have done with a letter from
home, he said, but I wanted to keep my sheepskin coat more
than I wanted a letter and I didn't know what he had in mind.
[Laughter]

SG: Was that any relation to Gerry Udy up Carbis?

JT: I suspect it might be . . .

JR: . . . they're distant [relations].[27]

There is a symbolic significance to this extract. Gregory's
intervention demonstrates how oral narrative can remove
rapidly over time and space, in this case by making sense of a
formerly unrecorded historical event in the USA by relating
the central figure of the narrative to a relation living in
modern Cornwall. Moreover, this concept helps to explain
Tonkin's seemingly contradictory remarks concerning
mobility. Migration in more recent times is perceived in
the context of change in Cornwall itself with immigration
apparently undermining the old homogeneity of the region.
For Tonkin the Cornish Diaspora was inherently different
since its cultural momentum was firmly rooted in the mother-
land.[28]

It would appear, therefore, that the interpretative section of
CAVA was now immersing itself deeply in popular memory theory and
in so doing had moved towards producing interviews through which the
interviewee's 'composure' is explored. 'Composure' is a term that was
coined by Graham Dawson and is used to describe how an individual
strives to constitute him or herself successfully within the framework of
a story. Involving oneself within composed stories is 'a cultural practise
deeply embedded in everyday life, a creative activity in which everyone
engages'.[29] And, furthermore, as feminist Penny Summerhill observes:

public memory is not drawn upon indiscriminately in the production of personal memory, the story that is actually told is always the one preferred amongst other possible versions. This is because the purpose of telling is to produce both a coherent narrative and a version of the self which can be lived with in relative psychic comfort, to enable in other words, subjective composure to be achieved.[30]

CORNISH BRAIDS

It follows from the above that if it is possible to gather enough material, then the process of reviewing numerous individuals' attempts at 'composure' could result in the creation of a reflexive subjective picture of Cornish society. However, for such wide-ranging research to be undertaken considerable amounts of interview material have to be sought out, recorded, collected, summarized and catalogued. It is partly for this reason, and to cement the Institute's outreach to Cornish communities, that the Cornish Braids project has been launched, an initiative that has already attracted substantial funding from the Heritage Lottery Fund.

The aim of the Cornish Braids venture is to create a multi-generational profile of Cornish life in the twentieth century. Through the medium of oral history, it will investigate key strands of cultural activity—in particular work, religion, politics, leisure and social relationships—to establish the first comprehensive study of this subject in Cornwall, or indeed the South-West of Britain, from a popular memory perspective. The project represents a timely study of all the changes that have taken place in Cornwall. For example, the distinctive symbols of economic and religious identity of the past are fast disappearing, the closure of South Crofty in the late 1990s symbolizing the final collapse of Cornwall's formerly dominant mining industry, and the loss of nearly 500 chapels since 1932 pointing to the long-term decline of Cornish Methodism. Cornish Braids will focus on three areas of activity: collecting oral testimonies; providing access to the archive; and interpreting the findings. Apart from creating and developing a public archive, it is intended to produce a book and CD based on the Cornish Braids recordings. Volunteers will play a key role in the project; two field work officers working in association with the Oral History Society and the College of St Mark & St John will organize regular training sessions for community volunteers associated with the Cornish project. This represents a deliberate 'volunteer strategy' that aims to develop oral history skills for individuals drawn from all sections of society.

CAVA: A BLENDING OF TRUFFLE HUNTERS AND PARACHUTISTS?

In conclusion, it is evident that CAVA has evolved into something more than Tregidga's original vision of an umbrella organization drawing together disparate groups and individuals from across Cornwall with an interest in 'oral history', becoming rapidly a movement for the introduction of new approaches to the collection and interpretation of oral narrative. Kate Tiller in a recent article advocating a multi-disciplinary 'new local history' chose to cite the work of the French *Annales* historian Emmanuel Le Roy Ladurie, whose work has centred upon interpreting the collected oral narrative in his study of fourteenth-century religious heresy.[31] Ladurie considers that there are two types of historian: 'truffle hunters' and 'parachutists'. Truffle hunters, Ladurie says, are:

> those supremely professional practitioners who are precise in their historical vision, addicted to their archives, and high minded in their search for what they believe to be the truth. They usually know a great deal about very little, are meticulously accurate in their footnote references, and deliberately eschew broad generalisations or speculative hypotheses, on the grounds that they are inconsistent with the exacting grounds of real scholarship.

On the other hand, the Parachutists:

> are by definition very different. They range more audaciously across the centuries, and survey a broader panorama of the historical landscape. They are concerned with the underlying causes rather than with superficial phenomena, they venture wide (and sometimes wild) generalisations, they move rapidly from one topic to another, and their work relies on secondary resources rather than on detailed research.[32]

Perhaps the success of CAVA lies in its ability to blend these differing perspectives, evident for example in both Tregidga's ongoing 'qualitative micro-politics' activities and Milden's postgraduate research into the relationship between Methodism and politics in which they rely heavily upon collected oral history recordings. Of course, the CAVA movement is still very much in its infancy and publications are only now starting to flow from the research that has been undertaken so far. However, if in another decade a similar review of oral history is commissioned it can be confidently predicted that oral history will still

be an important element of Cornish Studies, as Philip Payton acknowledges: 'CAVA has emerged against the background of the Combined
Universities in Cornwall project, an initiative in which the Institute (as
part of the University of Exeter) is poised to play a key role and where
there are exciting opportunities for building new partnerships and
significantly expanding CAVA's scope and resources'.[33]

NOTES AND REFERENCES

1. Allesandro Portelli, *The Death of Luigi Trastulli and Other Stories: Form and Meaning in Oral History*, New York, 1991, p. 46.
2. Portelli, 1991, p. 46.
3. Guy Beiner, *Bodhaire Ui Laoire: Oral History and Contemporary Irish Historiography*, Department of Modern Irish History, Trinity College Dublin, http://www.ucd.ie/pages/99articlesbeiner.html.
4. Beiner.
5. Philip Payton in *Cornish Voices*, 2000, p.1.
6. See reference to James Boswell, *Journal of a Tour of the Hebrides*, 1785, in P. Thompson, 'The Development of Oral History in Britain', in D.K. Dunaway and W.K. Baum (eds), *Oral History: An Interdisciplinary Anthology*, Walnut Creek/London/New Delhi, 1996, p. 351.
7. For examples of collected oral tradition see Robert Hunt, *Popular Romances of the West of England: Or the Drolls, Traditions, and Superstitions of Old Cornwall*, London, 1865.
8. Minutes of the Cornish Gorseth, June 1938.
9. Undated Tyr ha Tavas papers at the Institute of Cornish Studies reveal that the showing of this film to the London Cornish Association at Christmas 1936 was a sell-out and that a second presentation had to be organized.
10. Dr Slack has very kindly deposited copies of many of his recordings with CAVA.
11. Interview with Charles Thomas, May 2002, CAVA.
12. Rosemary Robertson, 'The Institute's Oral History Project: Family Farming in West Penwith, 1919–1939', in *Cornish Studies 7*, 1979, p. 67.
13. See 'A Life Story Interview Guide', in Paul Thompson, *The Voice of the Past: Oral History*, 3rd edn, Oxford, 2000, pp. 309–23.
14. Alessandro Portelli, *The Battle of Valle Giulia: Oral History and the Art of Dialogue*, Milwaukee, 1997, p. 32.
15. Interview with Garry Tregidga, May 2002, CAVA.
16. Interview with Garry Tregidga, May 2002, CAVA.
17. See Luisa Passerini, *Fascism in Popular Memory: The Cultural Experience of the Turin Working Class*, Cambridge, 1987.
18. Some of the information gleaned from Cecil Beer on this period appears in G. Tregidga and T. Crago, *Map Kenwyn: The Life and Times of Cecil Beer*, 2000.
19. Interview with Garry Tregidga, May 2002, CAVA.
20. For a definition of public history, see Jill Liddington, 'What is Public

History? Public Meanings and Their Pasts, Meanings and Practices', *Oral History* 30.1, 2002, pp. 83–93.

21. M. Frisch, *A Shared Authority: Essays on the Craft and Meaning of Oral History*, New York, 1990, p. 187.
22. Joanna Bornat, 'Reminiscence and Oral History: Parallel Universes or Shared Endeavour?' unpublished paper presented to the Oral History Society Regional Network meeting, Edinburgh, 2001.
23. Frisch, 1990.
24. A. Portelli, quoted in Alexander Stille, 'Prospecting for Truth Amid the Distortions of Oral History Ideas', *New York Times*, 10 March 2001.
25. Stille, 10 March 2001.
26. T. Crago, 'Highlighting the Social Dynamics of Oral History (An Investigation into the Changing Senses of Identity Occurring within Cornish Communities between the World Wars)', paper delivered at the 24th International Congress of Genealogical and Heraldic Sciences, Besancon, 2000.
27. CAVA Memory Day at Rescorla, St Austell, 4 December 2000, CAVA.
28. T. Crago and G.H. Tregidga, *Oral Narrative and Cornish Migration: Interpretations of Family, Place and Space*, Academie Internationale de Genealogie, forthcoming 2003.
29. Graham Dawson, *Soldier Heroes: British Adventure, Empire and the Imagining of Masculinities*, London, 1994.
30. Penny Summerfield, *Reconstructing Women's Wartime Lives: Discourse and Subjectivity of the Second World War*, Manchester, 1998.
31. Emmanuel Le Roy Ladurie, *Montaillou: Cathars and Catholics in a French Village, 1294–1324*, London, 1979.
32. Emmanuel Le Roy Ladurie cited in Kate Tiller, 'Past, Present, Future', *History Magazine* 3.5, 2002, pp. 30–2.
33. Payton, 2000.

CORNISH AT ITS MILLENNIUM: AN INDEPENDENT STUDY OF THE LANGUAGE UNDERTAKEN IN 2000

Kenneth MacKinnon

INTRODUCTION

An important aspect of the 'Good Friday Agreement' in 1999 was the recognition of the Irish and Ulster Scots languages in Northern Ireland, and the promise to sign and ratify the European Charter of Minority or Regional Languages. This very swiftly led to demands for inclusion of Welsh, Gaelic and Scots, which were rapidly accepted. As the result of prompt parliamentary action by Andrew George, MP for St Ives (on an adjournment motion on 23 February 1999), the government commissioned an independent academic study on Cornish. Its purpose was to provide a factual and officially accessible basis of knowledge about the Cornish language on which government policy could be based, and in particular consideration of the inclusion of Cornish within the United Kingdom's signature and ratification of the Charter. Accordingly, on 22 December 1999 the Secretary of State for the Environment, Transport and the Regions commissioned EKOS Limited (economic consultants, Inverness) and SGRUD Research (language-planning and research service in the Black Isle) to undertake an independent study of Cornish, reporting to the Government Office of the South-West.

The remit was to establish the position on the use and currency of the Cornish language historically and contemporarily, and to provide a sound factual basis for informing consideration of policy issues by various government departments. The study objectives were to report factually and impartially on: the historical position of Cornish to the present day; the ways in which Cornish is 'traditionally used' in Cornwall and elsewhere, including numbers, fluency and use in everyday life; learning, study, teaching and qualifications in the language; the body of literature; organizations promoting the language; and sources of funding and support.

The research was undertaken during January and February 2000 principally by the present author, involving desk research at research centres and archives in Cornwall and London, and face-to-face and telephone interviews of 50 organizations and individuals associated with the promotion of Cornish. Discussions with three focus groups of Cornish speakers (representative of the three main revived language varieties) provided contact with a further 48 persons. The principal researcher also attended and participated in Cornish-language events and meetings during (and subsequent to) this survey period.

The full text of the report is available from the Government Office of the South-West, and can be read and downloaded from its website.[1] The following summary of the report indicates the scope of its principal contents. Its inclusion in this volume of *Cornish Studies* is fortuitous and timely, for the last ten years or so have witnessed tremendous developments within the Cornish language movement, much of it considered within the pages of this series, and any 'taking stock' of the discipline of Cornish Studies must necessarily review the current state of Cornish and its future prospects. The report itself was not remitted to contain recommendations for the future. Its purpose was to provide an independent reference document as a basis for government policy. However, as its principal author, I do have views upon the current state of the Cornish language, issues relating to the language, and provisions which could be made for its further development, and I conclude this article with a commentary upon these.

SUMMARY OF MAIN FINDINGS

Historical Trends in the Development of Cornish
The Cornish language was the speech of Cornwall from Dark Age times through to the late Middle Ages. In the late medieval era it was weakening in eastern Cornwall but its substantial reverses came with the closer incorporation of Cornwall into the Tudor state. At its maximum size the speech community has been estimated at 38,000.[2]

During early modern times, Cornish initially held its ground as the majority speech of the Cornish people but the further dislocations of the seventeenth century (Civil War) and other rebellions destabilized the language considerably. By 1700, the year in which Edward Lhuyd visited Cornwall, he reported the language to be in substantial decline and limited only to the western extremities of Cornwall. This process of decline was considerably hastened by Cornwall's early industrialization and the inter-penetration of a previously autonomous speech community by adventitious economic enterprises reinforcing a new language. Nevertheless, knowledge of Cornish and some extent of speaking ability continued to be transmitted through family networks and individuals. These were the sources whereby scholars in the nineteenth century compiled the first dictionaries and learners' lessons in the language. A landmark for the language revival was Jenner's *Handbook* of 1904.

The beginnings of the revival pre-1914 produced a number of persons able to use the language—especially in writing. The inter-war years witnessed the formation of key institutions for the revival (Gorseth Kernow, the Old Cornwall Societies) and the establishment of classes both in Cornwall and in London. After the dislocations of the Second World War the language revival made initially slow but steady progress which gathered impetus as new journals were established. At this period the revival continued with Nance's revision of Jenner's original Cornish, which came to be called Unified (Ünys). The developing needs of the language grew beyond its patronage by the Gorseth and a Language Board was established in 1967 whose constitution was later reformulated to make it more representative of the body of speakers and users.

Disquiet with Nance's system was being voiced by the early 1980s. This was addressed linguistically by Ken George with regard to spelling, pronunciation and lexical problems. Also, at this time Richard Gendall was developing his ideas of basing the revived language upon its later vernacular and written forms. These were the seeds of the 'tri-partite split' between: Unified Cornish, which was based upon the late medieval classic texts; Gendall's Late/Modern Cornish; and those who adopted Ken George's version of Common Cornish (Kemmyn). The debate over the revival versions was addressed by public meetings and the Language Board adopted Kemmyn. The language controversies appear to have had a stimulating effect upon public awareness of the language and have attracted a new generation of learners. Linguistic research has been greatly stimulated in all three varieties, as has output of language resource publications and general reading material. The bulk of this publication has been in Kemmyn, the language variety which has produced most language activity and supporting institutions in terms of volume.

DOROTHY PENTREATH of MOUSEHOLE in CORNWALL
the last Person who could converse in the Cornish Language.

6. *Dolly Pentreath—certainly* not *the last person to speak
the Cornish language.*

Mode of Use

Traditionally, historically spoken Cornish extended across the whole
range of uses when it was the majority speech of the Cornish people. In
late medieval times it produced a literature which was chiefly religious
drama and verse. Cornwall had significant trading links with Brittany,
and Cornish was thus used in the tin trade, and in commercial and
economic life. The events of the sixteenth century resulted in the

Anglicization of the upper orders of society, with English becoming general in Cornwall's ruling classes. In its last phase, when the language was obviously fast retreating, efforts were made to secure its prospects by the production of a written literature in its Late/Modern form, largely by professional-class people. New industries implied the strengthening of English, but Cornish evidently remained strong amongst fishing communities in western Cornwall, which comprised its last body of speakers. There are reports of the language being used at sea into the nineteenth century, and for specific purposes even into the twentieth century.

In the revival, early use of Cornish was chiefly written, and from the beginning a conscious effort to produce a quality literature is evident. This has continued to strengthen from the pre-1939 period, as has the resolve to ensure Cornish as a spoken language. Today, the language is spoken in a wide variety of situations: the conduct of business in Cornish organizations; in cultural events; in a wide variety of social settings when speakers congregate; and most importantly in the homes and families of what is still a small number of cases. A reasonable estimate of the number of speakers able to use the language effectively for everyday purposes is approaching 300 in Cornwall itself (see Figure 3), with a further 50 reported for the London area. The survey found 10 families using the language in the home. It is also used increasingly in signage, public worship, ceremonies and ritual.

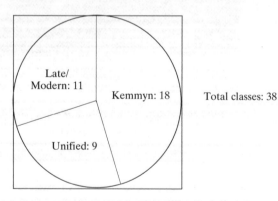

7. *Cornish language classes 1999/2000:*
numbers of classes by language-variety
(Source: Jane Ninnis, *State of the Language Statistics* 1999)

Availability and Take-Up of Learning and Study of Cornish
The 1984 Report *Kernewek Hedhyu* on the state of the language[3] had
noted that by 1983/4 the number of adult classes in Cornish had
increased to 18: in Bodmin, Camborne, Falmouth, Hayle, Helston,
Launceston, Lostwithiel, Liskeard, Newlyn East, Newquay, Padstow,
Penzance, Perranporth, Saltash, St Austell, St Just, Torpoint, and
Truro, with further classes reported outwith Cornwall.

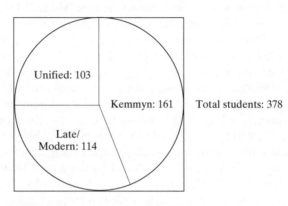

8. Cornish language classes 1999/2000:
estimated numbers of students by language variety
(Source: Jane Ninnis, State of the Language Statistics 1999)

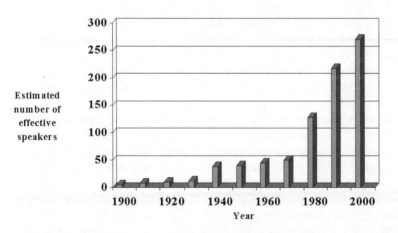

9. The revival of Cornish in the twentieth century
(Sources: A.S.D. Smith, *The Story of the Cornish Language*, Camborne, 1947
pp. 12–14; P. Berresford Ellis, *Cornish Language and Literature*, London,
1974, pp. 152–70; Treve Crago, Gorseth archives; Jane Ninnis, *State of The
Language Statistics* 1999)

The 2000 survey identified 36 formal classes in Cornish at adult education level. The figure was revised to 38 after the survey when further information was forthcoming. Eighteen classes were conducted in Kemmyn, at Callington, Four Lanes, Grampound Road, Helston, Jacobstowe, Launceston, Liskeard (two classes), The Lizard, Looe, Lostwithiel, Mullion, Newlyn East, Penzance, Pool, Saltash, St Austell and Truro. Nine classes were conducted in Unified, at Bodmin, Bude, Camborne, Newlyn, Penryn, Penzance (two classes), St Austell, and St Just. There were eleven classes in Late/Modern Cornish, at Falmouth, Menheniot, Pendeen (two classes), Redruth, St Agnes, St Austell, St Ives, Troon, and Truro (two classes). Enrolments for Kemmyn classes totalled 143, suggesting around 161 in total. Enrolments in 4 Unified classes totalled 46, suggesting around 103 in total. Enrolments in 9 Late/Modern classes totalled 93, suggesting around 114 overall. On this basis there was an estimated total of 378 students in the 38 classes (see Figures 1 and 2).[4] Other informal and self-help groups were reported, which would almost certainly suggest over 400 active learners. Most classes are held in and organized by further education colleges. Otherwise, they are locally organized by language activists and held in a variety of venues, such as village halls and pubs. There are also classes in Australia and London, as well as a correspondence course organized outside Cornwall. In 1999 some 297 corresponding students were registered for this distance learning service, *Kernewek dre Lyther*. Allowing for overlaps, active learners are likely to exceed 500.

At school level, Cornish was being taught as early as the pre-1939 period in local authority schools. After the war it featured in a private school at Camborne and subsequently developed in the local authority sector. A GCSE examination incentivized Cornish at primary and secondary level. The 1984 Report noted five primary schools and two secondary schools where Cornish was taught. Although the number of schools reporting the teaching of Cornish at some level has increased in recent years, the cessation of the GSCE scheme (due to low numbers), the introduction of the National Curriculum and local management of schools were often seen as set-backs. At primary level, four schools reported the teaching of Cornish within the school day, at Helston (St Michael's), Roskear, St Mawes, and Wendron. Extra-mural Cornish clubs were organized at eight schools: Coad's Green, Heamoor, Ludgvan, Godolphin, Saltash (Brunel), St Neot, St Mawes and Weeth (at Camborne). Four secondary schools taught Cornish: Liskeard Community College, Newquay Tretherras, Pool and Truro. Together with school pupils, numbers of active learners may probably approach 600.

A Body of Cornish Literature

Old Cornish is represented solely by a vocabulary and glosses in the Bodmin Gospels. A late medieval literature of religious verse, a charter, a mystery play cycle and two other dramas represent this period. Since the completion of the survey a further Middle Cornish manuscript has come to light. Late/Modern Cornish is said to commence with a collection of mid-sixteenth-century homilies. It continued in the subsequent two centuries with an extension of genres into secular verse, letters, and essays on various subjects including the language itself.

Revived Cornish literature has increasingly developed in quantity and quality. There have been a number of literary publications which have developed the essay, the short story and poetry in Cornish. More recently novels have been produced, along with an increasing amount of children's publications. In terms of output and publications per head of language users this may constitute a record even higher than Icelandic. The medieval drama has been revived in modern performance.

ORGANIZATIONS WHICH PROMOTE CORNISH

The survey contacted a wide range of organizations involved in or connected with the language. Our research has identified a total of about 50 such bodies, and contacted 42 of them. These can be broadly categorized as follows:

- Language organizations: Agan Tavas, Cornish Language Board, Cornish Language Council, Dalleth, Gorseth Kernow, Kowethas an Yeth Kernewek, Teere ha Tavaz. Total: 7. These represent the three main forms of the language and all are represented on the Cornish Sub-committee of the European Bureau for Lesser-Used Languages (EBLUL).
- Cultural organizations: Celtic Congress, Cornish Eisteddfod, Cornish Literary Guild, Cornish Music Guild, Cornish Music Projects, Federation of Old Cornwall Societies, Lowender Peran, Ros Keltek, Verbal Arts Cornwall. Total: 9.
- Educational Institutions: Cornwall Education Authority, London Association for Celtic Education, University of Dublin: Celtic Studies, University of Exeter: Institute of Cornish Studies, University of Plymouth: Modern Languages. Total: 5.
- Political and public life: the majority of local authorities had adopted a policy framework supportive of the language at the time of the survey. All have subsequently done so. Organizations interviewed comprised: Carrick District Council, Celtic League, EBLUL

(Cornish Sub-Committee), Cornish Bureau for European Relations (CoBER), Cornish National Committee, Cornwall County Council, Cuntelles Kysgwlasek Keltek, Kerskerdh Kernewek, Mebyon Kernow, North Cornwall District Council. Total: 10.
- Media (journals/magazines, radio and televison): *Agan Yeth*, *An Gannas*, *An Garrack*, Celtic Film and Television Festival, Pirate FM, Widwest Films. Total: 6.
- Private sector: Gwynn ha Du, Just Cornish, An Lyverji Kernewek. Total: 3.
- Religious life: the Bishop's Advisory Committee on Cornish Services, Bredereth Sen Jago. Total: 2.

The first two of these groups of organizations are, in the main, quite longstanding, have cross-membership, and exist on slight or very slight financial resources. Very active inter-Celtic links have been developed by the Gorseth, the Eisteddfod, the Celtic Congress, the Celtic League, and the Cornish Sub-Committee of EBLUL.

Funding and Support
It appears that organizations and individuals involved in the promotion and development of the Cornish language have received little in the way of funding over the last twenty years. We have identified third-party funding of approximately £50,000. This probably reflects the generally small-scale nature of these organizations over this time. However, there has been some funding activity during the 1990s, albeit for relatively small amounts. One of the main sources of funding has been local authorities. There has also been a small number of success-ful applications to the European Commission DG XXII, under the Minority Languages programme. Some organizations have depended on raising private funds to undertake their activities.

Whilst there has been a range of cultural funding programmes available through the European Commission during the 1990s, our consultations suggest that Cornish language organizations would have been able to access very little funding over the period, particularly as projects assisted tend to require partnerships between organizations from two or three member states. Our research indicates that over the last twenty years, Cornish language activity has not really been at the stage of critical mass where it could link up and exchange information with organizations in other member states. Further, these initiatives generally have relatively small budgets, with the bidding process being very competitive.

In addition, funding programmes delivered under Objective 5(b) and LEADER II during the 1990s generally required assisted projects to demonstrate an economic benefit for the area. Applications for specifically language-oriented projects were unlikely to be successful. The Department for Education and Employment (DfEE) was also consulted. It advised that two funds could potentially be sourced for Cornish language related activities: the Study Support Programme and the Standards Fund. The first of these is managed by the DfEE, and administered by local education authorities and provides funding for school activities such as learning Cornish out of school hours, including staffing costs.

A number of institutional and funding changes were currently taking place. Regional Development Authorities had recently been established in England, and the Cornwall and Scilly Objective 1 Programme was due to commence in 2000. Again, it seemed unlikely that specifically Cornish language and cultural related activities could be funded. A further programme had been developed called Culture 2000, which has been designed to replace some of the cultural programmes operated by the European Commission during the 1990s. It was due to operate from 2002 to 2004, and had a total budget of 167 ECUs over its five years of operation. However, the eligibility for funding from this programme includes partnership activities involving cultural operators from at least three eligible countries, and it may be difficult for Cornish language organizations to secure such funds, given the current level of critical mass. However, in 2000 Cornwall County Council was considering organizing training seminars for groups to advise them on fund application, form completion, etc. This could greatly benefit language organizations. Subsequent to the 2000 survey, the National Lottery Heritage Fund has initiated a Language Heritage Fund (commencing in 2002), with a remit for linguistic heritage starting with the indigenous non-English languages of the UK. This should be particularly relevant for Cornish-language applications.

COMMENTARY AND RECOMMENDATIONS

In undertaking this survey early in 2000, I was very conscious of 'following in the footsteps' of Edward Lhuyd, who had undertaken his survey of Cornish three hundred years earlier in 1700. Celtic Studies owe a great deal to Lhuyd, including their very name and identity.[5] In particular, Lhuyd's recording of the Cornish language when it was last a spoken vernacular, and his collecting of what was available of Cornish writings, have enabled subsequent scholars to attempt the revival of the language as a spoken medium once again.[6] Little specific attention was drawn to this tercentenary in Cornwall in 2000, although I prefaced my address to the second New Directions in Celtic Studies Conference[7] with this matter, as an acknowledgement of what we owe to Lhuyd. This article takes up the themes of that address, one of which was that we shall have a further opportunity to do justice to his memory on the tercentenary of his *Archaelogica Britannica*, which was published in 1707.[8] We shall also have a further commemorative opportunity to celebrate the centenary of the Cornish Revival in 2004, one hundred years on from Jenner's *Handbook*[9] and his 'Caernarfon Telegram'. The efforts of Lhuyd, and of Jenner, enabled the traditional transmission of Cornish in each of their generations to become available as a general resource for the language revival, and to ensure for it what Charles Thomas has termed 'apostolic succession'.[10]

The overall impression stemming from this survey is how much has been achieved with so little by so few. Most of the organizations were reported as subsisting on the slenderest of budgets, but were actively maintained by quite remarkable personal efforts. The survey team conveyed this verbally to the commissioning agency at the reporting meeting of representatives of English regions and administrations of other UK countries on 24th March 2000 at Eland House, Victoria, headquarters of the Department of the Environment, Transport and the Regions (DEFR). By this time the UK government had signed the European Charter without inclusion of Cornish on 2nd March 2000, and a year later on 27th March 2001 ratified the Charter, again without inclusion of Cornish. Additions to the Charter can be made at any time, but the round of consultations of other departments by the Government Office for the South-West has considerably exceeded the time taken for consultations on the other languages included. Subsequent to the 2000 survey, a study by Wella Brown[11] found that thirty-eight of the Charter's paragraphs for language use can be attested for Cornish. Thirty-five need to be in place to enable signature. A first priority and recommendation, then, would be to sign and ratify then European Charter on behalf of Cornish. Recently, the UK government has given assurance that it will sign and ratify Part II of the charter for Cornish (as it has done for Scots and Ulster Scots). Priority should then shift to securing signature and ratification in Part III (as for Welsh, Gaelic in Scotland, and Irish in Northern Ireland).[12]

The survey, in reviewing the historical development of Cornish, could have noted the need not only for status planning, but for corpus and acquisition planning also, linked to appropriate research. Languages in contact decline when their speakers experience the lack of presence in the social environment—especially linked to political and economic pressures to shift to another tongue. The languages under pressure then experience a shift in community and family usage. The survey has outlined these processes at work over the course of time. Cornish might have been buttressed by religious institutions but (unlike Welsh) was accorded no translation of scripture or prayer book—and Methodism came a century too late.[12] The language might have been buttressed by education, but it had ceased as a vernacular before the introduction of modern universal education. In reviving Cornish, there are three centuries of leeway to make up.

Corpus planning for Cornish is complicated by the three revived forms currently extant. The survey reported on the history and reasons for the three present language varieties. It made no value judgment concerning them, except to say that they had arisen to serve the needs and preferences of learners. The survey accepted these on the same basis as the presence of language varieties and dialects in other languages, such as the other Celtic languages and English. Revived Cornish is based on its literature at various historic periods. What is very much needed is the collation, editing and academic review of the whole corpus of the literature. A strongly worded plea for this—and for full diplomatic editions of all the mystery plays and historic Cornish literature—was made by Charles Thomas in 1963. Forty years later this work still remains to be done. I echo his views for the necessity of this as an inescapable basis for further corpus planning. This corpus has, however, recently been augmented by a newly discovered Middle Cornish text. Initiatives to edit and prepare these for publication should kick-start the process of scholarly editing and publication of the whole corpus. This should be capable of being funded from academic sources and the newly initiated Language Heritage Fund.

Language authorities for Cornish are essentially non-official and non-academic, although they are assisted by scholars and specialists. There is a quantum leap from this level of development to the provisions established for Welsh, e.g. the Welsh Language Board, and the University of Wales Board of Celtic Studies. The 'Good Friday Agreement' set up quite generously funded cross-border language authorities for Irish and Ulster Scots—the latter virtually *ab initio*. Even in the case of Scots Gaelic, government funding supports the language development agency Comunn na Gàidhlig—and a language board on the Welsh model is currently in the course of being established. Yet Cornish subsists within the same political state (the UK) as these other languages, and there is an argument for comparability of treatment all round—which may well be being met in the case of Gaelic.

The existence of three language varieties might complicate the establishment of language planning and development arrangements. These must obviously grow from acceptable principles within the language movement itself. There were indications during the research of some coming together after the 'tripartite split'. Keskerdh Kernow produced a three-variety 'Prayers for Cornwall' in 1999. The following year Gorseth Kernow accepted entries for its literary competitions in any of the varieties. Each of the varieties is represented on the Cornish Sub-committee of EBLUL. Amongst the three language movements there are various mutual recognitions, albeit partial at present but with every hope that they might become complete and all-round. The principal problem at the moment is in public signage—especially over the spellings of Cornish place-names. If Cornish is to have a public face, some form of consensus would need to develop. In the case of English place-names they have not necessarily been revised as the language has changed—and they preserve a variety of older forms. It might be that some form of agreement on such lines for Cornish place-names may be possible. It is an especially sensitive area, since name forms have been mostly what has survived of Cornish in current everyday speech and writing. The text of public signage presents a further problem, which perhaps only time can solve.

Together with corpus research, another research priority is in the sociology of the language. There has been no general survey of speakers, learners and users of Cornish in terms of numbers, abilities, usage and attitudes. Neither has there been any substantial assessment of general public attitudes towards the language. The three decennial CLAR surveys of Irish and the Welsh Housing Survey are good models of practice in this regard. I have myself undertaken similar—albeit smaller-scale—surveys of Gaelic speakers, and a recent survey of Manx[14] has provided an example for a language group of similar size to Cornish. These surveys have been conducted on similar methodologies and contain many similar questions. Comparisons of the case of Cornish with its neighbouring lesser-used languages would be feasible. Such a study would provide a foundation for language-planning initiatives, and would in itself be a consciousness-raising initiative.

The problem of consciousness-raising is crucial for the future development of Cornish. Its present body of speakers, learners and users is tiny. In the early twentieth century Nance was able to say of his and Jenner's efforts that his generation had put Cornish back in its feet but it would take another generation to get it to walk. In the later twentieth century Cornish was step-by-step making that transition. Considering that every development was practically a pulling of itself up by its own bootstraps, the achievements have been considerable. The next steps are not really feasible without a greater critical mass involving considerably more people, thus justifying a claim upon their own share of public funds for the development of language and cultural infrastructure. The problem is in creating greater public awareness of the language, securing a greater place for it in the social environment of Cornwall, and attracting a greater number of people effectively to learn it. The following suggestions are in no way prescriptive. As an outsider—however sympathetic—I may not be in the best position to assess how practical or successful they might be. But the Cornish language movement at the outset of a new millennium, and the Cornish language revival coming up to its centenary in 2004, needs to assess its position and discuss its options and possibilities. The following suggestions may serve then as a preliminary agenda—or indeed as points of departure.

One possibility might be a thorough look at the educational system and at the ways in which the National Curriculum can and should carry a distinctive Cornish component in history, culture and language. There have been Cornish Studies in Schools initiatives in the past, some led by the Institute of Cornish Studies, together with the Millennium Book *Cornwall For Ever! Kernow Bys Vyken* (presented free to every schoolchild in Cornwall in 2000), and there are currently renewed prospects for further initiatives. In particular, language acquisition planning deserves to be taken seriously. Increasing numbers seeking to acquire Cornish can also be the basis for encouraging the media to provide for their needs. The other Celtic languages can all provide good examples of popular language-learning series.

A second possibility might be in a renewed effort for critical mass to establish an effective form of Cornish-language pre-school education as a first stage, no matter how small and limited this might be initially. If it were well done, it would comprise a basis upon which school-level Cornish-medium education could be developed. Successful models for this can be found in Wales, Scotland and Northern Ireland. In the last case, parents came together in West Belfast, established their own community, and founded and ran their own school in the teeth of active opposition from the then regime. The story is well documented by Gabrielle Maguire.[15] The Isle of Man presents a similar language-situation to Cornwall's—and both Manx-medium pre-school and school-level education have recently been successfully established.

Gabrielle Maguire's account is a challenge to other language communities in revival. Attempts had been made in the Republic of Ireland to establish urban neo-Gaeltacht communities but the efforts had not succeeded. In the North, however, Gabrielle Maguire's group of young couples and parents created an Irish-speaking area with its own school, and from that beginning other community initiatives grew: a cultural centre, a secondary school, shops using Irish on façades and at the till, and a daily Irish-language newspaper. In Scotland, we are asking ourselves could something similar be done in urban Gaeldom? Could such a thing be done in the Isle of Man—or in Cornwall?

One way in which the language could effectively enter the social environment would be through cultural tourism. Its benefits would be shared with the home population. 'Tokenistic' Cornish is to be seen sporadically in all sorts of places. Were this to be systematized into an itinerary of Cornish language heritage, featuring all situations of significance to the language historically and contemporarily, it would enlighten both the visitor and the resident. Promotional literature, itineraries and guides, interpretation and information on site, 'blue plaques' and so on would greatly increase the visibility of the language and its place in the social environment. Forth an Yeth—the Cornish Language Trail—might be just the sort of initiative to get funding from the Language Heritage Fund.

There has been a great deal of 'new thinking' for Cornish at the recent turn of the century. Initiatives such as Keskerdh Kernow (Cornwall Marches On!), millennium events, the petition for a Cornish Assembly (Senedh Kernow), EU Objective 1 status, and the Eden Project have all bred a spirit of turning a new page. The South Crofty closure in 1999 was the end of a traditional industry, and the foot and mouth crisis in the countryside in 2001 was a threat to another, and to the more recent Cornish staple of tourism. These crises remind us that Cornwall is at the bottom of the UK league table for all economic indicators. Cornwall can demand special treatment.

In the preface to his *Handbook*, Jenner asked, 'Why should Cornishmen learn Cornish?'[16] His answer was that although 'there was no money in it, it serves no practical purpose, and the literature is scanty . . . the answer is simple: because they are Cornishmen'. Jenner went on to note that the Cornwall of his day, despite 'the few survivals of Duchy jurisdictions', was 'legally and practically a county of England . . . as if it were no better than a mere Essex or Herts'. Conventional wisdom has changed since his day, and now the Cornish might assert the right to their own Assembly, over and above the assertions of English counties such as Kent, simply because the elements of a distinctive local culture and identity can be demonstrated. The possession of a language is key to the status as one of the United Kingdom's distinctive and continuing nations. There is no doubt about it, there is now practical value to the Cornish language—and there is money in it. There are new agendas abroad in Cornwall today, and the role of the language and its enhancement in everyday life, in the Cornish economy, and in its politics deserves to be on those agendas. New ideas are called for on how this language can now not only walk (in Nance's phrase)—but live.

At the core of Jenner's ideas on reasons for learning Cornish was the kernel of identity, 'the outward and audible sign of his separate nationality'. He saw this as 'sentimental, and not in the least practical'. In revising his ideas to be inclusive by modern standards, we would also see real social and economic benefits in language revival. The County Council's Framework Policy for Cornish has been adopted by all Cornwall's district councils. This provides a groundwork for greater recognition: Cornish is at least officially recognized by all Cornish local authorities. Its place totally within the European Charter at both Part II and Part III levels, should be the next stage. Status can be important in strengthening the place of language within the social environment. Without it, attempts to advance the presence of the language in commercial life, public services, civic life and local civil society can always be countered with the objection that Cornish is not an 'official language'.

The struggle to reverse the process of language-shift for Cornish is important not only within Cornwall but internationally. Recent studies of world languages[17] have drawn to popular attention the precarious state of many of the 6,000 or so remaining spoken languages of the world. Every fortnight or so the last speaker of one of them dies and takes with him or her the history, traditions and cultural memory embedded in the language. Those working with endangered languages may well see this as the utter end for the languages in question. However, there may be real prospects of revival in some cases at least. Today great efforts are being made for Manx and for Cornish, whose last native speakers left behind spoken and written records from which the language can be learned.

We live in a globalizing, Anglicizing world in which the prospects for the littlest languages are not accorded much by way of prospects. Today even the smaller nation-state languages in Europe, such as Danish and Dutch, regard themselves as under threat. The French have always seen theirs as threatened— so now do the Germans. These peoples are not prepared to see their languages in contact with English go the way of earlier contacts: Irish, Welsh, Gaelic, Manx and Cornish. They will all certainly develop increasing demand for English—but this will not mean that their own must be sacrificed.

In the nineteenth century there was no place for non-English languages in the education systems of the United Kingdom. The other languages were seen as impediments to effective English acquisition. Bilingualism was not seen as a 'natural' state—and ordinary people were not thought to be fully capable of using two languages effectively. The average mind did not have sufficient space for two. Such notions still underlie much popular and press thinking about language in the modern world. In actual fact we are not proceeding into an altogether Anglicized world so much as into a bilingual one. Humanity sees the

need for at least two languages: one as a means of wider communication, and one as the medium of identity, expression and shared
fellow-feeling. In this process the monoglot-English societies may end
up without a language of their own in Gabrielle Maguire's sense. But
Cornwall can be different. Without Cornish, Cornwall might be seen, in
Jenner's sense, as part of just another typical English-speaking society.
But with a language of its own which truly lives within its social and
cultural life, Cornwall can be an effective example to the world of how
to take everything that the knowledge and use of English can impart
while retaining and developing everything that a language of its own
can do as well.

NOTES AND REFERENCES

1. Government Office of the South-West website at: www.gosw.gov.uk/gosw.
2. Ken George, 'How Many People Spoke Cornish Traditionally?' *Cornish Studies* 14, 1986, pp. 67–70.
3. Cowethas an Yeth Kernewek, *Kernewek Hedhyu: 1984 Report on the State of the Language*, Truro, 1984, p. 10.
4. Jane Ninnis, 'State of the Language Statistics' unpublished paper, 1999.
5. Simon James, *The Atlantic Celts: Ancient People or Modern Invention?*, London, 1999, pp. 44–50.
6. D.R. Williams, *Prying into Every Hole and Corner: Edward Lhuyd in Cornwall in 1700*, Truro, 1993.
7. At Boscastle, Saturday evening 4 November 2000, 7–9 p.m.
8. Edward Lhuyd, *Archaelogica Britannica*, London, 1707, republished Shannon, 1971.
9. Henry Jenner, *A Handbook of the Cornish Language*, London, 1904, republished New York, 1982.
10. Charles Thomas, 'An Dasserghyans Kernewek', *Old Cornwall* 6.5, Autumn 1963, pp. 196–205.
11. Personal communication from Wella Brown to Tony Steele, Government Office of the South-West, dated 24 October 2000.
12. *Western Morning News*, 22 July 2002.
13. Edmund Hambly, 1933, quoted in Garry Tregidga, 'The Politics of the Celto-Cornish Revival 1886–1939', in Philip Payton (ed.), *Cornish Studies: Five*, Exeter, 1997, pp. 125–50.
14. Philip Gawn, *Survey of Manx Speakers and Learners: Preliminary Findings*, Douglas, 1999.
15. Gabrielle Maguire, *Our Own Language: An Irish Initiative*, Clevedon, 1990.
16. Jenner, 1904, p. xi; see also Philip Payton, *A Vision of Cornwall*, Fowey, 2002, esp. chapter 6.
17. For example, see David Crystal, *Language Death*, Cambridge, 2000.

FATEL ERA NY A KEEL?
REVIVED CORNISH:
TAKING STOCK

Neil Kennedy

INTRODUCTION

Many people know just two overstated facts about Cornish, neither of them as straightforwardly true as they seem. Firstly, they know that the language died out. It is a 'dead language'. Secondly, they know that it's 'like Welsh'. The more informed may also know that it has been 'revived' and if they have taken a closer interest they know that there are several forms of revived Cornish. This splitting of the language into competing forms and factions has become during the last decade or so (the period under review in this volume) the overriding obsession of both revivalists and academic commentators, diverting attention from more pressing issues.

Cornish is now imagined in such diverse, seemingly irreconcilable ways that we have several, markedly different standards,[1] each based on a particular historical period and characterized by its own distinct orthography and recommended pronunciation. There are even important differences in grammar and vocabulary, making conversation between users of different versions problematic. Although the difficulties are not insurmountable, this is something of an absurdity for a language with few speakers and the situation has arguably hindered its promotion and teaching, giving ammunition to detractors and reducing economies of scale for publications. Competing organizations champion the various forms and seek to intervene in debates or regulate the language used at a grass-roots level. These debates are often acrimonious, preventing cooperation or the sharing of research.

Now, almost twenty years after the onset of this fragmentation, would seem to be an ideal time for Cornish speakers to take stock and reflect broadly upon their achievements and failures, as well as the challenges and needs of the revival. As a teacher of Cornish, my primary concern is for its present and future. How can we, as speakers, teachers and writers, move forward from a position of disunity and foster a sense of common purpose and shared strategies for teaching and promotion? Is it possible or even desirable to try to achieve, let alone impose, a single standard or should we seek a relativist acceptance of internal pluralism? What should the relationship be between historical Cornish and the revived language?

Here, I am attempting to reflect on the contemporary needs of the revival as a whole rather than getting bogged down in factional interests or the historical focus of most Celticists. My concern is that a small set of preoccupations and distractions is diverting the energies of revivalists from the task of constructing a social context for Cornish. Just what is the state of Revived Cornish (or Neo-Cornish as some prefer[2]) and what needs to be done in order for it to thrive?

THE STATE OF CORNISH

If Cornish has indeed been revived, what is the extent of that revival? In 1978 Myrna Combellack offered a review, reporting that there were thirteen 'official' evening classes and concluding that: 'with more than two hundred students enrolled at evening-classes each year, and with three regular magazines devoted entirely to Cornish . . . the cords which anchor us to our heritage never again shall be pulled apart'.[3] There have since been at least two notable progress reports from revivalists, each offering an upbeat assessment.[4] In their positive and optimistic portrayals, the impression is given that the future of Cornish is assured and that its resurgence continues apace. Nevertheless, it is hard to get beyond the subjectivity and 'spin' of the authors and gain a clear view. The wish to present Cornish as viable and vigorous has led revivalists to exaggerate their success whilst factional divisions have tempted them to belittle the achievements of competing forms.

More particularly, it is hard to gauge the concrete progress made since 1978 by comparing the figures quoted,[5] not simply because many of the figures are unreliable, but because the context and character of learning has changed, making statistical comparisons over time problematic. For example, the number of people sitting examinations of the Cornish Language Board or becoming 'language bards' of the Gorsedd no longer provides an accurate picture of recruitment or the extent of learning. Teachers point out that a smaller proportion of learners now sit examinations, interpreting this as evidence of wider socio-economic participation and greater emphasis on speaking and social use. My own observations lead me to agree. Learners from low-paid and manual jobs now form the majority in many classes, suggesting that Cornish has started to escape from the confines of romantic Celtic revivalism and become identified with popular Cornishness. Statistical analysis of the composition of classes is difficult because of the small numbers involved and a lack of recording. Nevertheless, as an example, a quick count of forty recent learners at Truro College reveals eleven who work in shops or service industries and twelve who work in manual or semi-skilled jobs. Only five work in typical middle-class professions. We are forced to interpret and supplement limited statistics with qualitative and impressionistic approaches. This trend was, nevertheless, obvious during the 1980s and 1990s, when Cornwall continued to experience the decline of traditional industries coupled with political marginalization, demographic change and perceived cultural loss. The language acquired a symbolic currency, not just as a marker of identity but also as a practice of dissent, appearing on anti-poll-tax posters as well as rugby ephemera.[6] This may have been an important turning point in the revival, altering its character and public perception but it has yet to manifest itself in terms of large numbers of fluent speakers.

When asked how many people speak Cornish, revivalists normally admit that they do not know. Perhaps they do not want to know, the absence of statistics serving as a convenient smoke screen for disappointing progress and allowing the luxury of wishful thinking; yet the alternative is that the numbers involved are now large enough for them to be genuinely unaware of who speaks Cornish or how well they do so. Certainly, we have emerged from the period when all speakers knew each other into one in which it is possible for them to be unaware of others living nearby, and this phenomenon is not entirely the result of fragmentation. We can, at least, be sure that the position has improved since 1981 when it was considered that there were around forty fluent speakers.[7]

Perhaps the real picture is lost somewhere between the triumphant claims of some enthusiasts and the dismissal of their opponents. Professor Ken MacKinnon (2000) has investigated the extent of Cornish learning and usage on behalf of the Government Office for the South-West, producing a well-researched report entitled *An Independent Academic Study on Cornish* (meant to inform government policy), a summary of which is presented in this volume.[8] This provides, for the first time, an external assessment of the situation that is probably more reliable than would be the census question that revivalists have demanded. According to MacKinnon, there are now '36 formal classes in Cornish at adult education level . . . and it is estimated that over 350 people attend'.[9] He identified other informal classes and self-help groups, concluding that the total number of learners was approximately 450. In other words, if the figures are correct, the number of adult learners may have almost doubled since Combellack's assessment in 1978. If the number of active learners has remained at a level between 200 and 350 in the intervening years then we might reasonably expect the number of speakers now to be in the thousands. From this point of view, MacKinnon's estimate of about 300 'effective speakers' seems disappointing, particularly if we accept Ken George's proposition that about 4,000 people would be necessary to maintain a sustainable community of speakers.[10] Some enthusiasts claim that Cornish is spoken with reasonable fluency by about 500 people, whilst a further thousand or so have either limited conversational competence or are actively engaged in learning, but even this hardly amounts to an unqualified success after a century of revivalist activity. I consider these figures to be generous and based on an undemanding definition of fluency, but the UK Committee of the European Bureau of Lesser Used Languages' website goes further, estimating that 840 people are 'fluent' and 2,900 'conversational'.[11] It is certainly the case that far more than 1,000 people have attempted to learn Cornish in the last twenty years, perhaps as many as 2,000, and it might well be the case that almost 1,000 of them are able to exchange politenesses and talk about simple everyday things, but few could be considered 'effective speakers' and from a revivalist perspective that is the objective. MacKinnon's sober estimate would seem to be fairly reliable, although we might put the number of 'semi-speakers' at about 500 in addition to the 450 active learners identified. Ultimately, though, my figures are as impressionistic as those of other revivalists.

Cornish learning defies statistical analysis. There are too many unknowns. But it is easy to see that few of those who enrol on beginners' courses become fluent. Wastage has been a strong feature, particularly in the intermediate stages, so urgent efforts have to be made to retain learners and encourage others to return.[12] Not all of this can be left to common-sense understandings of why they drop out and some attention needs to be given to research to identify reasons for giving up and the needs of learners outside the classroom. Although we might rejoice at the numbers enrolling for classes, many of us are sobered by the slowing down shown by most students once they pass the early stages. The progress of beginners is often rapid until the burden of new vocabulary and grammatical structure becomes too great for them to retain without frequent use. They reach a low-level plateau, going no further. This represents the amount of language that they can acquire aurally in a weekly class without intensive home study or the opportunities normally provided by a speech community and media. Many are not equipped to go further, in personal skills, learning resources or support outside the classroom.

Producing a large body of semi-speakers, i.e. people with limited conversational ability, may have benefits for the purposes of language revival. These people help to make the language viable in the community, so much so that I can now buy petrol in Truro and make purchases at several shops in Cornish. The people serving me might well get stuck if the conversation is extended beyond this simple exchange or comments about the weather, but they enable others to use the language and increase awareness. They also create a body of sentiment and support in favour of Cornish. For example, parents and teachers with only basic Cornish have been instrumental in introducing it to schools. Some have become school governors and councillors, helping to promote Cornish from new positions of influence. Nevertheless, this phenomenon of numerous, intermediate speakers, unable to proceed further, is the major failing of the revival.

Collectively, Cornish enthusiasts (or *Kernewegoryon/Kernowegorian*) form a sub-cultural 'scene' that differs from traditional speech communities. They speak Cornish as a deliberately learnt, second language, using it on a part-time basis, in some domains but not others. Transmission normally takes place in the adult education class rather than the home or primary school. Even those who succeed in speaking Cornish at home must use English outside. Using Cornish is, therefore, always a self-conscious, political act approaching performance. Gerald Priestland has described the revival as 'rather like putting a corpse on a heart-lung machine and claiming it is alive'.[13] Analogies between languages and organisms may be inappropriate but the tone of Priestland's comment provides a counterbalance to enthusiasts who talk as though their imaginary Cornish-speaking community has already come into being, claiming that new vocabulary is 'naturally generated'[14] amongst Cornish speakers, just as in English. Imagination merges with self-delusion and reality is confused with fantasy. Ken George, whilst asserting that Cornish is 'unquestionably a living language', has pointed out that 'revivalists must not get so carried away that they forget that Cornish is not in all respects like other tongues . . . Cornish is unlikely to be subject to the same socio-linguistic "laws" as those which govern major languages.'[15]

He argues that 'when speakers say that a certain feature . . . has now become part of Revived Cornish owing to popular usage, we should be suspicious. This argument is less valid for Cornish than for a major language like English or French.' It is hard to disagree. George's identification of the peculiar socio-linguistic position of Cornish is something that researchers need to investigate if the revival is to succeed. Cornish is currently taught as though a ready-made context exists for its use.

This is not to underestimate the extent to which Cornish is used socially. For several hundred people it is a part of everyday life, used in frequent face-to-face and telephone conversation with friends. For a solid core of advanced speakers it is no longer confined to organized events (such as the frequent 'yeth an weryns' or 'coozys' held in pubs) but has become normalized as the language of regular social activity. For a small number, perhaps as many as one hundred, it is one of the languages spoken at home. For the wider network of learners it is a language that is used often in brief social exchanges and arranged settings. Learners form friendships, meeting informally regardless of any intention to speak Cornish, and this may form a future social context for the revival.

In so far as Cornish speakers constitute a community, they do not inhabit a linguistically defined geographical space. This means that special efforts need to be made to create occasions for social use. In the absence of a normal speech community, teachers must act as social secretaries, organizing events outside the classroom and encouraging learners to form networks. Despite a substantial number of learners, the lack of opportunities for daily use is a major problem. Communication is more likely to take place via email and telephone than chance conversation in the street and it may well be that a virtual space is being created in which it is possible to imagine a Cornish-speaking future. Learners are starting to participate in email networks and visit the numerous Cornish sites that are being created. These include the site *Nowodhow Kernow*[16] that presents regularly updated Cornish and international news in Common Cornish (Kernewek Kemmyn). In recent years, revivalists have focused on the intermediate technology of well-printed books, seeing this as an advance from the 'rusty staples' syndrome that characterized publishing in the 1970s and 1980s when most teachers produced learning materials without access to word-processors or funds. Cornish speakers have campaigned, with very limited success, for brief radio and television broadcasts that do little to address the needs of learners.[17] Perhaps more energy should be targeted specifically at accessing the potential of new technologies to develop interactive teaching resources, multi-user domains and web-cast radio and television. These technologies have the added advantages of making Cornish available to a wider diaspora and combating images of Cornish as ancient, antiquated and deceased.

As well as the core of people who seriously attempt to learn, there is a host who pay lip-service to it and perhaps dabble in it. These have been neatly satirized by Pol Hodge in a poem about local councillors:

> Ty a lever dha 'Gorthugher da,'
> Kewsel yn Sowsnek rag hanter our,
> Ow korfenna gans dha 'Nos da'
> Hag ow kasa an yeth kernewek
> Dhe verwel yn diwleuv a'th konsel . . .

(You say your 'Gorthugher da', talk in English for half an hour, finishing with your 'Nos da', leaving/hating Cornish to die in the hands of your council . . .)[18]

Some, however, help to raise the profile and cultural capital of Cornish through artistic activities but are not themselves part of an emergent Cornish-speaking community. For example, Cornish films (including the recent *Hwerow Hweg*[19]) now appear every year. Unfortunately, most are short, 'arty' productions that involve non-Cornish-speaking actors learning their lines parrot-fashion.[20] Few of them benefit learners of Cornish and although they raise awareness, most do little to present it as a spoken language. Instead the language is served up for its novelty value to predominantly middle-class, quasi-bohemian audiences and the artificiality of the performance underlines the perception of Cornish as dead. Cornish-speakers themselves have been slow to take ownership of production and produce useful resources. There have been short broadcasts on television but these too are aimed predominately at non-Cornish-speaking audiences and often associate Cornish with unhelpful visual imagery drawn from stereotyped representations of the Celts and tourism.[21] Nevertheless, it would be wrong to belittle these achievements or fail to recognize that they represent a wider change in attitude. Amongst them are gems that provide visible manifestations of Cornish and act as effective commercials.

The tendency is for promoters of Cornish to hold up these symbolic usages as evidence for the advance of the revival and in one sense they are right to do so, but the inclusion of Cornish elements in the artistic activities of non-Cornish-speakers, primarily for the sub-titled consumption of English-speaking audiences, is not a reliable indicator of progress in the development of a Cornish-speaking community. For that reason I would like to avoid cataloguing the considerable artistic achievements of recent years and focus instead on the characteristics of Cornish learning. Rather than asserting the achievements of revivalists, I should like to pause and consider the needs of learners, asking why so many people begin to learn Cornish but fail to become fluent, regular speakers.

IMAGES OF CORNISH

The way in which Cornish is presented is closely related to the way in which it is imagined by its speakers and perceived by others. Until recently, Cornish has been almost entirely represented in terms of cultural practices and visual imagery from the Celtic Revival. Learners have had to embrace not only a new language, but also a set of sub-cultural activities and invented traditions that they do not necessarily encounter in their daily lives. Whilst this appeals to many, especially those on the indeterminate margins of popular Cornish identity, it also deters others. Language events present constructions of Cornishness that bear little relation to the cultural experiences of most Cornish people. One learner from a strongly Cornish background described her experience of attending a weekend event as 'culture-shock'. One challenge is to repackage the language in diverse ways that appeal to a broader range of cultural tastes, severing any automatic connections with revivalist Cornish folk music, for example, not by abandoning it but by providing choices. Some dusty corners of the scene are still characterized by a form of essentialism that is almost despotic in its insistence on one version of Cornishness.

This is something that can be helped by the publication of critical research. The process is already being helped by recent deconstructions of the Celtic Revival from within Cornwall.[22] These are enabling speakers to renegotiate the relationship between Cornish and the established visual practices of the Celtic Revival, rejecting images that they find unappealing whilst retaining others. At the same time, considerable progress has been made in incorporating cultural forms that associate Cornish with the lived experience of people today and add cultural capital. Whilst rooted in Celtic Revivalism, the recent invention of the *Noze Looan* ('happy night') combines elements of traditional music and singing in Cornish with an eclectic cocktail of jazz, funk, reggae etc. On promotional material, Celtic knot-work and uncial lettering is rejected in favour of styles imported from contemporary youth sub-cultures and surfing, one of the few activities that provides a source of local pride for the young. This, in theory, creates a cool space in which to speak Cornish. In literature, some are making a special effort to escape from the introspective and romantic narratives of the revival or stagnant nostalgia for a bygone Cornwall.[23] Some recent work addresses non-Cornish subject matter and everyday themes. In designing teaching materials, too, there has been some movement away from stereotypical and picturesque images.

Wind-turbines replace ruined engine houses and street scenes take the place of bardic circles.

Despite these positive trends, more thought has to be given to countering naturalized images of the language as variously bardic and ritualistic (confined to the Gorsedd), ancient and dead (for historians), eccentric and comic (for anoraks), dry and academic (confined to colleges).[24]

INSTITUTIONS

The tendency in assessments of the revival has been to focus on institutional aspects and cultural activities. Thus Combellack in 1978 emphasized the development of the Cornish Language Board, its examinations and publications. Judged from this viewpoint the revival has made great advances. Publications in and about Cornish amount to a small industry and the Board has grown in status, forming links with other institutions and achieving recognition for its examination scheme from Cornwall County Council. The revival has spawned numerous organizations and several councils have endorsed statements that support the language in principle. Cornwall County Council has, for three years, allocated a small budget for Cornish (£5,000 p.a.), the first regular funding that it has received. These institutional developments help to produce a climate in which people are encouraged to learn but are not themselves a measure of the extent to which the language is spoken. Instead, they are part of an infrastructure that may or may not be required for its advance. Campaigners have often become bogged-down in institutional considerations, concerning themselves with such issues as UK government recognition under the European Charter for Regional or Minority Languages. Such matters are important, opening the way to public funding and support, but they do not provide an automatic means to language learning. Indeed, the time invested in pursuing institutional issues may distract the small number of teachers and promoters from developing social spaces for Cornish and alternative opportunities for learning. This may serve as displacement activity that allows revivalists to apportion blame to others, constructing themselves as victims rather than taking responsibility and assuming agency. Whilst it is fair to say that central and local governments have been unresponsive and uninterested, revivalists have also failed to organize and grasp opportunities.

THE ACADEMIC GAZE

Revivalist preoccupations with historical study and 'the Holy Grail of authenticity' (as Bernard Deacon has dubbed it)[25] are fuelled by their difficult relationship with Celticists. Revived Cornish has been subject to the public comment of academics and amateur critics, forcing revivalists to participate in debates. The recent intensification of a critical academic gaze has coincided with grass-roots disquiet about the foundations of Robert Morton Nance's Unified Cornish (UC), the standard used by almost everyone until the mid-1980s. As Dr Ken George put it: 'now the whole basis . . . of revived Cornish is being called into question by Cornish speakers from within the language movement'.[26]

This has resulted in the fragmentation referred to above. Despite the damaging aspects of this division it is important to recognize some associated benefits. As a result we have more knowledge about historical Cornish and a climate in which more importance is given to such issues as pronunciation. The development of better learning resources and the expansion of classes is, in no small part, the result of competition between groups. However, the continuing obsession with division works against research in other areas. Revivalists have abused and misrepresented research to claim greater legitimacy for their preferred varieties in terms of 'authenticity', by which they normally mean closeness to historical Cornish. This is, in part, related to the relationship between revivalists and academics.

Some linguists are against the very idea of revival and have been quick to attack the project. Others are not against the principle but have criticized its basis. The prominent revivalist Ken George is also an academic whose second doctoral thesis examined the phonology of historical Cornish.[27] He considers that the problem of academic criticism is related to poor communication: 'Lack of communication between the two groups continues to cause problems'.[28] George has encouraged Cornish-speakers to engage in presentable research and engage academics productively. The first part of this process, i.e. the improved focus of revivalists, has been very productive, although the contribution of academics has remained minimal in terms of new understanding and knowledge. With notable exceptions, the academics who have contributed usefully are themselves Cornish revivalists. The academic gaze has generally been detached, casual and restricted to comment. It is enough to regurgitate common-sense views of Cornish as an extinct species of degenerate Welsh. Cornish has been a soft touch, allowing academics a parasitic relationship rather than a symbiotic one. This has a bearing on the way in which established discourses have been perpetuated and reshaped. Academics who are unable to speak or read Cornish have, like the antiquaries[29] that preceded them, owned knowledge about it and determined the veracity of discourse.

Such complaints date back to the early twentieth century when

Celticists opposed Cornwall's membership of the Celtic Congress and ignored the work of R.M. Nance. In his private letters, the revivalist A.S.D. Smith criticized the unwillingness of Welsh Celticists, such as Professor Ifor Williams, to engage with enthusiasts in Cornwall and learn from them:

> Trueth yu na vynnons-y keslafurya genen-ny: dhedha-y kepar ha dhyn-ny yma an coll. Mordon a wor moy. a Gernow ha Kernewek ages dyscajoryon Kembry oll warbarth; nyns yns mes fleghes orto-ef. Bytegens nefra ny weler hanow Mordon y'n scryvennow yn kever Kernewek a omdhysqueth trawythyow y'n Bulletin. [It's sad that they don't want to co-operate with us: it's their loss as well as ours. Mordon knows more of Cornwall and Cornish than all the Welsh academics together; they are but children compared with him. Nevertheless, one never sees Mordon's name in papers about Cornish that appear occasionally in the Bulletin.][30]

Smith was particularly scathing about the attitudes of Henri Lewis, author of *Llawlyfr Cernyweg Canol* (1946), a Welsh grammar of Middle Cornish:

> Nefra ny ve H. Lewis yn Kernow, ha nefra ny wruk scryfa Kernewek y honen, na'y gewsel. Yndella ef yu kepar ha'n dhyscajorian erel yn Kembry: examnya Kernewek y a wra kepar ha pan ve corf marow, ha namoy. [H. Lewis has never been in Cornwall and has never written or spoken Cornish himself. So he is like the other academics in Wales: they examine Cornish as though it were a dead body and nothing more.][31]

Charles Thomas picked up this theme in his address to the Celtic Congress in 1963, explaining that 'modern Celticists . . . unite in ignoring any of Nance's or Smith's work, and almost all of Jenner's'.[32] By contrast, the problem during the 1980s was that, in turning their attention to the revived language, academics focused on the work of Nance and his contemporaries, disregarding contemporary developments.[33] Some revivalists consequently developed an isolationist mentality, ridiculing academics as incompetent. In recent years, however, there have been positive developments. The new rigour within the 'Cornish scene' has led to a degree of respect and worthwhile input from academics. The opening of a productive dialogue has started to yield results. The practical engagement of individuals like Dr Nicholas Williams is testament to this change.[34]

WIDENING RESEARCH

Whilst we may be content that historical studies have expanded to inform the revival, other areas have received little attention. Research has, hitherto, been diachronic in focus, concerned, for example, with changes to pronunciation and grammar over time within the framework of comparative Celtic Studies. Current approaches are, furthermore, largely confined to the quantitative analysis of texts and the assumptions of technical/scientific rationality. Recent work has been based on the testing of hypotheses by means of corpus analysis, the assumption being that this methodology is objective and will lead to a correct interpretation of phonology, grammar and usage. Believers in the validity and infallibility of this approach seem to assume that errors will be revealed and eliminated by dispassionately testing theories against textual evidence. It needs to be recognized, however, that subjectivity is always present.[35]

Some still hide behind the myth of scientific objectivity and imagine that their selections are neutral and logically deduced, yet issues of aesthetic taste and powerful, subjective discourses about language and identity are at work.[36] When deconstructing 'scientific' analyses of Cornish, it is easy to discover inconsistencies and the partial use of evidence to support the ideological standpoint of individuals. In Foucauldian terms, the discursive practices of researchers create, rather than discover, the truth about Cornish, and their 'silences and the partial use of evidence' (as Deacon put it)[37] are as important as what they say. They have expressed themselves using a language of scientific certainty and truth that thinly disguises all manner of subjective and 'non-scientific' practices whilst convincing rank-and-file learners with its confidence. An intense, at times vitriolic debate has been conducted within the limits of scientific linguistics and Modernist assumptions. Nevertheless, corpus analysis and related textual research have advanced our understanding enormously and need to continue and expand, particularly after the recent discovery of a major historical text.[38] To benefit fully we simply need to engender a spirit of co-operation and reflection that recognizes subjectivity.

I am concerned personally with broadening the ways in which we consider the shape of Revived Cornish to include consideration of such previously excluded issues as taste and tacit or intuitive knowledge about language. These include such indeterminate issues as empathy with language and a 'feel' for what is right, based on experience. As Bernard Deacon put it: 'the language debate must move beyond the

scientific discourse and open up the debate to such things as specula-
tion, reflection, intuition and feelings. Such knowledge should be
admitted as equal and no longer, as assumed by modernism, inferior to
the knowledge produced by scientific method.'[39]

Hitherto, the strength of scientific discourse within language
circles, however loosely it might be applied, has rendered these alternative or supplementary approaches unreasonable, illogical, irrational,
unscientific and wrong. This is often apparent in criticisms of Richard
Gendall's work on Late Cornish,[40] yet to understand the fragmentation
of Cornish we need to appreciate that discursive issues are involved in
both research and the exercise of verbal hygiene. Far from being
culturally neutral, practices of 'language planning' involve questions of
taste and are themselves part of wider discourses surrounding Cornish
and notions of identity. It is, after all, discursive and ideological
issues that underpin the fragmentation of Neo-Cornish. As Payton has
argued, we can only begin to make sense of the selections involved by
considering a range of competing ideologies and discourses that have
an impact on the assumed, objective detachment of researchers.[41]
In particular, we might interrogate the various Cornish nationalisms,
pan-Celticisms and practices of differentiation from Englishness that
underpin linguistic purism and the desire for an unambiguously distinct
orthography.

Ken George partially acknowledged this in his discussion of
tensions between revivalists and academics: 'In principle, grammars
of the traditional language are descriptive and those of the revived
language are prescriptive'.[42] In other words, revivalists select from the
evidence in order to present the forms that they prefer and their
choices are not neutral. Accordingly: 'There is even an advantage in
the need to create new words in Cornish; they can be formed from
Celtic roots and thereby "purify" the language'. George's pleasure at
the prospect of 'purifying' Cornish is rooted in discourses that view
language as ideally pure. In other words, his is just one of a range of
possibilities for imagining and prescribing Cornish, rather than an
unassailably correct, scientific position. It presupposes the desirability
and possibility of purity and assumes the category of 'Celtic'. Richard
Gendall's practice has a similarly discursive element that assumes the
objective of descriptivism.

LEARNING

If historical research and factional politics have disproportionately
concerned revivalists, educational and social issues have been
neglected. There has been no corresponding research culture to
investigate strategies of learning and teaching and teachers have failed

to develop a coordinated, cooperative approach, even if some have developed their individual practices. The Cornish Language Board has given attention to issues of assessment and some teachers work together to improve their delivery, but there is no visible framework within which specifically Cornish educational research takes place. Our circumstances are unique but we seem content to pick-and-mix strategies from other language learning contexts without investigating their effectiveness. We need opportunities to review methods and resources by using them in practice, testing what does and does not work and exchanging experiences. Because the failure of most beginners to progress to fluency has not been addressed, I would like to outline some issues from personal experience that might require attention.

Firstly, who succeeds and do they share any characteristics? I have been recording observations of my students for seven years. A few have reached an impressive level of fluency. Two have become teachers and one is raising his children bilingually. Others have reached a level that falls short of full fluency but still enables them to engage in fluid conversation on everyday topics. These groups represent the more successful minority, so comparing them with less successful learners might suggest some ways forward for the majority. Successful learners mainly share these characteristics:

- They have commitment and motivation to their learning and the idea of reviving Cornish.
- They are independent, engaging in home study, often of a self-directed nature.
- They show empathy for the language, its idiomatic expression, rhythms, textures and sounds. One learner expressed this by saying 'It's like trying to remember something you've forgotten. It isn't like learning a new language.'

They are able to move their Cornish up to a level that cannot normally be achieved by attending classes and occasional social events. They get to grips with its workings, rationalizing information, recognizing patterns and links. This opens up the possibility of productive use, as they feel able to combine vocabulary in new situations and take risks, rather than being confined to formulaic structures and familiar phrases. They will often have been exposed to presentations of grammar at school, though few have succeeded in learning another language. Some acquire the ability to understand grammar descriptions whilst learning Cornish. They find it easier to use dictionaries and grammars, rapidly learning the conventions of presentation. It is apparent that most are unable to follow this route. They cannot distinguish between nouns, adjectives and verbs when using dictionaries and cannot cope with the supplementary notes and appendices. Most are intimidated and undermined by the technical presentation of information and have no grasp of the terms used in almost all course books. At the same time, there is no simple correlation between levels of previous education and the ability to deal with grammar. Anyone who can read a cake recipe or assembly manual can follow grammatical explanations once introduced to the terms and concepts.

Grammar is an area that I am rethinking in the light of experience, asking whether I have neglected its explicit teaching to the detriment of learning. Formerly, I avoided grammatical terminology, seeking to teach grammar without naming it. I took the view that people could learn a language without systematic overviews, internalizing the rules through use. I even went as far as regarding this route as 'natural' and inherently better. Like others I was drawn towards the naturalistic emphasis on learning by speaking, so much so that I tried to teach without written work. Now, in considering the slowing-down shown by intermediate students, I see significant shortcomings in this approach. Like Rod Lyon[43] I have produced 'plain language' grammar notes. Cornish teachers seem to divide into two camps, those who follow a grammatical progression and those who reject this in favour of current communicative approaches.[44] In effect, there has been a 'common-sense' reaction against the graded grammatical methods of older materials. The temptation is to equate these with an opposition between a dead language for study and one that may be spoken. In practice, both approaches have had limited success and the opposition is imagined. Part of the problem may lie in the previous schooling of teachers. Most endured foreign language learning during the 1960s and 1970s when behaviourist and audio-visual methods were combined with traditional presentations of grammar. Teachers continue to draw upon these experiences despite their poor success. In addition, they import methods from contemporary modern language teaching without considering their suitability to our circumstances. The lack of opportunities for immersion and the shortage of interactive materials makes learning Cornish different. Communicative approaches need to be adjusted or supplemented to compensate, whilst grammatical approaches alone do little to turn students into speakers.

I was interested to read Margaret Wells's account of teaching GCSE French grammar. She compares its implicit teaching through use and experience with its explicit teaching. In designing her research project she recognized that the 'implicit' teaching of grammar has limitations: 'Quite simply, we find that we are unable to teach implicitly all the time to our own and our pupils' satisfaction. Some grammar items have defied our attempts to convey them through example and practice, by naturalistic methods.'[45] She cites examples of grammar that seem to defy 'naturalistic' methods. Her colleagues were forced to redefine the term 'implicit' to allow any teaching done entirely in French and admit any grammatical explanation conducted in French 'without the aid of technical jargon'. This suggests the impossibility, within the constraints of the particular school system, of teaching without direct reference to grammatical rules. That is the point: we know that people can acquire language by immersion but that does not mean weekly or even daily classes. The constraints of our situation force us to take other routes and this is brought into sharp focus by the sizeable group of intermediate learners who fail to make headway within the limits of current provision. Without a grammatical vocabulary and an understanding of conventions, they are unable to access information. One response might be to teach them how to use resources, providing study skills and a specialist language of the classroom. Perhaps, for example, we should not reject supplementing communicative approaches with grammar explanations simply because that does not fit in with idealized models of learning.

Merely attending weekly classes is not enough. Fluent speakers have normally gone through some kind of intense activity. To achieve fluency it seems that a period of intense study or immersion is necessary. *Kowethas an Yeth Kernewek* has extended its residential *Pennseythun* (weekend) to cover several days. This, and shorter events run by other groups, provides the best opportunity for immersion but is insufficient on its own and learners who live in Cornwall often attend for one day rather than benefiting fully. If Cornish is to succeed, urgent attention must be given to the creation of permanent spaces where it is spoken. Attempts have been made to develop fledgling language centres and specialist shops but these have only gone a small way to providing opportunities. Some speakers have expressed an interest in the idea of a conveniently situated social club or café that might serve as a visible drop-in centre, precisely the sort of initiative that might provide a bridge between the classroom and spontaneous use.

Learners need to experience the phenomenon described by Professor Elizabeth Barber as 'the Din Phenomenon' and explored further by Stephen Krashen as 'the Din in the Head'.[46] Barber describes going to Russia with only basic Russian at her disposal. She was plunged in at the deep end and forced to sink or swim regardless of grammatical accuracy or social niceties: 'Any self-respecting adjective in Russian gives you on the order of forty possible categories of forms to choose from, according to the case, number, gender, and animacy, not to mention long and short forms and declension clauses'.[47] In a conversational setting, she could not consciously select appropriate forms because of the pace of conversation, concentrating instead on making herself understood functionally rather than holding up the conversation. This is difficult to achieve when learners have the easy option of speaking English, but we need to engineer the situation for more than a few weekends each year.

Richard Gendall advises teachers to adopt a 'little and often' approach: 'Ideally, language teaching should be by frequent, fairly short lessons; it is very easy for the brain to grow tired, and become less efficient, so that concentrated daily lessons of not more than forty minutes, perhaps less, achieve more than long lessons of an hour or even two hours, given twice or three times a week'.[48] It is hard to disagree when considering formal teaching, particularly when learners attend weekly sessions punctuated by long breaks. Gendall considers that the 'old fashioned grammatical approach' and 'direct method' teaching are both unsuited to the Cornish situation and he opts instead for 'a sort of compromise' that acknowledges the current inability to provide adequate facilities for immersion. He seems to have summed up the situation neatly, though I believe that classes of any timing and duration can do no more than prepare people for the kind of necessary, intense immersion described by Barber. That is what we lack.

CONCLUSION

The study of Cornish texts has advanced beyond recognition in the last twenty years, largely as a result of Ken George's intervention and responses to it. Richard Gendall has closely examined Late Cornish, revealing it to be a viable alternative to the medieval focus of R.M. Nance, and more recently Nicholas Williams has offered his repositioning of Unified Cornish around the Tudor texts. This new research culture has informed revisions and new codifications of the revived language. Despite an emphasis on disagreement, the research of Gendall, George and Williams is remarkable for its degree of correspondence. When applied, it enables us to speak and write 'Neo-Cornish' with far greater confidence about its proximity to the historical language. For this benefit to be maximized, research must expand within a mature spirit of collaboration that rejects the adversarial style of recent exchanges. For this to be possible we may need to actively foster the notion of a plural Cornish, coming to terms with the fact that no one can impose a standard. The publisher and teacher Ray Chubb warns against the imposition of uniformity and asks 'A yllyn ny gul agan dewys agan honen?' (Can we make our own choice?).[49] His answer is 'Prag na?' (Why not?). He argues that a measure of personal freedom is preferable to compulsion: 'If we make the mistake of forcing people to standardise in this way or that, then we will most certainly fail . . . Standardisation based on historic spelling will no doubt come eventually, but as a result of consensus rather than authoritarianism.' Despite Chubb's deterministic belief in the eventual selection of historic spelling, it is refreshing to encounter this open defence of personal choice, in effect an acceptance that, for the moment, it is impossible and probably undesirable to insist upon one standard. This is not to say that the current level of division is not harmful; it is rather a way of coming to terms with internal differences and recognizing that there is some value in other approaches. From a practical angle, it allows revivalists to co-operate on research and development.

We urgently need to supplement historical research with similarly developed studies of learning and teaching. Above all, we need to create an atmosphere of reflective, practice-based research amongst teachers and encourage the ongoing, critical examination of resources and methods. This needs to recognize that many, if not most, of the answers lie outside the classroom and may be addressed by revivalists themselves.

NOTES AND REFERENCES

1. Unified Cornish (Kernewek Unyes) codified by R.M. Nance c1920–38, Common (formerly Phonemic) Cornish (Kernewek Kemmyn) codified by Dr K.J. George c.1984, Revived Late (or Modern) Cornish (Kernuack Dewethas) codified by R.R.M. Gendall c1990 and recently revised, Unified Cornish Revised (Kernewek Unyes Amendys) codified by Dr N.J.A. Williams c.1995.
2. N.J.A. Williams prefers the term Neo-Cornish, which he distinguishes from Traditional Cornish, i.e. the historical language, stating in *Cornish Today: An Examination of the Revived Language*, Sutton Coldfield, 1995, p. 8, that 'Cornish cannot be revived'. Neo-Cornish 'is different from the speech of the last native-speakers and indeed of any speakers of traditional Cornish of any period . . . [It] is not Cornish in the way that the language of Dolly Pentreath and William Bodinar was Cornish.'
3. M. Combellack, in *Cornish Studies* 6, Redruth, 1978, p. 49.
4. B. Webb (ed.), *Kernewek Hedhyu—Report on the State of the Language*, Truro, n.d.; W. Brown, D. Chubb, R. Chubb, N. Kennedy and J. Ninnis, *The Cornish Language*, Truro, 1991.
5. See, for examples, Webb (ed.), n.d., and P. Payton and B. Deacon, 'The Ideology of Language Revival', in P. Payton (ed.), *Cornwall Since the War*, Redruth, 1993, p. 277.
6. For a discussion of fusion of popular and revivalist cultural forms see B. Deacon, 'And Shall Trelawny Die? The Cornish Identity' in Payton (ed.), 1993, pp. 200–23.

7. W. Brown, 'Stuth an Yeth Kernewek yn Jeth Hedhyu', 1991, cited in Payton and Deacon, 1993, p. 278.
8. K. MacKinnon, *An Independent Academic Study on Cornish*, EKOS Ltd and SGRUD Research for the Government Office for the South-West, 2000.
9. MacKinnon, 2000, p. 45, 7.3.
10. Unpublished remarks.
11. http://www.eblul.org.uk/ukmin.htm, 21 May 2002.
12. For a discussion of this phenomenon in the 1980s see Payton and Deacon, 1993, p. 278.
13. G. and S. Priestland, *West of Hayle River*, London, 1980.
14. Such opinions are regularly expressed. The distinction between 'natural' and 'artificial' change underpins attitudes to neologisms and requires critical deconstruction.
15. K.J. George, *The Pronunciation and Spelling of Revived Cornish*, Torpoint, 1986, p. 39.
16. *Nowodhow Kernow*, http://www.geocities.com/cornishnews/.
17. Television broadcasts are limited to about thirty minutes a year. BBC Radio Cornwall has a ten-minute weekly news feature and Pirate FM had discontinued its short-lived news broadcasts.
18. *Yeth Dhroag*, unpublished readings, 2000.
19. *Hwerow Hweg*, Antal Kovacs (Director), Penzance, West Coast Productions, 2002. Billed as the first feature-length Cornish film.
20. For example, *Splatt Dhe Wertha*, Bill Scott (Director), Falmouth, Wild West Films, 1997.
21. Such criticisms were levelled at the documentary *Kernopalooza!*, Helen Foster (Director), Carlton Westcountry, 1998.
22. For discussion see A. Hale and P. Payton (eds), *New Directions in Celtic Studies*, Exeter, 2000, pp. 1–14.
23. For a brief discussion of Cornish revivalist literature see B. Murdoch, *Cornish Literature*, Cambridge, 1993. For an anthology of revivalist poetry see T.S. Saunders (ed.), *The Wheel*, London, 1999.
24. See N. Kennedy, 'Imagination in Teaching Cornish', in R.F.E. Sutcliffe and G.O. O'Néill (eds), *The Information Age, Celtic Languages and the New Millenium—6th Annual Conference of the North American Association for Celtic Language Teachers*, Limerick, 2000, pp. 63–9.
25. B. Deacon, 'Language Revival and Language Debate: Modernity and Postmodernity', in Philip Payton (ed.), *Cornish Studies: Four*, Exeter, 1996, p. 98.
26. George, 1986, p. 4.
27. K.J. George, 'A Phonological History of Cornish', unpublished Ph.D. thesis, University of Western Brittany (Brest), 1984.
28. George, 1986, p. 36.
29. For discussion see E. Mitchell, 'The Myth of Objectivity: The Cornish Language and the Eighteenth-Century Antiquaries', in Philip Payton (ed.), *Cornish Studies: Six*, Exeter, 1998, pp. 62–80.

30. A.S.D. Smith, correspondence, 1940, in E.G.R. Hooper, *Kemysk Kernewek*, Camborne, 1977, p. 35.
31. Smith, 1940, p. 43.
32. C. Thomas, 'An Dasserghyans Kernewek: The Cornish Revival', *Old Cornwall* 6.5, 1963, p. 203.
33. G. Price, *The Languages of Britain*, London, 1984.
34. Williams, 1995; *Clappya Kernowek: An Introduction to Unified Cornish Revised*, Redruth, 1997; *English–Cornish Dictionary: Gerlyver Sawsnek-Kernowek*, Dublin and Redruth, 2000.
35. For discussion of subjectivity and ideology within Cornish research, see Deacon, 1996; P. Payton, 'The Ideology of Language Revival in Modern Cornwall', in R. Black, W. Gillies and R.O. Maolalaigh (eds), *Celtic Connections: Proceedings of the Tenth International Congress of Celtic Studies, Volume 1, Language, Literature, History, Culture*, Edinburgh, 1999, pp. 395–424; and P. Payton, *A Vision of Cornwall*, Fowey, 2002, chapter 7.
36. See N. Kennedy, Review of N.J.A. Williams, *Gerlyver Sawsnek-Kernowek*, in Philip Payton (ed.), *Cornish Studies: Nine*, Exeter, 2001, pp. 312–18.
37. Deacon, 1996, p. 96.
38. A two-part Late Middle Cornish play has been discovered recently, the first part a life of St Kea, the second part concerning Arthur's battle with the Roman emperor Lucius Hiberius and the relationship of Modred with Guenevere, increasing the corpus of Middle Cornish by about 20 per cent. Several overlooked Late Cornish MSS are also available now: see Payton (ed.), 2001, pp. 83–104 for example.
39. Deacon, 1996, p. 100.
40. R.R.M. Gendall, *A Students' Grammar of Modern Cornish*, Menheniot, 1991; *A Students' Dictionary of Modern Cornish*, Menheniot, 1995; *A Practical Dictionary of Modern Cornish, Part 1, Cornish–English*, Menheniot, 1997; *A Practical Dictionary of Modern Cornish, Part 2: English–Cornish*, Menheniot, 1998; *Tavas a Ragadazow*, Menheniot, 2000.
41. For discussion see Payton, 1999, and Payton, 2002, chapter 7.
42. George, 1986, p. 36.
43. R. Lyon, *Gero Nye Desky Kernuack, Let's Learn Cornish* (revised), Nancegullan, 2001. *Notiangow Kernuack rag Dallathorian—Cornish Notes for Beginners*, An Garrack, 1995, 1999 (or http://geocities.com/cornishlanguagecouncil/).
44. For discussion of communicative approaches see R. Mitchell, *Communicative Langauge Teaching in Practice*, London, 1988.
45. M. Wells, 'Reflecting on Grammar Teaching', in A. Peck and D. Westgate (eds), *Language Teaching in the Mirror*, London, 1994, p. 55.
46. S. Krashen, *Language Acquisition and Language Education*, London, 1989, pp. 35–42.
47. Krashen, 1989, p. 36.
48. Gendall, 1999, p. 001.
49. R. Chubb, in *An Gowsva* 8.3, Agan Tavas, 1996.

NOTES ON CONTRIBUTORS

Allen Buckley is editor of the *Journal of the Trevithick Society* and has written extensively on Cornish mining themes. He obtained a Master of Philosophy degree from Camborne School of Mines, University of Exeter, for his thesis on Cornish mine adits, and is a Fellow of the Royal Historical Society.

Treve Crago is Honorary University Fellow at the Institute of Cornish Studies, University of Exeter, and is currently completing a doctoral thesis on aspects of Cornish oral history. He is Network Representative for Cornwall of the Oral History Society and is Senior Researcher of the Cornish Audio Visual Archive, supported by the Heritage Lottery Fund. He is author (with Garry Tregidga) of *Map Kenwyn: The Life and Times of Cecil Beer* (2000).

Bernard Deacon is Lecturer in Cornish Studies at the Institute of Cornish Studies and the University of Exeter's Department of Lifelong Learning in Truro, Cornwall. He has recently (2001) completed his doctoral thesis at the Open University (Wales) on 'The Reformulation of Territorial Identity: Cornwall in the Late Eighteenth and Nineteenth Centuries' and is a frequent contributor to *Cornish Studies*. Amongst his recent publications is 'Imagining the Fishing: Artists and Fishermen in Late Nineteenth-Century Cornwall' in *Rural History* (12.2, 2000).

Amy Hale was formerly Lecturer in Contemporary Celtic Studies at the Institute of Cornish Studies and was co-editor (with Philip Payton) of *New Directions in Celtic Studies* (University of Exeter Press, 2000). Amongst her recent publications is her chapter 'Whose Celtic Cornwall? The Ethnic Cornish Meet Cornish Spirituality', in David C. Harvey, Rhys Jones, Neil McInroy and Christine Milligan (eds), *Celtic Geographies: Old Culture, New Times* (2002).

Edwin Jaggard is Professor of History at Edith Cowan University, Western Australia. He has published widely on Cornish political history, with articles in both *Cornish Studies* and the *Journal of the Royal Institution of Cornwall* as well as other scholarly editions, and is author of *Cornwall Politics in the Age of Reform* (1999) and *Liberalism in West Cornwall: The 1868 Election Papers of A. Pendarves Vivian* (2000).

Neil Kennedy is currently teaching in Brittany and was until recently Lecturer in Cultural Studies at Falmouth College of Arts. He has worked with Richard Gendall since 1985 to develop and promote a standard form of Revived Late/Modern Cornish and has written extensively on Cornish language issues. Amongst his recent publications is *Imagination in the Teaching of Cornish* (2000).

Alan M. Kent is a writer, lecturer and scholar living in Cornwall. He holds a doctorate from the University of Exeter (1998) and is the author of several collections of poetry. He has published widely on the literary and cultural history of Cornwall. His most recent works include *The Literature of Cornwall: Continuity, Identity, Difference 1000–2000* (2000), *Pulp Methodism: The Lives and Literature of Silas, Joseph and Salome Hocking* (2002), and *The Dreamt Sea: An Anthology of Anglo-Cornish Poetry 1928–2000* (2002).

Kenneth MacKinnon is Visiting Professor and Emeritus Reader in the Sociology of Language at the University of Hertfordshire, Honorary Fellow in Celtic at the University of Edinburgh, and an Associate Lecturer in social sciences, education and language studies with the Open University. He is the member for language planning and development on the Ministerial Advisory Group on Gaelic of the Scottish Executive. He was a war evacuee in Cornwall between 1940 and 1944 at Summercourt and St Ives.

Philip Payton is Professor of Cornish Studies at the University of Exeter and Director of the Institute of Cornish Studies in Truro, Cornwall. The author of numerous books and articles, his most recent publications include *Cornwall's History: A Brief Introduction* (2002) and *A Vision of Cornwall* (2002).

Ronald Perry is a frequent contributor to *Cornish Studies* and was formerly Head of the Faculty of Management at Cornwall College. He has written widely on Cornish and other themes, and is co-author of *Counterurbanisation: International Case Studies of Socio-Economic Change in Rural Areas* (1986).

Sharron P. Schwartz is Honorary University Fellow at the Institute of Cornish Studies, University of Exeter, where she is completing her doctoral thesis on the Cornish in Latin America. She is a part-time Lecturer in the University's Department of Lifelong Learning in Truro and has been a consultant for Cornwall's bid for World Heritage Site status for the Cornish mining districts. She has written widely on modern Cornish history and amongst her recent publications is 'Exporting the Industrial Revolution: The Migration of Cornish Mining Technology to Latin America in the Early Nineteenth Century', in Heidi Slettedahl Macpherson and Will Kaufman (eds), *New Perspectives in Transatlantic Studies* (2002).

Mark Stoyle is Senior Lecturer in Early Modern History at the University of Southampton. He has written numerous articles on early modern Cornwall and is author of *West Britons: Cornish Identities and the Early Modern British State* (University of Exeter Press, 2002). Other books include *Loyalty and Locality: Popular Allegiances in Devon during the English Civil War* (University of Exeter Press, 1994) and *From Deliverance to Destruction: Rebellion and Civil War in an English City* (University of Exeter Press, 1996).

Charles Thomas is Emeritus Professor of Cornish Studies at the University of Exeter and was formerly Director of the Institute of Cornish Studies. He was founder of both *Cornish Archaeology* and the first series of *Cornish Studies* and is the author of numerous articles and books, including *Tintagel, Arthur and Archaeology* (1993).

Garry Tregidga is Assistant Director of the Institute of Cornish Studies, University of Exeter, and is a founder of both the Cornish History Network (whose *Newsletter* he edits) and the Cornish Audio Visual Archive, the latter now the recipient of a substantial grant from the Heritage Lottery Fund. He has published widely on Cornish politics and history, and is author of *The Liberal Party in Britain Since 1918: Political Decline, Dormancy and Rebirth* (University of Exeter Press, 2000).

Colin H. Williams is Research Professor in Welsh at the University of Wales Cardiff and an Adjunct Professor of Geography at the University of Western Ontario, Canada. During 2002 he was a Visiting

Fellow at Jesus College and Mansfield College, Oxford. He has published widely in areas as disparate as political philosophy, comparative religion, ethnic nationalism and language planning and policy in Canada, the EU and Eastern Europe. He is a member of the Welsh Language Board, the government sponsored body which promotes the Welsh language.

Malcolm Williams is Principal Lecturer in Sociology at the University of Plymouth and Visiting Fellow at the Institute of Education in London. He is the author of four books in social research methdology, including *Science and Social Science* (2000). His research interests encompass migration and housing, with special reference to Cornwall.